The Corporate City

THE CORPORATE CITY

The American City as a Political Entity, 1800–1850

Leonard P. Curry

VOLUME I OF
THE EMERGENCE OF AMERICAN URBANISM, 1800–1850

CONTRIBUTIONS IN AMERICAN HISTORY, NUMBER 172

GREENWOOD PRESS
Westport, Connecticut • London

Library of Congress Cataloging-in-Publication Data

Curry, Leonard P.
   The corporate city : the American city as a political entity,
1800–1850 / Leonard P. Curry.
      p. cm.—(Contributions in American history, ISSN 0084–9219
; no. 172) (The emergence of American urbanism ; v. 1)
   Includes bibliographical references (p.   ) and index.
   ISBN 0–313–30277–4 (alk. paper)
   1. Municipal government—United States—History—19th century.
2. Municipal finance—United States—History—19th century.
I. Title. II. Series. III. Series: The emergence of American
urbanism ; v. 1.
  JS319.C87 1997
  320.8'5'097309034—dc20   96–29278

British Library Cataloguing in Publication Data is available.

Library of Congress Catalog Card Number: 96–29278
ISBN: 0–313–30277–4
ISSN: 0084–9219

First published in 1997

Greenwood Press, 88 Post Road West, Westport, CT 06881
An imprint of Greenwood Publishing Group, Inc.

Printed in the United States of America

The paper used in this book complies with the
Permanent Paper Standard issued by the National
Information Standards Organization (Z39.48–1984).

10 9 8 7 6 5 4 3 2 1

This book is dedicated to
my mother
and
the memory of my father

Contents

Maps follow page 193.

Acknowledgments

We tend to think of scholarship as a solitary undertaking, and in some measure so it may be, in the writing process. But the collection of data is, with rare exceptions, carried out in public depositories with the assistance of dozens of knowledgeable, skilled, and dedicated people, and publishing is always a group undertaking. And with the rarest of exceptions even in the process of composition the author relies upon other intellects and perceptions to clarify his understanding, his analysis, and his prose. So has it been with me and I am under great and continuing obligation to many people and institutions for physical, intellectual, and financial support.

I must acknowledge, first of all, my indebtedness to the members of the staff of the Ekstrom Library of the University of Louisville, the University of Louisville Archives, the Baltimore City Archives, the Free Library of Philadelphia, the City of Charleston Archives and Records, the Charleston County Library, the National Archives in Washington, D. C., and (above all) the Library of Congress, where I spent a substantial part of every year between 1966 and 1993. Among the divisional staffs in the latter institution who have been particularly helpful in the course of my research on this study are those of the Rare Books Division, the Microform Division, the Prints and Photographs Division, the Geography and Maps Division, the Newspaper and Periodicals Division, the Law Library, and, of course, on a continuing basis, the Stack and Reader Division and especially the Study Facilities Office (most notably, in recent years, Mr. Bruce Martin).

For financial assistance absolutely essential to the completion of this project I am indebted to the Smithsonian Institution for an appointment as Visiting Postdoctoral Research Associate in 1970–1971, the National Endowment for the Humanities for summer and senior scholar fellowships in 1985 and 1987–1988, the American Philosophical Society for grants in 1972 and 1976, the Southern Regional Fellowships Fund for grants in 1981 and 1986, and to the College of Arts and Sciences, the Graduate School, the Office of the Provost, and the Office of the President of the University of Louisville for numerous faculty research grants throughout this period.

For assistance in the publishing process I am grateful to several persons associated with Greenwood Publishing Group: to Mr. John Dan Eades, Ms. Lynn Zelem, and Mr. Bayard Van Hecke; and, especially, to Professor Jon L. Wakelyn, a loyal and patient friend. Additionally, my University of Louisville colleagues and friends Professor Justin A. McCarthy and Mrs. Rita E. Hettinger spent a great deal of time they could ill afford attempting to establish some measure of rapport between me and recalcitrant computer programs.

A final, and personal, note of appreciation must be added for my two sons, who accommodated, with great aplomb, the yearly uprootings associated with the research demands of this study and my wife, who would prefer to remain anonymous, but whose keen historical and literary skills have saved me from many missteps.

Series Introduction

It was during the first half of the nineteenth century that the growth patterns of urban America were set and cities in the United States reached early maturity. This was not when the seeds were sown, of course—that was earlier. And reference will be made repeatedly throughout these volumes to eighteenth- and even seventeenth-century origins of urban lifestyles and structures; to undertakings, successes, failures, and tentative gropings toward a form of existence and a consciousness that were both urban and American.

The differentiation between urban and rural came slowly. From beyond the sea the would-be controllers of colonial life and the colonists' destiny issued a stream of instructions directing the settlers to establish towns in the New World. These settlements were to keep the population penned in to smaller compass; encourage (perhaps make inevitable) the concentration on commercial activity, which theoretically promised the greatest and most immediate return to European investors (but which was, as the settlers accepted more quickly than the ''undertakers,'' impossible in the American economic and anthropological context); and make the colonists easier to control and more dependent upon the Old World. But it was successful agriculture that made permanent settlement possible and strained, weakened, and eventually broke the bonds of dependence (economic and political). The predominant exports were agricultural, sylvan, and mineral products that, for the first three-quarters of a century of colonial life, entered imperial trade via very small towns and private wharves along the broad tidewater rivers of the Chesapeake region.

Under these circumstances it was only natural that nonurban concepts and values should largely prevail in those areas of the colonies that fit most harmoniously into the mercantilistic pattern that structured the seventeenth-century (and, indeed, eighteenth-century) European empires. But in the more northerly colonies the pieces did not fit together so neatly—agriculture was carried on at a subsistence level; exports of local origin were much less frequently destined for other British colonies and even more rarely for the mother country; and, consequently, native commercial activities began to emerge early. These, in turn, encouraged, and benefited from, the concentrations of population and mercantile function in the small but developing towns. In the eighteenth century (for similar reasons—e.g., the partial replacement of tobacco by wheat in Maryland and rice in South Carolina) this embryonic urbanism emerged in the southern colonies as well.

It was hardly surprising that many nonurban cultural remnants persisted in those emerging urban centers. Cows were driven daily to Boston Common; in that town and elsewhere there was a distinct unwillingness to embrace the idea of a public market and the attendant requirement that commerce in fresh food be conducted there; hogs, slaughtered by the poor families for food in the fall, roamed the streets of almost every city; and Washington and other towns provided town or ward bulls for the benefit of residents who kept milk cows. Some of these anomalies persisted (Washington paid contractors to winter the ward bulls until the 1840s), but in the first half of the nineteenth century most were ended or efforts (e.g., re wandering hogs) were made to eliminate them. At the same time these cities were shaped by their American as well as their urban environment, in some cases moving in advance of the towns in the other sections of the world.

What had developed by the middle of the nineteenth century was an American urbanism—not an urban system; of that there was no persuasive evidence—appearing in various manifestations in a growing number of cities of increasing size scattered more and more widely and thickly across the land. The urban political entities shared many attributes—structure, distribution of function among executive and legislative elements, increasing democratization, sources of revenue and purposes of expenditures, integration into national partisan political structures, intergovernmental interaction particular to the United States, and a peculiarily American pattern of using urban entities as mechanisms to assist private mercantile economic activity, which, to a considerable degree, both rested on and fostered a close identification of residents with their cities. These and related matters are explored in the first of the four volumes that comprise this work.

The first five decades of the nineteenth century also saw the growth of the urban population of the United States accelerate (in relation to the whole population) to reach a level of growth (about 5 percentage points per decade in the percentage of the population urban) that would persist with almost no change until 1930. Moreover the great racial and ethnic and religious diversity in that population—a condition not ever known in non-U.S. cities and not even approximated until much later, though all urban populations are marked in some measure by diversity—was firmly established in that same era. In particular, the black population, the foreign-born population, the Catholic and Jewish populations (in a basically Protestant society), and the institutions to which these self-conscious and oppressed and threatened groups gave birth were firmly entrenched by 1850. The changes of the next three-quarters of a century were mostly replication of the earlier years; only the names were changed. These matters will be the subject of the second volume.

The third volume will examine the role of the city as provider. Starting with a well-established pattern from earlier decades of turning to the city in a corporate capacity to supply services demanded by urbanites which were difficult or at least inconvenient to obtain privately, the cities' functions expanded rapidly in response to greater social complexity and rising expectations to partly or wholly furnish a variety of services related to education, health, safety, transportation, and a number of other urban needs, some peculiarily American (e.g., education) and others generically urban (e.g., street paving). For a variety of reasons these activities increased dramatically during the half century—the growing numbers continuously enlarged the "market" for these services; the increasing density of the population made some services essential (e.g., fire protection) and others extremely helpful (e.g., sidewalks); and changes in technology made other activities more feasible (e.g., street lighting).

A much more generically urban—geographically and territorially—circumstance will be explored in the final volume in this work. From the most ancient times and in all climes cities have been centers of opportunity—social, cultural, educational, and, above all, economic. This is, of course, the major reason that cities continue to grow in population, activity, and complexity—in short, that urban areas continue to become more and more urbanized. In this respect the antebellum American city differed from the thirteenth-century Italian city, the fifteenth-century German city, or the seventeenth-century English city primarily in magnitude, technology, and details, not in the basic premise—cities offer to the residents far more opportunities (which the corporate city itself did not provide) than nonurban areas.

Thus, this work considers the antebellum American city with regard to several different aspects—as a political entity, as people, as a provider, and as an area of opportunity. In all of these categories—and in the topics addressed in each volume—the urban experience was frequently pronouncedly different from that of nonurban areas. That is to say that this work is an examination of American urbanism in the first half of the nineteenth century. To those who find this term offensive I can only say that to speak of the importance of urbanization, while denying the existence of urbanism because it is not sufficiently definable, is to posit a uniquely important process that has no product worthy of examination and is more of an indictment of a methodological construct than a convincing argument. Historians have a long and honorable tradition of describing and examining and, indeed, analyzing conditions that defy scientifically precise definition (e.g., frontier, nationalism). This work will not add materially to the definition, but it will add significantly to our understanding of, even if it does not cover every aspect of, antebellum American urbanism.

A NOTE ON METHOD

The analytical universe used to examine these topics will be the same in each of the volumes—the fifteen largest U.S. cities in 1850—Albany, Baltimore, Boston, Brooklyn, Buffalo, Charleston, Cincinnati, Louisville, New Orleans, New York, Philadelphia, Pittsburgh, Providence, St. Louis, and Washington. This array includes nine cities located in the free states and six in the slave area; six west of the Appalachian Mountains and nine to the east; a substantial mix of early and late developing cities; and all with populations in excess of 40,000.

A word needs to be added about the analytical process employed—comparative methodology. Unfortunately, many people interpret the term *comparative urban history* to mean multinational studies of urban development and (as I found to my great surprise) a few interpret a comparative approach to mean that only commonalities are sought or reported. But there is nothing esoteric or restrictive about the comparative method, though it does place certain limitations on the investigator in the interest of analytical rigor. In this instance it simply means that I have attempted to collect the same sorts of data on the same items for all of the fifteen cities in the analytical universe—this is, of course, by no means always possible. In attempting to generalize about these issues (including the tools of statistical analysis) the analysis is confined to that universe. Interpretative conclusions are reached by a more nearly interpolative (i. e., falling within given parameters) rather than extrapolative (i. e., falling anyplace) process, and potentially influential variables have also been collected from the same universe. It is, in short, designed to produce a more controlled identification and analysis of the commonalities and diversities in the American urban experience.

One final observation on method should be added to these comments. There is a fairly widespread manner of presentation that starts with the enunciation of a thesis that is then developed and elaborated, and in the process, or at some subsequent point, various accounts of events or circumstances are introduced to validate the thesis by virtue of being arguably extrapolatable from or illustrative of the premises of the thesis. This process tends to result in a product (book, chapter, article) that emphasizes the development and/or application of the theoretical aspects and that displays data sparingly.

With this type of historical writing—attractive and engaging though it undoubtedly is—the product of comparative research and analysis is at odds. The comparative method demands that comparable data be collected without conscious reference to a theoretical concept and that such data (not, of course, all of it) be presented and that interpolatively driven conclusions be derived, all in full view of the reader. The result is, thus, a product that presents far more data and is likely to give considerably less attention to the elaboration of a theoretical construct. To those readers who might find this display of data less to their liking than a more theoretical approach, I extend my sympathy, but not my apologies; the form of the book is the product of the method, and of the value of that method I am fully convinced.

Volume Introduction

The important thing about the political entity called a city (or town, or village, or borough, for that matter) is, of course, that it is a legal person and can do things that its residents could do individually, but not jointly (when not so incorporated) without great risk. It can buy, sell, and hold property; it can sue and be sued; it can borrow money. Moreover, the incorporation of the city enables it to do things that its residents could not do at all, individually or jointly, without incorporation. It can tax its residents and nonresident property holders and entrepreneurs; it can require residents and visitors to take (or not to take) prescribed action; and it can punish by fines and imprisonment failure to conform to these requirements.

Influencing all of these actions, during the period under consideration in this volume were a number of variables. Among them were the structure of this political entity, the ways in which its powers were distributed, and specific authorizations and restrictions concerning its actions. Particularly important were the ways in which it employed its most important tool—money. And an exploration of the way it raised its revenues and apportioned its expenditures tells us much about each of these political entities.

But the decisions on these matters, though reached corporately, were the aggregation of individual wills and wisdom, beliefs and biases, achievements and aspirations of the elected municipal officials. In turn, these attitudes and circumstances were shaped and modified by the life experiences (both in and out of office) of these people and the political process that brought them to office and shaped their conscious political environment.

The ability of both the corporate entity called the city and the officials that directed that entity to make choices and to put those choices into action was profoundly and continually influenced by other political entities—both coordinate and superordinate. These constituted the elements of power, knowledge, restraint, and conflict that made up the corporate political environment within which the cities existed and acted.

Out of the admixture of all of these elements of structure, resources, personnel, process, and relationship came not only the day-to-day functioning of the city but also a vision, however limited, blurred, and self-contradictory, of the city as it might be. And this both resulted from and further fostered an identification of the urbanites, especially the elite, with their city of residence and a willingness—in some cases, a determination—to use that political entity to capitalize activities perceived to be beneficial to the urban economy and to the financial well-being of the residents of the city.

This volume, then, will explore this urban ''person''—this political entity—and its corporate elements, relationships, and activities, as the necessary first step in the further investigations of other aspects of major American cities in the first half of the nineteenth century.

A Note on Sources

The number (and diversity) of sources that must be examined in the effort to explore the history of and life in fifteen cities over a period of half a century is enormous—my own estimate is just under 5,000 titles. By no means all of these have been utilized in writing this volume; but just the works cited must be in the hundreds, and the printing of a traditional bibliography of such magnitude would be prohibitively expensive. As an alternative, this brief essay is intended only to provide a superficial sketch (and a few examples) of some of the more extensively used kinds of materials.

A general overview of these cities (frequently accompanied by a considerable amount of useful detail) can be supplied by general histories, frequently multi-volume, of the individual cities. A few of these date from after the mid-twentieth century—for example, Constance M. Green, *Washington* (2 vols.; Princeton: Princeton University Press, 1962–1963)—but more frequently from the early twentieth or late nineteenth centuries—for example, Wilhelmus B. Bryan, *A History of the Nation's Capital* (2 vols.; New York: Macmillan, 1914–1916); J. Thomas Scharf, *History of Baltimore City and County* (Philadelphia: Louis H. Everts, 1881); Justin Winsor (ed.), *The Memorial History of Boston, Including Suffolk County, Massachusetts, 1630–1880* (4 vols.; Boston: James R. Osgood and Company, 1880–1881). Also useful are contemporary histories—for example, Ben Casseday, *The History of Louisville, from its Earliest Settlement to the Year 1852* (Louisville: Hull and Brother, 1852); Josiah Quincy, *A Municipal History of Boston, During Two Centuries* (Boston: Charles C. Little and James Brown, 1852).

Of particular value in the governmental and political areas are two compilations, one contemporary—David T. Valentine, *Manual of the Corporation of New York* (New York: various publishers, various dates)—and one retrospective—Joel Munsell, *The Annals of Albany* (10 vols.; Albany: J. Munsell, 1850–1857). Also useful are detailed specialized studies that often originated as doctoral dissertations—for example, J. H. Hollander, *The Financial History of Baltimore*, Extra Volume 20 of *The Johns Hopkins Studies in Historical and Political Science* (Baltimore: The Johns Hopkins Press, 1899); Charles P. Huse, *The Financial History of Boston, From May 1, 1822, to January 31, 1909*, Volume 15 of *Harvard Economic Studies* (Cambridge: Harvard University Press, 1916).

Of particular importance in the examination of governmental structures and financial operations are various government documents. City charters and amendments thereto are usually most easily found in consolidated city ordinances (see chapter 1, notes 21–22), but are sometimes published separately by city or, occasionally, state authority, and can always be found in state session laws. Financial records are sometimes published (regularly or intermittently) by cities, but can occasionally be found only in manuscript form or in fugitive publications or not at all.

The sources for the chapters on politics, elections, and city officers range from readily available to nonexistent. In some cities there were consolidated or annual listings of officers. City directories frequently contained lists of officers and, on rare occasions, election data (see, e.g., chapter 1, note 25). Melvin G. Holli and Peter d'A. Jones (eds.), *Biographical Dictionary of American Mayors, 1820–1980: Big City Mayors* (Westport, Conn.: Greenwood, 1981), is exceptionally useful on the cities' chief executives after 1820 in the nine of these cities that it covers.

When I began this study over thirty years ago (in 1966) I resolved (as a condition of completing the research in my lifetime) to utilize manuscript or newspaper sources only as a last resort. This proved to be the case for some financial data, which survive (if at all) only in manuscript form, and for city election returns, which frequently could be found only in contemporary newspapers. Thirty newspaper files were combed for election data, and a number of gaps remain unfilled. City directories, it might be noted, were also essential in establishing elected officials' occupations and connections with financial institutions, and frequently contained other valuable material as well.

With the exception of some fugitive pieces, the examination of the development of the city plan rests heavily on city ordinances, state legislation, and city maps. The latter have been indispensible and have been found largely in the Geography amd Map Division of the Library of Congress.

The last two chapters make extensive use of state session laws (see chapter 6, note 1, for an explanation) and the federal equivalent, *Statutes at Large*. Almost 1,000 volumes of these have been consulted.

Finally, an abundance of essential detailed information has been obtained from the federal census reports (see chapter 1, note 26), doctoral dissertations available on microfilm, and articles from a number of historical journals, primarily state quarterlies. Also of considerable value were several contemporary magazines, especially, *DeBow's Review* and *Niles' Register.*

Full bibliographic information is given at the point of first citation in each chapter.

Chapter 1

City Government

Though a corporate charter is not an absolute prerequisite to the existence of a city (Charleston had none for more than a century), urban residents find it exceedingly difficult to address the problems or exploit the opportunities of the urban condition without some means of acting both collectively and authoritatively. Urban governmental structures are, consequently, almost always provided at an early date in a city's life, either by the residents or by appropriate governmental authority, unless this normal pattern is disrupted by the interposition of other, and more powerful, interests (as was the case in colonial South Carolina).

As the nineteenth century dawned there were settlements at the location of each of the cities examined in this study, but they did not, in every case, legally exist as cities—not even some of the largest ones. Indeed, Brooklyn, Buffalo, Cincinnati, St. Louis, and Washington had no separate governments at all. There was, to be sure, a town of Brooklyn, but, as was common in the northeast, its boundaries extended well beyond the village and its population was predominantly rural. The other four settlements, all of which were, of course, quite small in 1800, lacked even this degree of local government. Not until 1804 would a "town" (Erie) be erected embracing the Buffalo settlement, and in that same year the new U.S. territorial government created the district of St. Louis (roughly comparable to a large county). Two years earlier, in 1802, the Ohio territorial legislature had incorporated the town of Cincinnati, encompassing a much smaller area than most northeastern "towns," but with boundaries that, nevertheless, extended considerably beyond the closely settled area. Washington-to-be remained under the control of federal commissioners and the Prince Georges County Court until Congress passed the initial city charter, also in 1802.[1]

The residents of New Orleans had been governed by a "Superior Council" (which was also responsible for the governance of the province) during the first French period, by a Cabildo during the Spanish years, and by an appointed mayor-council government on the French model in the three weeks of the second period of French control. This government was temporarily continued by a decree of U.S. territorial governor W. C. C. Claiborne, and the territorial legislature, in February 1805, passed the first act of incorporation for the city of New Orleans, which at this juncture had a population of perhaps 2,600.[2]

The other two trans-Appalachian towns in this group were new, raw, and small. Although the town of Louisville was established by an act of the Virginia legislature in 1780, the trustees named in that act (and their successors) were granted power extending only to the granting of land and the settlement of disputes arising from such grants. It was not until 1795 that a town government vested with tax and ordinance powers was created for the settlers at the falls of the Ohio by an act of the Kentucky legislature. Meanwhile, the Pennsylvania legislature, by an act of 1794, had established the borough of Pittsburgh.[3]

Two of the older eastern cities—New York and Albany—were, in 1800, still operating under city charters granted by colonial authorities, and in three others the governments had been established by acts of the post-Revolutionary state legislatures—Charleston (1783), Philadelphia (1789), and Baltimore (1796). Charleston and Baltimore were wholly new city incorporations. Philadelphia had received a charter in the colonial era, but its antiquated closed corporation government, already weakened by lack of popular support and the shifting of major urban governmental functions to elective boards, collapsed utterly during the Revolution.[4]

Finally, Boston and Providence, despite being the fourth and seventh ranking cities in size by 1800, not only retained the New England town form of government but would also continue to cling to these governmental systems well into the nineteenth century. The precise details of these structures varied in some minor particulars, but the basic repository of power and source of authority in each was the town meeting of all qualified voters (a more restricted body in Providence than in Boston). The growth in the size of the population had, by the end of the eighteenth century, produced a number of changes in structure and procedure in both towns. Greater authority to establish regulations and greater responsibility for oversight were assigned to the selectmen in Boston and the town council in Providence; the number of officers charged with specific responsibilities increased in both towns. By late in the period of town government the voters were electing, in addition to the major officers, members of school committees, overseers of the poor, fire wards, surveyors and measurers of boards and timber, cullers of hoops, fence viewers, hog reeves, hay wards, field drivers, sealers of weights and measures, surveyors of highways, members of boards of health, assessors, pound keepers, corders of wood, and a variety of others. Boston, under greater weight of population pressure, had introduced ward elections and written ballots with the polls being kept open for a number of hours. Additionally, "a *de facto* town council had been created" in 1813 consisting of the selectmen, overseers of the poor, and members of the board of health, who constituted a committee on finance and chose the town treasurer and the collector of taxes.[5]

The colonial charters of Albany (1686) and New York (1730), though differing in a number of particulars, provided for similar governmental structures for these cities; the only significant modification produced by American independence was the transfer of powers of appointment from the colonial governor first to the state governor and then to the state council of appointment. Each city had a mayor-council government with the mayor, recorder (a judicial officer), and clerk appointed by the council of appointment. The city council consisted of the mayor, recorder, and one alderman and one assistant alderman from each ward in New York and two aldermen and two assistant aldermen from each ward in Albany, sitting as a single body. The qualified electors—male residents who were freeholders or taxpayers—chose annually the aldermen and assistant aldermen in elections in each ward (six in Albany and nine in New York); in New York constables, assessors, and collectors were chosen in the same manner. The mayor had no veto power and, especially in Albany, controlled few appointments; the appointive powers of the council were more extensive. These charters, and particularly that of New York, reflected the increasing complexity of urban life even in the colonial period by providing for the appointment of a great number of persons to serve as city officers or to perform services for the citizenry. These ranged from deputy mayor, high constable, and chamberlain to common criers, bell ringers, beadles, scavengers, and garblers. In both cities the mayor was also clerk of the market and, in addition, served as coroner in Albany and as "bailiff and conservator of the water of the north and east rivers" in New York.[6]

The three city charters that emanated from the new state governments in the late years of the eighteenth century—those of Charleston (1783), Philadelphia (1789), and Baltimore (1796)—reflected a hesitant concern to make city governments patterned on Old World models both more reponsive to popular will and more in harmony with the political theories of the Revolutionary era. Nevertheless, they also bore the marks of a residual (and, indeed, renewed) distrust of "popular" government. The general determination to separate the executive and legislative functions was evidenced by the fact that the Baltimore and Philadelphia documents (as amended before 1800) excluded the mayor from the council. In neither Philadelphia nor Charleston were those officers vested with a veto power, a circumstance doubtless flowing from the pervasive distrust of the executive in the immediate postcolonial years. The intendant of Charleston, further, had no appointive power nor, initially, did the mayor of Philadelphia, but an act of 1799 assigned broad powers of appointment to the latter officer. In Baltimore, however, the mayor not only had the power to veto council ordinances (unless overridden by a two-thirds vote of both branches of the council) but also could fill by appointment all offices created by ordinance. This latter authority was much less broad than it appeared, however, for the Second Branch

of the council presented the mayor with two nominees for each office, from
which he was required to choose the appointee.

While these state legislatures did not continue the colonial practice (in New
York and Albany) of empowering the governor to appoint the city executive,
they nevertheless were not prepared to vest this choice unconditionally in the
voters of any of these three cities. In Charleston—where the three-shilling taxpayer requirement for voting was at least "high enough to be protested"—the
voters were given the most extensive voice in the executive's selection. There
the qualified voters each year first chose one warden (councilman) in elections
in each ward and then, in a citywide election later in the same month, named
one of those persons to serve as intendant. The selection procedure in Philadelphia most nearly resembled the colonial practice. There the governor appointed the aldermen, and the joint council annually selected one of these to
serve as mayor. In Baltimore, following a method earlier used to select certain
commissioners in Baltimore town, the voters chose electors who elected both
the mayor and the members of the Second Branch of the council for two-year
terms.

There were equally great variations in the legislative components of the city
government in these three towns. Charleston had a single council consisting of
the intendant and a single warden directly elected annually by the voters of each
of thirteen wards. As has been noted, the eight members of the Second Branch
of Baltimore's city council were named by the same electors who chose the
mayor, and for the same term; the First Branch was twice as large, consisting
of two members from each ward, elected annually by the ward's qualified
voters—that is, those entitled to vote for members of the Maryland General
Assembly. In Philadelphia (after the charter amendment of 1796) the freemen
qualified to vote for members of the state House of Representatives annually
cast their ballots at a single polling place in the city for all twenty members of
the Common Council and for one-third of the twelve members of the Select
Council (the aldermen appointed by the governor had only judicial, not legislative, power). Although Philadelphia's two councils had originally constituted
a single legislative body, by the end of the eighteenth century the councils were
sitting separately both there and in Baltimore.

These charters, unlike those dating from the colonial period, gave the governor almost no power to appoint city officials—in Philadelphia he directly
named only judicial officers (the recorder and aldermen) and, in effect, nominated the mayor by virtue of the requirement that that officer be selected from
the aldermen. In both that city and in Charleston nonelected officials were chosen by the council; the selection process in Baltimore, though more complex
(see above), was in the hands of local officers. As a safeguard, however, charter
provisions established qualifications that limited eligibility to serve on the councils. The wardens in Charleston and members of the Common Council in Philadelphia had to be qualified to vote for members of the state general assembly
and members of Philadelphia's Select Council were required to meet the higher

qualifications established to vote for state senators. In Baltimore members of the First Branch were selected from persons assessed "to the amount of one thousand dollars," and the requirement for members of the Second Branch was double that amount.

The clause in the Philadelphia charter granting general ordinance authority, coupled with those transferring to the new corporation the powers of the defunct city government and of various other bodies performing governmental functions in the colonial era, were apparently presumed to include sufficiently broad taxing powers. The Baltimore and Charleston charters included specific authority to tax in addition to the granting of general ordinance power. This taxing power was, at least insofar as it related to property, unrestricted in Charleston, but limited to two dollars per one hundred pounds assessment in Baltimore.[7]

During the first decade of the nineteenth century two more of these fifteen towns received their first city charters—Washington in 1802 and New Orleans in 1805. Perhaps it was because the charters were in neither case conferred by governments responsible to the local electorate that each returned to the colonial practice of appointive mayors: Washington's by the president and New Orleans' by the governor of Orleans Territory. Neither sat as a member of the city council and each could veto council ordinances, with a three-fourths majority being required to override the mayor of Washington while the more customary two-thirds sufficed in New Orleans. Both mayors had extensive appointive powers. The Washington charter flatly stated that "the mayor shall appoint all officers under the corporation." In New Orleans the mayor was empowered "to appoint all measurers, weighers, gaugers, marshalls [sic], constables, wharfingers, scavengers," and such other "officers and ministers" as "shall be directed by any ordinances of the . . . council." To prevent the more blatant exercise of presidential patronage, the Washington charter specified that the mayor must be "a resident of the city, prior to his appointment."

The New Orleans city council consisted of fourteen aldermen (two from each ward) chosen by the voters in ward elections for staggered two-year terms, and the recorder (appointed by the governor). Washington's two-house council was selected by a somewhat more complex procedure. The city's voters, in a general election, annually elected twelve "councilers." These twelve selected five of their number to form the "second chamber" and the remaining seven constituted the "first chamber." Probably because of the cumbersome nature of this arrangement, Congress amended the charter within less than two years to provide for the direct election by general ticket of nine members to each of the two chambers. The New Orleans council was specifically given the appointment of the treasurer, but no other appointive powers were assigned to that body or to the Washington council.

Neither charter established any other elective officers and, except for the recorder in New Orleans, no other officers in either city were appointed by the governor or the president. The electorate in each city was restricted to free white adult males resident in the city for one year. In the nation's capital voters also must have paid taxes within one year of the election and in New Orleans were required either to own real estate valued at $500 or to pay an annual rent of $100. In addition to general ordinance powers each corporation possessed broad authority to levy taxes, but that of Washington was limited to one-third of one percent of the assessed value of real estate.[8]

In two of the five initial charters granted in the fifteen years following the War of 1812 the governor was also, in some measure, involved in the process of selecting a mayor. In Pittsburgh (1816), as in Philadelphia, the city council, in joint session, selected the mayor from among the aldermen appointed by the state's chief executive. The procedure established by the Louisville charter (1828) provided a greater voice to the voters, but was more cumbersome than that in any of the other towns. In that city the qualified electors cast their votes for candidates for the mayoralty, and the names of the two persons receiving the greatest number of votes were then forwarded to the governor. That officer, with the consent of the state senate, named one of the two as mayor. In the event that the governor should decline to nominate either of the persons selected or the senate should fail to confirm, then a new election would be required. The Cincinnati charter of 1819 empowered the trustees (councilmen) to elect the mayor "from the inhabitants of the city," and the Boston and St. Louis charters—both enacted in 1822—each called for direct election of the mayor. In all of these cities except Cincinnati—where the chief executive served for two years—the mayors were chosen annually, and only in St. Louis did that officer possess a veto power; there it could be overridden by a majority of the whole number of the aldermen.

Bicameral councils were provided for in Pittsburgh and Boston, and single-chamber councils were specified in Cincinnati, Louisville, and St. Louis; the members were in all cities directly elected by the qualified voters. The electoral process was somewhat more complex in Pittsburgh than in the other towns. There the voters cast their ballots at a single polling place for nine members of the Select Council and fifteen common councillors. The former were required to meet the qualifications to serve in the state senate and the latter those for membership in the state house of representatives. Elsewhere ward elections were the rule, with the voters electing three trustees from each ward in Cincinnati, two councilmen per ward in Louisville, nine aldermen distributed among the wards according to their population in St. Louis, and four members of the Common Council from each Boston ward. In addition, votes were cast in Boston's ward elections for eight aldermen elected at large. Thus, the tendency toward small council bodies continued, with Boston's Board of Aldermen being only slightly smaller than that of St. Louis (nine), Pittsburgh's Select Council (nine), Louisville's council (ten), or Cincinnati's Board of Trustees (twelve); even Pittsburgh's fifteen-man Common Council was approximately of the scale provided for in these and earlier charters. A major exception, however, was Boston's Common Council, which numbered forty-eight—a decision that was doubtless influenced by that city's heritage of extensive direct participation in town affairs.

Boston was also unique in specifying that a majority of all votes cast was required for election of members of both councils and of the mayor, with re-balloting required in any case where candidates did not have a majority.

St. Louis required its aldermen to be at least twenty-one years of age, a U.S. citizen, resident in the city for one year, and possessed of a freehold estate in the municipality; its mayor had to be at least thirty years of age, a city resident for two years, and otherwise qualified as were the aldermen. The specific (and different) eligibility requirements to serve in Pittsburgh's two councils have been previously noted, but since the mayor was selected from the aldermen appointed by the governor, the charter specified no qualifications for that office. In the other two towns the requirements were less stringent. Boston's charter specified only that the mayor and aldermen be "inhabitants" of the city and the common councilmen of the wards from which they were elected, and the Louisville charter listed no qualifications for any city officers. This latter circumstance may well have been an oversight, however, for an 1830 amendment to the Louisville charter specified that every city officer be a taxpayer and "a housekeeper or freeholder," and that councilmen must reside in the wards that they represented—requirements that were substantially identical to those existing in Cincinnati.

There were charter provisions calling for the election of a city marshal in Louisville and overseers of the poor, firewards, and members of the school committee in the Boston wards, but (aside from Pittsburgh's governor-appointed recorder) other city offices were filled by internal appointment. In Pittsburgh, the joint councils possessed broad appointive powers by virtue of a clause in the charter assigning to them the powers previously held by the borough of Pittsburgh and "all the powers and authorities now vested in the select and common councils of the city of Philadelphia." In the other cities essentially unlimited appointive powers were vested jointly in the mayors and the councils (or some portion thereof) and potentially, by subsequent ordinances, in either alone. The Boston council was also specifically authorized to create other elective offices.

Although the phraseology of the charters differed, the electorate in all of these cities was probably quite similar. Pittsburgh's charter granted the suffrage to freemen who were citizens and taxpayers and had resided in the town for a year, and Cincinnati's to free white male freeholders or householders of at least one year's residence. Boston's voters had to be males who were taxpayers or exempt from taxation, and the charter further specified a residence requirement of one year in the state and six months in the city. In Louisville those persons qualified to vote for members of the state House of Representatives could vote in city elections if they had resided in the town for six months; a taxpaying requirement was added in 1831. Only St. Louis had no residence requirement, extending the suffrage to all free white male taxpayers "of the age of twenty-one years." The effect of these provisions was to produce in each city an electorate essentially consisting of free white resident adult male taxpayers, though some blacks certainly voted in Boston and may have qualified to vote in Pittsburgh.

In addition to broad general ordinance powers these charters also conferred (or confirmed) substantial taxing authority. No specific limits were placed on Boston's or Cincinnati's power to tax, but in the other towns the charters limited the rate of general property taxation—to four-tenths of one percent of the value in Louisville and one-half of one percent in St. Louis and Pittsburgh. In the latter city both the power and the limitation derived from the transfer to the corporation of all powers exercised by the former borough of Pittsburgh.[9]

The increasing tendency to rely on the direct electoral process, which is obvious in the charters drafted during these years, was manifest in ratification provisions attached to the Boston and St. Louis documents in 1822. Each provided that the charter should be valid only if approved by a majority of the persons voting in a special election on that issue. The Missouri legislature set a date three months after the passage of the charter, and that of Massachusetts requested that the election be held within twelve days. Boston voters, who had earlier approved a draft of this document prepared by a town committee by a vote of 2,805 to 2,006, approved the charter as passed by the Massachusetts legislature by a vote of 2,797 to 1,881. In St. Louis, where the "French" population tended to oppose the creation of the city (apparently fearing a loss of influence in the new government and an increase in taxes on real estate), the vote resulted in a narrow victory (107 to 90) for the charter.[10]

Providence, the second of the major metropolises that clung stubbornly to its town—as distinct from city—governmental system gave up the fight in 1831. Even given the restrictive suffrage established by Rhode Island's antiquated colonial charter, which served as the state's constitution, the growth in Providence's population had resulted in town meetings of an unmanageable size by the end of the first quarter of the nineteenth century. This circumstance, coupled with some perceived "injudicious expenditures of public money," moved a majority of the freemen to approve a proposed city charter in 1829. The state legislature dutifully passed the necessary act in January 1830, but provided that it should not be effective unless approved by three-fifths of the persons voting in a referendum on the charter. When only a small majority (383 to 345) supported the change, the town system was retained. But a confrontation between the town meeting and the council in 1830 and a destructive riot in 1831 apparently convinced many of the freemen that a change was imperative, and a repetition of the earlier process (i.e., voter appoval of a proposed charter followed by legislative action and a referendum) produced a large majority (459 to 188) for a city charter in November 1831.[11]

The Providence city government was quite similar to that provided for by the Boston charter of the previous decade. The mayor, aldermen, and councilmen were all chosen in ward elections by a majority of the qualified voters, and all served one-year terms. The twenty-four councilmen (four per ward) were elected from the wards; the mayor and six aldermen, at large. The mayor had no veto power and exercised only such appointive powers as might attach to his function as the presiding officer (with a vote only in case of a tie) of the Board of Aldermen, which appointed a number of city officals, with most of the remainder being named by the joint council. The voters were to be freemen—which meant that they were, among other things, possessed of a freehold valued at at least $134, or were the eldest sons of freemen possessing such estate—and the elected members of the city government were to be freemen and freeholders. The mayor and aldermen were to receive salaries but the councilmen were allowed no compensation. The executive powers previously possessed by the town council were transferred to the mayor and aldermen, and all authority formerly held by the town council or by the town meeting (including extensive taxing powers) were vested in the mayor, aldermen, and Common Council.[12]

The other two towns receiving their initial charters during the 1830s were Buffalo (1832) and Brooklyn (1834). The latter had for some years sought the establishment of a city government but had encountered the unremitting opposition of the New York City delegation in the state legislature. It would appear that this opposition rested primarily on the Manhattaners' hope that the counties of Kings and Richmond might be annexed to their city—a vision that foreshadowed the eventual consolidation of 1898. In 1833 the Brooklyn delegation managed to carry an incorporation act through the Assembly only to see it defeated in the Senate. But in the following year the legislature overrode the opposition of the state's major metropolis and passed the Brooklyn charter.[13]

The charters granted to the two New York cities were very similar. Each authorized ward elections in which the qualifed voters chose two aldermen (a total of ten in Buffalo and twelve in Brooklyn) as well as an assessor in Buffalo and a variety of ward officers in Brooklyn. The aldermen elected a mayor, who could not be an alderman but must be a "freeholder in said City" in Buffalo and a "freeholder and resident of said city" in Brooklyn. Aldermen were required to be freeholders and residents of the wards they represented. All elective and appointive officers served one-year terms. The mayor and aldermen constituted the Common Council, over which the mayor presided but in which he had no vote in Brooklyn and only a casting vote in Buffalo. The mayor's assent was not necessary to the passage of ordinances and resolutions by the Buffalo council, and his veto in Brooklyn could be overridden by a simple majority vote of the council. The councils were assigned extensive appointive powers and none were specifically vested in the mayors.

The Brooklyn charter defined the city electorate simply as those "who are and shall be authorized to vote at general State elections" and, by inference, were residents of the wards in which they tendered a vote. The Buffalo charter directed that poll lists "be kept in the same manner, as nearly as may be, as is provided by law for keeping poll lists at the general state election," and added the requirement that voters be residents of the ward in which they voted. Any person whose right to vote was challenged would be permitted to cast a ballot upon swearing that he was twenty-one years of age, a U.S. citizen, and had resided in the state for one year and in the county for six months. Blacks were required, in addition, to swear to the ownership of a freehold estate valued at $250 above any encumbrances thereon. This latter provision was in accordance with state law and, naturally, applied to voters in Brooklyn as well.

To each city was transferred the powers of the preexisting village government and each was, in addition, granted extensive ordinance powers. The Brooklyn council, however, was specifically forbidden to "prescribe the materials with which buildings in the said City shall be enclosed or covered." The provisions regarding taxing authority were somewhat more complicated. The Buffalo council could raise revenues of up to $8,000 annually in addition to assessments on landowners for local improvements (e.g., street paving). This limit was raised to $14,000 in 1835. The city of Brooklyn was divided into two units—the fire and watch district, comprising the fire wards of the old village and two adjacent wards, and the eighth and ninth wards, which lay outside the built-up area and adjoined the towns of New Utrecht, Flatbush, and Bushwick. The electors of the seven wards in the fire and watch district annually elected five—and those of the two outer wards, one—supervisors who met annually in May with the Common Council. This "Joint Board," by a majority of two-thirds of those present, established the sum (not to exceed $10,000) to be raised by taxation to defray city expenses, and "such further sum as they shall deem to be necessary" to purchase fire engines and land for firehouses. The Joint Board then specified what portion of the revenue to be raised was chargeable to the fire and watch district (Wards 1–7), what portion to the out wards, and what portion to the entire city. This information was then transmitted to the Board of Supervisors of Kings County (of which the city supervisors were members) and that body then levied the appropriate tax on the property in the two divisions of the city. The Common Council could, as in Buffalo, further assess real estate owners for the cost of local improvements from which they benefited.[14]

As might be expected, there were many changes in the charters of these cities throughout the remainder of the half century. One consistent pattern of modification was the movement in the direction of popularly elected mayors. At the beginning of the nineteenth century, as has been noted, voters in Charleston and Baltimore played the most direct role in the selection of the city's chief executive—in Charleston the intendant was directly elected in a two-step process, and in the Maryland metropolis the voters elected special electors who named the mayor. Charleston's electoral process was simplified in 1808 by permitting the voters to elect the mayor from among the whole body of citizens. In Baltimore the "electoral college" was finally eliminated by a charter change enacted by the state legislature in 1833 at the request of the city councils, and the city's voters thereafter elected the mayor directly.[15]

The preexisting or initial charters of four of these nineteenth-century cities, however—Albany (1686), New York (1730), Washington (1802), and New Orleans (1805)—provided for appointive mayors. Such a selection process was clearly inconsistent with the democratic trends in American political thought and practice in the first half of the nineteenth century, and it was doubtless inevitable that—despite many rural legislators' distrust of the city "mobs"—these charter provisions should be modified. New Orleans was unique in moving (in 1812) directly from an appointive to a popularly elected mayor. In each of the other three towns the first step was to vest the selection of the mayor with the city council rather than with the governor (or, in the case of Washington, the president)—a method of selection that was, it will be recalled, quite common in the 1820s and 1830s. Thus state legislation (or that of the Congress, in the case of the nation's capital) authorized councils to choose mayors in Washington in 1812, in New York in 1821, and in Albany in 1826. Additionally, similar changes took place in the charters of the Pennsylvania cities, where the mayors had originally been chosen by the city councils from among the aldermen (who were gubernatorial appointees). The power to elect the mayor from among the whole body of citizens was given to the council in Philadephia in 1826 and in Pittsburgh in 1833.[16]

In each of these five cities the selection of the mayor was transferred to the general electorate in due course. The change came quickly in Pittsburgh, when the state legislature enacted the necessary charter change in December 1833—some eight months after it had first lodged that power with the council. In Washington, Congress did not authorize the direct election of the mayor until 1820, eight years after establishing council election. In each of the other three cities rather more than a dozen years elapsed between the time the councils were empowered to elect the mayor and the transfer of that authority to the voters in New York (1834), Albany (1840), and Philadelphia (1839).[17]

In the meantime, all of the initial charters issued after 1816, except that of Louisville (1828), placed the mayoral electoral power either in the hands of the council—Cincinnati (1819), Buffalo (1832), and Brooklyn (1834)—or the general electorate of the city—Boston (1822), St. Louis (1822), and Providence (1831). Louisville's unwieldy selection process, involving voters, governor, and state Senate, was superseded by council election in 1836 and by direct election two years later. The state legislation (1840) that established the popular election of the mayor in Albany was general in nature and had the same effect in Brooklyn and Buffalo, and Cincinnati's new charter of 1827 contained a similar provision.[18]

The accelerating trend toward the popular election of the cities' chief executive officers can, perhaps, be shown more graphically in Table 1.1.[19]

Whereas in 1810 the voters selected the chief executive in only one city in seven, by 1840 that practice was universal in all fifteen towns.

As has been noted, there was apparently considerable reluctance on the part of state legislators—and the urban voters, where they were involved in framing their charters—to entrust the chief executive with a veto power. Here, as elsewhere, the framers of these enabling documents could find precedents for their course in the early state constitutions, a number of which had not granted the governors the veto power. It is common to attribute this circumstance to the

Table 1.1
Method of Mayoral Selection in Fifteen Cities, 1800–1840[a]

Year	External Apptmt.	Governor/ Other[b]	Electoral College	Council Election	Popular Election	Towns Not Yet Inc.
1800	2(40%)	1(20%)	1(20%)	0(0%)	1(20%)	10
1810	4(57%)	1(14%)	1(14%)	0(0%)	1(14%)	8
1820	2(22%)	2(22%)	1(11%)	1(11%)	3(33%)	6
1830	0(0%)	2(17%)	1(8%)	3(25%)	6(50%)	3
1840	0(0%)	0(0%)	0(0%)	0(0%)	15(100%)	0

[a]The percentages are of the total number of these cities
  incorporated as of that date.
[b]Mayor chosen by some form of combined action involving the
  governor and either the council or the electorate.

existence of a residual suspicion of the executive originating in the late colonial
experience. But the reluctance to grant the veto power to mayors continued long
after gubernatorial veto powers had become usual. Of the original charters of
these cities, dating from the colonial period to 1834, only five—Baltimore
(1796), Washington (1802), New Orleans (1805), St. Louis (1822), and Brooklyn (1834)—contained veto provisions. This unwillingness to grant the veto
power was not connected with the fact that in only a few cities in the first
quarter of the nineteenth century were mayors directly elected, for of the five
cities in which the veto was established by the initial charter, in only one—St.
Louis—was the mayor at that time chosen by popular vote. In Brooklyn the
council made the choice, and the initial charters of the other three towns provided for the mayor to be appointed by the governor (New Orleans) or the
president (Washington) or selected by an electoral college (Baltimore). Nor were
the charter changes providing for popular election accompanied by grants of
veto power. In Albany the mayor was made elective in 1840 but was not granted
the veto power, and the same circumstances existed in Cincinnati in 1827, Pittsburgh in 1833, Louisville in 1838, Philadelphia in 1839, and Buffalo in 1843.
By 1840 the mayors were directly elected in all of these fifteen cities, but at
that date—and at all other times during the first half of the nineteenth century—
more than half of the city charters withheld the veto power from the mayor.
Indeed, when Washington's mayor was made elective in 1820 the council vote
required to override his veto was reduced from three-fourths to two-thirds. There
was only slight growth (from three to five—there were charter changes in New
York in 1830 and in New Orleans in 1836) in the number of mayors vested
with veto power in the 1820s and 1830s, when the number of cities with elective
mayors increased fivefold. Again, the situation can be most clearly depicted by
a tabular presentation (see Table 1.2).[20]

It is readily apparent that the rapid expansion of mayoral veto powers occurred
in the years immediately following 1850. This doubtless resulted from the increasing concern for peace and order in the cities. Their communities racked by
riots and their society and culture under attack by hoards of turbulent newcom-

Table 1.2
Veto Power of Mayor in Fifteen Cities, 1800–1855[a]

			Majority Required to Override Veto				
Year	No Veto	Simple Majority	Majority of Members	2/3 of Present	2/3 of Members	3/5 of Members	3/4 of Present
1800	4(80%)						1(20%)
1810	4(57%)			1(14%)			2(29%)
1820	6(67%)			2(22%)			1(11%)
1830	7(58%)		2(17%)	2(17%)			1(8%)
1840	10(67%)	1(7%)	2(13%)	1(7%)			1(7%)
1850	10(67%)		2(13%)	1(7%)		1(7%)	1(7%)
1855	4(27%)	1(7%)	1(7%)	3(20%)	3(20%)	2(13%)	1(7%)

[a]The percentages are of the total number of these cities incorporated as of that date.

ers, the disturbed native-born urbanites, who still dominated city governments, hoped that a strengthened chief executive—possessing a greater degree of political independence than the ward-elected councilmen—could suppress the endemic violence, undercut the efforts of the immigrants and their native allies to seize political power, and restore a modicum of tranquility to the cities. The enlargement of mayoral veto powers was only a part of the strengthening of the urban executive that marked the beginning of the emergence of the "strong mayor" urban governmental structure. Veto powers were finally granted to the mayor in Louisville in 1851, in Buffalo in 1853, and in Philadelphia, Boston, and Providence in 1854. Only in Louisville could a simple majority of the council override the mayoral veto; a majority of all members elected was required in Providence, a two-thirds majority in Boston and Philadelphia, and two-thirds of the elected members in Buffalo. During the same period the vote required to override a veto was increased from a majority of elected members to two-thirds of the elected members in New York in 1853 and in Brooklyn in 1854. And when the veto was restored to the mayor of New Orleans in 1852 (with the abandonment of the municipality system) the majority required to override was set at three-fifths of the elected members rather than the earlier (1805–1836) two-thirds of those present.[21]

There was also a less pronounced tendency to increase the terms of mayors during these years. As late as 1830 there were only four of the cities in which the mayoral term was longer than a single year—Cincinnati and Baltimore, where a two-year term had been specified in the original charters, and New Orleans and Washington, where identical terms had been established when the office had been made elective in 1812 and 1820, respectively. Similar action was taken in Louisville in 1838, where the transformation of the mayoralty into an elective office was accompanied by an extension of the term of office to three years. But it was not until the end of the half century—during the same years that saw the expansion of the mayoral veto powers—that the trend away from single-year terms became apparent. Two-year terms were established in New York in 1849, in Albany in 1851, in Brooklyn in 1853, and in Buffalo and Philadelphia in 1854.[22] These changes—as the grants of veto power, and for like reason—were doubtless intended to strengthen the mayoral office.

So, too, were a number of charter provisions enacted primarily during the early 1850s that vested the mayors with greater or nearly exclusive control of the cities' expanding police forces. Such changes took place in Louisville in 1836 and 1851, in New York in 1849 and 1851, in New Orleans and Philadelphia in 1854, and in Buffalo in 1856.[23]

As might be expected, the charter provisions relating to the city councils also underwent some change, though these modifications were not as extensive or significant as those relating to the mayors. One observable shift was a modest tendency toward the establishment of bicameral councils. The original charters of three-fifths of these cities had provided for councils with a single chamber, but by the early 1850s two-thirds of the cities had two-house councils. The changes came in New York in 1830, in St. Louis in 1839, in Louisville in 1850, and in New Orleans in 1852.[24]

One would anticipate that the size of the councils would tend to increase as the urban populations grew and the wards (which were usually the electoral districts for council members) became more numerous. Such was, however, by no means universally the case. Washington's Common Council, to be sure, tripled in size, from seven in 1802 to twenty-one in 1850, and Cincinnati's trustees increased in number from ten in 1819 to forty-eight in 1851. The situation in New Orleans was peculiar. The one-house council originally consisted of fourteen members. When the municipality system was established in 1836 (see pp. 25–26, below) the city council consisted of the municipalities' councils sitting together—a much larger number. But when this system was abandoned in 1852 the size of the Board of Assistant Aldermen (the more numerous body in the bicameral council) was set at twenty-four. Elsewhere the numbers were more stable. Though ward boundaries were repeatedly redrawn, both the number of wards and the representation per ward remained the same in Boston and Providence; consequently, the size of the Common Council in each city was constant—forty-eight in Boston and twenty-four in Providence. Buffalo's Board of Aldermen numbered ten from 1832 to 1850, and Philadelphia's Common Council held steady at twenty throughout the entire half century. There were very modest increases in several other cities. Charleston's thirteen wardens (later aldermen) of 1800 had grown to only fourteen by 1850 despite many changes in the wards and a substantial annexation in 1848. New York's two equally sized councils had numbered fourteen each in 1800 and only increased by four during the five decades. Louisville's single council grew from ten in 1828 to sixteen in 1850 by virtue of the creation of three additional wards. When the nine-man single council of St. Louis had been replaced by a bicameral body in 1839, the Board of Delegates (the larger of the councils) was assigned a membership of twelve, which remained constant throughout the remainder of the half century.[25]

In a few cities the authorities indicated a determination to restrain or prevent the expansion of council membership. In Albany, where the colonial charter had provided for a council consisting of two aldermen and two assistant aldermen from each ward, each new ward added four members to the council, which reached twenty early in the nineteenth century. The number was maintained at that level only by holding the number of wards steady at five while the city's area and population both increased. As a result of this policy the average ward population roughly tripled between 1815 and 1840. By that date an increase in the number of wards had become imperative, but when the number of wards was doubled in 1841, the office of assistant alderman was abolished, and, since each ward would subsequently be represented by two aldermen, the size of the council remained constant at twenty.[26]

The situation in Baltimore was similar. There the number of wards had been held stable at twelve from 1818 until 1842 while the average ward population rose from about 5,000 to roughly 9,000. The creation of two new wards in the latter year only increased the size of the First Branch of the council from twenty-four to twenty-eight, but still left the average ward population at over 7,700 and increasing at a rate of about 500 per year. In 1846, consequently, the number of wards was increased to twenty and the representation in the Second Branch reduced to one per ward.[27]

Pittsburgh's Common Council membership, originally set at fifteen in 1816, had grown to twenty-three in 1839 as the number of wards increased from two to five. Although council representation was not originally based on wards, the increasing clumsiness of conducting at-large elections of growing numbers of councilmen by a population that burgeoned from perhaps 6,000 in 1816 to 21,000 in 1840 eventually resulted in ward elections with five members of the Common Council (and three of the Select Council) sitting from each ward. When, in the mid-1840s, the sixth, seventh, eighth, and ninth wards were created in quick succession the Common Council membership soared to forty-five. To diminish this unwieldy number state legislation was secured in 1847 that assigned two Select Council seats to each ward but froze the Common Council membership at thirty, to be apportioned among the wards according to population.[28]

In the sixteen years after the city's founding Brooklyn's Board of Aldermen had increased in size only slightly—from eighteen to twenty-two. Since the voters in each ward elected two aldermen, this limitation was accomplished by restricting the number of new wards created to two. But a concomitant of this restraint in a period of enormous population growth was a dramatic increase in the average ward population, which rose from about 2,200 to over 8,800 between 1834 and 1850. When, in 1854, Brooklyn, Williamsburg, and Bushwick were consolidated, it was obvious that new wards would have to be created. Initially the number of wards rose only to eighteen, but additional creations, of necessity, followed. In anticipation of these changes, the legislature had reduced the council representation to one alderman per ward, initially reducing the size of the Board of Aldermen below the 1850 level. But ward populations were still very high—in 1855 the average ward population in Brooklyn exceeded 11,400.[29]

The inevitable result of population growth coupled with efforts to limit the

Table 1.3
Changes in Population per Councilman in Fifteen Cities, 1830–1850

Cities Ranked by Pop./Cnclm.[a] in 1850	Rank by Population in 1850	Pop./Cnclm.[a] in 1850	Pop./Cnclm.[a] in 1830	% Change 1830-1850
1. New York	1	28,642	14,471	+98%
2. Baltimore	2	8,452	3,359	+152%
3. St. Louis	8	6,488	556 (1828)	+1085%
4. Philadelphia	4	6,069	4,023	+51%
5. Brooklyn	7	4,402	1,219 (1834)	+261%
6. Buffalo	13	4,226	1,058 (1832)	+299%
7. Cincinnati	6	3,498	2,069	+69%
8. Charleston	12	3,070	2,524	+22%
9. Boston	3	2,852	1,279	+123%
10. New Orleans	5	2,771[b]	3,286	-16%[b]
11. Louisville	11	2,700	1,034	+161%
12. Albany	9	1,905	1,046	+110%
13. Washington	15	1,905	1,046	+82%
14. Providence	14	1,730	728 (1831)	+138%
15. Pittsburgh	10	1,553	628	+147%
Mean:		5,393	2,566	+110%
Median:		3,070	1,219	+152%

[a]Total population divided by membership of the largest council chamber
[b]In 1850 the New Orleans city council consisted of all members of the three municipality councils sitting jointly.

size of city councils was an increase—sometimes a dramatic increase—in the ratio of population to councilmen. This progression constituted a major change of scale in the area of urban government and may well have had a significant impact on many residents' perceptions of the city as a political institution and the relationships between that institution and the citizenry. The nature of this change in the last two decades of the half century is indicated by the data in Table 1.3.[30]

Several things are readily apparent from an examination of these data. First, there were substantial increases in the population/councilman (P/C) ratios in most of these cities. The mean P/C ratio increased by 110% and the median by 152%. In only six of the cities was the increase less than 100%. The explanation for the slower growth of the P/C ratios in these cities varies. New York's P/C ratio, of course, almost doubled in any event and the numerical increase was actually well over twice that in St. Louis. But since the P/C index in New York was already so extremely high in 1830 the percentage growth was smaller. Philadelphia and Charleston had the lowest population growth rates (1830–1850) of any of the cities—51% and 42%, respectively. Since the council membership remained unchanged in Philadelphia, the percentage increase in the P/C ratio was identical with that of the population. The number of aldermen in Charleston increased by two, dropping the P/C ratio increase below that of the population. In Cincinnati and Washington increases in the council membership—from twelve to thirty-three in Cincinnati and from eighteen to twenty-two in Washington—partially offset population increases of 365% and 112%, respectively.

The New Orleans figure is an aberration produced by the fact that the 1836 charter had created a large—and largely powerless—council (see note b, Table 1.3). When, in 1852, a new charter reestablished a single city government, the Board of Assistant Aldermen had twenty-seven members—almost twice the number in 1830—with a resulting P/C ratio of 5,251, based on a population expanded by the annexation of Lafayette.[31]

Second, although the variation in the size of the P/C ratios appears to be enormous, that appearance is deceptive. It is true that the range of P/C ratios in 1850 was 5.0 times the mean of those ratios and 8.8 times the median. But the range is monstrously skewed by the New York figure, which is considerably more than three times the second highest ratio (its population is also more than three times as great as the next largest city's). If the New York P/C ratio is removed from the array, the remaining fourteen towns show a range of ratios that is only 1.8 times the mean of those ratios and 2.3 times the median. Moreover, the range was, in relative terms, narrowing in the last two decades of the half century—in 1830 the fourteen-city array (excluding New York) of P/C ratios had shown a range of 2.0 times the mean and 2.9 times the median. This shift was occasioned, of course, by the disappearance of the very low P/C ratios that were so common in 1830, when nine of the fifteen cites showed ratios smaller than the lowest figure in 1850.

Third, the size of the P/C ratio is, to a considerable degree, a function of the size of the city population. The first five cities listed in Table 1.3 include three of the five largest ranked by total population (four of the top five if we adjust the New Orleans figure to conform to the changes accomplished by the 1852 charter) and the last five include three of the five smallest. While there are some obvious discrepancies—Boston, which ranks ninth in P/C ratio and third in population size and St. Louis, which ranks third in P/C ratio and eighth in population size—the tendency for P/C ratio ranking to conform generally to rank by population size is obviously pronounced. The rank order correlation (Spearman's rho) between P/C ratio and population size is .654—.723 if the New Orleans figures are adjusted. This tendency is less pronounced than in 1830, however, when the rank order correlation was .875.

The central point at issue in shaping the actions of urban governmental leaders and state legislators affecting the P/C ratio was the inherent and inevitable conflict in a democratic political entity with an expanding population between the desirability of the fullest representation of the electorate in the governing process and the fear that bodies deliberating on local and mundane matters would become unable to function when the membership exceeded some finite but as yet undetermined number. Obviously, the issue was most commonly resolved by limiting council sizes.

In three cities, however, the size of the largest council was dramatically increased in the early 1850s. In two cases this change produced an equally significant drop in the P/C ratio; in the third the ratio, nevertheless, rose. The increase of the number of.wards in Cincinnati from eleven to sixteen in 1851, with the constant assignment of three trustees to each ward, increased the number of trustees from thirty-three to forty-eight and dropped the P/C ratio to 2,500—29% below the 1850 figure. New York's continued reliance on two equally sized councils with the electorate of each ward electing one alderman and one assistant alderman, coupled with an unwillingness to consolidate the older wards, had by 1850, created two problems—a P/C ratio rapidly approaching 30,000 and a grossly disproportionate representation of the electorate in the councils depending on the ward of residence. Ward populations at midcentury varied from 6,655 to 52,882, and the average ward population of the first six wards (at the southern tip of Manhattan) was 17,900 as compared to 31,396 for the remainder. Consequently, by a charter amendment of 1853, the Board of Assistant Aldermen was replaced by a Board of Councilmen of "sixty members, to be elected from as many districts . . . of contiguous territory, and as near as may be of equal population." The result was a drop of the P/C ratio by 59% to 10,043 (based on the estimated 1853 population) and, obviously, a much more equitable distribution of seats.[32]

The increase in the size of Philadelphia's Common Council in 1854 from twenty to seventy-four (with the membership to be determined by the number of taxable inhabitants after 1855) was, however, produced by wholly different considerations. In that year all of the municipalities in Philadelphia County were consolidated into a single city and the population of Philadelphia was, thus, enormously increased. With the number of councilmen increasing by 270% and the city's population (estimated in 1854) by 388%, the P/C ratio actually increased by 5% to 6,371.[33]

The general democratic trends of the period that contributed to making the mayoral office elective also had an impact on other areas of municipal government. One evidence of such influence was the growth in the number of the municipal officers who were chosen by direct election. Generally speaking, there were few elected officials (aside from the members of the city councils, who were almost always directly elected) in these fifteen cities at the beginning of the century or, alternatively, at the time of the granting of their first city charters. Indeed, more than half of them—Baltimore, Charleston, Cincinnati, New Orleans, Philadelphia, St. Louis, and Washington—had none at all. Only one such office[34] was to be found in Buffalo and in Louisville, two in Providence, and three in New York. In only three of these towns, thus, did the number of these elective offices exceed three—in Albany there were four; in Brooklyn, the last of these cities to be chartered, one city and five ward offices were filled by direct election; and in Boston (with its long heritage of town meeting government) the charter provided for the election of a minimum of 132 persons (see note 34) to fill five ward offices.[35]

If Boston was a notable exception to the generalization that there were few or none of these elective offices established in the initial charters, it was, to an even greater degree, an exception to the rule that the number of such offices tended to increase by the middle of the nineteenth century. Indeed, by virtue of the elimination of the firewards, the 1854 Boston charter provided for the filling of only four ward offices by direct election (excluding public school officers, who were almost universally elected in these cities).[36] Bostonians appear to have taken quite literally the provision in their original city charter transferring to the city government the power previously exercised by the town meeting, and the very great number of officials previously elected by that body continued to be selected by the mayor and city council. Additionally, the city governments of Baltimore, Charleston, and Pittsburgh continued, as they had initially, to appoint or elect a variety of officials who were elsewhere directly elected.

In the other eleven cities, however, there were, in varying degrees, increases in the number of the elective offices. The officials most commonly removed from the control of the councils by making them elective were those dealing with or overseeing the cities' financial affairs. Many of these offices had not existed in the earlier years of the half century and when first created were frequently filled by council appointment. But by the early 1850s the treasurer was an elective officer in seven of these towns and the controller in six. Assessors were also directly elected in six of the cities, as were overseers of the poor (or comparable officers), who controlled the disbursement of the not inconsiderable relief funds. Additionally, in five towns the voters chose the collectors or receivers of taxes and in four named the city auditors. Among those city officials not directly concerned with financial operations, those most commonly chosen at the polls were city attorneys or solicitors or counselors, in six cities; marshals, in four cities; constables, in four cities; inspectors of elections, in four cities; street commissioners, in four cities; and city surveyors, in four cities. In addition, the voters in six cities filled one or more judicial offices.

In some urban centers the growth in elective offices was modest—an increase of three in Albany, four in Washington and Brooklyn, and five in New Orleans. But in others the additions were more numerous—fifteen in Buffalo and Philadelphia and twelve in Louisville. In the City of Brotherly Love, for example, the 1789 charter had provided for no elective officers with the exception of the members of the city council. Under the provisions of the consolidation charter of 1854, however, the voters elected (in addition to the mayor, councilmen, and school directors) a marshal of police, a treasurer, a receiver of taxes, a controller, three city commissioners, a solicitor, twenty-four members of the board of health, twenty-four prison inspectors, twenty-four guardians of the poor, forty-eight aldermen (the equivalent of justices of the peace), forty-eight constables, twenty-four judges of elections, forty-eight inspectors of elections, forty-eight assessors, and (by an amendment of the next year) twelve surveyors—a total of 308 officials. Overall, the number of such elective offices (see note 34) in these cities increased by almost 400%, from 23 to 113.[37]

These democratic impulses were also reflected in other changes during the period. Suffrage is an obvious case in point. Since many state constitutions or statutes, in the first half of the nineteenth century, specified property ownership or payment of taxes as a prerequisite to voting, it is clear that such requirements would also prevail in the election of city officials. But it must also be remembered that city charters frequently established more stringent requirements for participation in municipal elections. For instance, New York's 1777 constitution extended the right to vote for state assemblymen to adult males with freehold estates of fifty dollars, renters who paid at least five dollars rent annually, and freemen of the city of New York created in or before 1777. But that city's charter excluded renters entirely, limiting the suffrage to fifty-dollar freeholders and freemen. It has been estimated that of the 13,018 adult white males in the city in 1801, more than 8,000 could vote for state assemblymen, while fewer than 3,000 could participate in the municipal elections. In 1804, despite substantial opposition within the city government, the state legislature extended suffrage in city elections to renters paying at least twenty-four dollars rent annually.[38] The city subsequently established a broader electorate by authorizing voting by taxpayers, but when the state, in 1826, eliminated all property and tax qualifications for voting for adult white males (with a $250 property requirement for blacks), the municipality again lagged behind and did not drop the taxpayer requirement until 1842. Nevertheless, before the end of the half century the nation's largest city had moved from a quite restrictive electorate to universal white (but including black property holders) manhood suffrage, qualified only by age, residence, and citizenship requirements.[39]

In Brooklyn and Buffalo—with very late initial charter dates—the state legislation of 1826 proved determinative; each began its metropolitan life with free white male suffrage. The situation in Louisville was somewhat more complicated. Kentucky had pioneered white manhood suffrage in the late eighteenth century, and the city's initial charter (1828) had specified a metropolitan electorate identical with that of the state. Nevertheless, in a little over two decades the state legislature rewrote the voting requirements for the city at least four times, including a taxpaying requirement in 1831 and 1838 and omitting it in 1833 and 1851. Similar charter provisions tying city suffrage requirements to those in the state dated from 1796 in Baltimore and Philadelphia, from 1817 in Charleston, and from 1834 in Cincinnati and—when not modified by subsequent state legislation, as was the case in Louisville—carried all of these cities except Philadephia into the universal white male suffage column before the end of the half century.[40]

In Albany, too, the impact of the 1826 change in state suffrage requirements was determinative, but not immediate. Its charter of 1801 had created an unusual—indeed, to the best of my knowledge, unique—municipal electorate. The franchise was extended not only to freeholders, renters paying at least five dollars annually in rent, and taxpayers, but also to every adult male who was "an inhabitant and born within the said city." These provisions were repeated in the 1826 charter, and the state suffrage provisions of that year were not extended to Albany municipal elections until 1828. In St. Louis, too, where the payment of a city tax was a requirement for voting under the provisions of the first three city charters (1822, 1835, and 1839), adult white male suffrage was eventually established by a clause in the 1841 charter making the municipal electoral qualifications indentical with those of the state.[41]

The progression in New Orleans, though moving from a more restrictive base, was quite similar. By the 1805 charter voting in the Crescent City had been limited to adult white males owning real estate valued at $500 or more or paying at least $100 annually in rent. An amendment in 1812 reduced the rent requirement by one-half and added taxpayers to the electorate, and in 1818 all the requirements except the payment of a state tax were eliminated. These conditions prevailed until the new Louisiana constitution of 1845 established universal white manhood suffrage throughout the state, including municipal elections.[42]

In five of these cities, however, some form of property ownership or taxpaying qualification for voting still existed at the middle of the nineteenth century. The situation in Boston was rather more complex than in the other four towns. There, in 1800, voters were required to possess a $200 freehold; but when Massachusetts adopted taxpayer suffrage in 1821, voting in the town of Boston was clearly affected. This was reflected in the initial city charter of the next year, which specified that every adult male citizen, meeting certain residence requirements, "who shall have paid . . . any state or county tax, which . . . shall have been assessed upon him . . . , and also every [such] citizen who shall be, by law, exempted from taxation" should be entitled to vote in city elections. The practical effect of the "exempted" clause, which was repeated in the 1854 charter, was apparently insignificant, for it was not even mentioned in a published statement of voting qualifications in 1851.[43]

The situation in Philadelphia and Pittsburgh was quite simple; suffrage followed the state law, which required men twenty-two years of age and older to have paid a state or county tax. Between the twenty-first and twenty-second birthdays no tax payment was required. The initial charter of Washington (1802) established a taxpayer suffrage which continued throughout the half century, but a significant modification was made by the 1848 charter. In that document the council was authorized to levy a school tax of one dollar on every adult white male citizen, and the payment of that tax (together with any others assessed) was declared to be sufficient to qualify individuals to vote. Thus, as a practical matter, all adult white male citizens could vote in the nation's capital in the mid-nineteenth century, unless they were delinquent in paying their taxes.[44]

Rhode Island's colonial charter, which continued to serve as the constitution of the state for sixty-five years after independence, limited voting to "freemen"—that is, persons holding a $134 freehold—or their eldest sons. When, after the "Dorr War," Rhode Islanders adopted a new constitution opening the polls to adult males who paid a one-dollar registry tax, these new voters were specifically excluded from participating in Providence city elections. Consequently, Providence alone, among these cities, entered the second half of the nineteenth century with a property qualification for voting.[45]

Thus, the national political tendencies of the Jacksonian era had worked to expand vastly the suffrage in almost all of these cities in the first half of the nineteenth century. Only Providence can be seen as an exception and even there another tendency—the rapid rise in urban property values—had produced a similar (though less pronounced) result. More specifically, the electoral changes illustrate the rapid erosion of the commonly accepted and often closely linked concepts that property deserved representation in government and that the votes of non–property owners were peculiarly susceptible of corrupt purchase. In the movement to exalt people over property in representative government, the major cities frequently lagged well behind the vanguard. As has been noted, at various times a number of these towns—for example, Albany, New York, Providence, Louisville, and St. Louis—maintained suffrage requirements that were more restrictive than those of their states. Indeed, even nonresident property holders could vote in municipal elections in Charleston throughout this period and in St. Louis before 1841, and until 1804 New York residents could cast votes in each ward in which they held the requisite amount of real estate.[46]

Closely related to these property or tax requirements for voting were the qualifications established for municipal officeholders. It was usual, of course, for charters to require that the mayors and council members (and, frequently, other officers as well) be drawn from the qualified electors. But many municipal charters established additional property ownership requirements for citizens holding these offices. This was not, however, universally true; Albany, New York, and Boston never had such additional requirements, and Providence's specification that the mayor and councilmen must be both freemen and free-holders differed only slightly from the state suffrage requirements. Other cities—Pittsburgh, Philadelphia, and Charleston (for wardens only)—washed their hands of the matter by early tying the qualifications for municipal office holding to those for state officers.[47]

The original charters of Charleston and Washington established no special property qualifications for officeholders; that of Baltimore set none for the mayor but required members of the First and Second Branches of the council to be holders of property assessed at $1,000 and $2,000, respectively. In 1807 the Baltimore council qualifications were reduced to $300 and $500 and a qualification of property assessed at $500, was added for the mayor. In the following year, when Charleston's electors were permitted to choose someone other than a warden as intendant, a substantial property qualification was established for that office—a freehold valued at 1,500 pounds sterling, free of debt. And in 1812 Washington's city officers were required to be freeholders. These qualifications appear to have been retained throughout the remainder of the half century.[48]

The initial charters of Brooklyn, Buffalo, and St. Louis required the mayor and council members to be freeholders. In Cincinnati the mayor and the trustees (i.e., council members) had to meet the more modest requirement of being free-holders or householders. These requirements were dropped from the second charters of Buffalo (1853) and Brooklyn (1854), but were retained (except that for the mayor, which was eliminated in 1834) in successive Cincinnati charters until omitted from the Ohio general municipalities incorporation act of 1852. In St. Louis the freehold requirement was made more specific in the 1839 charter— "a lot or part of a lot of ground within the city, containing not less than two thousand square feet"—before being dropped two years later.[49]

New Orleans' 1805 charter required aldermen to be freeholders but established no property qualifications for the mayoralty (an appointive office at this date). When the mayor was made elective in 1812 a very substantial property qualification—$3,000 in real estate—was attached to that office. In 1818 the aldermanic property qualification was set more specifically as real estate valued at $1,000. These requirements remained unchanged throughout the period of "municipalities" government and until they were dropped in the 1852 "reconsolidation" charter and replaced by the requirement that the mayor and council members should meet the qualifications mandated for members of the state House of Representatives.[50]

As in a number of other cities, Louisville's initial charter had established no property qualifications for city officers. But three years later, in 1831, the mayor and council members were required to be taxpayers and either freeholders or householders. An 1836 amendment specified that the mayor must be a freeholder but eliminated all except the taxpayer qualification for councilmen. Two years later, however, a council member was required to be either a freeholder or "a housekeeper with a family." The city's second charter, in 1850, eliminated all these qualifications.[51]

In general, then, the trends in relation to office holding qualifications were like those relating to suffrage—the elimination of property requirements and the admission to power (at least in theory) of an ever broadening portion of the whole population. Given social and political realities of the first half of the nineteenth century—that is, that in all cities the mayoral and council offices would, in any event, almost certainly have been filled from the upper socioeconomic segment of the population—a freehold requirement probably did not exclude very many serious contenders for municipal office. In this respect, at least, the office holding requirements differed from the suffrage requirements, for the latter clearly excluded large numbers of potential participants. In only three cities—Baltimore (before 1807), Charleston (after 1808), and New Orleans (between 1812 and 1820 for mayor and after 1818 for aldermen)—do the property qualifications appear to have been sufficiently high to create even a modest barrier to those individuals with any likelihood of election. But there was no headlong rush to eliminate these requirements. Of the eleven cities which had additional qualifications for office holding (this includes those cities whose charters merely referenced state assembly qualifications) only two (New York and St. Louis) had eliminated these before 1850; five others (Brooklyn, Buffalo, Cincinnati, Louisville, and New Orleans) dropped these provisions from new charters written between 1851 and 1854; and four (Baltimore, Charleston, Providence, and Washington) retained some property ownership or taxpaying qualifications beyond the mid-1850s.

The democratic tendencies of the antebellum era were further reflected in the fact that the urban electorates were involved in some manner in the preparation of, or ratification of, modifications in the charters which served as the cities' constitutional documents. These governmental entities were, of course, creatures of the state (or, in the case of Washington, national) governments, and any change in their basic law must, of necessity, emanate from those governments. But in the later years of the half century more charter changes resulted from, or were made dependent upon, actions of the voters in the affected city, though this practice was by no means universal.

It is true that even at an early date charter changes frequently—probably usually—followed a petition from citizens or a request from a city government, and that such requests were sometimes quite detailed as to the changes, and even the wording, desired. Such applications were, in fact, not infrequently recited in the preambles to acts affecting the governmental structure of these towns, as was the case, for example, with state legislative acts relating to Philadelphia in 1796, Albany in 1801, Pittsburgh in 1804, and Baltimore in 1807. But the major concern in these early years would appear to have been with corporation rights, not popular will. It is worthy of note that perhaps the most detailed and extensive assertion of the desirability of legislative deference to the wishes of the city corporations was inspired by the passage of the April 5, 1804, act of the New York legislature enlarging the New York City electorate by the extension of the suffrage to twenty-five-dollar rent payers "without the application or consent of the Mayor, Aldermen, and Commonality of the city." Certainly no charters were prepared by popularly elected conventions or ratifed by popular vote in the first two decades of the century.[52]

One action of the Maryland legislature on a charter issue during this period did reflect some concern for voter—but not necessarily corporation—approval. In 1807 that body amended the Baltimore charter of 1796 to provide for the direct election of members of the Second Branch of the city council and, at the same time, the reduction of the property qualifications for membership in both branches by 70 to 75%. The legislature (probably because the reduction of property qualifications was "a strict party consideration" in the city) uncharacteristically provided that the changes should not be effective unless ratified by a convention consisting of two delegates from each ward elected by general ticket. Current council members and other corporation officers were specifically prohibited from serving as delegates.[53]

In the years after 1820, however, direct or indirect participation by the urban electorates in accomplishing charter changes became much more common. In Boston, for example, a committee previously raised by the town meeting reported a charter proposal to its parent body on the last day of 1821. The citizens debated the proposal in town meeting for three days, making a number of amendments, and submitted to the citizens five questions involving the approval of the proposal and some of its constituent parts, to be determined by ballot. On January 7, 1822, all five questions were decided in the affirmative, and before the end of February the state legislature enacted the first charter of the city of Boston, providing, however, that the act should be effective only if approved by the town's voters. This approval was given by a three-to-two margin and the city of Boston was legally established.[54] The situation was substantially identical in Providence in 1829–1831. The major difference was that the state legislature, when it enacted in 1830 the charter that had been proposed by the town and approved by its electorate, required the document to be approved by three-fifths of the town's voters. The majority in 1830 was substantially below that figure, but when the whole process was repeated the following year the final vote was more than 70% favorable and the charter became effective.[55]

In the cities that had already been incorporated local conventions of elected delegates sometimes drafted new charters in the second quarter of the nineteenth century. This was the case in New York in 1830 and 1849, in Washington in 1848, in Brooklyn in 1848–1849, and in Louisville in 1851. Moreover, four of these charter proposals (all except that of Brooklyn) were approved by the voters of the city before being transmitted to the appropriate legislative bodies, which in every case enacted the requested legislation. In two instances—Brooklyn and New York in 1849—the legislature made the new charters subject to ratification by the voters. Some charters that were not initiated by local conventions—for example, those of St. Louis in 1822 and Cincinnati in 1826—were also required to be ratified by the local electorate before becoming effective.[56]

The Louisville charter of 1851 was unique in incorporating specific provisions for the electorate to initiate charter changes or propose an entirely new charter. Two alternative methods were authorized. The city council might submit proposed charter changes to the voters at any general election of city officers or provide by ordinance for the election of delegates to a convention to propose amendments to the present charter or to draft a new charter. In the latter case, the results of the convention deliberations must be submitted to the voters at a general election. If approved by the voters and enacted by the state legislature the proposals would "form a part of or supersede" the existing charter. But "if the majority of votes cast be against the same, the said Council shall not present the same to the Legislature for enactment." Several amendments to the 1851 charter were initiated by the city and enacted by the legislature under these provisions during the 1850s.[57]

Nevertheless, opposition by the city government or rejection by the voters did not inevitably prevent changes in the governing documents of the cities. An 1847 act requiring the city of Baltimore to pay the salaries of certain judicial officers appointed by the state authorities was adopted despite the vigorous protests of the city officials. Indeed, state legislatures sometimes adopted entire charters immediately after their rejection by the voters. The Cincinnati charter of 1826 and the Brooklyn charter of 1849 had both been enacted by the legislatures subject to their ratification by the electorates of those cities. In Cincinnati about 56% of the voters at a town meeting cast negative votes, and in Brooklyn the negative vote was about two-thirds—in both cases in a very light poll. But both charters were repassed without a voter ratification provision—Cincinnati's in 1827 and Brooklyn's (after the removal of the provision that was presumed to have been most objectionable to the electorate) in 1850.[58]

It is probable that these democratic tendencies of the era influenced, in some measure, certain elements of geographic decentralization in the urban governmental structures. The prevalence of ward election of a number of officers has previously been noted (see pp. 18–19), and these practices doubtless reflected a desire to keep the oversight of certain crucial functions—particularly elections, assessments, tax collection, poor relief, and public education—close to smaller units of the electorate, in the hands of one's "neighbors." But in some cases geographic decentralization of governmental functions also was clearly the product of distrust, fear, or hostility on the part of geographically concentrated elements of the city's population. The clearest case in point is New Orleans.

The 1836 charter of the Crescent City did not destroy the city government, but it did divest it of almost all of the powers associated with a municipal corporation, including the taxing, police, and (with a few exceptions) ordinance powers. These powers were, instead, lodged in three "municipalities," each of which

shall possess separate corporate rights, and are hereby declared to be distinct corporations, and possess generally all such rights, powers and capacities as are usually incident to municipal corporations; . . . and in general shall possess and exercise within their respective limits, all such powers, rights and privileges as are now possessed and exercised by the Corporation of New-Orleans.

Each municipality was governed by a council consisting of a recorder and aldermen elected for two-year terms by the voters; these councils possessed "all the powers now vested by law in the City Council of New-Orleans." The boundaries of the First Municipality encompassed the "Old City," or the Creole section; and those of the Second Municipality embraced the "upper suburbs," or Faubourg Ste. Marie, or the "American" sector. The Third Municipality—the "lower suburbs," or Faubourg Marigny—was a slightly more diverse area inhabited primarily by more recent arrivals from Spain and France and a sizeable number of Creoles, but few "Americans." The "American" sector had developed rapidly in the 1820s and early 1830s, and by 1835 rivaled the "Old City" in population and surpassed it in wealth and commercial importance. These circumstances created a situation in which the "Americans" chafed under the control of the still dominant French, who, in turn, felt threatened by the growth, prosperity, and potential power of the "Americans." The ensuing arrangment left each "population" free to follow its own dictates: each provided for public improvements at rather different rates; each created a bonded indebtedness for these and other purposes; and each (or at least the First and Second Municipalities) became even more unlike the other.[59]

In other instances some elements of geographic decentralization of taxation and expenditure would appear to have resulted primarily from a suspicion that, for certain areas, the benefits of the metroplitan government might be significantly less than the costs. Specifically, residents of outlying wards feared that their taxes might be used primarily to improve streets and services in the more heavily built-up area, particularly in the central business district, and that the city authorities would be slow to extend those services to the outer and more sparsely populated wards, where the costs would be great and the voters few. In a number of cases, doubtless, residents of these peripheral areas did not perceive the need for some of those services in their neighborhoods or the justice of paying taxes to provide such services to other residents of the city. Hence, limits of direct taxation were established in Baltimore in 1817 and a fire and watch district in Brooklyn by the initial charter of 1834, and city taxing authority was severly limited in the area outside these boundaries. In St. Louis similar concerns produced a sightly different result; a tax differential for the outer wards was established in 1841 and later a quarter and then a half of all revenue derived from those wards was mandated to be spent on improvements there, under the direction of the council members from the affected wards. And an 1850 legislative act required each municipal council in New Orleans to prepare separate budgets for the ''urban'' and ''rural'' areas, thus further fragmenting that already trifurcated city.[60]

In Washington the fear that the revenues of the entire city would be committed to the improvement of the Capitol–White House area, coupled with the persistent reluctance of Congress to contribute to public improvements in the capital city, led to the centering of much taxation and expenditure power in the wards. The most extensive tax revenue—that derived from real estate—was collected and retained by the wards. The general government collected a variety of license and other taxes but derived most of the funds needed to support general expenses from transfers from the wards. Improvements were carried out by the wards, which maintained separate budgets and, eventually, created ward debts. This system came into existence as early as 1812 and persisted throughout the half century.[61]

Thus, the democratic trends of the era and persistent localism combined to introduce a considerable measure of geographic decentralization into the American urban governmental experience in the first half of the nineteenth century. But another public attitude was also influential here and in a concurrent movement toward functional decentralization within these city governments. Integrally associated from an early date with the attempts to establish and expand greater popular participation in government was a pervasive distrust of government institutions—a belief that governments and their officers were inherently repressive in nature and a conviction that their exercise of power must be monitored, checked, and limited to prevent them from exalting the concept of public order at the expense of personal liberty and popular rule. It is illustrative that the 1826 controversy in Cincinnati over the new charter passed by the legislature and submitted to the city's voters for ratification was perceived by a visitor as a confrontation between ''the City Council, with the wealthier class of inhabitants'' and ''the multitude,'' over the issue of ''a stricter police and its necessary regulations.'' The charter went down to defeat because a narrow majority of the voters opposed ''abridging public liberty.''[62]

Consequently, even when geographic and cultural differences were not involved there was a pronounced and increasing tendency to disperse rather than concentrate governmental authority, to create new and independent loci of power, and to cling to single-purpose elective boards and commissions (e.g., boards of health, overseers of the poor) that had existed prior to the incorporation of the city. One clear result of these attitudes was the dramatic increase during the half century in the number of city officials who were elected (and, hence, more nearly independent of mayoral and council authority) and charged with specific duties (see pp. 18–19). Even when these officers were appointive, as was true during most of the half century in many of these towns and throughout the period in some, their mere existence, however necessary, tended to diffuse executive power.

New York's 1830 charter mandated that "the executive business of the Corporation of New York, shall hereafter be performed by distinct departments, which it shall be the duty of the Common Council to organize and appoint." The council not only discharged this responsibility but, in addition, through its standing committees intruded its influence still further in executive matters. This circumstance precipitated a confrontation in 1842 between Democratic mayor Robert H. Morris and the Whig-dominated council, in the course of which the mayor asserted that the exercise of executive power by the council committees was in violation of the city's charter. But by that time the practices he condemned were more than a decade old and firmly engrafted onto the governmental structure, and, indeed, Mayor Morris had not complained of these procedures during his first term when his own party controlled the council. In the 1849 charter the legislature attempted to bring some order to the confused and confusing administrative practices in the city by providing that "neither the Common Council nor any Committee or member thereof, shall perform any executive business whatever." But though the charter vested the executive powers in the mayor and the heads of departments it, at the same time, made seven of the nine department heads elective, thus giving them a greater degree of independence and continuing a diffusion of executive function.[63]

In Philadelphia, too, the councils secured significant influence in administrative affairs. After the creation (at least as early as 1833) of a full range of standing joint committees of the two boards, whose responsibilities paralleled the major functions of urban government, a *de facto* departmentalization of executive responsibilities developed. The administrative role of the council was further increased and that of the mayor concomitantly reduced in 1839; when the state legislature made the mayoralty elective the city councils, by ordinance, transferred the appointive power previously exercised by the mayor to the councils or the standing joint committees. Moreover, throughout this period these committees submitted departmental budget estimates and authorized departmental expenditures. Thus, the provision in the 1854 charter that directed the councils "to provide by ordinance for the establishment and regulation of all the departments" and further specified that "through the mayor and proper committees, the said councils shall maintain a supervision of each department" did little more than confirm existing practice.[64]

Even in cities where the councils were not as actively involved in executive affairs as in New York and Philadelphia they frequently exerted considerable influence through the appointment of various city officers. The charters of Brooklyn (1834), Boston (1854), Louisville (1851), and Providence (1833), for example, vested extensive appointive powers exclusively in the councils. In other cases elective boards or officials had extensive budgetary authority. The guardians of the poor and the controllers of schools in Philadelphia could establish their own budgets under the terms of the 1854 city charter, and it appears to have been assumed that the councils would make the requested appropriations. In New York, under the 1849 charter, appropriations were required to be "based upon specific and detailed statements, in writing, of the several heads of the departments," through the comptroller, and under the 1853 amendment the governors of the almshouse transmitted their budgetary requests to a special board of commissioners composed of city officers. If that body rejected the request the governors could, by a two-thirds vote, cause it to be transmitted directly to the supervisors, whose duties were confined to establishing the tax rates necessary to fund the requests. And the 1853 charter of Buffalo gave the elected comptroller a major role in shaping the budget. A politically important function was removed from the control of the mayor and councils by the terms of the charters of Brooklyn (1850) and Buffalo (1853), which provided for elected commissioners of excise to control the issuance of liquor licenses.[65]

Even when they did not possess budgetary independence or exercise power previously vested in the councils or the mayors, elective boards with limited responsibilities could often be excessively jealous of their prerogatives, touchy about their autonomy, and aggressive in defining their areas of responsibilities. Boston's second mayor, Josiah Quincy (the elder), found it difficult to discharge his concept of his mandated responsibility "to inspect the conduct of all subordinate officers" when members of these independent bodies (whose existence antedated that of the city) refused to acknowledge that they were "subordinate" to the mayor. Quincy believed the existence of those boards to be a major barrier to efficient administration of the city. Quincy's views only partially prevailed. The 1854 charter vested the powers of the surveyors of highways in the council, but the overseers of the poor and almost all members of the school committee continued to be elected. And although the mayor was granted a veto at this time, the power of that office was not otherwise strengthened—indeed, was somewhat weakened by removing the mayoral vote in the appointment of city officers—and (with the exception noted below) until well after the middle of the century "the administration of Boston was practically in the hands of the committees of the City Council."[66]

Structure, of course, is not inevitably determinative of function. An energetic and aggressive chief executive could sometimes exert great influence in the governance of a city even when the charter did not appear to provide him with the necessary powers or instruments. Boston, during the administration of Josiah Quincy, is an excellent case in point. Boston's initial charter denied the mayor a veto, restricted his appointive powers to presenting nominations to the board of aldermen, placed some appointive powers in the hands of the joint council, and, as has been noted, provided for a number of independent boards. The charter, it has been asserted, "was, in fact, not an effort to establish a new form of government, but simply intended to perpetuate, so far as possible, the old regime in an attempt to substitute delegated for direct control.'' Quincy, moreover, had vigorously opposed the abandonment of town government in 1822. Nevertheless, by taking the chairmanship of all major committees, by proposing courses of action, and by sheer force of personality, he made himself one of the most important and influential mayors of the antebellum era.[67]

It is readily apparent that the trends of development in urban government in the first half of the nineteenth century were not, in all cases, entirely harmonious, complementary, and mutually supportive. On the contrary, some clearly appear to have been contradictory. This is hardly surprising. Even before the outbreak of the American Revolution the traditional, closed structures of urban governments on the European model had clashed gratingly with the rapidly developing participatory and representative local governmental practices in at least some of the colonies. Elective had begun to replace appointive officials in the chartered cities, and in Boston and Providence the participatory town systems were partially adapted to the larger populations and more complex activities of those urban centers. At no time during the three-quarters of a century after the Revolution were there any theoretical models of urban government that appeared wholly appropriate to the needs and aspirations or entirely harmonious with the wishes and attitudes of the urban populations or capable of fully allaying their distrust of government. The attempts to develop acceptable urban governmental structures, of course, confronted the same contradictory claims for precedence as did the efforts to organize other governmental entities in the late eighteenth and early nineteenth centuries—the balancing of the needs and demands for order and freedom, for individualism and corporateness, and for participation and effectiveness. To attain acceptability and support, governmental control had to accommodate the concept (and, in so far as possible, the practice) of personal liberty. A minor example of such accommodation involves the ancient concept of freemanship. Originally instituted to afford economic protection to the mercantile and artisan elements in largely static urban populations, the exclusion from these trades of persons who were not freemen of the city (a right obtainable by birth, local apprenticeship, or purchase) never made much economic sense in the New World and became primarily a source of revenue for the corporations and (because freemen were voters) a means of restraining the electorate, especially at the lower end of the economic scale. But such a governmental restriction on personal liberty appeared inappropriate even before the Revolution and was increasingly viewed as oppressive in the post-Revolutionary era. Consequently, the economic restrictions on nonfreemen disappeared well before the legal provisions were changed and the political restrictions were submerged in the rising tide of suffrage extension.[68]

But although the attempt to balance the sometimes contradictory claims of order and freedom—of corporateness and individualism—influenced the efforts to formulate acceptable governmental structures at all levels in antebellum America, the imperative need for order and corporateness loomed ever larger in the thinking of urbanites seeking to establish and modify their governments. For the size and diversity of the urban populations required more restraints on individual liberties than was the case in smaller towns and rural areas. Such practices and omissions as throwing garbage randomly upon the ground, discharging firearms, building structures of flammable materials, allowing chimneys to go unswept and take fire, and permitting privy vaults to overflow would, in urban areas, endanger the property, health, and lives of persons other than the offenders and must, of necessity, be restrained, regulated, or prohibited. The more extensive commercial and manufacturing activities in the city made it desirable, if not essential, that some corporate power intervene to protect both the entrepreneurs—whose activities formed the economic base of the community—and the consumers. Also, the diversity of the urban populations and the anonymity provided by their size meant that the restraints and controls exercised by nongovernmental institutions and entities—families, churches, neighbors, communally shared values—operational in smaller populations became, in some measure, inoperative or at least weakened in the cities and needed to be replaced by corporate—almost certainly governmental—regulation. Mob violence, for example, was largely an urban phenomenon, and the strengthening of police powers and concentration of police control that occurred in the period after 1830 was clearly a response to the threats presented by the increasing frequency and scope of such activities. It is difficult to imagine that the chief executive of a nonurban community would have been granted the police powers which a city shaken to its foundations by a fierce and deadly riot the previous year conferred upon the mayor of Providence in 1831—powers that included search without warrants and imprisonment without charges, hearing, or trial.[69]

Still, if the need for corporate order appeared dominant among the factors influencing the structuring and restructuring of urban governments in the middle years of the nineteenth century, neither the urban residents nor the state legislators who usually (but not always) were guided by their wishes were blind to the potential problems presented by concentrating in fewer hands the increased power necessary to preserve that order. They were, moreover, justifiably concerned about the potential for laxity, mismanagement, and fraud that grew in proportion to the size of the city budgets and the expansion of city functions. To guard against these potential abuses they increasingly spread the direct responsibility for the exercise of power among a larger number of officials and made more of them directly elective, diminishing (or attempting to diminish) the influence of the mayor and council. The 1854 Philadelphia charter required that all offices subsequently created dealing in any way with the assessment, collection, appropriation, or expenditure of city funds be filled by election, and that document and the New York charter of the previous year incorporated provisions dealing with bribery and fraud.[70]

The trends in the development of urban governmental institutions were, thus, diffuse—strengthening here, limiting there. The universal shift to directly elected mayors and the more widespread granting of veto powers, together with a tendency to concentrate police powers in the hands of a single official, assuredly indicated a growing rejection of the old strong council–weak mayor formula. But exactly what form of government would take its place was by no means clear. In the charters of mid-nineteenth-century cities can be found the seeds of both the strong mayor and the commission forms of urban government. Faced with the continuing necessity to maintain public order, the undiminished distrust of governmental power, the need to respond effectively to new demands for communal action, and a burgeoning and increasingly heterogeneous population, the urban residents groped—with a clearer vision of what they feared and repudiated than of what they desired—for a structure of government that would serve well their needs and aspirations. They acted, nevertheless, with assurance and optimism—pessimism would come later—and were by no means prepared to view the government of its cities as "the one conspicuous failure of the United States."[71]

Chapter 2

Financing Urban
Government

The creation of urban governmental structures may suggest at least something about the aspirations urban residents have for their cities and what they expect from their officials, or about the aspirations and expectations of some influential portion of those residents, or of the state or federal officials that shaped those structures. A detailed examination of the fiscal affairs of urban governments provides fairly conclusive evidence about what they were willing to pay for (or were perceived as being willing to pay for) and what services they obtained or, at least, were publically promised. Few government services are without cost. Even the fire protection initially provided by volunteer companies soon generated charges upon the corporation for firehouses, engine upkeep, and new equipment. And however large a role volunteerism may have played in village life, as the urban population grew in size and complexity—often well before the issuance of city charters—that volunteerism faded into insignificance. Those of large or at least modest estate—the only segment of the urban population for whom the voluntary participation in government or the voluntary provision of service to the community was ever a genuine possibility or held any significant measure of attractiveness—found the burden too onerous as the duties of office multiplied, involved more attention to detail, required more nearly continuous oversight, and conferred less honor upon and brought less public gratitude to the officeholder. Concurrently, residents of lesser economic standing required remuneration if they were to become the primary providers of urban services, and this remuneration could not, in every case, be provided by user fees.

It might be suggested that, in regard to the public monies that supported urban government, there were three basic areas of inquiry indicated by three simple questions: How much money was involved? Where did it come from? And where did it go? But to these simple questions simple answers are always difficult and often impossible to obtain. In 1899 J. H. Hollander, attempting to bring some sort of order to the historical financial data of the single city of Baltimore, candidly cautioned that his laboriously constructed tables could only be used for rough comparisions. "Owing to the multiplicity of items in the Comptroller's Reports," he lamented, "and the absence of descriptive detail, it has been impossible to compile an accurate balance sheet, and in certain years the discrepancy is large."[1] In dealing with a relatively large number of cities the difficulties are compounded. Some cities appear rarely or never to have published comprehensive data; figures are wholly missing for many years; the categories of revenues and expenses were frequently modified without explanation; and the dates of the fiscal year fluctuated widely both in individual cities and among the urban centers. The list could be extended almost infinitely, but a substantial body of data has been collected for a number of these cities from which some tentative conclusions can be cautiously drawn.

Limited information on governmental revenues has been located for nine of these cities in the second decade of the nineteenth century—Albany (1811), Baltimore (1817), Boston (1818), Louisville (1819), New Orleans (1820), New York (1817), Pittsburgh (1817), Providence (1815), and St. Louis (1819). The Pittsburgh data consist of a gross revenue figure only, but for the other towns full or partial detail is available showing the sources of the receipts. These urban centers differ greatly from one another in many particulars. Their populations range in size (in 1820) from 4,012 for Louisville to 123,706 for New York, with four having populations in excess of 25,000. Four are located in slave states and four lie west of the Appalachian Mountains. Only four—Albany, Baltimore, New Orleans, and New York—had been granted city charters; the remainder were operating under some form of town government. And it is clear that size and governmental structure had some considerable influence on the amount of revenue raised and the sources of that revenue.[2]

As Table 2.1 reveals, there were significant disparities among the cities in the amount of revenue raised in relation to the size of their populations. The per capita amount of revenue generated by the government of New York in 1817 was more than six times as great as the similiar figure for Pittsburgh in the same year.[3] But the variations are by no means random. Of the four cities with populations (in 1820) in excess of 25,000, only in Baltimore did the revenue raised amount to less than $5.96 per capita, while among the five smaller cities it was only in the largest—Albany (12,630)—that the per capita revenue exceeded $2.09. Indeed, when the rankings of these urban centers by size and by per capita revenues are compared there is a very close correlation between size and revenue levels throughout the array of cities, with Baltimore (second in size and fifth in per capita revenue) presenting the only significant anomaly; there is no other instance of a deviation of more than two rank positions. A statistical examination of the two lists yields a rank correlation coefficient (Spearman) of .817 (or, if we exclude Baltimore from the analysis, of .881).

It is clear, thus, from an examination of the gross and per capita revenue

Table 2.1
Revenues in Nine Cities, 1811–1820

City (year)	Per Capita	Gross
New York (1817)	$7.46	$862,128.77
New Orleans (1820)	6.15	167,130.00
Boston (1818)	5.96	242,322.99
Albany (1811)	5.48	53,085.17
Baltimore (1816)	2.28	118,085.56[a]
Providence (1815)	2.09	22,800.00
Louisville (1819)	1.60	5,995.18
St. Louis (1819)	1.22	5,224.77
Pittsburgh (1817)	1.21	7,844.31
Median	2.28	
Mean	3.72	
Range	6.25	
SD	2.35	

SD   Standard deviation.
[a]Aggregate of detail; $400 greater than
statement of gross.

levels in these nine cities, not only that city revenues rose with the increase in the population of the urban centers, but also that the increase in revenue levels was grossly disproportionate to the growth of the population. Doubtless much of the increase in the per capita levels of urban revenue was a reflection of the expansion of responsibilities of the goverments of larger cities, which, in turn, resulted from the increasing diversity and complexity of function and rising expectations of their populations.

Since an increase in population size and complexity was normally accompanied by the grant of a city charter, which, in turn, tended to increase the urban residents' expectations for the delivery of city services, the chartered city governments tended to raise larger per capita revenues than the town governments in the other urban centers. Thus, in the chartered city of Albany, with a population of 9,683 in 1811, per capita revenue was more than two and one-half times that in the town of Providence, with a slightly larger population of 10,919. Nevertheless, there are anomalies. The town of Boston ranked third among these nine cities in population (1820) and third in per capita revenues. But the city of Baltimore, the second largest of these cities, ranked fifth in per capita revenue, with a figure less than two-fifths that of Boston. All of which leads to a statement of the obvious: the revenues raised are related to (though not always identical with) the anticipated expenditures, which, in turn, are a function of the responsibilities that have been assumed by or assigned to the urban government.[4]

The structure of urban government would appear to have been definitive, however, in determining the sources from which revenue was raised. As the figures in Table 2.2 show, each of the four urban centers with town governments (disaggregated data are not available for Pittsburgh) relied on property taxes for more than three-quarters of its total revenue. In only one of the four chartered

Table 2.2
Percent of Revenue Derived from Property Taxes in Eight Cities, 1811–1820

City (year)	Percent
Louisville (1819)	88.7
Providence (1815)	87.7
St. Louis (1819)	85.3
Boston (1818)	75.8
Baltimore (1816)	27.2
New York (1817)	23.1
Albany (1811)	15.1
New Orleans (1820)	9.6

Median	51.5
Mean	51.6
Range	79.1
SD	33.4

cities (Baltimore—27.2%) did the dependence upon property taxes reach one-quarter. The latter, of course, had other legally authorized sources upon which to rely. New Orleans, which derived less than a tenth of its receipts from property taxes, raised well over three-fifths of its income from the sale and rent of corporate property and from wharfage, and almost another eighth from license fees for taverns and boarding houses. Albany, too, relied heavily on land sales and rentals (which constituted more than two-thirds of that city's revenue) and resorted to borrowing to supply another fourteenth. Baltimore, on the other hand, drew one-half of its receipts from a variety of specific license and auction taxes and about one-ninth from the rental of city property and market stalls. Rather more than 8% of that city's revenue consisted of special assessments on property holders to defray (in part) the costs of constructing and repairing streets, sidewalks, wells, and pumps. In New York such assessments accounted for almost a third of the total revenue with another eighth coming from the sale and rental of city property. License and other nonproperty taxes supplied another thirteenth, and more than a fifth of the city's total receipts came from the sale of city stock and three loans from the Mechanic's Bank.[5]

Property tax rates during this era, though varying considerably, would appear to have been uniformly below $1 per $100 of assessed valuation. For the ten cities for which such data have been located (see Table 2.3)[6] the rates ranged from 20 cents per $100 in New Orleans to 82 cents in Boston, with eight of the cities taxing property at 50 cents or less. The per capita property tax collections varied much more widely, with the figure for Boston being almost eight times that for Baltimore, despite the fact that Boston's tax rate was only a little higher than that of Baltimore. The size of the tax yields was, obviously, heavily affected both by the actual differences in real estate values in the various towns and by the nominal values for tax purposes as reflected in the assessments (see Table 2.4).[7] Baltimore officials during this period commonly assessed property at about one-fifth of its market value. When raising funds to pay the federal direct tax of 1816, the state assessor valued the real estate in Baltimore at almost 15.5

Table 2.3
Property Tax Rates and Per Capita Yields in Eleven Cities, 1811–1819

City (year)	Tax Rate per $100	Per Capita Property Tax Collections
Boston (1818)	$0.82	$4.51[a]
Baltimore (1816)	0.75	0.62
Pittsburgh (1816)	0.50	n.a.
Washington (1819)	0.50	n.a.
Cincinnati (1811)	0.35	n.a.
St. Louis (1819)	0.30	1.04
New York (1817)	0.275	1.73
Providence (1815)	0.245	1.83
Louisville (1819)	0.22	1.42
New Orleans (1812)	0.20	n.a.
Albany (1811)	n.a.	0.83
Median	0.325	1.42
Mean	0.416	1.71
Range	0.62	3.89
SD	0.21	1.22

n.a. -- Not available for this year.
[a]Probably includes a small amount of poll
taxes.

million dollars despite the fact that it was assessed for city tax purposes only three years earlier at rather less than 3.5 million dollars. Boston assessors, on the other hand, entered the property of residents of that city on their books at one-half the actual value—slightly over 19.5 million dollars in 1818. Moreover, the assessment rolls included widely disparate components of personal property, ranging from none in Philadelphia and Louisville to between 40% and 50% of the total figure in Boston and Providence. Finally, tax delinquency rates varied from city to city and from year to year.[8]

By the 1830s the increasing urban populations and, in at least some cases, the increased responsibilities of the urban governments had driven the city budgets upward significantly (see Tables 2.1 and 2.5).[9] In such older established cities as New York (1817–1834), Baltimore (1817–1835), and Providence (1815–1835) the gross receipts had more than doubled. In Albany (1811–1832) receipts had almost tripled and in Boston (1818–1835) had more than quintupled.[10] In the towns that were small and unincorporated in the second decade of the nineteenth century the increase had been greater still, with the receipts in Louisville (1819–1832) and St. Louis (1819–1836) being seven and eight and two-thirds times, respectively, as great in the fourth decade as in the second.

The increase in per capita receipts was much less pronounced. There was practically no increase in Albany and New York, but the figures more than doubled in Baltimore and Louisville, almost tripled in Boston, and more than tripled in St. Louis. In Providence the increase was roughly one-third.

The revenue figures for Charleston and Boston are so disproportionately large as to require comment. In this fiscal year almost half of Charleston's expendi-

Table 2.4
Property Assessments in Nine Cities, 1813–1824

City (year)	Gross Assessment	Per Capita Assessment
Providence (1815)	8,163,265[a]	747.62
New York (1817)	78,895,735[b]	683.04
Washington (1819)	6,403,125[c]	502.48
Boston (1818)	19,600,600[d]	481.84
Brooklyn (1818)	2,902,338[e]	438.42
Philadelphia (1824)	21,136,215[f]	300.21
St. Louis (1819)	1,132,164	263.42
Louisville (1821)	1,189,664[f]	256.12
Baltimore (1813)	3,325,848	76.05
	Median	438.42
	Mean	416.58

[a]Estimated. On the basis of later data, probably a little less than one-half of this figure was personal property.
[b]On the basis of later data, probably about 35% of this figure was personal property.
[c]On the basis of later data, probably less than 10% of this figure was personal property.
[d]About 43% of this figure was personal property.
[e]About 9% of this figure was personal property.
[f]Real estate only.

tures went for capital improvements (including such items as street and walkway paving, the acquisition of land for the White Point Gardens, and street widening and wharf construction) and another sixth was disbursed in the form of loans and stock subscription to the Charleston, Louisville, and Cincinnati Railroad. These unusual expenditues forced the city to resort to borrowing for well over half of this year's revenue. Boston, too, derived more than one-half of its revenue from loans, most of which apparently went to service the existing debt. But while Boston's 1835 revenues conformed closely to the usual pattern in the Massachusetts metropolis in this period, the same was clearly not the case in Charleston. There the 1838 figures were almost double those for the early 1840s. Thus, the Charleston figure is clearly aberrant. If Charleston is excluded from the calculations, the median per capita receipts for the remaining ten cities drops to $4.88 and the mean to $5.81. Hence, the median per capita receipts for the cities analyzed (excluding Charleston) more than doubled between the 1810s and the 1830s (see Tables 2.1 and 2.5).

The general reliability of these findings about the shift in per capita receipts is further supported by an analysis of the changes in the per capita revenues in the seven cities common to both lists—Albany, Baltimore, Boston, Louisville, New York, Providence, and St. Louis. The mean per capita receipts for these cities increased rather less than three-quarters and the median more than doubled.

Table 2.5
Receipts in Eleven Cities, 1832–1838

City (year)	Per Capita	Gross
Boston (1835)	$16.96	$1,308,843.71
Charleston (1838)	15.38	453,281.00[a]
New York (1834)	7.74	1,908,496.60
Philadelphia (1835)	5.86	510,466.73
Albany (1832)	5.85	152,787.51
Washington (1832)	4.94	97,466.37[b]
Baltimore (1835)	4.82	440,512.01
St. Louis (1836)	3.70	45,262.94[c]
Louisville (1832)	3.36	42,059.59
Providence (1835)	2.83	56,700.00
Cincinnati (1837)	2.06	82,182.20

Median	4.94	
Mean	6.68	
Range	14.90	
SD	4.73	

[a]Aggregate of detail; $882 less than statement of gross.
[b]Includes ward receipts (all property taxes); figures include property taxes <u>levied</u> and other taxes <u>collected</u>.
[c]Aggregate of detail; exceeds statement of gross by $1,001.

As in the 1810s, there is an observable tendency in the 1830s for the larger cities to have larger per capita revenues. Per capita receipts exceeded five dollars in three of the four cities in Table 2.5 with estimated 1835 populations above 50,000, and the revenues in Baltimore fell below that figure by only eighteen cents. Among the six cities (if we exclude Charleston) with populations of less than 50,000, only the per capita revenue of Albany exceeded five dollars. Nevertheless, the relationship between city size and per capita receipts was much less close than in the 1810s. The rank correlation (Spearman) between city size in 1835 and per capita revenues among the cities in Table 2.5 (excluding Charleston) is only .485, significantly below the figure derived from an analysis of the cities in Table 2.1.[11]

It will be recalled that the analysis of the sources of urban revenue in the second decade of the nineteenth century (Table 2.2) revealed wide variations in the extent of reliance on property taxes and clear differences between the chartered cities and the urban centers still operating under the more restrictive town governments. By the 1830s all of the cities analyzed had received city charters, but there were still wide variations in the reliance on property taxes (see Table 2.6).[12] Nevertheless, some significant changes had taken place during the two decades. While the percent of revenue raised by property taxes had ranged over 79.1 percentage points (from 9.6% to 88.7%) in the 1810s, the range in the 1830s was only 59.3 percentage points (from 18.0% to 77.3%). Even more significant was the dramatic drop of the standard deviation from 33.4 to 18.88.

Table 2.6
Percent of Receipts Raised from Property Taxes in Eleven Cities, 1832–1838

City (year)	Percent
Washington (1832)	77.3[a]
Providence (1835)	73.7
Louisville (1832)	52.0
New York (1834)	47.4
Baltimore (1835)	46.1
Philadelphia (1835)	39.0
Cincinnati (1837)	35.9
Boston (1835)	30.0
St. Louis (1836)	25.7
Albany (1832)	19.8
Charleston (1838)	18.0[b]
Median	39.0
Mean	42.3
Range	59.3
SD	18.9

[a]Entirely ward receipts.
[b]Estimated.

The distribution in the earlier decade was strongly bimodal with one-half of the cities deriving more than 75% of their revenue from property taxes and all but one of the others relying on property taxes for less than 25% of their receipts (Baltimore's figure of 27.2% placed it just barely outside of the lower range). By the fourth decade the figure for all but three of the cities examined lay *between* 75% and 25% (Washington's figure of 77.3% is barely above the cutoff). Another type of change is indicated by the fact that the median percentage of revenues derived from property taxes dropped from 51.5% in the 1810s to 39.0% in the 1830s and the mean from 51.6% to 42.3% (cf. Tables 2.2 and 2.6).

Two major shifts are obvious from an examination of these data. First, the major cities were becoming much more similar in the extent of their reliance on property taxes. Second, the general tendency clearly was to rely less heavily on property taxes than at an earlier date.

These tendencies are further confirmed by examining the changes in the seven cities common to both lists (Tables 2.2 and 2.6). For these towns the median percentage of revenue derived from property taxes declined from 75.8% in the 1810s to 46.1% in the 1830s, while the mean dropped somewhat less precipitously from 57.6% to 42.1%. The range of percentages, meanwhile, declined from 73.6 percentage points in the second decade to 53.9 in the fourth, and the standard deviation from 31.4 to 17.1.

The unusually heavy reliance on property taxes in Washington partially reflects an idiosyncrasy in the urban financial structure. Many Washington property holders feared that the "out wards" would be heavily taxed to improve the streets in the northwestern section of the city. Consequently, the 1812 charter had specified that "after providing for all objects of a general nature the taxes raised on the assessable property in each ward shall be expended therein, and in no other," largely for local improvements. While assessments for major improvements were also authorized (though referred to as "taxes" and levied according to the value of the property), this circumstance doubtless resulted in at least some improvements being funded by property taxes that in other cities were financed by assessments on the property directly benefited. Moreover, a variety of other expenditures (e.g., the laying of water pipes and the purchase of fire engines) were made specifically chargeable to these ward revenues. A major reason for the heavy reliance on property taxes in 1832, however, was the collection of a tax of $40,123.02 (53% of the total property tax revenue) "for the purpose of the Chesapeake and Ohio Canal."[13] The other two cities drawing more than one-half of their gross receipts from property taxes in the 1830s—Providence and Louisville—had relied even more heavily on this source of revenue two decades earlier (see Table 2.2). In the interim both had received city charters (and, consequently, access to additional sources of revenue). Thus, their reliance on property taxes diminished sharply, though such receipts continued to constitute a major portion of their gross revenues.

At the other end of the scale, Albany's reliance on property taxes for less than a fifth of that city's total receipts represented little change from practices of twenty years earlier, while the low figure in Charleston was largely the result of the heavy reliance on loans previously noted. The situation was somewhat similar in Boston, which derived more than 54% of its revenue from loans, as compared to less than 12% in 1818. In St. Louis, the only other city in which property taxes accounted for less than a third of revenues, the 1836 figure (25.7%) represented a decline of almost 60 percentage points from that of 1819. This circumstance clearly reflected the broadening of the revenue base that accompanied the chartering of the city, for in the fourth decade of the nineteenth century license, water works, and wharf receipts provided almost five-eighths of the city's total income.[14]

The increased reliance on property taxes in New York, where the portion of the revenue derived from this source roughly doubled between the 1810s and the 1830s, reflected a rather abrupt shift in the early 1820s, followed by a gradual upward movement thereafter. The more modest increase in the percentage of municipal revenue derived from property taxes in Baltimore over these three decades resulted from an even more dramatic jump in 1819 to a figure approximating that of 1835. In the succeeding years (with a single exception) reliance on property taxes in the Maryland metropolis fluctuated within a range of roughly 10 percentage points on either side of the 1835 figure.[15]

The general tendencies of American cities to rely less heavily on property taxes for their receipts meant, of course, that other sources of revenue became more important (see Table 2.7).[16] Eight of these cities in the fourth decade of the nineteenth century derived more than a tenth of their income from various types of city-owned property. Such receipts included the proceeds from the sale

Table 2.7
Percentage of Receipts Derived from Various Sources in Eleven Cities, 1832–1838

City (year)	City Property	Loans	Assessments	Other Taxes & License fees
Albany (1832)	24.7	8.9	34.0	a
Baltimore (1835)	10.8	6.9	21.3	6.1
Boston (1835)	10.5	54.3	0.1	0.1
Charleston (1838)	7.7	55.4	0.0	14.7
Cincinnati (1837)	17.0	0.0	0.0	45.3
Louisville (1832)	17.7	5.0	1.1	12.8
New York (1834)	5.9	18.7	20.1	2.4
Philadelphia (1835)	31.0b	25.8	0.0	0.0
Providence (1835)	13.2	1.9	0.0	4.6
St. Louis (1836)	32.7bc	a	a	29.3
Washington (1832)	1.8	0.0	0.0	16.1

aInsufficient degree of disaggregation of data to determine amount.
bIncludes income from water works.
cProbably understated because of limited level of data disaggregation.

and rental of real estate owned by the corporation, market stall rental, wharfage fees, dividends on and proceeds from the sale of city-owned stocks in private corporations, interest on loans and bank deposits, ferry recipts, and user charges collected by municipal water works. Receipts from these sources approached a third of the total municipal revenues in Philadelphia and St. Louis (the only two cities reporting the collection of water rents). Five of these eleven cities raised more than a tenth of their total revenue from license fees and taxes other than those levied on property, and four realized a similar proportion from loans. In three cities assessments for improvements on streets, sidewalks, sewers, pumps, and wells accounted for a fifth or more of the receipts; in most of the towns, however, such collections were apparently not cycled through the regular budget.

Some slight attention should be given to the increasing importance of non-property taxes and license fees. Not only did the income from such sources constitute a larger and larger portion of the total city revenues in succeeding decades, but the activities affected also expanded dramatically. Almost universal were the specific taxes on theatrical performances and exhibitions, as were the licenses required for the operation of taverns, ordinaries, groceries, and other retailers of spirituous liquors, and of public transportation vehicles (e.g., carts, wagons, drays, carriages, hacks, and stages).[17] License requirements for coffee houses, billiard tables, victuallers, and confectioners were almost as common, and the port cities (as well as some others) usually either licensed auctions or levied an *ad valorem* tax on sales at venue, or both, unless this potentially lucrative source of revenue had been preempted by the state government. A few cities licensed other retail trades (Washington's ordinances were perhaps the most comprehensive), and Charleston taxed retail sales and some incomes.[18]

Table 2.8
Property Tax Rates and Per Capita Yields in Thirteen Cities, 1832–1838

City (year)	Tax Rates per $100	Per Capita Property Tax Collected
Baltimore (1835)	$4.78	$2.22
Cincinnati (1837)	1.85	0.74
Washington (1832)	1.10[a]	3.82
Boston (1835)	0.97	5.08
Albany (1835)	0.769	1.16
Pittsburgh (1835)	0.70	n.a.
Philadelphia (1835)	0.70[b]	2.29
New York (1834)	0.45	3.67
Louisville (1832)	0.40	1.75
St. Louis (1835)	0.375	0.34
Providence (1835)	0.30	2.09
Brooklyn (1835)	0.233[c]	n.a.
Charleston (1838)	n.a.	3.94
Median	0.70	2.22
Mean	1.05	2.46
Range	4.55	4.74
SD	1.20	1.42

n.a. -- Not available.
[a]Includes $0.60 per $100 tax for C & O Canal
   stock.
[b]Rate for 1838.
[c]Estimated.

Nevertheless, the property tax remained an important—usually the dominant—element in the revenue structures of major American cities in the 1830s.
For some cities for which full financial data are not available during this period
it is possible to obtain information on property tax rates and assessments. In
these particulars, then, the range of cities examined can be extended beyond
those included in Tables 2.5, 2.6, and 2.7. On the other hand, property tax rate
and assessment data have not always been located for the specific years for
which disaggregated revenue information is available in all of the eleven cities
examined in the tables for the 1830s, though such materials have been located
for at least one year in this decade. Tables 2.8[19] and 2.9[20] display the results of
the analysis of these data in the form of property tax rates, per capita property
tax collections, and gross and per capita property assessments in these cities.

It is obvious that property tax rates in the nation's largest cities had increased
significantly during the previous two decades. The average rate for cities in the
1830s (Table 2.8) was roughly one and one-half times greater than in the 1810s
(Table 2.3). If we confine our analysis to the nine cities common to both lists,
the increase is even greater—just over 175%. The variations were also much
wider than two decades earlier—then all tax rates had been between 20 and 82
cents per $100; by the later period they ranged between 23 cents and $4.78 per
$100 and exceeded the 1810s mean in eight cities. Baltimore's rate was five
and a third and Cincinnati's four and a quarter times greater than in the second

Table 2.9
Property Assessments in Fourteen Cities 1832–1839

City (year)	Gross Assessment	Per Capita Assessment
Brooklyn (1835)	$26,390,151[a]	$1,085.12
New York (1834)	186,548,511[b]	756.37
Providence (1835)	13,333,333[c]	666.60
Boston (1835)	39,651,300[d]	513.86
New Orleans (1834)	27,339,430[e]	446.81
Charleston (1839)	13,031,698[e]	443.80
Washington (1832)	7,795,760[f]	395.04
Louisville (1832)	4,694,655[g]	375.12
Albany (1835)	9,653,108[d]	333.27
Philadelphia (1835)	27,514,167[g]	316.02
Pittsburgh (1835)	4,402,401[h]	261.39
St. Louis (1832)	2,221,888	199.08
Cincinnati (1837)	6,378,900[i]	159.68
Baltimore (1835)	3,787,762	41.41

Median	385.08
Mean	428.11
Range	1,043.71
SD	257.94

[a]About one-eighth personal property.
[b]About one-third personal property.
[c]Estimated. On the basis of later data, probably a little less than one-half personal property.
[d]About two-fifths personal property.
[e]Real estate only.
[f]About 9% personal property.
[g]Almost entirely real estate.
[h]Estimated.
[i]About one-quarter personal property.

decade of the century. In Boston, Providence, and St. Louis, on the other hand, property tax rates had grown by one quarter or less.

The increase in the per capita property tax yield, however, was considerably more modest, with the mean rising from $1.71 (for seven cities) in the 1810s to $2.46 (for eleven cities) in the fourth decade—just over a quarter. Baltimore's per capita property tax collection was slightly over two and one-half times greater in the 1830s than in the second decade—a rate of increase less than half that of the tax rate. Among the other five cities for which per capita property tax yield data are available for both the second and fourth decades of the century, only in New York was the increase in the per capita property tax collection (112.1%) greater than the growth in the tax rate (63.6%). Boston, Providence, and Louisville showed per capita yield increases of 13%, 14%, and 23%, respectively, compared to tax rate increases of 18%, 22%, and 82%. And in St. Louis the per capita property tax collections actually declined by two-thirds, despite a one-quarter growth in the tax rate.[21]

It is clear that significant changes must have been occurring in the assessed valuation of property in these cities, in collection processes and delinquency rates, in the prevalence of property ownership, or in some combination of these. Despite obvious increases in the market value of much urban real estate, many cities showed only modest increases in gross property assessments over a twenty-year period, and in a number the per capita assessed value of property actually declined. The mean per capita assessment in the fourth decade (Table 2.9) was a few dollars above that of the 1810s (Table 2.4), while the median value dropped by almost an eighth. Among the nine cities present on both lists the mean per capita assessment showed about a 16% increase, but this was largely because the gross assessment in Brooklyn jumped more than 800% and that of Louisville almost 300%, resulting in per capita increases of 148% and 46%, respectively. Among the other seven towns, only three—Boston (7%), New York (11%), and Philadelphia (5%)—showed increases in the per capita assessed property value; the other four suffered declines ranging from 11% in Providence to 46% in Baltimore. Obviously such changes did not accurately reflect property value trends in these cities. In the 1830s it was estimated that Philadelphia assessors' returns did not represent more than one-sixth of the real value of the property in that city. Baltimore's assessors were supposed to enter property on the tax books at one-fifth of the market value, but the "real value" assessment of 1836 recorded a gross valuation more than eleven times as great as that of the previous year.[22] It is, of course, entirely possible that, in some cities at certain stages of development, property values genuinely did not increase proportionately to the population. Thus, gross assessment increases during these years of almost two-thirds in Providence and nearly 100% in St. Louis lagged behind the influx of people and left Providence with an 11% and St. Louis with a 24% decline in per capita assessments. In any event, the nearly static or declining per capita property valuations, coming at a time when higher per capita revenues were required to provide the demanded urban services and prevent the fiscal collapse of the cities, caused the urban governments to exploit more extensively other sources of urban revenue.

By the middle of the nineteenth century urban revenues had expanded dramatically; there was a decline only in Charleston. In the 1830s only two of the cities examined (New York and Boston) raised a revenue in excess of 1 million dollars, and the third largest gross receipts figure (for Philadelphia) was just barely over a half million. By midcentury, however, gross revenues exceeded 1 million dollars in three metropolises and was over a half million in more than one-half of these cities (see Table 2.10).[23] New York's revenues increased by almost two and a half times and were, in 1850, almost a third larger than the combined 1830s receipts of all eleven of the towns in Table 2.5. Receipts continued to expand more rapidly than the urban population, with the per capita revenues roughly doubling in Providence and Cincinnati, and increasing between a fifth and four-fifths in most of the other cities. The only exceptions (among the cities common to both Tables 2.5 and 2.10) were Washington, with essentially no change in the per capita revenues; Baltimore, which showed a small

Table 2.10
Receipts in Fourteen Cities, 1846–1851

City (year)	Per Capita	Gross
Boston (1850)	$25.80	$3,531,416.64
New York (1850)	12.88	6,640,813.85
Albany (1850)	10.47	513,406.05
New Orleans (1846)	9.84	1,017,568.67
Charleston (1849)	9.46	393,511.00
Providence (1850)	7.00	290,500.00[a]
Philadelphia (1850)	6.92	839,756.80
St. Louis (1850)	6.65	518,132.06
Pittsburgh (1851)	5.73	269,250.00[a]
Washington (1850)	4.99	199,450.64
Cincinnati (1850)	4.64	536,038.00
Baltimore (1850)	4.59	775,194.15
Louisville (1850)	4.58	198,040.04
Brooklyn (1847)	4.46	350,419.14

Median	6.79
Mean	8.43
Range	21.34
SD	5.44

[a]Projected.

shrinkage; and Charleston, with a dramatic drop of over one-third. The mean per capita revenue increased from $6.68 to $8.43 between the middle of the fourth and the end of the fifth decades.

While there was still some relationship beteen city size and per capita revenue, that relationship (as expressed statistically) continued to deteriorate. Of the six cities with populations in excess of 100,000 in 1850, four had per capita revenues above $6.00; of the six with populations below 50,000, three had per capita revenues below $6.00 and for one of the others the data are not available. But the rank order correlation (Spearman) between city size and per capita receipts was only .256, down from .623 in the 1830s and .817 in the 1810s. The older, established (and mostly northeastern) cities tended to raise more revenue in proportion to their populations than did those more recently achieving major rank; eight of these cities ranked in the most populous ten in 1810 and seven of the eight occupy the top seven positions in Table 2.10.[24]

It was not, of course, a simple function of age that produced the higher per capita revenues, though it is true that the development of city services (and the concomitant need for increased revenues) frequently lagged behind population gain in the more rapidly growing newer cities. The major factor influencing the amount of revenue raised in the various cities was obviously the level of expenditures generated by the services provided (retrospectively, currently, and/or prospectively). Expenditures are addressed later in this chapter but a brief consideration of a single municipal service will illustrate this point. Of the fourteen cities listed in Table 2.10, disaggregated data exist for twelve and partially disaggregated data for a thirteenth (St. Louis).[25] Of these thirteen cities, six re-

Table 2.11
Percent of Receipts Raised from Property Taxes in Thirteen Cities, 1847–1851

City (year)	Percent
Baltimore (1850)	78.4
Cincinnati (1850)	65.5
Washington (1850)	64.3[a]
Louisville (1850)	53.2
Providence (1850)	52.8
Philadelphia (1850)	49.9
St. Louis (1850)	49.8
New York (1850)	48.6
Brooklyn (1847)	43.0
Boston (1850)	35.2
Charleston (1849)	34.2
Albany (1850)	25.3
Pittsburgh (1851)	23.3
Median	49.8
Mean	48.0
Range	55.1
SD	15.3

[a]Entirely ward revenues.

corded receipts from city water works and/or bonds sold for the construction, expansion, or improvement of these systems. All these six cities had gross revenues in excess of five dollars per capita. Water works–related income comprised almost a sixth of Pittsburgh's total revenues, more than a fifth of Philadelphia's, more than a third of Boston's, and almost two-fifths of Albany's.[26]

The overall growth of city revenues throughout the half century, though consistent, was quite irregular. The mean per capita receipts, as shown in Tables 2.1, 2.5, and 2.10, increased by just under four-fifths between the second and the fourth decades of the century and by somewhat less than one-quarter between the middle of the fourth and the end of the fifth decades.

An examination of the sources of revenue does not reveal the same simple regularity, however. It is true that some tendencies observable between the second and fourth decades continue to operate to the middle of the nineteenth century. For example, the major cities continued to become more similiar in regard to the percentage total revenue derived from property taxes. A comparison of the data displayed in Tables 2.6 and 2.11[27] show the range diminishing from 59.3 percentage points (18.0 to 77.3) to 55.1 percentage points (23.3 to 78.4) and the standard deviation dropping from 18.88 to 15.34. The figures for all but one of the cities now fall between 25% and 80%, and that for Pittsburgh falls barely outside this range. At midcentury the percentage of revenues raised from property taxes lay between 25% and 70% for eleven of the thirteen cities; this was true for only seven of eleven cities in the 1830s and one of eight in the 1810s.

At first glance this centripetal process would appear to be illustrated even more dramatically by an examination of the changes in the eleven cities common to both Table 2.6 and Table 2.11.[28] In the 1830s three of these cities raised more, and eight less, than one-half of their revenue from property taxes. By 1850 the top two—Washington and Providence—had reduced their reliance on property taxes by 13 and 21 percentage points, respectively, while seven of the bottom eight—all but fourth-ranked New York (47.4%)—had increased their dependence on this tax by from 5 to 32 percentage points. In both Louisville and New York the percentage of revenue derived from property taxes rose by roughly 1 percentage point. But there was an anomaly in that the movement was sometimes through, rather than to, the center, resulting in a shift in the rank order of Baltimore (within the eleven cities) from fifth to first, of Cincinnati from seventh to second, and of Providence from second to fifth. Thus, the changes in individual cities have an air of randomness not entirely compatible with the statistically demonstrable, successively tighter clustering of these cities around the mean throughout the half century.

In one other respect the tendencies observable by comparing Tables 2.6 and 2.11 differ from those observable in the entire period. While the mean and median percentages of the revenue derived from property taxes had dropped by roughly 9 and 12.5 percentage points between the 1810s and the 1830s (see Table 2.2), the comparable figures rebounded upward by 5.7 and 10.8 percentage points by midcentury.[29]

The increased reliance on property taxes to produce higher per capita gross revenues required larger per capita property tax collections, and this, in turn, could result only from higher property tax rates or increased per capita assessments, or both. As a matter of fact, it was both (see Tables 2.12[30] and 2.13[31]).

True, the mean property tax rate was about a seventh lower in 1850 than a decade and a half earlier (see Table 2.8), but that was an aberration produced by the inordinately high tax rate for Baltimore ($4.78 per $100 assessed value) in the 1830s—more than two and one-half times the next highest level of taxation and almost seven times the median. This inflated tax rate was, in turn, the result of per capita tax assessments in Baltimore that were lower than those for any other of the cities ($41.41) in 1835—about a quarter of the next lowest figure and less than a ninth of the median (see Table 2.9). Tax rates had increased (often substantially) in six of the eleven cities with rate data common to Tables 2.8 and 2.12, almost doubling in St. Louis, more than doubling in Albany, rising 150% or more in Louisville and New York, and more than trebling in Brooklyn.[32]

As was the case with the data on the extent of reliance on property taxes, property tax rates in the individual cities often changed dramatically over the decade and a half. Among the eleven cities for which tax rates are available for the periods covered by both Tables 2.8 and 2.12 there were rather extreme changes in the rank ordering—Baltimore dropped from first to fifth, Washington from third to sixth, Boston from fourth to ninth, and Philadelphia from sixth to tenth, while Albany moved from fifth to second, New York from seventh to

Table 2.12
Property Tax Rates and Per Capita Yields in Thirteen Cities, 1847–1851

City (year)	Tax Rate per $100	Per Capita Property Tax Collected
Cincinnati (1850)	$1.70	$3.04
Albany (1850)	1.563	2.65
New York (1850)	1.14	6.27
Louisville (1850)	1.00[a]	2.44
Baltimore (1850)	0.82	3.60
Washington (1850)	0.75[b]	3.20
Brooklyn (1847)	0.722[c]	1.91
St. Louis (1850)	0.721[c]	3.31
Boston (1850)	0.68	9.08
Philadelphia (1850)	0.58	3.45
Providence (1850)	0.53	3.69
Charleston (1850)	0.48	3.23
Pittsburgh (1851)	n.a.	1.34
Median	0.74	3.23
Mean	0.90	3.63
Range	1.22	7.74
SD	0.37	1.92

n.a. -- not available.
[a]Tax rate for 1851.
[b]Tax rate for 1849; computed.
[c]Computed.

third, Louisville from eighth to fourth, and Brooklyn from eleventh to seventh. In short, eight of the eleven cities moved more than two positions in ranking. But the result of this movement was to produce a much tighter clustering of the tax rates in the cities around the common center—the range dropped from $4.55 to $1.22 and the standard deviation from 1.20 to .37.

There was also a general upward movement in per capita assessments. Between the fourth decade and the middle of the nineteenth century (cf. Table 2.9 and Table 2.13) the median remained essentially unchanged while the mean rose by 18.5%. The per capita assessment increased in seven of the thirteen cities common to both tables, sometimes dramatically—almost doubling in St. Louis, much more than doubling in Cincinnati and Boston, and increasing well over tenfold in Baltimore. Among the cities showing declines the changes were, with a single exception (Brooklyn), of the magnitude of roughly a quarter or less. But the rank order shifts were more extreme, with nine of the thirteen moving more than two positions and four in excess of four positions. Nevertheless, all these shifts left both the range and the standard deviation largely unchanged.

The per capita property tax collected is, of course, the product of the interaction of the property tax rate and the per capita assessment, mediated by delinquency. Property tax yields clearly increased between the 1830s and midcentury (cf. Tables 2.8 and 2.12). The mean and median per capita property tax collections both rose by roughly one-half, and the individual figures increased for nine of the eleven cities for which data are available in both periods.

Table 2.13
Property Assessments in Thirteen Cities, 1846–1852

City (year)	Gross Assessments	Per Capita Assessments
Boston (1850)	$180,000,000[a]	$1,315.02
Providence (1850)	31,958,900[b]	769.85
New Orleans (1852)	66,631,937[c]	574.94
New York (1850)	286,085,417[d]	554.94
Philadelphia (1850)	62,000,000[e]	510.81
Baltimore (1850)	80,166,992	474.21
St. Louis (1850)	29,676,649	381.15
Brooklyn (1847)	29,365,189[f]	373.33
Cincinnati (1850)	42,862,726[g]	371.32
Louisville (1851)	16,000,000[e]	350.24
Washington (1846)	11,450,923[h]	343.40
Charleston (1850)	14,192,750[i]	330.18
Albany (1850)	12,601,689[j]	248.25
	Median	381.15
	Mean	507.51
	Range	1,066.77
	SD	267.71

[a]41.62% personal property.
[b]44.20% personal property.
[c]5.70% slave property; all other real estate.
[d]27.59% personal property.
[e]Projected.
[f]12.35% personal property.
[g]20.22% personal property.
[h]10.83% personal property.
[i]Real estate only.
[j]25.17% personal property.

In 1850 only one of these eleven cities (Louisville—$2.44) had a per capita property tax yield below $2.50; a decade and a half earlier seven had fallen below that figure. Both the range and the standard deviation increased significantly (by almost two-thirds and one-third, respectively), indicating increasing diversity among the cities in this respect.

Nevertheless, on the average these cities relied on property taxes for less than one-half of their revenues (see Table 2.11); in only one instance (Baltimore) did the figure exceed two-thirds. It should be kept in mind that the data here presented are subject to some error because in some cities loans and/or public improvement assessments are not included in city budget figures. Additionally, in some cases certain fees or other income are specifically dedicated to debt service (through sinking funds) or to the provision of particular governmental services, and are sometimes not passed through the city budgetary accounting process.

The most notable shifts during this period (ca. 1835–ca. 1850) have to do with receipts from city property, loans, and other governmental units. A comparison of these figures (Table 2.14)[33] with those in Table 2.7 shows income from city property forming a much smaller percentage of the gross receipts at

Table 2.14
Percentage of Receipts Derived from Various Sources in Twelve Cities, 1847–1851

City (year)	City Property	Loans	Public Imp'v't. Ass'm'ts	Other Taxes and Licenses	Other Govt. Units
Albany (1850)	6.4[a]	56.6	2.5	1.5	6.7
Baltimore (1850)	6.6	--	4.7	5.3	0.8
Boston (1850)	9.5[a]	51.9	0.4	0.1	1.3
Brooklyn (1847)	0.5	23.7	30.8	--	--
Charleston (1849)	7.5	22.2	--	8.8	2.3
Louisville (1850)	12.3	--	--	25.5	2.2
New York (1850)	19.8[a]	17.0	10.4	1.1	--
Philadelphia (1850)	27.7[a]	19.8	--	0.9	--
Pittsburgh (1851)	22.0[a]	51.5	--	0.8	--
Providence (1850)	3.4	35.7	--	0.6	2.8
St. Louis (1850)	15.0[ab]	c	c	12.0	c
Washington (1850)	9.4	--	--	15.6	8.9

[a]Includes receipts from water works.
[b]Probably understated because of limited level of
   disaggregation.
[c]Insufficient disaggregation to determine.

midcentury than in the 1830s. Of the ten cities common to both tables[34] only in New York and Washington did the percentage of receipts derived from city properties increase. But it must also be noted that the *actual* income from city-owned property had, with rare exceptions, *not* declined; among these ten cities, only Albany and Charleston, in fact, showed any falling off of such receipts— there they slipped by $3,900 and $5,600, respectively, between 1832 and 1850. Such income, in fact, increased by more than 50% in Philadelphia (1835–1850), more than trebled in Boston (1835–1851) and Louisville (1832–1850), quintupled in St. Louis (1836–1850), increased by almost ninefold in Washington (1832–1850), and more than tenfold in New York (1834–1850). Yet because of the very great increase in total revenues every one of these cities except New York registered a decline in the percentage of receipts derived from city properties.

The income from loans was, of course, much more irregular, and single-year figures must be approached cautiously. It is likely, however, that the absence of loan receipts in such cities as Baltimore and Louisville was, by the mid-nineteenth century, less typical than the level of such receipts elsewhere. Certainly loans had supplied the Baltimore city goverment with more than $150,000 (almost a sixth of the total revenue) only a couple of years earlier.[35] In one-half of the cities in which there was identifiable loan revenue it accounted for more than a third of the gross receipts. In every city with recorded loan receipts in both the 1830s and 1850,[36] with the exception of Charleston, the amount of such income increased, usually dramatically, but in only two of these towns (Albany and Providence) did the portion of the city's gross revenue derived from loans also rise. In the other five cities (excluding Charleston) the actual amount of

Table 2.15
Summary of Revenue Changes over Time

Mean of Data Re:	1810s	1830s	c1850	Source (tables)
Per Capita Gross Receipts	$3.72(9)	$6.68(11)	$8.43(14)	2.1, 2.5, 2.10
% of Receipts From Property Taxes	51.6(8)	42.3(11)	48.0(13)	2.2, 2.6, 2.11
Property Tax Rate (per $100 Assessed Value)	$0.416(10)	$1.05(12)	$0.90(13)	2.3, 2.8, 2.12
Per Capita Property Tax Collected	$1.71(7)	$2.46(11)	$3.63(13)	2.3, 2.8, 2.12
Per Capita Property Assessment (rounded)	$417(9)	$428(14)	$508(13)	2.4, 2.9, 2.13

(0) The number of cities for which data are available for analysis.

loan income grew by 26% in Philadelphia, more than trebled in New York, increased by 1,388% in Boston, by 2,110% in Albany, and by 9,327% in Providence; in Boston borrowing provided more than $1,800,000 in 1850 and in New York more than $1,100,000.

The most common intergovernmental transfers involved the distribution of state funds to assist local public education. Additionally, states, counties, and commissions of immigration made payments to city almshouses, hospitals, houses of industry, and overseers of the poor to underwrite (in part) the costs of providing welfare services to nonresidents. Federal transfers were rare, and apparently limited to support for Marine hospitals (to provide care for sailors and riverboat men) and occasional partial funding of public improvements in Washington. Given the quasi-independent status of a number of boards controlling schools, hospitals, poor relief, and, in some cases, building construction, it is not unlikely that intergovernmental transfers were more extensive than these data suggest, with a number of such payments not being passed through the city's governmental budget process or captured in its financial reports.

One way of summarizing the patterns of urban governmental receipts in the first half of the nineteenth century is to examine the central tendencies of the group of cities for which data are available at various points throughout the period (see Table 2.15). Such analysis shows a slowing growth in the per capita gross receipts and an increasing growth in per capita property tax collected and, predictably, a very slight fluctuation (within a range of 9.3 percentage points) of the percentage of receipts derived from property taxes. Meanwhile, property tax rates leaped by more than 150% between the 1810s and the 1830s and then declined modestly by midcentury, as the per capita assessments remained stable throughout the mid-1830s and inched upward by less than a fifth by 1850. But in individual cities the shifts were more irregular. Some of these irregularities can be perceived by an examination of the data for each of the seven cities that appear in almost every table (see Tables 2.16.1, 2.16.2, 2.16.3, and 2.16.4).

What these tables vividly illustrate is the enormous diversity within the general patterns. Indeed, these seven cities tended (but in no regular pattern) to

Table 2.16.1
Composite Analysis of Revenue in Seven Cities

City	A. Per Capita Receipts			B. Gross Receipts ($000s)		
	1810s	1830s	c1850	1810s	1830s	c1850
Albany	$5.48	$5.85	$10.47	$53.1	$152.8	$513.4
Baltimore	2.28	4.82	4.59	118.1	440.5	775.2
Boston	5.96	16.96	25.80	242.3	1,308.8	3,531.4
Louisville	1.60	3.36	4.58	6.0	42.1	198.0
New York	7.46	7.74	12.88	862.1	1,908.5	6,640.1
Providence	2.09	2.83	7.00	22.8	56.7	290.5
St. Louis	1.22	3.70	6.65	5.2	45.3	518.1

Sources: Tables 2.1, 2.5, 2.10.

become less, rather than more, homogeneous in regard to the various measurable aspects of their financial operations. Only in the table dealing with the property tax revenues as a percentage of the gross receipts (Table 2.16.2) were both the range and the standard deviation smaller in 1850 than in the 1810s. This circumstance is doubtless, in part, the result of the fact that these seven cities include three of the largest, three of the smallest, and one very rapidly changing metropolis. In the larger universe—with more midrange towns—there is, as we have previously observed, a tendency toward tighter concentration around the mean.

A few additional observations about property taxes should, perhaps, be added. The property tax rate recorded for a given city (and, consequently, the property tax receipts) sometimes—but by no means always—included state, county, or township levies. Records are by no means precise, but this would appear to have been the exception rather than the rule.[37]

In some cities taxes actually were, or appeared to be, levied to meet anticipated expenditures in a number of specific areas. In the fiscal records of Albany, for example, the receipts as well as the expenditures figures were consistently categorized by function and showed specific amounts of property tax revenue assigned to a number of functional divisions; in 1840 the budget included such amounts as $16,000 from "a tax on account of" the city watch, $7,000 for city lamps, $10,000 for interest on and reduction of the city debt, $2,500 for construction of school houses, and $20,000 from a "tax for contingencies."[38]

This practice probably originated as a means of avoiding the limitations which state legislatures frequently placed upon the general property-taxing powers of the city corporations, and in many cases was doubtless illusory, for there is little evidence that receipts were rigorously segregated in practice. But there was also a potent element of reality in the process. It is likely that such functionally designated taxation was, in some instances, intended to insure that the residents of the cities were taxed only for those services that were actually provided. This certainly was a product of such tax procedures, for the tax rate levied upon property was determined by its location inside or outside of often overlapping special service districts. By 1849 nine different property tax rates were levied

Table 2.16.2
Composite Analysis of Revenues in Seven Cities

City	C. % of Revenue From Property Taxes			D. Property Tax Rate per $100 Assessed Value		
	1810s	1830s	c1850	1810s	1830s	c1850
Albany	15.1	19.8	25.3	n.a.	$0.769	$1.563
Baltimore	27.2	46.1	78.4	$0.75	4.78	0.82
Boston	75.8	30.0	35.2	0.82	0.97	0.68
Louisville	88.7	52.0	53.2	0.22	0.40	1.00
New York	23.1	47.4	48.6	0.275	0.45	1.14
Providence	87.7	73.7	52.8	0.245	0.30	0.53
St. Louis	85.3	25.7	49.8	0.30	0.375	0.721

Sources: Tables 2.2, 2.3, 2.6, 2.8, 2.11, 2.12

in New York, ranging from $0.91549 to $1.1832 per $100 of assessed valuation, depending on the property's location in relation to the water, lamp, and streets districts.[39]

A final aspect of property tax collections has to do with the question of arrearages. It is frequently difficult (and sometimes impossible) to determine the extent to which property owners delayed paying the taxes assessed. In many cases the reports of the responsibile officals lumped together all property taxes collected in a given year without indicating the amounts collected as arrears of taxes unpaid in previous years. Some collectors and treasurers did make such distinctions, however, and in other cases indicative (if not precise) figures can be calculated from data derived from different sources. The tendency to postpone tax payments would appear to have been most pronounced in Baltimore and New York. At the end of the third decade of the nineteenth century about four-fifths of the property taxes levied in a given year in New York remained unpaid at the end of that year. This was roughly double the figure for Baltimore in the same period. Five years later the arrearage figure was closer to a half in Baltimore and over nine-tenths in New York; at the end of the fourth decade the New York figure remained essentially unchanged. But the late 1830s (in Baltimore) and the 1840s (in New York) saw a dramatic decline in these figures to roughly two-fifths in Baltimore and, more spectacularly, to about 15% in New York. Most of the arrearages were, as might be expected, discharged in the year subsequent to that in which the taxes were levied. Throughout the 1830s and 1840s less than a tenth of the taxes remained unpaid in New York at the end of the second year. In Baltimore the figure varied more widely between about one-fourteenth and almost a quarter.

Although the data are less specific for Washington, it is certain that large amounts of property taxes sometimes went unpaid for considerable periods of time. Between 1829 and 1833, for example, the accumulated arrearages at the end of each tax year were always greater—up to 80% greater—than that year's total tax levy. The figures for 1831 are illustrative. In that year taxes in the

Table 2.16.3
Composite Analysis of Revenues in Seven Cities

City	E. Per Capita Property Tax Collections			F. Per Capita Property Assessments		
	1810s	1830s	c1850	1810s	1830s	c1850
Albany	$0.83	$1.16	$2.65	n.a.	$333.27	$248.25
Baltimore	0.62	2.22	3.60	$76.05	41.41	474.21
Boston	4.51	5.08	9.08	481.84	513.86	1,315.02
Louisville	1.42	1.75	2.44	256.12	375.12	350.24
New York	1.73	3.67	6.27	683.04	756.37	554.92
Providence	1.83	2.09	3.69	747.62	666.60	769.85
St. Louis	1.04	0.34	3.31	263.42	199.08	381.15

Sources: Tables 2.3, 2.4, 2.8, 2.9, 2.12, 2.13.

amount of $48,839.74 were levied upon property in the city; the total collections (current and delinquent) amounted to $38,866.72; and the city's books showed accumulated arrearages (1820–1831) of $75,686.82 at the end of the year. The Cincinnati data are even less precise, with widely divergent figures on tax collections appearing in different sources. It seems certain, however, that *at a minimum* the property taxes unpaid at the end of tax years between 1830 and 1845 only once dropped below 30%, was usually above 40%, and occasionally in excess of one-half.

At the other end of the spectrum, first-year arrearages in Boston throughout the period 1820–1850 were often as low as 2% or 3% and rarely above 6%, while the figure was consistently below 5% in Charleston in the 1840s.

Scattered data suggest that a number of the other cities fell between these extremes. First-year delinquencies in Louisville in the 1830s and 1840s would appear to have ranged from just under a tenth to almost 30%, and most commonly about a fifth. The comparable figures for Philadelphia in the 1840s were usually between 11% and 18%, but dropped as low as 6% on occasion; they were a little over a quarter in St. Louis in 1827, 38% in Brooklyn in 1847, and a little more than a sixth in Providence in 1850.[40]

As has been previously noted, data on the amount of revenue derived from loans in a single year may not accurately reflect the extent of reliance on borrowing to finance the cities' governmental operations. Borrowing tends to be highly erratic because a great portion of urban indebtedness (there were exceptions) was not incurred by the slow accretion of annual deficits, but, rather, by decisions to resort to the city's credit to fund nonrecurring major expenses. Hence, information on levels of debt accumulation are likely to be much more reliable indicators of trends throughout the half century.

The data in Table 2.17[41] show per capita debt levels (with the single exception of Albany)[42] below $9.00—indeed, one-half at $2.05 and below. Among the three cities with debts in excess of $100,000, only Albany's appears to have been largely the result of an accumulation of deficits in operating expenses, and

Table 2.16.4
Composite Analysis of Revenues in Seven Cities

G. Gross Assessments

City	1810s	1830s	c1850
Albany	n.a.	$9,653,108	$12,601,689
Baltimore	$3,325,848	3,787,762	80,166,992
Boston	19,600,600	39,651,300	180,000,000
Louisville	1,189,664	4,694,655	16,000,000
New York	78,895,735	182,548,511	286,085,417
Providence	8,163,265	13,333,333	31,958,900
St. Louis	1,132,164	2,221,888	29,676,649

Sources: Tables 2.4, 2.9, 2.13.

even there the purchase of $15,300 worth of water company stock and appropriation of $34,200 to the construction of the state capitol contributed measurably to the level of indebtedness. Philadelphia's debt was largely incurred in financing the construction of the water works, and New York's resulted primarily from extraordinarily heavy street-paving costs.[43] In a number of the other cities for which no data have been located, it is likely that there was no debt or nothing more than an occasional temporary deficit that was covered by a local bank and quickly repaid. The debt of New York remained largely unchanged to the mid-1830s, and the same was true of Albany until the mid-1820s, after which it declined during the ensuing decade. In Pittsburgh and Providence the corporate indebtedness gradually increased, but was still below $100,000 by the end of the 1820s. Boston's debt changed little before the early 1820s but began to increase rather dramatically a few years after the city's incorporation. The indebtedness of Philadelphia and Washington rose at a relatively rapid rate into the 1820s, largely because of continuing ward deficits in Washington and the construction of the Fairmont water works in Philadelphia. The year 1818 saw an increase of more than 600% in Baltimore's debt, as the city embarked on an ambitious program of street openings and paving, and then remained fairly stable through the 1820s.[44]

There would appear to be no discernable relationship between population size and debt levels among these eight cities. The four largest (1815 population)—New York, Philadelphia, Baltimore, and Boston—ranked second, third, eighth, and sixth in per capita indebtedness. Three of the towns with substantially identical populations (between 10,700 and 11,000)—Albany, Providence, and Washington—ranked first, seventh, and fifth. The three cities whose initial charters antedated the Revolutionary era all had debts in excess of a quarter of a million dollars and were the only ones with gross indebtednesses above $65,000 or per capita indebtednesses in excess of $3.02. The other two chartered municipalities—Baltimore and Washington—were, on the other hand, randomly intermixed with the three unincorporated towns at the lower end of the debt spectrum, however measured.

Table 2.17
Reported Debt in Eight Cities, 1810–1820

City (year)	Total Debt	Per Capita Debt
Albany (1817)	$268,847	$23.08
New York (1812)	900,000	8.84
Philadelphia (1810)	360,000[a]	6.70
Pittsburgh (1820)	21,904	3.02
Washington (1814)	21,000	2.05
Boston (1815)	62,500	1.65
Providence (1815)	17,601	1.61
Baltimore (1817)	54,695	1.05
	Median	2.54
	Mean	6.00
	Range	22.03
	SD	6.57

[a]Estimated.

By the mid-1830s the debt position of the major American cities had changed dramatically, though not only the levels, but the trends, diverged from the norms in some cities. All eight cities listed in Table 2.17 also appear in Table 2.18.[45] Among these cities there was a reduction in total indebtedness only in Albany; the per capita debt declined by more than 85% in that city and by more than a quarter in New York. In all of the other metropolises the per capita indebtedness increased significantly, more than trebling in Philadelphia, Pittsburgh, and Providence and increasing by 800% in Boston, more than 1,000% in Baltimore, and more than 4,000% in Washington. The mean per capita indebtedness for the cities in Table 2.18 was almost triple that for those in Table 2.17, while the median was more than triple, the range almost quadruple, and the standard deviation more than triple.

Washington was the obvious "outlier" in the mid-1830s. That city had recently issued more than 1.25 million dollars in bonds in aid of the Chesapeake and Ohio canal. In 1836 the federal government agreed to pay off 1 million dollars of this debt (the so-called Holland Loan) if the city would convey to the Treasury Department the C. & O. stock for which the bonds had been exchanged. This transfer was promptly accomplished.[46] If the amount of the federal assumption is excluded from the Washington debt figure, the mean per capita indebtedness for these cities drops to $12.63, the median remains unchanged, the range falls to $35.30, and the standard deviation to 10.73. Even so, the adjusted mean is still more than triple that for Table 2.17 if we omit the data for Albany—the "outlier" in that table (see note 42)—the median is more than four times as large, the range more than quadruple, and the standard deviation almost quadruple.

The higher debt levels in these cities generally resulted from decisions to embark upon programs of capital expenditures that could not be funded from normal revenue sources, though, admittedly, the continuing rise in Philadel-

Table 2.18
Reported Debt in Ten Cities, 1832–1835

City (year)	Total Debt	Per Capita Debt
Washington (1835)	$1,817,422	$86.15
Philadelphia (1835)	2,210,600	25.39
Boston (1835)	1,147,600	14.86
Baltimore (1835)	1,070,756	11.71
Pittsburgh (1832)	152,773	10.70
New York (1835)	1,639,978	6.37
Louisville (1835)	91,165	5.78
Providence (1835)	102,993	5.15
Cincinnati (1835)	148,658	4.18
Albany (1835)	100,000	3.45

Median	8.54
Mean	17.37
Range	82.70
SD	23.77

phia's indebtedness (after the funding of the Fairmont water system) appears to have been largely the product of repeated annual deficits for "many years past." Pittsburgh's debt, like that of the Quaker City, was incurred primarily to supply the city with water. In like manner, more than one-half of the debt of New York represented the cost of the construction (up to 1835) of the Croton water system. Most of the increase in the debt of Providence resulted from the construction of the Dexter Alms House, on which the city expended some $43,000 between 1825 and 1828. The major part of Boston's debt—indeed, almost the whole of it—represented expenditures on various municipal improvements (e.g., the construction of Quincy Market), and the same circumstances prevailed in Louisville. The late 1820s and the 1830s saw a considerable increase in municipal investment in transportation works. More than half of Baltimore's debt ($500,000) resulted from subscriptions to the Baltimore and Susquehanna and Baltimore and Ohio railroad companies, and by 1835 Washington had borrowed more than one and a third million dollars to assist canal corporations.[47]

Not only had there been, in general, a significant increase in urban debt levels by the end of the first third of the nineteenth century, but many American cities were just entering a period of rapidly escalating indebtedness. The last years of the 1830s saw pronounced—often dramatic—rises in the debts (both gross and per capita) in a number of these metropolises.

Table 2.19[48] displays municipal indebtedness figures for eleven cities in the period between 1837 and 1839. A comparison of the measures of central tendency for Tables 2.19 and 2.18 (using the adjusted Washington figures) shows an increase of more than three-quarters in the mean, nearly a trebling of the median, and very slight downward shifts in the range and standard deviation. A still clearer perception of what was taking place in these years can, perhaps, be derived from an examination of the changes in the urban centers for which data are available for both the middle and the end of the decade.

Table 2.19
Reported Debt in Eleven Cities, 1837–1839

City (year)	Total Debt	Per Capita Debt
Washington (1839)	$822,260	$35.89
Philadelphia (1837)	2,950,600	32.89
Baltimore (1839)	3,111,045	31.07
St. Louis (1839)	437,112	28.37
New York (1839)	8,130,335	26.95
Louisville (1838)	465,979	24.48
Charleston (1838)	706,608	23.98
Boston (1839)	1,596,000	17.78
Albany (1839)	386,687	11.80
Cincinnati (1839)	305,673	6.92
Providence (1839)	99,690	4.42
	Median	24.48
	Mean	22.23
	Range	31.47
	SD	10.12

Of the nine cities included in Table 2.19 for which 1835 data were located (see Table 2.20),[49] seven showed at least a 20% increase in per capita debt by 1839 (or slightly earlier for Louisville and Philadelphia); in four cases the increase was 165% or more. The only exceptions were Washington and Providence, where slight declines were registered. In the latter city, where the debt had fluctuated narrowly around the $100,000 mark for a decade (having declined from $102,993 in 1835 to $99,690 in 1839), there would be an increase of almost $83,000 in 1840, which would produce a per capita indebtedness in 1840 that was 53% higher than in 1835 (as compared with 14% lower in 1839). This increase was produced by the creation of a "school loan fund," and the dramatic rise was unique in antebellum Providence's financial history. The relatively high debt level in Charleston reflected a program of municipal improvements (including the development of White Point Garden and the Battery) and a modest purchase of railway stocks. Borrowing in St. Louis was primarily to fund the water distribution system and secondarily to prevent the buildup of sandbars, which threatened the city's river commerce.[50]

To put the matter in a different perspective, the total reported municipal debt in these nine cities (using the adjusted Washington figure for 1835) much more than doubled during the closing years of this decade, rising from $7,328,572 to $17,868,269. Although the percentage changes were quite large in some of the smaller cities (Louisville recorded the largest percentage increase in both actual and per capita debt), the four largest metropolises in the nation—New York, Baltimore, Philadelphia, and Boston—accounted for more than nine-tenths of the growth in the total debt of these nine cities. As might be expected, there is a moderate relationship between city size and gross debt among these cities in the 1830s, with the rank order correlation (Spearman) being .582 for 1835 and .700 for 1839.[51]

Table 2.20
Changes in Per Capita Reported Debt in Nine Cities, 1835–1839

City	1835	1839	% Change	$ Change
Albany	$3.45	$11.80	+242%	+$8.35
Baltimore	11.71	31.07	+165%	+19.36
Boston	14.86	17.78	+20%	+2.92
Cincinnati	4.18	6.92[a]	+66%	+2.74
Louisville	5.78	24.48[a]	+324%	+18.70
New York	6.37	26.95	+323%	+20.58
Philadelphia	25.39	32.89[b]	+30%	+7.50
Providence	5.15	4.42	-14%	-0.73
Washington	38.75[c]	35.89	-7%	-2.86
Mean:	12.85	21.36	+66%	+8.51

[a]Figure for 1838.
[b]Figure for November 1837.
[c]Excluding debt assumed by the United States in 1836.

The largest of these increases—that of New York, nearly 6.5 million dollars—was almost wholly accounted for by the continued funding of the Croton water system, public building construction, and two public service loans (the fire loan and the fire indemnity loan) associated with the great fire of 1835. The second largest increase—about 2 million dollars in Baltimore—would appear to have gone almost entirely to the purchase of stock in such internal improvement corporations as the Susquehanna Canal Company, the Baltimore and Susquehanna Railroad, and the Baltimore and Ohio Railroad. Roughly three-sevenths of Philadelphia's $740,000 rise went to finance a variety of municipal improvements, while the remainder resulted from an excess of general expenses over revenues. In like manner, it would appear that the entire increase of indebtedness in Boston was occasioned by the persistent annual deficiencies in the general revenue. Roughly 80% of the $375,000 growth in Louisville's debt can be attributed to some land purchases for public building construction and the purchase of stock in the Lexington and Ohio Railroad and the Ohio Bridge Company.[52]

At the end of the fourth decade of the nineteenth century urban debt levels, though often springing from similar types of expenditures, would appear to have resulted from distinctly individualistic decisions by the different governmental bodies rather than from any identifiable pattern. There was, for instance, no significant relationship (Spearman: .350) between per capita debt levels and city size, and similarly unimportant negative relationships of those debt levels to percentage of population growth between 1820 and 1840 (Spearman: −.250) and between 1830 and 1840 (Spearman: −.133). Cities that had received charters early did tend to have higher per capita debt levels. Six of the eleven cities in Table 2.19 had been initially chartered before 1810, and four of these six had debt levels above twenty-five dollars per capita, compared to only one of the other five towns. There was also a tendency for cities located in the slave area to have higher per capita debt levels. In all of the five slave area cities in Table 2.19 the indebtedness was above the table mean; this circumstance prevailed in only two of the remaining six towns. It must also be remembered that these figures are based on the whole population, including slaves; if the analysis should be restricted to free persons the debt levels would be much greater. This geographic division may reflect efforts on the part of southern commercial cities (and would-be commercial cities, such as Washington) to supplement the more limited available private capital in financing the construction of turnpikes, bridges, canals, and railroads—certainly such ventures accounted for substantial portions of the debts of Washington, Baltimore, and Louisville, and constituted a smaller element in Charleston's indebtedness.

The patterns of municipal indebtedness varied considerably in the different cities in the fifth decade of the nineteenth century. In Baltimore, Cincinnati, New York, and Providence the debt levels rose sharply in the early years of the decade; thereafter indebtedness declined slightly in Providence, while the other three cities registered slight to modest increases. Boston's debt dropped slightly through 1847 and then escalated rapidly in the closing years of the decade. Washington showed a slow decline throughout the period, while a dramatic increase in the Philadelphia debt in 1846–1847 was preceded and followed by periods of slight growth. And Louisville recorded a substantial increase early in the decade followed by successive periods of stability and decline before its indebtedness moved upward sharply late in the decade to a level rather above the 1841 figure.

By the middle of the century the gross reported debt in the cities listed in Table 2.19 had considerably more than doubled, with every city except Washington recording increases of 50% or more. The growth was greater than 90% in seven of the metropolises, reaching 473% in Cincinnati and 386% in Albany. But because of the continued—often dramatic—increases in the urban populations the growth in per capita indebtedness was much smaller. In addition to Washington, Louisville and St. Louis also recorded declines (of a little over one-third and somewhat less than one-half) in per capita indebtedness, and the increases in Baltimore, Providence, and Charleston were less than 10%. In only three cities did the figure more than double—Albany (+214%), Boston (+155%), and Cincinnati (+118%). The average figure for these eleven cities in 1849–1851 was only modestly ($4.09, or 18%) above that for 1837–1839.

The mean per capita indebtedness for all of the metropolises listed in Table 2.21[53] was rather more than a quarter larger than for those listed in Table 2.19, and the abnormally large figure for New Orleans accounted for a preponderant portion of the increase. If that city is excluded from the calculations, the average per capita indebtednes for the remaining thirteen cities drops to $25.11. By this date the municipal indebtedness was greater than 1 million dollars in more than two-thirds of the towns, and the per capita debt exceeded twenty-five dollars in more than one-half.

Unlike the situation in 1839 there was a discernable (though not strong) re-

Table 2.21
Reported Debt in Fourteen Cities, 1847–1851

City (year)	Total Debt	Per Capita Debt
New Orleans (1847)	$7,409,954	$69.48
Philadelphia (1850)	5,885,800	48.49
Boston (1850)	6,195,000	45.26
Albany (1850)	1,877,688[a]	36.99
Baltimore (1850)	5,454,389	32.26
New York (1850)	15,803,433	30.65
Pittsburgh (1851)	1,349,570	28.80
Charleston (1849)	1,059,834	25.47
Washington (1850)	776,470	19.41
Louisville (1851)	723,810	15.84
St. Louis (1850)	1,192,992	15.32
Cincinnati (1850)	1,750,000	15.16
Brooklyn (1848)	690,000	8.14
Providence (1850)	194,351	4.68
	Median	27.14
	Mean	28.28
	Range	64.80
	SD	16.98

[a]Does not include $100,000 in loan
guarantees.

lationship in 1850 between municipal debt levels and the size of the urban populations, with the calculations yielding a rank order correlation (Spearman) of .534 for per capita debt and .815 for gross reported indebtedness. The five largest cities in 1850 are to be found among the six with the greatest per capita indebtedness and occupying the top five positions in total reported debt. The weak-to-modest negative relationship observable at the end of the 1830s between urban growth rates and per capita indebtedness was much more pronounced a decade later. Among the five cities at the top of the list in Table 2.21 are to be found four of the five towns that had the lowest growth rates between 1840 and 1850 and between 1830 and 1850. Four of the five metropolises with the highest growth rates over both the last decade and the last two decades are to be found among the five at the bottom of the list. The rank order correlations (Spearman) between per capita debt and growth rates are −.837 (1840–1850) and −.556 (1830–1850).

All of this suggests that the greatest increase in municipal indebtedness in the 1840s was taking place in the long-established major metropolises, which continued to experience substantial, though not (in percentage terms) dramatic population growth. This was assuredly the case. The four cities that consistently occupied the four top spots in terms of size in every census between 1800 and 1850—New York, Baltimore, Boston, and Philadelpia—accounted for more than four-fifths of the 22-million-dollar increase in municipal indebtedness recorded in the eleven cities common to both Tables 2.19 and 2.21.[54]

The major portion of this debt increase in the 1840s in the largest American

Table 2.22
Composite Analysis of Per Capita Debt in Ten Cities

City	$ 1810s	$ c1835	% Change	$ c1839	% Change	$ c1850	% Change	Total % Change
Albany	23.08	3.45	-85	11.80	+242	36.99	+213	+60
Baltimore	1.05	11.71	+1,015	31.07	+165	32.26	+4	+2,972
Boston	1.65	14.86	+801	17.78	+20	45.26	+155	+2,643
Cincinnati	n.a.	4.18	--	6.92	+66	15.16	+119	+263[a]
Louisville	n.a.	5.78	--	24.48	+324	15.84	-35	+174[a]
New York	8.84	6.37	-28	26.95	+323	30.65	+14	+247
Philadelphia	6.70	25.39	+279	32.89	+30	48.49	+47	+624
Pittsburgh	3.02	10.70	+254	n.a.	--	28.80	--	+854
Providence	1.61	5.15	+220	4.42	-14	4.68	+6	+191
Washington	2.05	86.15	+4,102	35.89	-58	19.41	-46	+847
Median	2.54	8.54		24.48		29.73		
Mean	6.00	17.37		21.35		27.75		
Range	22.03	82.70		31.44		43.81		
SD	6.96	23.77		10.95		13.24		

[a]Increase from c1835 to c1850.

Sources: Tables 2.17, 2.18, 2.19, 2.21.

cities represented municipal capital investment in three areas—water supply systems, gas lighting facilities, and extra-urban transportation works (railways and canals). In all six cities (cf. Tables 2.19 and 2.21) recording debt increases of more than 1 million dollars during this decade there were heavy expenditures for these purposes. Of the total indebtedness in 1850, water loans accounted for over 90% in New York and aid to railroad and canal corporations for over 92% in Baltimore. Water loans in Boston, though constituting a smaller percentage of the total indebtedness than in New York, accounted for over 97% of the increase in the 1840s. Debts contracted for providing water to the city and aiding transportation works made up more than 88% percent of the decennial increase in Albany and over 87% percent in Cincinnati, while railway, water, and gas loans constituted almost 93% percent of Philadelphia's increase.[55]

Ten cities appear in at least three of the four tables (2.17, 2.18, 2.19, 2.21) dealing with municipal indebtedness; seven in all four. Per capita debt figures for these ten cities are displayed in Table 2.22. Aside from the general upward trend that is readily apparent, there are few, if any, generalizations that can be drawn from these data. There is some evidence, however, of tighter clustering over time of the debt levels in these cities. The mean and the median consistently draw much closer together (in relative terms) throughout the half century. The highest per capita figure for an individual city, which was almost four times the mean in the 1810s and nearly five times the mean in circa 1835, had shrunk to about two-thirds to three-fourths greater than the mean circa 1839 and circa 1850.

One other minor aspect of city debts should be mentioned briefly. At one time or another during this half century, at least two-thirds of these cities issued certificates of indebtedness that circulated (at least in some measure) as currency. Such certificates appear to have been issued bearing either no interest or very low rates—typically 1% (the most common interest rates for municipal bond issues were 4% to 6%). Several considerations doubtless moved the city governments to issue such securities. Since the certificates were paid out to discharge claims against the city, the low interest rates and instant "marketability" (without the costly discounts insisted upon by bankers) were doubtless attractive to the city officials. It is also likely, however, that such issues were, at least in part, a response to the needs of the urban populations. Bank notes were, throughout this period, both largely unsecured and variable in supply and often shrank in number during times of financial unrest. City certificates, moreover, were frequently issued in very small denominations and were obviously designed to replace the minor coins, which tended to disappear quickly in periods of panic. Pittsburgh issued one-, two-, and three-dollar certificates; those circulated by Baltimore ranged from five cents to two dollars in value; the New York notes were worth from six and one-quarter to fifty cents; and Philadelphia appears to have issued notes in denominations as low as ten cents. In New York, Pittsburgh, and Cincinnati these certificates were issued as early as the 1810s, when the War of 1812 and the panic of 1819 created some severe financial stringencies; and Louisville's issues of 1822–1825 were probably related to continued banking and currency disorders in Kentucky. In Washington and Albany the issues of 1823 and 1826 may have been called into existence by the same financial unrest. Clearly the next major panic—that of 1837—and its predecessor uncertainties were similarly influential in triggering note issues in New Orleans (1836, 1837), Baltimore (1837), Pittsburgh (1837), Philadelphia (1837–1838), and, perhaps, even in St. Louis (1842). These certificates comprised the greater part of the total unfunded debt for the remainder of the half century in Pittsburgh, peaking at $224,000 in 1849; and the note issues of New York eventually amounted to almost $250,000, while the Second Municipality of New Orleans issued $300,000 in bonds in 1838 to redeem its small notes. In most of the cities, however, the issues were much more restricted. Baltimore authorized the issuance of $350,000 worth of certificates in 1837, but it would appear that less than a third of that amount was ever circulated. In the other cities the outstanding certificates appear rarely to have exceeded $50,000 and to have been, in many instances, much lower. In Washington, for example, although the corporation had issued almost $380,000 in notes by 1836, only a little over $25,000 had not been redeemed, and more than half of that amount was estimated to have been lost or destroyed.[56]

Urban expenditure data are more difficult to obtain than revenue figures and, when found, are frequently not sufficiently disaggregated to provide a clear picture of expenditure patterns. The problems of analyzing urban expenditure data comparatively is further complicated by the considerable diversity of practice among local governmental entities in assigning the responsibility for funding various activities. Public education expenses, for example, might be a charge upon the general city funds, or upon the county, or upon a separate school board budget, or upon some combination of these. Poor relief might be administered by the city government or the county court, or by overseers of the poor, who contolled an independent budget not incorporated into the reports of city officials. External public health activities (e.g., quarantine operations) were often (but not always) state responsibilities, while the expenditures associated with internal health functions (e.g., hospitals, dispensaries, street cleaning, removal of "nuisances," vaccination, and the work of city physicians) might be chargeable to the city, the county, a charitable bequest, an independent board of health, or (often) some combination of all these. And while the expenses of construction and repair of streets, walkways, gutters, sewers, and the like were usually paid from city funds (whether raised by taxation or assessment), it would appear that some or all of these activities sometimes fell under the purview of separate commissioners whose expenditures were not reported in city budget documents. None of the Philadelphia documents available, for example, show any expenditures for education, or for public health (except for street cleaning), or (with rare and obviously partial exceptions) for poor relief. Nevertheless, the Quaker City had excellent educational, relief, and public health facilities.

The data that follow, therefore, must be viewed as indicative rather than definitive. I have attempted to indicate the most obvious likely discrepancies wherever it is possible to observe them. In many cases, however, an inadequate level of disaggregation of the data makes it impossible to determine clearly the pattern of expenditures for municipal purposes.

At least some data on expenditures have been located for ten of these fifteen cities at some point during the period 1809–1821 (see Table 2.23).[57] The data for New Orleans and St. Louis are almost completely undisaggregated but for the other cities some detail is available. Aside from the fact that the city with the largest population has the highest per capita expenditures and that the two smallest towns are to be found in the ninth and tenth positions, there is little relation between population size and expenditure levels—the second and third largest cities rank third and fourth from the bottom in expenditures. The rank order correlation (Spearman) between per capita expenditures and population size in 1815 is a very modest .521. It should be noted, however, that the Philadelphia expenditure figure is obviously incomplete, but even if the listed gross expenditure is used instead of the sum of the given detail, the resulting figure for per capita expenditures ($2.38) would only move the Quaker City one step higher in the rank order. Boston's expenditure figure, on the other hand, is somewhat inflated by the inclusion of all county expenses and a substantial payment to the state of state property taxes collected by city officials. If these items were excluded, Boston's gross expenditures would drop to $158,109.80 and the per capita expenditures to $3.89.

In theory—though not always in practice—the exclusion of debt service charges from the expenditure figures of the various cities should give a more nearly accurate picture of the levels of expenditures for governmental services

Table 2.23
Expenditures in Ten Cities, 1809–1821

City (year)	Per Capita Expenditures	Total Expenditures
New York (1817)	$7.45	$860,278.43
New Orleans (1820)	7.20	195,597.00[a]
Charleston (1821)	6.04	152,940.57[b]
Albany (1811)	5.51	53,310.24[c]
Boston (1818)	5.41	219,903.13
Providence (1815)	3.54	38,700.00[c]
Baltimore (1816)	2.26	117,358.67[b]
Philadelphia (1809)	2.08	109,057.37[d]
Washington (1819)	1.70	21,692.84[e]
St. Louis (1817)	0.41	1,503.43[a]
Median	4.48	
Mean	4.16	
Range	7.04	
SD	2.35	

[a]Inclusiveness undeterminable because of very limited disaggregation.
[b]Includes no expenditures for education.
[c]Includes no expenditures for public health.
[d]Sum of detail; $15,808.18 less than statement of gross. Includes no expenditures for education, poor relief, or public health (except street cleaning).
[e]Includes no expenditures for debt service.

in the various cities. For eight of the ten cities listed in Table 2.23 the expenditure data are sufficiently disaggregated to permit the separation of debt service expenditures from what might be thought of as more nearly constituting current expenses. An examination of these data, presented in Table 2.24,[58] shows no changes in the rank order of the cities, although there are substantial differences among the cities in the changes in per capita expenditures produced by the exclusion of debt service charges. The percentage reduction produced by the exclusion was clearly directly related to the size of per capita expenditures, ranging from 22% in New York to 0% in Washington and (with two exceptions) following the same pattern as that for per capita expenditures.[59] This indicates that the cities with the larger per capita expenditures committed larger percentages of their budgets to debt service, a conclusion confirmed in greater detail by the figures in Table 2.25.

The data displayed in Table 2.25 give some indication of the manner in which the cities' budget makers committed their funds. Officials in Philadelphia, Baltimore, and New York, for example, placed the greatest emphasis (more than 40% of their available funds) on the improvement of physical facilities—streets and drainage in all three cities, with additional commitments to water delivery facilities in Philadelphia and harbor improvements in Baltimore and New York. Officials in Providence, Boston, and Washington, on the other hand, assigned primary position to human services, with Boston emphasizing education and the

Table 2.24
Expenditures, Excluding Debt Service, in Eight Cities 1809–1821

City (year)	Per Capita Expenditures	Total Expenditures
New York (1817)	$5.81	$670,779.38
Charleston (1821)	4.93	124,973.51[a]
Albany (1811)	4.66	45,154.64[b]
Boston (1818)	4.26	173,280.92
Providence (1815)	3.09	33,700.00[b]
Baltimore (1816)	2.17	112,496.67[a]
Philadelphia (1809)	1.95	103,415.37[c]
Washington (1819)	1.70	21,692.84
Median	3.66	
Mean	3.57	
Range	4.11	
SD	1.45	

[a]Includes no expenditures for education.
[b]Includes no expenditures for public health.
[c]Sum of detail; $15,808.18 less than listed gross.
  Includes no expenditures for education, poor
  relief, or public health (except street cleaning).

other two towns stressing poor relief. In Albany and Charleston the strongest emphasis was on public safety, with particular concern for policing in both cities, but the South Carolina metropolis funded the human services area (in particular, poor relief) almost as heavily.

An analysis of these sets of data using rank order correlation (Spearman) reveals some interesting relationships. There is, for instance, a quite strong correlation (.833) between population size and per capita expenditures on urban physical facilities, but city size is only moderately related (.429) to debt service expenditures, and apparently wholly unrelated (.048) to expenditures on human services. Thus it can be seen that the need for physical facilities is closely related to the size of an urban population, and it should be further noted that the extent of indebtedness—and, hence, the amount of money required for debt service—is often strongly influenced by the need to finance the construction of streets, bridges, markets, and water works. On the other hand, it might be suggested that the commitment of resources to fund human services flows more from philosophical or ideological commitment or traditional practices than from a clearly perceived "need" generated by an accretion of residents. But a word of caution should be inserted. It must be remembered that it is in relation to expenditures on human services that the data are least complete. For two of the four largest cities important areas of human services are clearly "off budget" insofar as the city authorities are concerned.[60]

By the end of the first third of the nineteenth century a number of differences in the patterns of governmental expenditures can be observed (see Table 2.26).[61] Not only is the mean per capita expenditure for the twelve cities analyzed up more than four-fifths from the comparable figure two decades earlier, but each

Table 2.25
Per Capita Expenditures by Category[62] in Eight Cities, 1809–1821

City (year)	Total	#	Physical Facilities	#	Human Services	#	Public Safety	#	Debt Service	#
New York (1817)	$7.45	1	$3.03	1	$1.15[a]	3	$0.82	3	$1.64	1
Charleston (1821)	6.04	2	0.66	5	1.83[b]	1	1.88	1	1.10	3
Albany (1811)	5.51	3	1.09	3	0.66[c]	5	1.78	2	0.84	4
Boston (1818)	5.41	4	0.39	6	1.47	2	0.49	5	1.15	2
Providence (1815)	3.54	5	0.17	7	1.12	4	1.75[d]	4	0.46	5
Baltimore (1816)	2.26	6	1.06	4	0.19[b]	6	0.43	6	0.09	7
Philadelphia (1809)	2.08	7	1.11	2	0.16[e]	8	0.37	7	0.13	6
Washington (1819)	1.07	8	0.28	8	0.29	7	0.23[f]	8	0.00	8
Median			0.86		0.89		0.62		0.65	
Mean			0.97		0.86		0.84		0.68	
Range			2.75		1.67		1.65		1.64	
SD			0.85		0.59		0.60		0.56	

\# -- Indicates rank order in magnitude of per capita expenditures.

[a]Includes some undisaggregated expenditures for corrections.
[b]Includes no expenditures for education.
[c]Includes no expenditures for public health.
[d]Includes militia expenditures.
[e]Includes no expenditures for education. poor relief. or public health
   (except street cleaning).
[f]Includes no police or watch expenditures.

of the two highest figures is more than double the highest figure in Table 2.23. The New York total expenditure figure for 1834 is considerably more than the combined total for all ten cities listed in Table 2.23. But where the 1817 New York figure was almost as great as the combined total of the other nine cities in the earlier analysis, in the 1830s the combined total of the second and third largest city expenditures (Boston and New Orleans) is greater than the expenditures of the Empire City.

As was the case two decades earlier, there was little observable relationship between population size and per capita expenditure (Spearman: .378). There is roughly the same degree of negative correlation (−.322) between per capita expenditures and rate of population growth during the period 1820–1840. There was, however, a clearly observable tendency for cities in the slave area to have higher per capita expenditures than those in the free states. The average for the five southern cities was $8.70, while that for the seven northern cities was $6.65—almost a quarter less. Two decades earlier (see Table 2.23) the average for the southern cities had lagged about a quarter behind that of the cities of the free states, but most of the differential in the 1810s had been accounted for by the very incomplete data for St. Louis. Or, to put it another way, the average per capita expenditure of cities in the slave area increased by almost 150% while the growth was a little over a third for the northern states. This differential is even more unusual when we remember that the slave component in these south-

Table 2.26
Expenditures in Twelve Cities, 1834–1838

City (year)	Per Capita Expenditure	Total Expenditure
Boston (1835)	$16.86	$1,300,813.43
Charleston (1838)	14.93	439,859.00[a]
New Orleans (1835)	12.00	779,626.33[b]
New York (1834)	8.29	2,045,445.74
Albany (1835)	8.08	233,921.00[c]
Washington (1836)	6.12	131,945.58[d]
Philadelphia (1835)	5.81	505,461.61[e]
Louisville (1835)	5.63	88,885.55[f]
Baltimore (1835)	4.84	442,455.98
Cincinnati (1835)	4.09	145,601.26[g]
Providence (1835)	2.50	50,000.00[h]
Brooklyn (1833)	0.92	17,921.88[i]
Median	5.97	
Mean	7.51	
Range	15.94	
SD	4.65	

[a]Sum of detail; exceeds statement of gross by
   $2,829.00.
[b]No expenditures for education disaggregated.
[c]No expenditures for fire protection or public
   health disaggregated.
[d]No expenditures for police or public health
   disaggregated.
[e]Includes no expenditures for education, poor
   relief, or public health (except street
   cleaning).
[f]Sum of detail; $99.98 greater than statement of
   gross.
[g]No expenditures for poor relief, public health,
   or debt service disaggregated.
[h]Includes no expenditures for public health.
[i]No expenditures for street lighting, education,
   or poor relief disaggregated.

ern urban populations had practically no access to the human services facilities and programs (e.g., hospitals, poor relief) of these cities. It might be suspected, on the other hand, that the presence of a servile population necessitated (psychologically, if not practically) heavier expenditures in the public safety area (see Table 2.28).

Over the two decades per capita expenditures more than trebled in Washington (+260%) and Boston (+212%) and more than doubled in Philadelphia (+179%), Charleston (+147%), and Baltimore (+114%). The increase was about two-thirds in New Orleans, almost one-half in Albany, and a little over a ninth in New York. Per capita expenditures declined more than a quarter in Providence. In these nine cities, common to both Table 2.23 and Table 2.26, the average increase in per capita expenditures was 93%—97% in the southern towns and 73% in the northern.

As might be expected, the elimination of debt service charges (see Table

Table 2.27
Expenditures, Less Debt Service, in Twelve Cities, 1834–1838

City (year)	Per Capita Expenditures	Total Expenditures
Charleston (1838)	$11.66	$343,561.00
Boston (1835)	8.42	649,954.69
New Orleans (1835)	8.32	540,730.00[a]
Albany (1835)	6.63	191,924.40[b]
New York (1834)	6.03	1,488,356.32
Louisville (1835)	5.39	85,012.75
Cincinnati (1835)	4.09	145,601.26[c]
Baltimore (1835)	3.98	363,666.21
Philadelphia (1835)	3.85	335,493.04[d]
Washington (1836)	2.22	47,940.47[e]
Providence (1835)	2.10	42,000.00[e]
Brooklyn (1833)	0.85	16,637.20[f]

Median	4.74
Mean	5.30
Range	10.81
SD	2.98

[a]No expenditures for education disaggregated.
[b]No expenditures for fire protection or public
  health disaggregated.
[c]No expenditures for poor relief, public health,
  or debt service disaggregated.
[d]Includes no expenditures for education, poor
  relief, or public health (except street
  cleaning).
[e]Includes no expenditures for public health.
[f]No expenditures for street lighting, education,
  or poor relief disaggregated.

2.27)[63] from the data in Table 2.26 does not much change the patterns of expenditures. The mean per capita expenditure is $5.30, about half again as large as the equivalent figure two decades earlier. Charleston, Boston, New Orleans, Albany, and New York occupy the top five positions, as they did in Table 2.26, though in somewhat different order, and Providence and Brooklyn still bring up the rear. Only two cities moved more than two rank order positions—Cincinnati, with a dramatic rise from tenth to seventh position, and Washington, with an even more pronounced drop from sixth to tenth. The first shift was occasioned by the fact that the 1835 Cincinnati budget identified no debt service expenditure, and the latter by the committing of almost two-thirds of the Washington budget to debt service in 1836.

When we turn to an examination of expenditures by categories (Table 2.28)[64] we are immediately struck by the fact that average per capita expenditures for physical facilities had more than doubled and those for debt service more than trebled as compared to the levels two decades earlier (see Table 2.25). Even more remarkable is the fact that average per capita expenditures for human services and public safety remained essentially unchanged—the former rose by one cent and the latter declined by three cents. This circumstance was admittedly

Table 2.28
Per Capita Expenditures, by Categories, in Twelve Cities, 1834–1838

City (Year)	Total	Physical Facilities	#	Human Services	#	Public Safety	#	Debt Service	#
Boston (1835)	$16.86	$2.43	5	$2.60	1	$1.39	2	$8.43	1
Charleston (1838)	14.93	5.20	1	1.06	5	2.05	1	3.27	4
New Orleans (1835)	12.00	5.12	2	0.48[a]	9	1.18[b]	4	3.86	3
New York (1834)	8.29	2.50	4	1.40[c]	2	0.97	5	2.26	5
Albany (1835)	8.08	3.92	3	0.74[d]	6	0.50[b]	9	1.45	7
Washington (1836)	6.12	0.84	6	0.29[d]	11	0.02[e]	12	3.90	2
Philadelphia (1835)	5.81	1.76	7	0.34[f]	10	0.75	6	1.95	6
Louisville (1835)	5.63	1.17	8	1.15	3	1.29	3	0.25	10
Baltimore (1835)	4.84	2.02	9	0.50	8	0.60	7	0.86	8
Cincinnati (1835)	4.09	0.68[g]	10	1.10[g]	4	0.24[g]	10	0.00[g]	12
Providence (1835)	2.50	0.35	11	0.73[d]	7	0.53	8	0.40	9
Brooklyn (1833)	0.92	0.05	12	0.04[d]	12	0.22[h]	11	0.07	11
Median		1.89		0.74		0.68		1.70	
Mean		2.17		0.87		0.81		2.21	
Range		5.15		2.56		2.03		8.43	
SD		1.68		0.65		0.56		2.31	

-- Indicates rank order in magnitude of per capita expenditures.

[a] Includes no expenditures for education.
[b] Includes no expenditures for fire protection.
[c] Includes some expenditures for corrections, not disaggregated.
[d] Includes no expenditures for public health.
[e] Includes no expenditures for police or street lighting.
[f] Includes no expenditures for education, poor relief, or public health (except street lighting.
[g] Very limited disaggregation, with more than half of all expenditures listed under "other"; only streets, fire protection, police, and education listed separately.
[h] Includes no expenditures for street lighting.

Table 2.29
**Cities for Which Disaggregated Data Are Available for Human Services by
Categories, Rank Ordered by Per Capita Expenditures, 1834–1838**

Rank	Education	Poor Relief	Public Health
1	Boston -- $1.56	Charleston -- $0.77	Boston -- 0.482
2	Cincinnati -- 1.10	Albany -- 0.61	New York -- 0.478
3	Louisville -- 0.62	New York -- 0.565	New Orleans -- 0.26
4	New York -- 0.36	Boston -- 0.558	Charleston -- 0.241
5	Providence -- 0.30	Providence -- 0.42	Louisville -- 0.239
6	Albany -- 0.13	Louisville -- 0.29	Baltimore -- 0.20
7	Washington -- 0.10	Baltimore -- 0.24	n. a.
8	Baltimore -- 0.07	New Orleans -- 0.22	n. a.
9	Charleston -- 0.06	Washington -- 0.19	n. a.
Median	0.30	0.42	0.25
Mean	0.48	0.43	0.32
Range	1.50	0.58	0.28
SD	0.50	0.19	0.12

influenced by the inclusion of data on additional cities in the 1830s, some of which (e.g., Brooklyn and Cincinnati) had very low levels of identifiable expenditures for human services and/or public safety. But that by no means constitutes a satisfactory explanation, for among the eight cities common to Table 2.25 and Table 2.28, the same phenomenon is observable. The mean per capita expenditures for these eight cities rose only ten cents (from $0.86 to $0.96) in the human services category and one cent (from $0.84 to $0.85) in the public safety area.

There is little indication of any relationship between city size or rate of growth and expenditures in any given area, with rank order correlations (Spearman) ranging between .40 and −.40, with one exception. There is a weak negative correlation (−.483) between per capita debt service expenditures and rate of population growth during the period 1820–1840. Differences are also observable between northern and southern cities; the mean per capita expenditures for the five cities from the slave area are larger than the means of the seven northern cities in all areas except human services—72% larger for physical facilities, 56% for public safety, and 15% for debt service. In the area of human services the average per capita expenditures of the northern cities was 43% larger than the southern.

It is true that a full understanding of this whole area is greatly inhibited by inadequately disaggregated data (especially in the northern cities), but the conclusion that the southern cities lagged behind those of the north in expenditures on human services is inescapable. We can, in some measure, minimize the difficulties produced by the inadequacies of the budget-reporting procedures by looking only at those cities with the highest reported per capita expenditures in the fields of education, poor relief, and public health (see Table 2.29).[65] Data are available on differing numbers of northern and southern cities in each of these subcategories, but in every case the tendency of the cities from the non-slave states to occupy the top rank order positions is pronounced. In the area of educational expenditures, the five northern cities for which satisfactory data are available occupy five of the top six positions in per capita expenditure. In the poor relief subcategory all four of the included northern cities are ranked in the top five, and in the public health area the only two northern cities available for analysis are ranked first and second.

As previously noted, the southern cities, on the average, committed much more urban resources per capita to public safety, with the average per capita expenditures in this category by southern towns being almost three-fifths greater than in the northern cities. Particularly notable in this area is the greatly dispro-portionate amount spent for policing and lighting the metropolises of the lower south (Charleston and New Orleans), where the average per capita expenditures of $1.38 were almost four times the average for the remaining ten cities (see Table 2.28). It is likely that the determination to prevent, insofar as possible, slave (or black) gatherings, slave disorders, and the possibility of slave revolt accounted for the decision by the governmental authorities to commit such rel-atively large amounts of money to efforts at social control. Significantly, in the upper south cities—which had much smaller slave populations—the average per capita expenditures for policing and lighting were much lower—about half those in New York and New England cities.

At least at first glance, the changes in the expenditures of the metropolises over the next decade and a half were less dramatic than those between the second and fourth decades. For instance, the mean per capita expenditure increased by only about one-fourth between the mid-1830s and the end of the fifth decade, as compared to more than 80% between the 1810s and the 1830s (cf. Tables 2.23, 2.26, and 2.30),[66] and the range of individual city expenditures, which had more than doubled in the earlier period, increased by considerably less than one-half in the later block of time. Around 1850, as in the mid-1830s, there were only three cities in which the per capita expenditures exceeded $10.00, and in only one city in the latter period (as compared to two in the former) did that figure fall below $4.00. Of course, the cities were now larger and their gross expenditures were concomitantly greater. New York's expenditures almost quin-tupled, approaching 10 million dollars, more than half again as great as the combined expenditures of all twelve of the cities examined in Table 2.26. But for the first time the level of expenditures per capita actually declined in several cities and there was even a drop in gross expenditures in one town.[67] Four southern cities recorded such declines in per capita expenditures in the decade and a half before 1850—Charleston (−39.18%), Louisville (−19.36%), Wash-ington (−7.19%), and Baltimore (−1.24%). Charleston also recorded a 14.09% reduction in gross expenditures. The Charleston experience doubtless repre-sented a "rebound" effect from the exceptionally high expenditures of 1838, which included sizeable purchases of land and corporate stocks. In like manner, almost two-thirds of Washington's 1836 expenditures (a grossly abnormal

Table 2.30
Expenditures in Thirteen Cities, 1847–1852

City (year)	Per Capita Expenditures	Total Expenditures
Boston (1850)	$25.50	$3,490,059.42
New York (1850)	19.03	9,808,608.85
New Orleans (1852)	17.28	2,282,200.00[a]
Albany (1850)	9.91	503,107.20
Charleston (1849)	9.08	377,885.29
Providence (1850)	6.90	286,600.00[b]
Philadelphia (1849)	6.41	759,949.19[c]
Pittsburgh (1851)	6.02	282,093.59[d]
Washington (1850)	5.68	221,093.59
Baltimore (1850)	4.78	807,544.82
Cincinnati (1850)	4.73	545,633.23
Louisville (1850)	4.54	196,233.82[e]
Brooklyn (1847)	2.73	214,480.68[f]

Median	6.41
Mean	9.43
Range	22.77
SD	6.60

[a]Projected; no debt services expenditures listed.
[b]Sum of detail, $100 less than statement of gross.
[c]Includes no expenditures for education or public
    health (except street cleaning); poor relief figure
    obviously incomplete.
[d]Includes no expenditures for education, poor relief, or
    construction or repair of streets, walkways, gutters,
    sewers, or bridges.
[e]Sum of detail, $330.45 less than statement of gross.
[f]Includes no expenditures for education, poor relief,
    or debt service.

amount) had gone for debt service, and some downward "correction" was only to be expected. But in Baltimore and Louisville the decline would appear to reflect a failure of expenditure levels to keep pace with population growth. It is perhaps worth noting, in this regard, that as a result of the long-cycle economic depression following 1837, the wholesale price index in 1850 stood at barely more than five-sixths of the 1835 figure, less than three-quarters of the 1836 and 1837 levels, and just over three-quarters of that of 1838.[68]

An examination of the nine cities common to Tables 2.23, 2.26, and 2.30 reveals the existence of two groups of towns. Throughout the antebellum period, Albany, Boston, Charleston, New Orleans, and New York occupied the first five positions in per capita expenditures, while Baltimore, Philadelphia, Providence, and Washington consititited the group with lower levels of expenditures. Among the top group there were greater and increasing variations (at least in the second quarter of the century), with the range of expenditure levels rising from $2.04 ($5.41 to $7.45) in the 1810s to $8.78 in the 1830s to $16.42 at midcentury. Among the cities in the bottom group of four the range was much smaller, rising between the 1810s and the 1830s from $1.84 ($1.70 to $3.54) to

$3.62 and declining to $2.12 by about 1850. These tightly concentrated figures, then, might be seen as constituting the bare minimum of acceptable urban governmental expenditures, with means of $2.40, $4.82, and $5.95 at the previously stated intervals. The means for the upper group of five at the same intervals were $6.32, $12.03, and $16.16.

Like previous data sets, there is an insignificant correlation between levels of per capita expenditure and city size (Spearman: $-.308$) and still no significant correlation with the rate of recent (1830–1850) population growth (Spearman: $-.404$). However, the tendency observable in the 1830s for southern cities to rank higher than their northern counterparts in per capita expenditures was no longer observable; by midcentury the average per capita expenditure among nothern cities was almost a quarter larger than among southern metropolises.

Two items of potential interest might be noted. First, the very modest negative correlation between city size and per capita expenditures suggests that the larger cities were, perhaps, beginning to realize some economies of scale in furnishing urban services to their populations. Second, the increasing range and standard deviation, each of which almost tripled between the 1810s and midcentury, would suggest that the nation's largest cities were becoming increasingly diverse rather than more homogeneous, probably because of divergent levels of expectations on the part of the residents.

The elimination of debt service charges significantly diminishes the expenditure levels in this array of American cities, and it is clear that borrowing was playing a larger and larger role in the fiscal operations of the towns. Among the thirteen cities for which financial data have been located, only two (New Orleans and Brooklyn) showed no specific provision for debt service in their budgets. In the 1830s (see Table 2.27) the mean per capita expenditures, excluding debt service costs, of the cities examined was rather more than 29% less than the mean per capita gross expenditures; by midcentury this figure had risen to almost 37%. In the fourth decade only two cities budgeted as much as 35% of gross expenditures to debt service; at the beginning of the sixth decade six cities (more than one-half of those reporting any such expenditures) exceeded that figure. Only one of the cities listed in Table 2.31[69] (excluding New Orleans and Brooklyn) allotted less than 20% of its expenditures to debt service; in the 1830s (see Table 2.27) five did.[70]

Nevertheless, so universal was the reliance on loans and the concomitant appropriation of debt service funds that relatively few major changes can be seen in the rank order placement of the cities in Tables 2.30 and 2.31. The same cities are to be found in the first five places. New Orleans (which budgeted no funds for debt service because its newly reconstituted city government placed the responsibility for redeeming outstanding bonds on the old "municipalities") moved from third to first but the relative positions of the remaining four towns were unchanged. Among the other eight cities, Providence and Pittsburgh, with 43% and 73%, respectively, of their budgets going to debt service, dropped three and five places, but otherwise the changes were minor. The elimination of

Table 2.31
Expenditures, Less Debt Service, in Thirteen Cities, 1847–1852

City (year)	Per Capita Expenditures	Total Expenditures
New Orleans (1852)	$17.28	$2,282,200.00[a]
Boston (1850)	14.04	1,922,285.39
New York (1850)	7.04	3,629,865.19
Albany (1850)	6.57	333,475.46
Charleston (1849)	4.80	199,536.83
Philadelphia (1849)	4.61	546,258.44[b]
Washington (1850)	4.15	172,668.25
Louisville (1850)	4.00	172,668.25
Providence (1850)	3.90	161,900.00
Cincinnati (1850)	3.68	424,433.23
Baltimore (1850)	2.88	487,047.77
Brooklyn (1847)	2.73	214,480.68[c]
Pittsburgh (1851)	1.63	76,520.00[d]
Median	4.15	
Mean	5.95	
Range	15.65	
SD	4.42	

[a]Projected.
[b]Includes no expenditures for education or public health (except street cleaning); poor relief figures obviously incomplete.
[c]Includes no expenditures for education or poor relief.
[d]Includes no expenditures for education, poor relief, or construction or repairs of streets, walkways, gutters, sewers, or bridges.

the debt service expenditures makes little change in any correlation with either population size or recent (1830–1850) population growth (Spearmans of .250 and −.412, respectively).

An analysis of the expenditures by categories (Table 2.32)[71] shows, as the data just discussed would suggest, the largest increases in average per capita expenditures since the 1830s (70.6%) occurring in the debt service area (cf. Tables 2.28 and 2.32). More unexpected is the very small shift in the physical facilities category—here the mean per capita expenditures increased by only 8.3% and the median actually declined by more than a quarter. Even this figure is grossly skewed upward by the New Orleans figure, which is more than twice the next highest figure. If the Crescent City expenditure is excluded, the mean for physical facilities expenditures drops to $1.80, 17% less than in the 1830s. Increases in expenditures for human services and public safety were substantial, with the per capita averages rising by 68% and 61%, respectively, above the 1830s levels. But in all categories the range of expenditure levels rose dramatically—by 42% for debt service, 61% for physical facilities, 68% for public safety, and 72% for human services—indicating wider diversities among the cities than earlier.

There was no significant correlation between levels of expenditures in these

Table 2.32
Per Capita Expenditures by Category in Thirteen Cities, 1847–1852

City (year)	Total	#	Physical Facilities	#	Human Services	#	Public Safety	#	Debt Service	#
Boston (1850)	$25.50	1	$4.46	2	$4.51	1	$3.47	1	$11.45	2
New York (1850)	19.03	2	2.28	4	1.87	3	1.39	3	11.98	1
New Orleans (1852)	17.28	3	9.01	1	1.64	5	3.41[a]	2	0.00[b]	12
Albany (1850)	9.91	4	4.38	3	0.95	9	0.87	7	2.34	5
Charleston (1849)	9.08	5	0.90	10	1.03[c]	8	1.38	4	4.29	4
Providence (1850)	6.90	6	0.89	11	2.55	2	0.68	10	3.00	6
Philadelphia (1849)	6.41	7	1.37	7	0.17[d]	11	1.33	5	1.80	8
Pittsburgh (1851)	6.02	8	0.64[e]	13	0.10[f]	12	0.56	11	4.39	3
Washington (1850)	5.68	9	2.27	5	1.12	7	0.07[g]	12	1.52	9
Baltimore (1850)	4.78	10	0.93	9	0.59	10	0.75	9	1.90	7
Cincinnati (1850)	4.73	11	0.76	12	1.77	4	0.76[h]	8	1.05	10
Louisville (1850)	4.54	12	1.08	8	1.23	6	0.96	6	0.55	11
Brooklyn (1847)	2.73	13	1.62	6	n.a.[i]		n.a.[i]		n.a.[i]	
Median			1.37		1.81		0.92		2.48	
Mean			2.35		1.46		1.30		3.77	
Range			8.37		4.41		3.40		11.98	
SD			2.28		1.14		1.02		3.79	

-- Indicates rank order in magnitude of per capita expenditures.

[a]No lighting expenditures disaggregated.
[b]No debt services listed.
[c]Educational expenditures probably incomplete.
[d]No expenditures listed for education, poor relief, or public health (except street cleaning).
[e]Expenditures for markets and water works only; no expenditures listed for constuction or repair of streets, walkways, gutters, sewers or bridges.
[f]No expenditures listed for education or poor relief.
[g]Very limited disaggregation for police and lighting.
[h]Expenditures for street lighting not disaggregated.
[i]Level of disaggregation insufficient to permit analysis.

areas and the size of the urban populations (the Spearman correlation ranged from −.363 to .490) or between levels of expenditures and the percentage of population growth between 1830 and 1850 (Spearman: −.259 to .336). Moreover, there is, rather surprisingly, no significant relationship (Spearman: .377) between per capita debt levels and per capita expenditures for debt service. While there are observable regional differences, they are by no means as pronounced as in the 1830s. Southern expenditure levels were higher for physical facilities (+38%) and public safety (+2%, or +26% if the obviously flawed Washington data are excluded). These figures are significantly lower than the +72% and +56% margins recorded by southern cities in the 1830s (see page 72, above). As earlier, the northern cities spent more heavily in the area of human services—52% more than their southern counterparts (or 108% if we exclude the wholly unrealistic Philadelphia and Pittsburgh data). This constitutes an increase over the 43% margin for northern cities in the 1830s. The most extensive change in comparative regional urban expenditures was for debt service. In the 1830s per capita expenditures for this purpose by southern cities was 15% greater than those in the northern towns. This circumstance had been diametrically reversed by midcentury, when debt service expenditures were 220% greater in the northern than in the southern cities (or 156% larger if the two "zero expenditure" cities of Brooklyn and New Orleans are excluded).[72] It appears likely that these differences in human services and public safety continued to reflect the facts that 1) neither free blacks nor slaves had equal access (indeed, rarely *any* access) to southern educational or public welfare services and 2) the fear of "servile insurrection" moved southern civic leaders to fund police and fire departments more generously than their northern counterparts.

When attempting to examine more detailed expenditures at midcentury, we are, as at earlier dates, plagued by unsatisfactory levels of disaggregation. It is possible, as in the 1830s, to break out the subcategories in the human services area. Moderately satisfactory data have been located for ten cities in each of the first two subcategories (education and poor relief) and for twelve in the third (public health). The most immediately obvious observation (see Tables 2.29 and 2.33[73]) is that the levels of expenditure had increased significantly in the first two categories. The mean per capita expenditures for education, for example, increased by more than three-quarters and the expenditures by the first-ranking city (in this instance, the same city—Boston) by more than one-half. In poor relief the mean increased by a third and the first-ranking town by six-sevenths. It is probably safe to say that public health expenditures remained essentially unchanged between the 1830s and midcentury. To be sure, the mean for this category diminished by three-eighths, but that was primarily a result of a doubling of the number of cities for which data are available. The mean for the top six cities in Table 2.33 is $0.33, only one cent above that in Table 2.29, although the figure for the first-ranking city in 1850 was more than two-fifths greater than in the 1830s. The slightness of the growth of the mean is attributable to

Table 2.33
Cities for Which Disaggregated Data Are Available for Human Services, Rank Ordered by Per Capita Expenditures, 1849–1852

Rank	Education	Poor Relief	Public Health
1	Boston --$2.38	Boston --$1.43	Boston --$0.69
2	New Orleans -- 1.51[a]	New York -- 0.83	Cincinnati -- 0.38
3	Providence -- 1.13	Cincinnati -- 0.70	Louisville -- 0.30
4	Washington -- 0.75	Charleston -- 0.62	New York -- 0.23
5	New York -- 0.73	Louisville -- 0.55	Charleston -- 0.19
6	Cincinnati -- 0.69	Providence -- 0.53	Philadelphia -- 0.16
7	Albany -- 0.45	Albany -- 0.46	Baltimore -- 0.13
8	Louisville -- 0.38	Washington -- 0.28	Pittsburgh -- 0.10
9	Baltimore -- 0.28	Baltimore -- 0.19	Washington -- 0.09
10	Charleston -- 0.26	New Orleans -- 0.08[a]	Albany -- 0.042
11			New Orleans -- 0.038[a]
12			Providence -- 0.01
	Median 0.71	0.54	0.145
	Mean 0.86	0.57	0.20
	Range 2.12	1.35	0.68
	SD 0.63	0.36	0.18

[a]Projected.

the fact that the expenditures for the 1830s were greater than in the later period in four of the six top positions.

If we look only at changes in the nine cities listed in Table 2.29 in the first two subcategories, there is little overall difference. The increase in the means is somewhat smaller, the ranges are identical, and the standard deviations almost unchanged. A comparison of individual cities does reveal that per capita expenditures for education actually declined in two cities and that for poor relief in four. These declines were rather more than a third in educational funding in Cincinnati and Louisville and more widely variable in poor relief support—just under two-thirds in New Orleans and from a fourth to a fifth in Albany, Baltimore, and Charleston. These declines must be seen in the context of fairly significant increases in the other cities—increases ranging from 53% (Boston) to 650% (Washington) in educational support and from 47% (New York and Washington) to 90% (Louisville) in poor relief funding.

As was the case a decade and a half earlier, the expenditures of northern cities were significantly higher than those of the southern towns in all three of these subcategories. In Table 2.33 as in Table 2.29 the three lowest positions in educational and poor relief funding are occupied by three of the five southern cities. In the public health area northern dominance is not quite so clear, with southern cities occupying third, fifth, seventh, ninth, and eleventh positions in Table 2.33. In relative terms, there was some growth in the funding of educational activities by the southern cities; their mean per capita expenditure for this purpose rose from 30% of the northern figure in the 1830s to 58% by midcentury.[74] There was, on the other hand, a distinct decline in relative southern

Table 2.34
Summary of Changes in Expenditures in U.S. Cities

Mean of Data Re:	1810s	1830s	c1850	Sources (Tables)
Per Capita Expenditures	$4.16(10)[a]	$7.51(12)	$9.43(13)	2.23,2.26,2.30
Per Capita Expenditures, Less Debt Service	3.57(8)	5.30(12)	5.95(13)	2.24,2.27,2.31
Per Capita Expenditures for:				
Physical Facilities	0.97(8)	2.17(12)	2.35(13)	2.25,2.28,2.32
Human Services	0.86(8)	0.87(12)	1.46(12)	2.25,2.28,2.32
Public Safety	0.84(8)	0.81(12)	1.30(12)	2.25,2.28,2.32
Debt Service	0.68(8)	2.21(12)	3.77(12)	2.25,2.28,2.32
Debt Service, Less "Zero Funding" Cities	0.77(7)	2.41(11)	4.12(11)	2.25,2.28,2.32

[a]Figures in parentheses indicate the number of cities for which data are available.

support for poor relief. In this subcategory the mean per capita expenditures of southern cities remained unchanged at thirty-four cents while mean northern expenditure levels increased by almost one-half, resulting in a relative decline in southern funding from 63% of the northern level in the 1830s to only 43% in 1850. In the public health area the southern position improved despite a pronounced decline in expenditures, because of an even greater drop in northern urban funding levels. By midcentury mean southern per capita expenditures, despite a drop of three-eighths, had risen from one-half (in the 1830s) to almost two-thirds of the northern levels.

In summary (see Table 2.34), the mean per capita expenditures of American cities (with a single exception) increased in every category examined in each of the time intervals utilized. The sole anomaly is the slight decline in public safety expenditures between the 1810s and the 1830s. But the increases are by no means regular in all categories (see Table 2.35). For instance, except in the areas of human services and public safety increases in per capita expenditures were, in percentage terms, considerably larger in the 1810s-to-1830s era than in the later period—usually three to four times as large. These figures must be viewed with caution, however, since, in some of the more extreme cases (e.g., debt service) the extent of the differential is a statistical product of calculating percentages from smaller actual bases for the earlier period. Nevertheless, it remains true that *actual* per capita increases were, in a number of categories, greater in the earlier than in the later interval. Gross per capita expenditures, for instance, grew by $3.35 between the 1810s and the 1830s and by $1.92 between the 1830s and circa 1850. For "expenditures, less debt service" the figures were $1.73 and $0.65 and for physical facilities expenditures, $1.20 and $0.18.

More notable are the differential increases for the whole period in the various categories. In the areas of public safety, human services, and "expenditures, less debt service," the increases over the entire period were tightly clustered, ranging from a little over two-fifths to two-thirds. The remaining categories displayed

Table 2.35
Percentage Changes in Expenditures in U.S. Cities

Mean of Data Re:	1810s-1830s	1830s-c1850	1810s-c1850
Per Capita Expenditures	+80.5%	+25.6%	+126.7%
Per Capita Expenditures, Less			
Debt Service	+48.5%	+12.3%	+66.7%
Per Capita Expenditures for:			
Physical Facilities	+123.7%	+8.3%	+142.3%
Human Services	+1.2%	+55.2%	+57.0%
Public Safety	-3.6%	+48.1%	+42.9%
Debt Service	+235.0%	+86.4%	+411.8%
Debt Service, Less			
"Zero Funding" Cities	+213.0%	+71.0%	+435.1%

Table 2.36
Summary of Changes in Expenditures in U.S. Cities
in Constant (1835) Dollars

Means of Data Re.:	1810s	1830s	c1850
Per Capita Expenditures	$3.24 (10)[a]	$7.41 (12)	$11.29 (13)
Per Capita Expenditures,			
Less Debt Service	2.63 (8)	5.24 (12)	7.10 (13)
Per Capita Expenditures for:			
Physical Facilities	0.71 (8)	2.15 (12)	2.80 (13)
Human Services	0.65 (8)	0.87 (12)	1.75 (12)
Public Safety	0.66 (8)	0.81 (12)	1.56 (12)
Debt Service	0.51 (8)	2.17 (12)	4.51 (12)
Debt Service, Less			
"Zero Funding" cities	0.58 (7)	2.36 (11)	4.92 (11)

[a]Figures in parentheses indicate the number of cities for which
data are available.

in Tables 2.34 and 2.35 showed much higher increases, with gross expenditures and expenditures for physical facilities growing by 127% and 142%, respectively, and debt service expenditures more than quintupling. These increases are, of course, closely interrelated. Much of the urban debt was incurred to pay for new or improved physical facilities, and the increased borrowing necessitated higher (though not necessarily proportionately higher) expenditure levels for debt service.

An accurate comparison of expenditure levels across time is, of course, rendered difficult because of changes in price levels. The wholesale price index for the years for which data were calculated for these analyses ranged from 82 to 170. Changes of this nature are usually of minor importance in analyzing data within the narrower time frame embodied in the earlier tables.[75] But across a period of several decades such changes can create distortions. To overcome these difficulties Tables 2.36[76] and 2.37 have been constructed on the basis of constant (1835) dollars.

A comparison of Tables 2.34 and 2.35 with Tables 2.36 and 2.37 reveals two major changes accompanying the conversion to constant dollars. First, the in-

Table 2.37
Percentage Changes in Expenditures of U.S. Cities in Constant (1835) Dollars

Means of Data Re.:	1810s-1830s	1830s-c1850	1810s-c1850
Per Capita Expenditures	+128.7%	+52.4%	+248.5%
Per Capita Expenditures,			
Less Debt Service	+99.2%	+35.5%	+170.0%
Per Capita Expenditure for:			
Physical Facilities	+202.8%	+30.2%	+294.4%
Human Services	+33.8%	+101.1%	+169.2%
Public Safety	+22.7%	+92.6%	+136.4%
Debt Service	+325.5%	+107.8%	+784.3%
Debt Service, Less			
"Zero Funding" Cities	+306.9%	+108.5%	+748.3%

creases in funding across the whole period are appreciably greater when measured in constant, as opposed to current, dollars; second, because of substantial increases in the percentage of change between the 1830s and circa 1850 and decreases in those figures for the 1810s–1830s period, there is some "smoothing out" of the rates of increase in some categories across the entire period.

Tables 2.38 and 2.39 summarize expenditure patterns for eight cities across the half century in current and constant dollars. Here, again, the picture is one of great diversity. The increases throughout the half century in gross expenditures in current dollars, for instance, range from 147% to 1,487% and in constant (1835) dollars from 207% to 2,677%. In per capita gross expenditures the figures are much smaller, but the range is still considerable—from 50% to 371% in current dollars and from 88% to 725% in constant (1835) dollars. Nor does every comparison of funding levels at successive time periods show an increase; in more than 20% of the cases involving current dollars and almost 10% of those based on constant (1835) dollars the later figure was smaller than the preceding one, indicating declines in funding levels.

Diversity is seen also in the rank ordering of these eight cities in the various categories at different times. In the areas of per capita gross expenditures and per capita expenditures, less debt service, there is, to be sure, considerable consistency—Albany, Boston, Charleston, and New York occupy the first four positions in all time periods in both categories whether measured in current or constant dollars. But in all of the other subtables only one element of significant regularity emerges—Boston, Charleston, and New York occupy the first three positions in per capita debt service, whether stated in current or constant dollars, with a single exception in each of the two subtables. Elsewhere, though there may be consistency in a single city (Providence always ranks last in per capita expenditures for physical facilities in current or constant dollars) the general impression is one of randomness (e.g., Boston ranks sixth, fourth, and first in per capita current dollar physical facilities expenditures).

Indeed, there would appear to be few generalizations to be drawn from an examination of urban financial practices in the first half of the nineteenth century, although, as has been previously noted, there were some centralizing trends

Table 2.38
Summaries of Expenditure Patterns in Eight Cities

A. Gross Expenditures ($000)				B. Per Capita Gross Expenditures ($)			
City	1810s	1830s	c1850	City	1810s	1830s	c1850
Albany	53.3	233.9	503.1	Albany	5.51	8.08	9.91
Baltimore	117.4	442.5	807.5	Baltimore	2.26	4.84	4.78
Boston	219.9	1,300.8	3,490.1	Boston	5.41	16.86	25.50
Charleston	152.9	439.9	377.9	Charleston	6.04	14.93	9.08
New York	860.3	2,045.4	9,808.6	New York	7.45	8.29	19.03
Philadelphia	109.1	505.5	759.9	Philadelphia	2.08	5.81	6.41
Providence	38.7	50.1	286.6	Providence	3.54	2.50	6.90
Washington	21.7	131.9	221.1	Washington	1.70	6.12	5.68

C. Per Capita Expenditures, Less Debt Service ($)				D. Per Capita Expenditures for Physical Facilities ($)			
City	1810s	1830s	c1850	City	1810s	1830s	c1850
Albany	4.66	6.63	6.57	Albany	1.09	3.92	4.38
Baltimore	2.17	3.98	2.88	Baltimore	1.06	2.02	0.93*
Boston	4.26	8.42	14.04	Boston	0.39	2.43	4.46
Charleston	4.93	11.66	4.80*	Charleston	0.66	5.20	0.90
New York	5.81	6.03	7.04	New York	3.03	2.50	2.28*
Philadelphia	1.95	3.85	4.61	Philadelphia	1.11	1.76	1.37
Providence	3.09	2.10	3.90	Providence	0.17	0.35	0.89
Washington	1.70	2.22	4.15	Washington	0.28	0.84	2.27

E. Per Capita Expenditures for Debt Service ($)			
City	1810s	1830s	c1850
Albany	0.84	1.45	3.34
Baltimore	0.09	0.86	1.90
Boston	1.15	8.43	11.45
Charleston	1.10	3.27	4.29
New York	1.64	2.26	11.98
Philadelphia	0.13	1.95	1.80
Providence	0.46	0.40	3.00
Washington	0.00	3.90	1.52

0.00 -- Decline from previous time period.
*Decline for entire period (1810s-c1850).

in the rising revenues. The most obvious general tendency was the continuing growth in urban revenues and expenditures, both gross and per capita, whether measured in terms of current or constant dollars. Although some regional trends were occasionally observable, this growth (except in the gross figures) would appear to be largely unrelated to such matters as city size or rapidity of population growth. The increased reliance on borrowing is reflected in both the growth of city debts (see Tables 2.17, 2.18, 2.19, and 2.21) and expenditures for debt service (see Tables 2.34, 2.35, 2.36, and 2.37). But the nature of the expenditures, the means of raising the revenue, and even the extent of the cities' financial commitments seem to have been a product of often decidedly different priorities about city services and operations.

Nevertheless, these circumstances were related to a shared group of interre-

Table 2.39
Summaries of Expenditure Patterns for Eight Cities in Constant (1835) Dollars

A. Gross Expenditures ($000)				B. Per Capita Gross Expenditures ($)		
City	1810s	1830s	c1850	City	1810s	1830s	c1850
Albany	42.3	233.9	589.9	Albany	4.37	8.08	11.80
Baltimore	77.7	442.5	961.3	Baltimore	1.50	4.84	5.69
Boston	149.6	1,300.8	4,154.9	Boston	3.68	16.86	30.36
Charleston	149.9	399.9	460.9	Charleston	5.92	13.57	11.07
New York	569.7	2,272.7	11,676.9	New York	4.93	9.21	22.65
Philadelphia	83.9	505.5	926.7	Philadelphia	1.60	5.81	7.82
Providence	22.8	50.1	341.2	Providence	2.08	2.50	8.21
Washington	17.4	115.7	263.2	Washington	1.36	5.37	6.76

C. Per Capita Expenditures, Less Debt Service ($)				D. Per Capita Expenditures for Physical Facilities ($)		
City	1810s	1830s	c1850	City	1810s	1830s	c1850
Albany	3.70	6.63	7.82	Albany	0.87	3.92	5.21
Baltimore	1.44	3.98	3.43	Baltimore	0.70	2.02	1.11
Boston	4.26	8.42	16.83	Boston	0.27	2.43	5.31
Charleston	4.83	10.60	5.82	Charleston	0.65	4.73	1.10
New York	3.85	6.70	8.38	New York	2.01	2.78	2.71
Philadelphia	1.50	3.85	5.62	Philadelphia	0.85	1.76	1.67
Providence	1.82	2.10	4.62	Providence	0.10	0.35	1.06
Washington	1.36	1.95	4.94	Washington	0.22	0.74	2.70

E. Per Capita Expenditures for Debt Service ($)			
City	1810s	1830s	c1850
Albany	0.67	1.45	3.98
Baltimore	0.06	0.86	2.26
Boston	0.78	8.43	13.63
Charleston	1.08	2.96	5.23
New York	1.09	2.51	14.26
Philadelphia	0.10	1.95	2.20
Providence	0.27	0.40	3.57
Washington	0.00	3.42	1.81

0.00 -- Decline from previous time period.

lated changes. As the years passed in the nineteenth century these cities not only became more populous but, in addition, the communal concepts of the role of city governments were modified and expanded; the perceived need for public health, public safety, and educational facilities and services burgeoned; and the demand for water delivery, street lighting, and public transportation capacity escalated dramatically (see volume 3 of this study). Although these changing perceptions lagged behind the population growth, all of the urban officials eventually had to confront these rising expectations, which, in turn, fueled increased expenditures and, thus, revenues. The demands were compounded by the explosive expansion of the desired boundaries of the urban commercial hinterlands and the resultant involvement in urban mercantilistic activities (see chapter 7) with a consequent increase in governmental expenditures and, especially, indebtedness and related debt service charges.

From first to last, then, the perception of governmental roles, by citizens or officials, was the initial impetus which drove the expenditure increases which eventually (and despite some reluctance on the part of the taxpayers) impacted revenue production. The nature of urban fiscal policy was essentially the formulation of the mechanics and choice of alternatives to meet these demands.

Chapter 3

Urban Politics

In the framing of city charters and other statutes state legislators and (in a number of cases) city residents invested time, energy, thoughtful consideration, knowledge of the experiences of other urban centers, and a fair amount of ingenuity, for the purpose of indicating with considerable specificity the structure of government they thought most likely to operate satisfactorily in a given place and time. Such charters and other acts did not, however, create a government any more than an engineer's drawings created an efficiently operating steam engine. The transformation of concept into reality required activities of a less theoretical, more mundane, and continuing nature. And just as a careless or unskilled artisan could mar the envisaged product of the designer, or an ignorant or venal operator could render the machine less efficient or even dangerous, while a skillful and intelligent worker could suggest practical improvements and make necessary adjustments, so, too, did much depend upon the nature and ability of those chosen to create and operate the urban governments. As an operational matter the much-vaunted American concept of a government of laws and not of men was not even a theoretical possibility.

The process by which government officers are selected, then, becomes a matter of great practical importance. Since none of these cities entered the nineteenth century with a government of the old closed corporation format, popular elections, at least in some measure (and increasingly widely throughout the half century) constituted the process by which governments were made realities. But the urban electoral process was not confined to the selection of officers of the corporation. Cities also became electoral districts for the choice of state legislators and members of the federal House of Representatives; additionally, they constituted individual voting units in presidential and gubernatorial elections.

By 1800, of course, the two-party structure that would become the national norm in the United States had already emerged; indeed, one of the two major components of that "first American party system"—the Federalist party—was at the edge of the downhill slope that would lead to its collapse on the national level in the second decade of the nineteenth century. But in the cities in which the Federalists had established a significant presence in the late eighteenth century they showed unusual survival abilities. At the turn of the century Washington did not exist as a political entity, New Orleans and St. Louis still lay beyond the national boundaries of the United States, and Brooklyn, Buffalo, Cincinnati, and Louisville were small villages whose votes were rarely separately recorded. Of the remaining eight cities, only in Baltimore were the Jeffersonian Republicans clearly in a dominant position at the end of the eighteenth century—there Jeffersonian Samuel Smith was elected five successive times to represent the Baltimore district in Congress.[1] There was, however, clear indication of Republican strength in Philadelphia during those years. Federalist control of the city's congressional seat was broken by Republican John Stanwick's narrow (51.2% of the vote in each year) victories in 1794 and 1796. But the Federalists were clearly stronger, carrying their Assembly ticket with over 61% of the vote even as Stanwick was winning his second term. In 1797, 1798, and 1799 the Federalists stacked victory upon victory, the most lopsided being Robert Waln's congressional race in 1798, in which he polled 69.2% of the vote and carried every ward. More commonly the Federalist vote percentage was in the upper fifties, and the Republicans were usually victorious in the two or three most northerly wards (i.e., North Mulberry, South Mulberry, and Upper Delaware).[2]

The political situation in New York was at once more complex and a clear example of the effects on electoral success of both the role of different issues in city, state, and federal elections and also of the impact of differing suffrage requirements. In the Empire State not only did voters for governor and state senators have to possess real estate valued at at least $250—a provision not mandated for voters for members of the state Assembly—but the charter of its largest city (and of other cities as well, for that matter) also specified a rather high property qualification for voting for charter officers. At the turn of the century more than 8,000 residents of the city met the requirements to vote in state elections, while fewer than 3,000 were qualified to vote for city officers. The federal Constitution, of course, made the qualifications for voting in congressional elections the same as for the state Assembly.[3] Consequently, although the Federalists maintained a "preponderant majority" in the city councils throughout the 1790s and Federalist John Jay carried the city with 57.2% of the vote in the 1795 gubernatorial election, Republican Edward Livingston represented the city district in Congress throughout the latter half of the decade. The election of 1800 gives a pretty clear picture of the existing political situation. The Federalists won ten of fourteen seats in the city council and lost only the two northernmost "out wards" (the sixth and seventh) to the Republicans. In the Assembly contest, however, the Jeffersonians added three more wards (the fourth, fifth, and sixth) to their ranks and elected their entire ticket.[4]

In Albany, Boston, Charleston, and Providence the Federalists would appear to have been in firm control in the 1790s, and it is likely that the same was true of Pittsburgh. The latter town was, of course, quite small during this period and disaggregated electoral data, consequently, are very sparse. But county figures, contemporary observations, and subsequent performance certainly strongly suggest Federalist preponderance.[5]

There are several circumstances that inhibit the collection of detailed information about political alignments in some of these cities in the first fifth to a quarter of the nineteenth century—the period of the decline of the Federalist party and the emergence of the "Era of Good Feeling." Several of the towns remained so small throughout these years that the vote cast in them was almost never separately reported. Brooklyn, Buffalo, Cincinnati, Louisville, and St. Louis can be seen as falling into this category in the early years of the century. Moreover, even when the results of the city elections were reported such reports frequently merely listed the names of the persons elected and gave no particulars about the votes or the opposing candidates. Indeed, local elections would appear to have been frequently conducted without reference to national parties until, in some cases, well after 1830. Meanwhile, the votes in the state and national contests conducted along party lines were often not disaggregated below the county level. Finally, in a number of these cities—especially those in the south and west—the dominance of the Jeffersonian Republican party was so thorough that no party opposition emerged in most elections, and contests, when they existed, were among Republicans. In Baltimore, Brooklyn, Cincinnati, Louisville, New Orleans, St. Louis, and Washington, certainly, anti-Republican opposition was rarely visible before the rise of the "second party system." The case of Buffalo is less clear, for the data are so few for the early years as to preclude any conclusions. As a sort of afterword it might be noted that only local elections were held in Washington and that throughout the half century no popular contests for governor or for presidential electors took place in Charleston, where these offices were filled by the state legislature.

Until there was a change in city suffrage requirements in 1804, the Federalists continued to control the city council of New York, carrying five of seven wards in 1801 and 1802 and five of nine in 1803, and in 1802 mustering almost 56% of the vote. But during the same period the Jeffersonians consistently won the Assembly elections with more than 55% (and sometimes over 60%) of the ballots. The Federalist victories were clearly produced by the restricted charter electorate—the rather hotly contested city election of 1802 attracted almost 1,600 voters, while more than 6,200 turned out for the 1803 Assembly contest. The Federalist mayor Richard Varick was even accused (probably correctly) of improper activities designed to keep the charter electorate smaller still.[6]

The impact of the 1804 change in New York charter suffrage requirements— extending the vote to £25 ($62.50) leaseholders—was immediate and dramatic.

Table 3.1
New York City Elections

Votes Cast (year)	% Federalist
10,629 (1810)	50.1
10,595 (1814)	50.3
9,985 (1813)	50.7
9,431 (1815)	50.8
9,305 (1812)	52.2
9,209 (1811)	57.5

The twelve-to-six Federalist margin in the city council in 1803 was converted into Republican majorities of fourteen to four in 1804 and fifteen to three in 1805. Only in the first two wards at the southern tip of Manhattan did the Federalists elect any of their candidates. By 1806 the total vote cast in the charter elections had risen to 6,161 (despite the absence of any recorded votes in ward one, where the Federalist candidate was unopposed) compared to 7,449 in the Assembly race.[7]

Except for Aaron Burr's victory by about 100 votes in the 1804 gubernatorial race and the Federalist successes in the tenth and eighteenth wards in the 1806 city council race (but with only 40% of the total vote), the Republicans dominated New York politics for the next five years, though by relatively slight margins (from 50% to 55%). But 1809 ushered in an abrupt change, probably because of unrest in the nation's major port city occasioned by the intensifying maritime problems associated with the European war and the Jefferson and Madison administrations' response to those difficulties. By 1808 the increase in the number of wards and the changes in ward boundaries had produced four wards (the first, second, third, and tenth) that were reliably Federalist; four that were reliably Republican (the fifth, seventh, eighth, and ninth); and two (the fourth and sixth) that were marginal. The Federalists carried the state for the first time in a decade, and, although the Republicans narrowly (50.6%) carried their Assembly slate in the city in 1809, the city council that year went to the Federalists by fifteen seats to five. This latter was an exceptionally large margin. In the years that followed, through 1815, the Federalists usually controlled twelve of the twenty city council seats (thirteen in 1812 and ten in 1814) by carrying the marginal fourth and sixth wards with 50% to 51% of the votes there. The Federalists were successful in the Assembly races (except in 1814) by capturing between 50.1% and 57.5% of the vote. During this period the proportion of the Federalist (or, in 1814, non-Republican) vote varied inversely with the total votes cast (see Table 3.1).[8]

In Philadelphia, as in New York, the turn of the century brought success to the Jeffersonian Republicans. Although as late as 1798 the Federalists had carried all twelve wards and garnered almost 70% of the vote, in 1800 William Jones, the Republican congressional candidate, polled 50.2% of the vote and had majorities in six of the city's fourteen wards. To the traditionally Republican northern wards (Upper Delaware, Lower Delaware, North Mulberry, and South Mulberry) he had added the two new southwestern wards (Locust and Cedar). The Federalists carried the legislative and council contests by greatly reduced margins—about twenty-five vote margins compared to almost two-to-one majorities in the same races the year before. By the following year the Republicans were able to carry both the council (Select and Common) and state legislative (Assembly and Senate) races with from 51.5% to 53% of the vote and to add two more wards (South and New Market) to their ranks. This position the Republicans held and expanded through 1804, carrying the city for Thomas McKean in the 1802 gubernatorial race by 1,943 to 1,517 (56.2%) and choosing the Jeffersonian electors in the 1804 presidential contest with only about 700 votes going to the opposition.[9]

The future, moreover, appeared bright for Philadelphia Republicans, for the wards they carried were the peripheral (and more rapidly growing) ones, while the Federalists drew their strength from the more stable central wards. In 1801 the Republicans carried every ward north of Mulberry Street and (with the exception of Dock Ward) south of Walnut Street. The one worrisome consideration was that the Republicans in that year polled less than 52% of the vote in both New Market and Locust wards—a degree of marginality unmatched in any of the Federalist wards.[10]

But these animating reflections proved illusory. The emergence into greater prominence of the *tertium quids* in 1805 (dissident Republicans with whom the Federalists made common cause) produced new alignments that blunted the Jeffersonian offensive. In that year the antiadministration candidate for governor—Thomas McKean—garnered just over 51% of the vote in Philadelphia, and two years later the Constitutionalist (i.e., Federalist and Quid) candidate for the state Senate carried ten of the fourteen wards (all but the two most northwestern and the two most southwestern) with over 60% of the vote. What followed was a period of political flux, extending at least to the end of the War of 1812, during which neither party could achieve lasting dominance. In 1808 and 1809 the Republican candidates for governor (Simon Snyder) and Congress (Adam Seybert) carried the city with 51.4% and 53.5%, respectively, of the vote. Then, successively, the Federalists took the 1810 congressional race and the 1811 state Assembly contest; the Republicans won the 1812 and 1813 presidential and Assembly elections; and the Federalists were again successful in the gubernatorial contest of 1814 and the council elections of 1815.[11]

Though not quite as precisely as in New York, there was in Philadelphia also a direct relationship between voter participation and the Republican percentage of the vote. In each of the elections listed above between 1807 and 1815 (inclusive), the Republicans won whenever the total voter turnout exceeded 5,000 and lost whenever it was below that figure. When the vote dropped below 4,500 the non-Republican percentage closely approximated or exceeded 60%.

In Albany and Providence the specific data are very sparse for the first decade and a half of the nineteenth century, but both seem to have been thoroughly (probably over 70% in the case of Providence) Federalist. The areas of greatest Republican strength would appear to have been Providence's north end and Albany's south end. The data to establish Boston's allegiance to the Federalist party are much more complete. To be sure, Republican Elbridge Gerry managed to eke out narrow victories (50.4% and 52.9%) in Boston in the gubernatorial races of 1800 and 1801. But for the remainder of the period through 1815 Bostonians voted consistently for the Federalist candidates for chief executive of the state. Indeed, only twice (1808 and 1810) in these fourteen elections were the Jeffersonians able to muster as much as 40% of the Boston vote.[12]

Pittsburgh, too, was predominatly Federalist during these years. The century opened on an erratic note, to be sure. The Federalist candidate for borough inspector won by a single vote in 1800, while the Republican candidate took that office in 1801 by a two-to-one margin. This was, however, an aberration that would not be soon repeated. The Federalist congressional candidates carried the borough in 1802 and 1804 with 65.9% and 59.5% of the vote, respectively. The developing split in Pennsylvania's Republican ranks now worked to the Federalists' advantage. Thomas McKean, the Federalist-Quid gubernatorial candidate, carried Pittsburgh in 1805. At the beginning of the next decade the Federalists continued to benefit from Republican factionalism. In 1810 the Pittsburgh district congressional seat was contested between two "Republican" candidates; the victor in Pittsburgh (but not in the district) was Adamson Tannehill, a former Federalist. In the next two years local elections were won by a Republican faction and a "Friends of Peace, Union, and Commerce" ticket containing a number of individuals associated with antiadministration activities, while the borough officers, chosen in 1813 in a nonpartisan election, included several of like persuasion. In that same year the Federalist candidate for the state Senate polled almost 52% of the votes in Pittsburgh.[13]

The shift to Republicanism in Charleston was, in the early nineteenth century, probably more pronounced than in any other of these cities. As late as 1803 the city was viewed as the major center of Federalist strength in South Carolina. The Federalist candidate for Congress in February of that year—Thomas Lowndes—polled almost 57% of the vote to defeat Republican Robert Marion. But in October of the next year Marion captured more than 55% of the vote and inaugurated an almost uninterrupted string of Republican victories in congressional races. Marion won again in 1806 (51%) and 1808 (66.5%), and in 1810 "the Federalists neither held caucuses nor formed a ticket for the election." This observation appeared, at first glance, to indicate a resigned acceptance by the Federalists of their inability to mount effective opposition to the Republicans, their share of the vote in a losing cause having declined from 47.5% in 1806 to 33.5% in 1808. They had also lost the state Senate race in 1808 to Republican John Drayton by essentially the same margin. But this appearance was deceptive. In the 1806 legislative election, eight of the city's fifteen legislative seats were filled by candidates from the "Federal Republican" ticket, four from the "Democratic Republican" list, and three candidates endorsed by both parties. These labels, incidentally, were not uncommon in other cities as well. In 1810 the Republican nominees for Congress and the state Senate seat were Langdon Cheeves and Henry Middleton, both of whom had been endorsed by the "Federal Republicans" for the state legislature in 1806. This circumstance probably accounted, in part, for the absence of a party challenge in the latter year. In 1812 the Federalists contested elections for federal representative (under the name of "Friends of Union, Commerce, and Honorable Peace"), state representative, state senator, and intendant (mayor) and marshaled over 40% of the votes in three of the four contests; and in 1813 Republican Thomas Bennett, Jr., defeated the Federalist candidate by only 3 votes in a total of 933 cast. In the following year Thomas Rhett Smith led the Federalists to victory in the intendant's race, with 54.2% of the vote. In the same year, however, Smith failed to carry Charleston in the congressional race, mustering only a little more than 38% of the vote against Henry Middleton, a Republican whom the Federalists had not only endorsed in the state legislative race of 1806 (as noted above) but to whom they had also given tacit support for the state Senate in 1810.[14] Thus, by the end of the War of 1812 the Federalists in Charleston still preserved a presence in federal, state, and local elections and could occasionally win a contest, though their strength in recent nonvictories had ranged between 38% and 46%. They had also sometimes employed open or tacit endorsement with a measure of success.

A decade and a half into the century, then, Baltimore, Brooklyn, Washington, and all of those cities west of the Atlantic tier of states were so thoroughly Republican that a Federalist presence could hardly be detected except in the form of individuals. The northeastern cities of Albany, Boston, and Providence were solidly Federalist; but the Republican presence was clear and continuing, though hardly threatening, and Pittsburgh was apparently equally devoted to the Federalist cause. Charleston had abandoned its earlier commitment to Federalism and was firmly under Republican control, though the Federalists continued to contest the elections and on rare occasions emerged victorious. The two most politically ambivalent cities were New York and Philadelphia. The former, whose expanded electorate had earlier been predominantly Republican, appeared, by the end of the period, to be narrowly, though continuingly, Federalist. The Quaker City swung back and forth between the two parties with occasional variations of as much as 10 or 15 percentage points in successive elections.

During these early years of the nineteenth century—indeed, in some measure in the 1790s—organizations had emerged in several of these cities that served to provide leverage to enable a relatively small number of individuals to exert disproportionate influence on party affairs. In both New York and Philadelphia Tammany societies had existed well back into the eighteenth century and were Federalist in orientation in the late 1780s and early 1790s. By 1794, however, both bodies had been abandoned by their Federalist members and were thoroughly and actively Republican. The General Society of Mechanics and Tradesmen in New York had a similar history; founded in 1785 as an anti-Clinton (later Federalist) instrument, it nevertheless entered the nineteenth century as a Republican organization. With the Washington Benevolent Societies the Federalists were more successful. Founded in 1808 in New York and Philadelphia, these constituted a late and almost desperate effort to reinvigorate the failing party. They spread rapidly, though they were most numerous in New York and New England, and were to be found before the middle of the second decade of the nineteenth century in such additional cities as Boston, Providence, Albany, and Baltimore.[15]

In the two decades following the Treaty of Ghent changes in national party structures—the national collapse of the Federalist party, the development of Republican factions in the aftermath of the Panic of 1819, and the emergence of Jacksonianism—had, as might have been expected, significant impact on urban political alignments. To facilitate the examination of the urban responses to these changing conditions it might be noted that antirelief partisans (particularly in the western areas), the anti-Jacksonians, and the Whigs can be seen as sucessors to the Federalists in concepts, tendencies, and practices, though not necessarily in personnel or even, in a number of cases, leadership. That is to say, they tended to be probank, pro–protective tariff, progovernment, and, in a vague but observable way, conservative. If this is kept in mind elements of both continuity and change across these time periods will be more readily distinguishable.

The most immediate and striking shift on the political scene was the dramatic and obvious collapse of the Federalist party on the national level. This circumstance had differing effects in the local urban context. In some cases change was immediate, in others, delayed, and in several cities no real partisan shift occurred during these decades. Providence's allegiance to the Federalist party and its successors remained unshaken. In 1815 and 1816 the Federalists garnered well over three-quarters of the vote, although that party's margin in the state at large was more than 30 percentage points less. By 1830 the political balance seems to have undergone no significant change in Providence, as the National Republican gubernatorial candidate, Asa Messer, carried that city with 74.5% of the vote, although his Jacksonian opponent, James Fenner (a former Federalist) took the state by a margin of over 1,000 votes. The only unusual shift in the next five years came in 1833, when the National Republican vote for governor in Providence rose to 87.4% and the Jacksonians actually lost the state by a wide margin. In 1832 the National Republican proportion of the Providence vote was at the more common levels of 73.1% and 74.6% in the gubernatorial and presidential contests, and in the mayoral election (in which no party labels were displayed) National Republican Samuel W. Bridgham took 66.2% of the vote. In the next three years the Providence National Republican (Whig) vote was 71.8% (1833), 79.0% (1834), and 75.3%. Until 1834 the Jacksonian Democrats were able narrowly to carry the sixth ward in the city's extreme west end, but thereafter the Whigs prevailed in every ward, amassing from 76% to 87% of the votes in the first five wards. It seems certain that the brief appearance of the Anti-Masons in those years made no impact upon Providence's Whig (and proto-Whig) party; in that city these third party adherents appear almost entirely to have come from, and returned to, the Democratic party ranks.[16]

Republicans were no more successful in Boston than in Providence. For seven years beginning in 1816 the Federalists polled more than 60% of the Boston vote in successive annual gubernatorial elections—indeed, in only one contest (1816) did the victors poll less than 67%. But even before that date evidence of some political instability could be discerned. Upset by what they perceived as inept fiscal management of the town as the Panic of 1819 swept the country, Bostonians gave enough support to the Republican selectmen candidates in that year to bring the incumbent board members to the brink of defeat. The following year (1820) a union ticket of dissident Federalists and Republicans wholly displaced the former selectmen, and that same group was reelected in 1821. In 1822 a bipartisan political movement surfaced denominated the "middling interest" party, which combined the concerns that produced the union ticket in 1820 with resentment of the long-standing dominance and arrogance of the group of Federalist leaders known as the "Junto." The "middling interest" candidates for city council and aldermen swept into office with about 55% of the vote. It seems likely that it was this same coalition of Republicans and dissident Federalists that brought forward Josiah Quincy as a candidate, in opposition to the regular "caucus federal candidate," Harrison G. Otis, in Boston's first mayoral election in that same year. As a result of this political confusion Quincy picked up about 47% of the vote, Otis almost 10 percentage points less, and Thomas L. Winthrop, the regular Republican candidate, was left with between a third and a half of the usual Republican vote in the city. Quincy, Otis, and Winthrop all withdrew (no candidate having received a majority and, hence, no choice having been made under Massachusetts law) and John Phillips was elected unanimously in the second trial. When, in the next year, the Federalists (or at least some of them) set aside their differences and nominated Quincy as the "federal union" candidate for mayor, some of the discontent obviously remained, for Quincy polled only 52.6% of the vote and Republican George Blake attracted the suffrage of an unwonted 45.7% of Boston's voters. This destabilization of Boston politics—which was, at least in part, a reflection of party flux on the national scene—produced an effect in state races as well. William Eustis—a perennial Republican gubernatorial candidate—saw his share of the Boston vote increase from 32.3%, 29.7%, and 31.3% in 1820, 1821, and 1822 to 48.4% and 47.7% in 1823 and 1824. In 1825 a "union or amalgamation ticket" for Boston's legislative seats, comprised of equal numbers of Federalists and Republicans, was defeated by the straight Federalist ticket. But the next year, when one Republican, one union, and two Federalist tickets (with much overlap) were presented to the electorate, two trials produced majorities for fourteen Republicans, ten of whom had also been on the unionist or one of the Federalist tickets. In 1827, Levi Lincoln, a Federalist who supported the Adams administration, who had received 82% and 64% of the Boston vote in 1825 and

1826, was presented for reelection as the union or administration candidate. He was opposed by William C. Jarvis, the Boston-Charleston Free Bridge candidate, and Harrison G. Otis for the straight-out Federalists. At the same time legislative slates were presented in Boston under the designation of Union (or Administration), Federal Republican, Democratic, Free Bridge, and Brokers (with much overlapping). Lincoln took over 60% of the Boston vote but the Union legislative slate polled only 44.6% of the vote. Only eight of the thirty seats were filled in the first election and none were added in the second trial.[17]

This strange interlude in Boston's political history was apparently brought to an end by the mayoral election of 1828. Josiah Quincy, after initially failing to be elected as an intraparty opponent of the Federalist caucus candidate in the first mayoral election in 1822, was subsequently elected six successive times to that office and proved to be one of the most notable mayors of any American city in the antebellum era. But upon narrowly failing to obtain a majority in two trials for reelection against Federalist Thomas C. Amory in 1828, Quincy (and Amory as well) withdrew, and on the third trial Bostonians gave Federalist (later Jacksonian) Harrison Gray Otis two-thirds of the vote against Jacksonian Caleb Eddy.[18]

But this period of partisan instability still left the political balance in Boston largely unchanged. In 1828 the Adams presidential electors polled 78.8% of the vote, and they took more than three-quarters of the ballots in every ward except the second and third, where the figures were 65.5% and 63.6%. National Republicans and Whigs continued to dominate the city. In successive gubernatorial races, Levi Lincoln, the National Republican incumbent, took over 75% of the Boston vote in 1828, 1829, 1830, and in April 1831, and 70.7% and 61.2% in his last races in November 1831 and in 1832. Until 1831 Lincoln never lost a single ward, and even with the appearance of multiple candidates in that year and in 1832 he mustered a plurality in the second ward in the former year and the second and third wards in the latter, to complement his majorities in all the other wards. It was not until 1833 that a Democrat managed to win a major election. In that year Theodore Lyman, Jr., the nominee of the Democrats and Workingmen, defeated Whig candidate William Sullivan for the mayoralty with 59.3% of the vote. But Lyman had attracted much Whig support for this office and, indeed, was nominated by the Whigs for reelection in 1834. The other city officers, however, were Whig, and when Lyman ran for the congressional seat in 1833 he garnered less than a third of the vote in Boston. This may, in part, have reflected a local split in the Whig party on the issue of the state liquor-licensing law. But in the meantime Whig gubernatorial nominee John Davis took a plurality of the Boston votes in 1833 and an almost two-thirds majority in 1834 against Democrat Marcus Morton, Anti-Mason John Quincy Adams, and a Workingmen candidate. Adams would seem to have attracted some Whig support in 1833, but except for that interlude the Anti-Masonic and Workingmen's movements seem to have done little except attract more participants to the elections by their presence and redistribute the anti-Whig vote. In 1835 the

Whig candidates for mayor (Samuel T. Armstrong) and governor (Edward Everett) polled a little over two-thirds of the vote.[19]

The predominantly Federalist position of Pittsburgh was apparently only slightly modified in the 1815–1835 period, though, of course, party labels changed. The first Select Council, elected in 1816, consisted of four Federalists, two Republicans, and three members whose party alignments are now unclear. Two years later the "Independent Republican" candidate for Congress, Henry Baldwin, polled almost three-quarters of the vote against Regular Republican nominee Samuel Douglas. In the 1819 legislative races Pittsburgh gave majorities to three Federalists and one Republican, with the average Federalist vote being more than twice the average Republican poll; and the following year the "Heisterite" or Independent Republican candidates for city officers rolled up "respectable majorities" in their wards. This block continued to command majorities in Pittsburgh in 1822 and 1823—substantial (almost 70%) in the 1822 congressional elections, and narrow (barely over 50%) in the state legislative and charter elections.[20]

Here, as elsewhere, the appearance of Jackson on the national political scene perturbed existing political alignments. Jackson electors polled three-quarters of the 1824 Allegheny County vote (and probably about the same percentage in Pittsburgh), and by a narrow (eleven to nine) margin the Pittsburgh city council chose Jacksonian John M. Snowden as mayor in 1825. Snowden was reelected two years later and in 1828 Jackson electors took two-thirds of the city vote. The next year more than two-thirds of the Pittsburgh voters supported Democratic gubernatorial nominee George Wolf over his Anti-Masonic opponent, Joseph Ritner, and gave Democrat James S. Stevenson a 53.4% margin in the congressional race over Harmar Denny, the Anti-Masonic candidate. On the other hand, the administration forces carried the charter elections in 1828 and Snowden could muster only three of twenty votes in the council for reelection. Only Ross Williams, of the three Democratic candidates, was successful in the 1827 state legislative races.[21]

In Pittsburgh, as elsewhere, in the early 1830s two other political movements emerged—the Workingmen's party and the Anti-Masons. To some degree in Boston, New York, and other eastern cities—but to a greater extent in Pittsburgh—the Workingmen's party was an artificial organization designed to attract and control artisan and shopkeeper votes rather than a movement emerging from those elements of the city's population as they attempted to make their political weight felt. As one historian of the movement in Pittsburgh has said, "Clay and Jackson partisans were its midwives and in the ensuing struggle for the control of the 'child' the supporters of Jackson won out." Even this statement may exaggerate its significance. Lasting but a single year, the Workingmen did not, even in that short period, act in concert. In the congressional race of 1830 the "original" Workingmen nominated Robert T. Stewart, who was endorsed by some Democratic Republicans, but other Workingmen endorsed the regular Democratic Republican nominee, John Gilmore. The previous year had

Table 3.2
Pittsburgh Vote, 1830–1835

Total Vote (year)	"Conservative" Percentage
2,061 (1830)	50.8
1,722 (1832)	51.7
1,621 (1835)	54.9
1,619 (1832)	59.5
1,565 (1834)	63.4

seen the emergence of the other "third party" of the period—the Anti-Masons. In Pittsburgh, as in most other cities (except Boston), the Anti-Masons, in addition to being political dissidents, were primarily opponents of the Jacksonians and forerunners of the Whig party, some of whom, at least, were not yet prepared to embrace the National Republicans. Harmar Denny carried the Anti-Masonic banner in the 1830 congressional race and polled more of the Pittsburgh vote (30.9%) than either Stewart (27.1%), Gilmore (22.1%), or the Clay candidate, Walter Forward (19.9%). The Anti-Masons did even better in the charter elections of that year and their control of the councils resulted in the choice of Matthew B. Lowrie as mayor over Democrat Magnus M. Murray. Murray was victorious in the next year's mayoral contest but the Anti-Masonic candidates piled up majorities in Pittsburgh in the gubernatorial (51.7%) and congressional (59.5%) races in 1832 and the congressional race in 1834 (63.4%) with Whig endorsements. Three more races indicate the transitional nature of Pittsburgh's politics at the middle of the fourth decade of the nineteenth century. In the first general election for mayor in January 1834, incumbent Samuel Pettigrew, presented as a "Jackson and Clay" candidate, garnered almost 60% of the vote against an Anti-Mason and an independent Anti-Masonic candidate. A year later the moribund Workingmen party emerged (at least in name) to second the Democratic nomination of Pettigrew, who took about 52% of the vote against Anti-Mason Walter B. Lowrie. Finally, in the fall of 1835, the gubernatorial nominee of the Whig party, Joseph Ritner, polled almost 55% of the Pittsburgh vote against Independent Democratic (probank) candidate George Wolf (39%) and Regular Democrat Henry A. Muhlenberg, Jr. (6.3%). The Whigs took 60% of the vote in the north and west wards and 49% in the south and east wards. Thus, it would appear that in 1835 Pittsburgh was at the end of the formative period of the "second American party system," and a continuation of the anti-Republican/anti-Democratic tilt in that electorate was likely.[22]

In the period after 1830 there appeared in Pittsburgh evidence of a phenomenon that has been noted elsewhere—an inverse relationship between the size of the vote cast and the "conservative" (e.g., National Republican/Whig) percentage of the vote. The data in Table 3.2 illustrate this pattern.

Albany, like Pittsburgh, suffered some perturbation of its normal partisan alignment during the two decades of political transition between 1815 and 1835.

The earlier Federalist inclinations of the town were undisturbed in the immediate postwar years. That party controlled the city council in 1817 and 1819 by at least a three-to-two margin; but in 1820, for the first time, the Republicans secured a majority in the councils, carrying sixteen of nineteen contested seats in a remarkable political turnaround. The Albany voters also gave the Republicans a modest margin (53.3%) in the election of delegates to the state constitutional convention in 1821, but Federalist Stephen Van Rensselaer collected over three-fifths of the votes in Albany in the congressional by-election of the following year. For the next several years the anti-Jackson forces (e.g., People's party, Clintonians, Republicans, National Republicans) were victorious, carrying the legislative slate in 1823, the entire city council in 1824 and 1825, and an overwhelming majority in the council in 1826 and 1827, as well as polling almost two-thirds of the city's vote for governor in 1824.[23]

The charter election of 1828 marked a dramatic, if short-lived, shift of party power. In that and the following year the Jacksonians captured control of the city council, losing only the third ward in 1828 and carrying all five wards in 1829. In 1829 and 1830 both the Workingmen and the Anti-Masons appeared on the scene, both making common cause with the anti-Jacksonian National Republicans, with varying success. Albanians gave more than 54% of their votes to Democratic gubernatorial candidate Enos T. Throop over Anti-Mason Francis Granger, but the Workingmen (who at least nominally headed an anti-Jackson coalition) took fourteen of the twenty council seats in the charter election, losing the second ward and splitting the fourth. Even a cursory glance makes clear the fluid nature of Albany's partisan politics in 1830. The fifth ward returned the largest Democratic majority (60.3%) in the gubernatorial race and the largest anti-Jacksonian majority (61.3%) in the council contest. Ward one voters cast 54.4% of their ballots for Throop but 55.6% for Ralph Pratt, the anti-Jackson aldermanic candidate.[24]

This was probably the peak of Democratic ("Regency") power. In 1831 the party managed to retain control of the council with a slightly diminished majority (thirteen of twenty seats)—again losing the fifth ward and now electing only one of four candidates in the third ward—and split the council in 1833. But in between (1832) the anti-Jacksonians filled sixteen of the twenty council seats and narrowly (50.8%) carried the city in the congressional race of the same year. In 1834 the Whigs garnered 52.2% of the Albany vote, carried the first three wards in the gubernatorial contest, and took all five wards and 56.5% of the vote in the spring elections of town officers (supervisors and assessors). The following year the Whigs elected their Assembly ticket with 51.8% of the vote and had about the same margin (51.5%) in the charter elections, though the council seats were split evenly.[25] Albany thus ended the transitional period with its adherence to the Federalist/National Republican/Whig alignment largely unchanged but with the level of that dominance somewhat diminished. The first and third wards were reliably Whig, the fourth normally Democratic, and the second and fifth shifting, though they rarely went Democratic at the same time.

Indeed, all the cities that had pronounced Federalist alignments in the late years of the "first American party system" emerged from the transitional decades still committed to a similar (or successor) political orientation.

The nation's two largest cities—New York and Philadelphia—had had a rather mixed political experience in the early years of the nineteenth century. In the last half dozen years ending in 1815 the Federalists seemed to have established a continuing, if narrow, control of New York City. But with the end of the War of 1812 that party went into sudden eclipse. In 1816 the Republicans carried the gubernatorial race and elected twelve of twenty aldermen. In the years that followed Republicans (usually the Bucktail faction) again took twelve council seats in 1817, thirteen in 1818, fifteen in 1819, seventeen in 1820, sixteen in 1821, seventeen in 1822, and sixteen (of twenty-four) in 1825. In this period (1816–1825) the opposition—the People's (Clintonian) party—managed to take a bare majority of the aldermanic seats only in 1823 and 1824. DeWitt Clinton also carried the Empire City in the 1824 and 1826 gubernatorial races, but with very rare exceptions the "Bucktail" or "Regency" faction was in control. At the beginning of this period the Federalists could usually be counted on to carry the extreme southern wards one, two, and three and occasionally prevailed in wards four and nine as well; by the end of the first quarter of the century no opposition candidate except DeWitt Clinton himself could be expected to show any significant strength outside of the first two wards and the newly reshaped fifth ward on the upper west side.[26]

In 1826 DeWitt Clinton sought election as governor—his last political effort (he died before the end of his term)—and carried New York City with a comfortable 56.5% of the vote. The disappearance of Clinton and the coalescence of political leaders in anticipation of the Jacksonian presidential candidacy in 1828 clarified divisions and, in some measure, simplified (insofar as it was possible for anything in New York politics to be simplified in this era) political alignments in the Empire City on state and national issues. But city politics and charter elections became even more confusing for several years. David T. Valentine, whose careful collection of electoral data less than thirty years later has been of immense value to historians of New York City, despaired of assigning accurate partisan labels to council candidates during these years (in particular, 1826, 1828, 1829, and 1831). He employed such comments as "Although several candidates were run in some of the wards, it is difficult to define the precise basis upon which the division existed"; and "We have not been able to procure precise returns"; and "The division of parties was of too complicated a character to assign them an exact position."[27]

By 1828 something more closely approximating a bipartisan sorting of the political elements in New York City was beginning to be visible through a haze of sometimes conflicting, often overlapping, and always confusing nominations and endorsements. In that year, although the clarity of alignments was potentially obscured by bipartisan antiauction endorsements in congressional races, the outlines were fairly clear. In the governor's race Martin Van Buren (Jackson) easily won the city with over 60% of the vote over Adams candidate Smith Thompson, who was able to carry only the first three wards (the old Federalist strongholds). The vote for the Jackson presidential electors was substantially identical in scope and distribution to that of Van Buren. In the congressional races the Jackson candidates were so strong that even those without the antiauction endorsement easily defeated (by about 3,000 votes) the Adams nominees who had endorsements. It would appear that the antiauction endorsement was worth a little more than 4,000 votes to Adams men and a little less than 4,000 votes to Jacksonians. The one Jacksonian who received an endorsement carried all fourteen wards; the two unendorsed Jacksonians lost wards one, two, and three.[28]

The 1829 legislative races constituted superlative examples of the confused politics of the 1820s. To fill the eleven Assembly seats New Yorkers elected eight members of the regular Tammany slate (which eight were also on the seceding Tammany slate), two candidates from the seceding Tammany slate (one of whom was also slated on the Mason's Hall National Republican ticket), and one Workingmen's nominee. To the state Senate were sent one Democrat and one National Republican endorsed by the Workingmen. The Workingmen's nominations attracted rather more that 6,100 voters in the Assembly races (compared to more than 10,000 for the ''straight'' Tammany ticket), and something over 4,200 (compared to a little less than 8,900) in the Senate races.[29]

By 1830, despite the continuing presence of Anti-Masonic and Workingmen's nominations (until ca. 1832) as well as National Republicans (until 1832) and Whig opposition, the Democrats were clearly firmly in control. Beween that date and 1835 the opposition managed only a single victory, when they took seventeen of thirty council seats (and 50.3% of the vote) in 1834. The city's Democrats, on the other hand, carried the 1830 gubernatorial race (51.8% against two opponents), the 1831 state Senate race (61.9%), the presidential (59.2%) and gubernatorial (58.6%) races in 1832, and the gubernatorial race (53.2%) in 1834. In charter elections the Democrats took twenty-four of thirty council seats in 1832, nineteen in 1833, and twenty-two in 1835. Finally, between 1815 and 1835 none but Republicans (though a couple of Clintonian Republicans slipped in in the early 1820s) filled the congressional seats from New York City.[30] New York, then, emerged from these two transitional decades more firmly attached than ever before to the Republican/Democratic cause.

In the years just before 1816 the partisan pattern in Philadelphia was somewhat similar to that in New York. But where the Federalists had carried almost everything before them in the latter city, in Philadelphia, though the Federalists had dominated, the Republicans had been successful in the early years of the War of 1812. In the first years of the transitional period (1816–1835) the differences between the two metropolises became much more pronounced. Where New York became solidly Republican, Philadelphians continued to lean, more heavily than before, toward the Federalists, who maintained a vigorous presence under their old name (though often cooperating with dissident Republicans) in the Quaker City until the end of the first quarter of the century. These transitional decades, in fact, divide themselves into three fairly distinct periods in Philadelphia—a time of increasing Federalist dominance (1816–1825), an interval of shifting and uncertain party loyalties (1826–1831), and the rapid emergence of solid Whig control of the city (1833–1835).

In 1816 the Federalists won control of the city council (despite the formation of a temporary coalition by the Old School and the New School Republicans), which they continued to control until 1825, except for the Republican success (by about a 300-vote margin) in 1819.[31] In addition, Federalist John Sergeant won reelection to Congress with almost 58% of the vote and the anti-Madison (in effect, Clinton) presidential electors took almost 60% of the vote in the city. Sergeant was subsequently returned in 1818 and 1820. In 1817 Joseph Heister, the Old Style Republican gubernatorial nominee endorsed by the Federalists, took almost 72% of the city vote, a feat he repeated in 1820. Andrew Gregg, with similar political backing, took 62% of the Philadelphia vote in the gubernatorial election of 1823. Only in presidential races did the Republicans/Democrats succeed, and even here Philadelphians gave 39% of their votes to a hopeless Clinton electoral ticket in 1820 and supported Jackson in 1824 only by a bare majority (50.6%). Normally, throughout this period the Federalist (or the equivalent) vote in the city fluctuated 3 or 4 percentage points on either side of 60%, and Republicans usually carried (at most) only the far northern North and South Mulberry wards and the extreme southern Cedar ward. By 1824 and 1825, however, it was clear that Federalist strength was fading. In addition to narrowly losing the 1824 presidential contest, the Federalist candidate, William Lehman, led the ticket in the Assembly race with less than 54% of the vote. In 1825 the Federalist vote for state senator shrank to 50.8% and the Common Council split thirteen to seven for the Federalists.[32]

Although the Jacksonian influence (except when Jackson was a candidate) came a little later and the hardening of political lines after the inception of the "bank war" came a little quicker, Philadelphia's electorate between 1826 and 1832 reflected the instability that marked the national political scene. In 1826 Henry Horn (Jacksonian) and John Sergeant (administration) each polled 1,597 votes for U.S. representative, with 1,393 votes going to Thomas Kittera, the Federalist candidate. In the same year Federalist Stephen Duncan won the state Senate race with 51.6% of the vote, but the Republican candidate carried an almost unprecedented six of the fifteen wards—the northern South and North Mulberry wards, the southern Cedar and New Market wards, and the central Middle and North wards. In addition, the Republicans lost Locust ward by one vote and South ward by nine votes. Thus, in addition to taking one ward (New Market) in the eastern range, the Republicans carried or nearly carried every ward in the western range.[33] The next year John Sergeant (Adams) defeated Jacksonian Joseph Hemphill for the major city congressional seat (consisting of twelve of the city's fifteen wards) with 51.5% of the vote. Even this small margin overstates the administration strength in Philadelphia; two of the three wards not included in the congressional district (New Market and Cedar) were solidly Jacksonian. Moreover, the leading Federal candidate in the state Assembly contest managed only a plurality (47.2%) in a three-way race against Jacksonian and administration men that resulted in the election of four Federalists and two Jacksonians. In 1828 the city went "hell bent" for the Jacksonians, who took the presidential contest, the Assembly seats, the Common Council, the Select Council, and the Philadelphia vote for two congressional seats, all by margins of between 55.4% and 58.2%. The Adamsites could only carry five wards—Lower Delaware, High Street, and Walnut on the Delaware and North and South on the Schuylkill. The Workingmen's movement made its appearance in this year, endorsing eighteen Jacksonians and eight administration nominees in the Assembly and council slates and making four independent nominations. The three independent nominees for the Assembly and the Common Council averaged 241 votes while the Select Council nominee polled 539 votes.[34]

The various elections of 1829 show that year to have been a most faithful reflection of the political turbulence of the times. Philadelphians elected one Democratic and six Federal Republican assemblymen, three Democratic and two Federal Republican select councilmen, and sixteen Federal Republican and four Democratic common councilmen. Democratic gubernatorial candidate George Wolf carried Philadelphia with almost no opposition (93.1%). The Workingmen ran separate (though abbreviated) tickets in all local races and polled (with a single exception) between 828 and 889 votes. Some very strange voting patterns, which doubtless resulted from endorsements of several of the candidates by the Workingmen, make it difficult to speak with precision about party divisions of the vote, but the basic electorate appears to have been split 44.3% Federal Republican, 42.8% Democratic, and 12.9% Workingmen in the Assembly race and 43.4% Federal Republican, 43.7% Democratic, and 12.9% Workingmen in the Select Council contest.[35]

In 1830 and 1831 the Democrats appeared to have achieved solid control in the Quaker City. In the 1830 Common Council races they took a majority (50.6%) of the vote in a three-way contest and ran almost 12 percentage points ahead of the anti-Jacksonians. In the two-party congressional race of that year the Democratic candidates garnered 57.3% of the Philadelphia vote. In the following year the Democrats took almost 63% of the vote in the state Senate contest and captured all of the city's state Assembly seats, Select Council vacancies, and Common Council seats, with margins of 55.6% and 56.2% in the three-party Assembly and Common Council races and 59.6% in the two-party Select Council contest, discounting Workingmen's endorsements in both races. Here, as elsewhere, the Workingmen aided the anti-Jacksonians more than the Jacksonians. They endorsed ten Federal Republicans in the 1830 races and ten more (together with three Democrats) in 1831. During these years the independent Workingmen's vote shrank from more than 800 in 1830 to less than 400 in 1831. By 1831 the Democrats controlled twelve of Philadelphia's fifteen wards (taking more than two-thirds of the vote in six) leaving only three eastern wards—Lower Delaware, Walnut, and Chestnut—in the hands of the Federal Republicans.[36]

In no other city was the shift from Democratic control to anti-Jackson dominance quite so abrupt and decided as in Philadelphia. There was no transition like that which had preceded the Democratic sweep of the early 1830s. One can only surmise that the debate on the tariff issue in 1831 and 1832 and the veto of the Bank recharter bill in 1832 touched Philadelphians at very sensitive points.

In 1832 the anti-Jackson forces won all the electoral contests in Philadelphia: state, local, and national. They took 62.6% of the vote in the presidential race and 61.2% in the congressional contest. National Republican Joseph Ritner polled 58.2% of the vote in the gubernatorial election, and the anti-Jackson candidates swept the state Assembly (61.0%), Select Council (59.4%), and Common Council (59.5%) races. Able to win only three wards in 1831, the National Republicans now carried thirteen of fifteen wards, leaving only the North Mulberry and Cedar wards to the Jacksonians. The Democrats made a partial comeback the next year, reducing the National Republican margins to 51.5% in the Assembly races and in the Select and Commmon Council elections to about 51%. The Jacksonians upped their ward control to seven—North and South Mulberry and Upper Delaware to the north, New Market, Locust, and Cedar to the south, and Middle in the center of the western range of wards. The Whigs (as the anti-Jacksonians were now most commonly called) came storming back to take 60% of the city vote in the Assembly, Common Council, and Select Council contests and reducing the Jackson-controlled wards to three—North Mulberry, Upper Delaware, and New Market—at the extreme northern and southern ends of the city. In 1835 Joseph Ritner, the Anti-Mason/Whig nominee, took 61.4% of the city vote in the gubernatorial election and carried all fifteen wards. The Whig victories in the state senatorial, Assembly, Common Council, and Select Council races were slightly larger than in the governor's contest.[37] There could be no doubt that they had taken firm control of politics in the Quaker City.

The early Federalist dominance in Charleston, it will be remembered, had given way to Republican control about the middle of the first decade of the century, which control was hardly challenged in the following years. After 1815 (and, indeed, frequently before) in many races Republicans were pitted against each other, party labels were absent, alignments of candidates were identifiable only by reference to earlier or later loyalties (an alternative particularly unsatisfactory in periods of party flux), and contemporaries noted that candidates' support disregarded party lines. In 1816, for example, Republican Henry Middleton carried Charleston in the congressional race over Federalist William Crafts, Jr. But the editor of the *Charleston Courier* observed that Crafts had received "very handsome and honorable support" from Republicans but had been defeated by the desertion of the Federalists. In 1818 the Federalist *Courier* pushed a slate of state representative candidates under the heading "Independent

Republican Ticket," a label the Federalists also used elsewhere. Of the sixteen persons nominated, six were identifiably Republicans and five were Federalists. Nine of the "Independent Republican" nominees were elected, including five Republicans and one Federalist. The vote distribution suggests that eight of the "Independent" victors (including the five Republicans) were on another slate as well. In the same year two Republicans contended for the state Senate seat and in 1820 a similar circumstance prevailed in the congressional race; the votes were relatively close in both elections. In the latter year two Republicans and a Federalist contested the state Senate race, and Republican Philip Moser took 46.8% of the vote to Federalist Thomas Lowndes' 41.4%, leaving 11.8% for Republican George W. Cross. At the "downtown" poll at the Court House (Broad and Meeting streets) Lowndes took a majority (54.4%); the "midtown" poll at the Market House returned a majority (64.8%) for Moser, who also garnered a plurality (47.5%) at the "uptown" poll at the Tobacco Inspection House. In state Senate races in January 1821 and October 1822 Federalist William Crafts, Jr., managed to carry a plurality (38.5%) of the city's votes, and pluralities in all three polls, against three Republican opponents (in a *very* light poll) and then a bare majority (50.6%) in a head-to-head battle with Republican John Geddes (although Geddes carried both the "midtown" and the "uptown" polls). But these were aberrations; Republicans were generally victorious. Indeed, so dominant were the Republicans that clear-cut political divisions became obscure in local council and state Assembly races as Federalists resorted to creating bipartisan slates in the hope of sneaking a few of their own into office, and Republicans, feeling no real pressure from the opposition, abandoned party organizational control over nominations and engaged in a free-for-all process of nomination and slate making. In 1822, for instance, there were at least ten ostensibly nonpartisan slates for the sixteen Assembly seats, on which appeared the names of forty-two persons. Obviously, there was a great deal of overlap among the lists. No person's name appeared on all ten slates but one appeared on nine and seven people were named on only one; thirteen appeared on five or more slates and six slates contained no name that did not appear on at least one other list. In the election votes were cast for thirty-eight of these citizens (four having apparently withdrawn) and for five others whose names had appeared on a composite list of all persons nominated, which was published just before the election. One of the latter—incumbent H. F. Dunkin—was elected (finishing eighth), and the single person named on nine slates—*Courier* editor A. S. Willington—failed of election, finishing twenty-fifth. Between these extremes, voters elected one (of two) appearing on eight lists, four (of five) on seven, three (of three) on six, one (of two) on five, four (of five) on four, and two (of eight) on three.[38]

It was from this apparent chaos that there emerged a brief period of real two-party conflict. In Charleston, as elsewhere, the arrival of Andrew Jackson (a native son of the state—at least so said South Carolinians) on the national political scene served as a precipitant for a coterie of supporters that eventually developed into the Democratic party; the opposition remained, for several years, more fluid, but clearly antipathetic to the Jacksonians. Republican Joel R. Poinsett was returned to Congress in February 1823 and October 1824, carrying all three polls and 60% and 65%, respectively, of the vote. In the charter and Assembly elections of this date multiple slates, not identified by party but frequently with occupations listed, still appeared. But among the successful candidates in the Assembly contest, those who were identified (or would shortly be identified) with the Jackson camp greatly outnumbered the Adams supporters. By 1826 Charleston voters were presented with moderately identifiable party candidates, despite the existence of multiple Jackson slates and some overlap, for the Assembly seats, and returned a clear majority (ten of sixteen) of unquestioned Jacksonians and four others (two of them almost certainly administration men) whose names appeared on tickets of both factions. Thomas S. Grimke, the administration candidate for the state Senate, however, managed to secure that seat with a plurality of sixteen votes over the higher vote of the two Jacksonian contenders. Grimke had a majority in the Court House and Market House polls, while the leading Jacksonian candidate, Richard Cunningham, had a majority in the smaller Tobacco Inspection House poll.[39]

Charlestonians ended the decade with Jacksonian victories in 1828 and 1829. In the former year there were multiple Assembly tickets bearing both the Jackson and Union labels, with some names appearing on opposing slates. But the names of all of the ten victors apeared on Jackson tickets, though five had also been presented on Union lists. The next year Jacksonian H. L. Pinckney took 55% of the vote to defeat Unionist Thomas S. Grimke for the intendancy. Among the twelve wardens only three were not listed on a Jacksonian ticket. A month later Charlestonians elected sixteen state assemblymen, all of whom had been associated with Jackson forces.[40]

With the beginning of the fourth decade of the nineteenth century the emerging nullification crisis overshadowed all other political considerations in South Carolina. In the years that followed, Charleston elections were contested by the Nullification and Union parties. In 1830 the balance of forces was very narrow. Nullificationist Richard Cunningham won the state Senate seat over Unionist James L. Petigru by twenty-five votes in a total of over 2,500 cast. In the concurrent Assembly elections Charlestonians selected eight candidates from the Unionist slate, five from the Democratic ticket, and three whose names appeared on both lists. Petigru carried the Court House and Guard House (uptown) polls, but Cunningham took the Market House poll with 59% of the vote. A month earlier the Unionist candidate for intendant, James R. Pringle, carried three of the four wards (all except the southwestern Ward two)—and took 56% of the total vote to defeat Nullificationist Henry L. Pinckney. But this was the high tide of Charleston Unionism.[41] In 1831, 1832, 1833, 1834, and 1835 the Nullification candidates won election after election to local, state, and federal offices. In 1831 Henry L. Pinckney won the office of intendant over Unionist incumbent James R. Pringle with 52.7% of the vote and carried every ward except the first (southeast)—an almost exact reversal of the outcome in 1830. The following year Pinckney's share of the vote increased to 53.9% and he carried all four wards, though he had margins of only five votes each in wards one and four (northwest). In 1833, 1834, and 1835 there was no Unionist opposition to E. H. North for this office. Indeed, in the latter year there were no Unionist candidates for any of the city offices, and the Nullifiers had carried all the council seats since 1831 in any event. The same conditions prevailed in the legislative races. Although the margin in 1831 was slight—M. I. Keith, the Nullification candidate, took the state Senate seat by only eight votes over John Robinson—the Nullifiers' share of the vote grew to 52.4% in the Assembly and 52.8% in the Senate races in 1832 and reached almost 55% in 1834. Aside from narrowly losing ward four (northwest) in the 1832 legislative race, the Nullifiers controlled all sections of the city. As a practical matter the direct political confrontation between Nullifiers and Unionists was at an end in Charleston after 1835, though the alignments of individual political leaders produced by this controversy persisted for a much longer period of time.[42]

In several of these cities the electoral data for the early years of the century are so scant as to prohibit us from reaching any conclusions about political alignments. But during these transitional decades (1815–1835)—often *late* in the period—patterns began to emerge. Brooklyn, Buffalo, and Washington are cases in point. Slight data suggest that Brooklyn voters tended to vote Republican/Democratic through 1830, with the Jacksonian gubernatorial candidate, Enos T. Throop, in that year polling almost 72% of the Brooklyn vote over Anti-Mason Francis Granger. But in 1834 the vote for the Democratic nominee for governor, William L. Marcy, was down to 57.4%, and the city council consisted of seven Democrats, six Whigs, one Native American (doubtless of Whig proclivities), and five members supported as bipartisans. The next year John Dikeman, the Native American candidate, won the state Assembly seat by seventy-eight votes, though the Democrats did marginally better in the council elections, taking three of the four bipartisan seats in the previous council.[43]

Unlike many frontier areas, western New York had a substantial Federalist presence early in the nineteenth century. The Republicans carried Genesee County, in which the village of Buffalo was then located, in 1802 but the Federalists were successful in 1804. At least the "leading early settlers in Buffalo" are supposed to have been Federalist. The region would appear to have been favorably disposed to the 1812 declaration of war, however, though the Erie Canal project doubtless created some Clintonian strength in the area later. In the late 1820s Anti-Masonry was very strong in Erie County, which had by then been carved out of Genesee County. In 1830 Democrat Enos Throop took 52% of the Buffalo vote in the gubernatorial contest against the Anti-Masonic candidate Francis Granger, but four years later Whig William H. Seward took almost 60% of the vote in Buffalo over the ultimately successful Democratic candidate, William L. Marcy. It was hardly surprising that, with this background,

Buffalo entered the era of the "second American party system" with a strong two-party orientation.[44]

By the middle of the second decade of the century Washington's Republicanism was apparently of the most elitist variety. Benjamin G. Orr and Samuel N. Smallwood, who were elected (by the council) mayor in 1817 and 1819, clearly drew on the same support; and those supporters obviously were *not* enthusiastic when Thomas Carberry, the spokesman of the "Poor Man's Party," won the first contested popular mayoral election in the nation's capital (in the only previous one the incumbent, Smallwood, was essentially unopposed) with a plurality (43.1%) of the vote over three opponents. Carberry's victory was the product of both the split in his opposition and the voting of a number of residents who had been excluded from suffrage by the practice of not entering personal property holdings of less than $100 on the tax books, thus effectively preventing such property owners from satisfying the taxpayer suffrage requirement. Once in office, Carberry ordered that owners of small amounts of personal property be added to the tax lists, only to be confronted by a council ordinance prohibiting city officers from placing on the tax rolls the names of any residents who were not real estate owners and owned less than $100 worth of personal property. Carberry refused to sign the ordinance, but he was defeated in 1824 by Samuel Smallwood, who signed the "$100 Bill." This situation remained unchanged until 1848. Incidently, in his 1822 victory Carberry had garnered majorities in the first and second wards (between Tenth Street, northwest, and Rock Creek) and the sixth ward (in the extreme eastern section of the city), as well as a plurality in the fourth (Capitol Hill) ward.[45]

This series of events apparently played a major role in shaping partisan divisions in Washington. In the years that followed, although multiple overlapping slates were the rule in the council elections, the mayoral contests were much more clear-cut. And in those mayoral races through 1835 the anti-Jackson and Whig candidates were, with two exceptions, successful, occasionally with little or no opposition. In 1826 Roger Weightman (who had been elected mayor by the council when Smallwood died in 1825) defeated Carberry by a three-to-two margin, carrying every ward except the first (far northwest). Joseph Gales, Jr., the anti-Jackson editor of the *Intelligencer*, was subsequently named mayor by the council upon Weightman's resignation. In 1830 the local Jacksonian leader, John P. Van Ness, polled 37.5% of the vote over Jacksonian George Sweeny (31.8%) and anti-Jacksonian Willam A. Bradley (30.7%), with the combined Jackson vote constituting a majority in wards one, two, three, and six. Van Ness was reelected in 1834, barely defeating Thomas Munroe with 50.7% of the vote and majorities in only the first and third wards. The political transitional period ended with an all-Whig election in 1834 after Democrat Thomas Carberry withdrew late in the campaign, and Whig editor Peter Force lost to William A. Bradley, who was "said to be a Whig." Bradley polled 55.3% of the vote in a contest in which both Whig candidates apparently actively sought Democratic votes after Carberry's withdrawal.[46]

In these three cities, then, by 1835 the "second Americn party system" was very much alive. The partisan loyalties of the Brooklyn and Buffalo electorate seemed rather unclear, while in Washington the future looked more promising for the Whigs than for the Democrats.

In the period of the "first American party system," Baltimore, Cincinnati, Louisville, and St. Louis appeared to be Republican strongholds, though the data are admittedly sparse in the latter three cases. In Baltimore, of course, there had been a vigorous (if unsuccessful) Federalist party in the pre–1815 years. In the political transition decades (1815–1835) this opposition sometimes seemed almost to disappear. Certainly the Republican/Democratic dominance was unchallenged before the mid-1820s. Between 1808 and 1826 only three persons— Edward Johnson, George Stiles, and John Montgomery—occupied the mayoral chair. All Republicans, they won election after election, often defeating one another in the process. In 1822, for instance, the Johnson electoral ticket defeated that for Montgomery by 3,518 to 3,150, but two years earlier the positions had been reversed when Montgomery's electors, with 53.2% of the vote, had defeated Johnson's slate. The Federalists did run candidates in some races; a single Federalist candidate was entered in the contest for state Senate seats in 1818, collecting but 31% of the vote. The Federalists complained that the Republicans voted the soldiers from Fort McHenry and relied on foreigners still loyal to the countries of their nativity. But the Federalists' vehement opposition to increasing the Baltimore representation in the state Assembly was hardly likely to attract strong support in that city. The Federalists did manage to win a bare majority (50.4%) for one congressional seat in the city portion of the district in 1824 (carrying five of the twelve wards), On the other hand, the Jackson presidential electors took 56.5% of the Baltimore vote in that year; but since here, as elsewhere, some Federalists supported Jackson as an antiadministration candidate, that vote hardly clarifies the murky political scene that had developed by the mid-1820s. The elections of 1826, indeed, would seem to suggest that the Jacksonians might be in trouble in the Maryland metropolis. In the congressional race they put forward John P. Kennedy as a "straight-out" Jackson supporter in opposition to incumbent John Barney, a Federalist elected with Republican suport, and Republican Peter Little, both of whom were seen as at best uncommitted in the Jackson-administration conflict; but Kennedy finished a poor third in the three-man race. The mayoral contest of that year was, as usual, between two Republicans—incumbent and perennial officeholder John Montgomery and Jacob Small, a builder and architect (hence, not of the legal-mercantile urban elite) who had polled almost 1,000 votes in the 1824 mayoral race running on the "Mechanics" ticket. Small's victory, with almost two-thirds of the vote and majorities in eleven wards, might be thought to be a favorable omen for the Jacksonians. But, contrary to received wisdom, urban artisans and mechanics tended, in most cities, *not* to support Jackson, and Small, indeed, ended up in the Whig camp.[47]

Actually, the Jacksonians stood on the brink of almost complete dominance of Baltimore's political scene. Jacob Small, to be sure, was an exception. Identifying himself with the Native Americans and, later, the Whigs, he nevertheless won reelection as mayor in 1828 and 1830 with 59% and 56% of the vote, before falling to Jacksonian Jesse Hunt, who took 60% of the vote in 1832 and 55% in 1834 against Small. Additionally, the Whigs carried the 1834 Assembly races in Baltimore with 51.7% of the vote, and the Workingmen took those races in 1833 with 59.1% of the vote and majorities in eleven of the twelve wards. But aside from these aberrations, Baltimore's political performance was unreservedly Democratic. For example, Jackson electors took 52.6% of the city vote and carried nine of twelve wards in 1828; Democratic candidates took the city's Assembly seats in 1829 (58.1%), 1830 (52.1%), and 1832 (52.6%), carrying eight to ten wards; and the Baltimore vote in the congressional elections went to Democratic candidates in 1829 (56.2%) and 1833. In the latter contest the regularly nominated Democratic candidate Isaac McKim won in one district and an Independent Democrat (pro-Jackson, anti–Van Buren), James P. Heath, in the other. Finally, in 1835 Democrat Samuel Smith took the mayoral election in an overwhelmingly one-sided vote (76.3%) over Moses Davis, in a very light poll.[48]

Cincinnati's undifferentiated Republicanism began to sort itself into contending factions in the 1820s. In 1822 Jacksonian (later) James W. Gazlay won the Cincinnati district congressional seat, taking 65% of the city vote. While most candidates were still at least nominally nonpartisan, that guise was impossible to maintain in the presidential race of 1824, which the Jackson electors won in Cincinnati with a clear majority (51.6%) of the vote in a three-way race with Adams and Clay supporters. Gazlay carried Cincinnati in the congressional race again in 1824, but by a reduced margin (51.5%), and Jacksonian Andrew Mack, in 1827, took the city's state Senate seat with 56.1% of the vote. But the sorting process also produced an anti-Jackson faction that would eventually—indeed, shortly—prove to be the dominant element in Cincinnati politics. Throughout this transitional (1815–1835) period only National Republicans and Whigs occupied the mayoral office in Cincinnati. In 1828 the Cincinnati electorate gave 52% of its votes to Jackson, but four years later Jackson's vote dropped to just over 40% as Clay carried all five wards. Meanwhile, the Adams party took the township trustees' election in 1828 with 56.5% of the vote; the National Republican gubernatorial nominee, Dorius Lyman, carried 57.9% of the city's vote in 1832; and the Jacksonian mayoral candidate, Andrew Mack, garnered only 37.7% of the ballots in 1829. But Jacksonian Samuel R. Miller took 57.8% of the vote in Cincinnati for state senator in the latter year.[49]

The year 1832 marked the beginning of an era of almost unbroken National Republican/Whig dominance. The Democrats won the sheriff's race in 1832 (75.2%) and the state legislative contest in 1833 (56.9%), but everywhere else the anti-Jacksonians ruled. In addition to the presidential election of 1832, they also took the gubernatorial, congressional, legislative, and various charter races with from 57.9% to 61.4% of the vote. The next year the Whigs carried a variety of charter contests, many without Democratic opposition. The years 1834 and 1835 saw Whig victories in Cincinnati in the elections for governor (64.9%), congressman (65.6%), state senator (65.3% and 56.2%), and state legislator (64.8% and 53.4%); while the 1835 mayoral election attracted (as usual) multiple Whig candidates, with the Democratic contender, John C. Avery, taking only 35.6% of the vote. By the middle of the 1830s the Democrats had regained enough strength to carry the third and fourth wards, but with a substantial majority (59.4%) only in the third. The first, second, and fifth wards returned Whig majorities of over 60%.[50]

Cincinnati's downstream neighbor, Louisville, experienced a similar political realignment. There, too, the first two decades of the nineteenth century had seen no significant—often no visible—opposition to the Jeffersonian Republicans. Indeed, Federalists were much more scarce in the Falls City than in Cincinnati. The emergence of a two-party—or, at least, two-faction—system began earlier in Louisville because of the controversies associated with the passage of the relief, stay, and replevin laws after the Panic of 1819 and, later, with the Old Court–New Court battle.[51] In the gubernatorial election of 1820 John Adair, the primary Relief candidate, carried Jefferson County with a clear majority of the vote in a four-way race in which two of the other candidates were also pro-Relief. Perhaps an even more revealing figure was the 76.5% of the county vote polled by Relief lieutenant gubernatorial candidate William T. Barry in a two-man race. But two considerations need to be kept in mind. First, a number of pro-Relief partisans of 1819 went over to the opposition when the Relief party's efforts to oust the justices of the Court of Appeals raised troubling legal and constitutional questions and, some believed, threatened property rights. Second, while Relief and New Court partisans probably *tended* to support Jackson, there was no clear continuity between the earlier state-issue based parties and the national parties that formed the "second American party system." The subsequent elections illustrate these points. In 1821 three of the four candidates for state legislative seats from Jefferson County who polled the larger numbers of votes in both Louisivlle and in the county as a whole would be anti-Jacksonians. In August of 1824 the Old Court gubernatorial candidate, Christopher Tompkins, carried just over 50% of the Louisville vote, and in the November presidential election Jackson carried the city over Henry Clay with almost two-thirds of the vote.[52]

Political alignments and strength in Louisville remained uncertain and volatile in 1825 and 1826. In the first of these years three Old Court partisans swept the state legislative races in the city by almost a two-to-one majority. These candidates were endorsed by the *Louisville Public Advertiser*, which had by now become a major Jackson organ in the state and had earlier championed the anti-Relief, Old Court cause. The next year Thomas Joyes led a New Court sweep of the legislative seats. By 1828 the new party lines were drawn and the Jacksonians swept all before them in Louisville, taking 59.2% of the city vote for their gubernatorial candidate, William T. Barry, and 60.5% in the legislative race; while the Jackson presidential electors took 57.2% of the Louisville ballots.[53]

By 1828, however, the bloom was already beginning to fade on the Democratic victories. The National Republican nominee took a majority of the congressional vote in Louisville as well as two of the three legislative seats— Democrat James Guthrie was the exception, as he would be repeatedly in the years ahead. The Democrats rebounded in 1830, when Guthrie led a sweep of the Assembly seats in the Louisville polls. The charter elections, incidentally, were apparently still wholly divorced from the new national political structure, with four candidates announced for mayor, six for marshal, and three to five for councilmen in the various wards. But by 1831 the Jacksonians had been pushed aside and the National Republicans garnered majorities in Louisville in the congressional (63.8%), state Senate (55.1%), and legislative (59.6%) races. Even James Guthrie lost his bid for reelection to the state Senate, and except for that these elections pretty much set the pattern for the last years of the transition decades. In 1834 the Whigs took the legislative seats, with almost two-thirds of the votes, carrying all five wards; and in 1835 they won by a much narrower margin (51.1%), carrying the second, third, and fourth wards. Democrat James Guthrie did manage to recapture the Senate seat, but except for this aberrant victory, Louisville was a solidly Whig city.[54]

Like Cincinnati and Louisville, St. Louis would appear to have been thoroughly Republican during the era of the "first American party system"; like them also, there is very little information available on these early years. Factions emerged within St. Louis Republican ranks (probably on the basis of local issues and conflicting ambitions) in the second decade of the century. A group, united primarily in their support for the interests of large landholders, called the "Junta" generally dominated the elections in St. Louis County until well into the 1820s, though the membership in the group was neither stable nor significantly related to later party alignments. Both David Barton and Thomas Hart Benton, for instance, were at one time included in this faction but ended up respectively opposing and supporting Jackson's presidential candidacy. Generally speaking, the "Junta" candidates were successful in St. Louis County in the territorial elections of 1816, 1817, and 1818, and the town elections of 1819. In the contest for constitutional convention delegates in 1820 the proslavery "Junta" candidates carried both the township (64.6%) and the county (69%) over a slate of persons opposed to the further introduction of slaves into Missouri. While there were more proslavery candidates than delegates seats available, the effect of slating was very clear among the first six candidates, all of whom received between 452 and 477 votes in the township; the votes were much more widely scattered among the antislavery candidates, suggesting a lower level of organization and activity. Not even this loose factional organization carried over to the town election. Before 1819 the trustees races attracted very little interest, with frequently only fifteen to twenty votes being cast. But in January 1819 168 voters cast ballots, electing five trustees, none of whose names had been prominently associated with either faction, and defeating such proven "Junta" men as Thomas H. Benton and Alexander McNair as well as leading anti-"Junta" leader Joseph Charless.[55]

By the early 1830s factions other than the old "Junta"–anti-"Junta" division began to reshape St. Louis politics. In 1822, in the aftermath of the 1819 panic, the Relief issue was a major factor in state elections. The lines were somewhat blurred in St. Louis, however, where electors gave 53% of their votes to the anti-Relief aspirant for the state Senate seat, John S. Ball; and among the eleven candidates receiving the largest number of votes in the Assembly elections were six Relief proponents, four anti-Relief partisans, and one whose position was not announced. In the congressional race John B. C. Lucas, longtime anti-"Junta" leader, defeated "Junta" member John Scott by a margin of three to two. In the first mayoral election, in 1823, William Carr Lane, a former Federalist, later a Jacksonian, and ultimately Whig, who had been a St. Louis resident for only four years, polled 55.5% of the vote over two "Junta" associates. Although party lines were still vague, the 1824 state elections were at least primarily conducted in relationship to the presidential candidacy of Andrew Jackson, but in St. Louis the alignment was still fuzzy. Jackson gubernatorial candidate William H. Ashley polled less than 40% of the vote in St. Louis, while George F. Strother, the Jacksonian candidate for mayor, took 50.7% of the vote in a three-man race. To the state Senate the St. Louis district (with the support of the city electorate) sent one Jacksonian and one anti-Jacksonian and to the state House of Representatives three Jackonians, two anti-Jacksonians, and one whose position is not clear. All except one of the persons elected as state senators and representatives appeared on a slate presented by "MANY VOTERS" in a local newspaper two weeks before the election—four Jacksonians and three anti-Jacksonians. Finally, the city's voters cast 42.4% of their ballots for presidential electors supporting Henry Clay, 33.6% for Adams electors, and 24.1% for Jackson electors, in a very light poll. Clearly, the St. Louis political scene was very muddled as late as the mid-1820s.[56]

By 1826 it was clear both that St. Louis was leaning toward the anti-Jackson camp and that party organization was still embryonic. No Jacksonian contested the congressional seat, which Edward Bates took in a two-way race with John Scott, with a margin of almost four to one in the city. Anti-Jacksonians also won the state Senate (61.1%) and sheriff (55.2%) races, but three of the four state representative seats went to Jackson partisans. A majority of the city council, on the other hand, were anti-Jacksonians. Two years later Edward Bates was reelected to Congress with two-thirds of the vote over Jacksonian Spencer Pettis, and three of the four state Assembly candidates receiving the largest number of votes were anti-Jacksonians. The sheriffalty, on the other hand, went to Jacksonian Robert Simpson with 70.6% of the vote. In 1833 the Democrats seized one last victory, electing Samuel Merry as mayor with 53.1% of the vote. Merry's qualifications were challenged, however, because he held a federal office—receiver of public monies in St. Louis. When the courts upheld the challenge and ousted Merry, the voters elected Whig John W. Johnson by a majority of 286 to 252 (53.2%) and reelected him in 1834. The Whigs then closed out these transitional decades by electing John F. Darby as mayor in 1835 and subsequently reelecting him for three more years.[57]

By 1835, then, the "second American party system" was firmly established in the nation, and these fifteen cities were, with the single exception of Charleston, integral parts of that system. This should not be taken to mean that local elections were, in every instance, contested on the basis of national party divisions, though that was usually the case. But the urban centers were units—frequently vital units—in the national party structure, and their voters were mustered to their party's drummer for at least a majority of the electoral contests.

The period 1835–1850 was the heart of the active life of the "second American party system"—a period when political power in the nation was delicately balanced between two energetic, well-organized national parties. Naturally, this degree of balance was by no means reflected in every locality. On the contrary, individual states, counties, and cities tended much more frequently to give their political allegiance, with greater or less consistency, to one or the other of these parties. And generally speaking, this was at least as true of the cities as of the other local political units.

One city—Charleston—must be viewed as, to a considerable degree, separate from this party structure. To be sure, the city's electorate was nominally overwhelmingly Democratic—however Charlestonians might understand that label at any given time. But as a practical matter elections were rarely contested on national party terms. When the Unionists' narrow victory in 1830 was followed by ever larger victories by the Nullifiers, tempers frayed and violence erupted in Charleston in October 1834, with shots being exchanged between the Unionists and their opponents. This episode—or, more accurately, a subsequent conference in Columbia later in the year between Nullification leader James Hamilton and revered Unionist spokesman James Petigru—marked the end of open political conflict between the two factions, both of which were appalled by the danger of mob violence in a city with a large, and to a considerable degree, unsupervised, slave population. In the charter election of 1835 no Unionist slate was presented, though the carefully unlabeled slate, composed largely of merchants, contained the names of persons who had earlier been endorsed by both parties. The year 1836 saw a return to previous practice as at least five heavily overlapping tickets were published for the charter elections in September (with Robert Y. Hayne the sole candidate for intendant) and two overlapping slates (Independent and United Republican) for the state representative races in October. The six nominees on both slates received, understandably, the highest number of votes of the sixteen elected, and counted both Nullifiers and Unionists among their number. The next year a Democrat, Henry C. Pinckney, defeated (54.7%) an anti–Van Burenite, James Lynah, for mayor, though that race was not, apparently, contested on the presidential issue. The same candidates, joined by two others, contested the mayoralty in 1838, with Pinckney again victorious with 39.5% of the vote; four overlapping slates of aldermanic aspirants were published. Such multiple tickets with considerable duplication of candidates continued to be common in charter elections, notably in 1840 (five slates), 1841 (two slates with half the aldermanic candidates the same on both), 1842 (three slates), 1843 (thirteen slates), 1845 (five slates), 1846 (five slates), 1848 (five slates), and 1850 (three slates with identical candidates for more than a third of the positions). Nor was the practice rare in the state representative contests. In 1842, for example, at least ten slates containing a total of twenty-eight candidates were presented, and three-fourths of the names appeared on at least five lists. And in 1850 such political fragmentation reached its apex when twenty-four slates of representative candidates, containing a total of forty-two names, were presented. Twenty-two of these aspirants appeared on at least ten slates.[58]

But political appearance was not always political reality in Charleston. Beneath the apparent chaos was solid Democratic dominance. In the legislative election of 1842 the voters were presented with ten slates of candidates. But of the seventeen persons elected only one was clearly identifiable as a Whig, though two or three others received Whig endorsements at one time or another. Even when elections appeared to swing on particular issues they rarely transcended party loyalty. In 1846, for example, the candidate slates for state representatives were printed in the *Charleston Courier*, and the issue upon which some of the slates were constructed was that of the method of selecting presidential electors. South Carolina law still provided for the choice of electors by the legislature, but many citizens urged direct election. The retention of legislative selection was a device by which the political power of the "Low Country" (including Charleston) was enhanced, for the legislature was grossly malapportioned to the detriment of the "Up Country." Nevertheless, nine of the seventeen candidates elected were pledged to support popular election of electors, while eight favored the status quo. But all were, so far as we can tell, Democrats. This was all the more remarkable because it was only briefly, in the mid-1840s, that open two-party races occurred. In 1844 Whig and Democratic legislative tickets were run, with the Democrats taking over 60% of the vote and carrying all four wards.[59]

Genuine, acknowledged systems of party competition existed in all of the other fourteen of these cities, though the dominance of one or the other of the major parties was common and it was not unusual for charter elections to be conducted without open reference to the national parties. These cities may be divided into four groups—solidly Democratic, solidly Whig, contested but leaning toward the Democrats, and contested but leaning toward the Whigs. In this first category—solidly Democratic—is a single city, Baltimore. The Whigs managed to eke out a narrow win in 1850, by a plurality over two Democratic mayoral candidates; and in noncharter elections they took a narrow (52.4%) victory in the 1844 congressional race and squeezed out a one-vote margin in the 1846 state Senate contest, in otherwise Democratic years. Only 1838 and 1843 could be considered Whig years. In the former (perhaps as an aftermath of the 1837 "Democratic" panic) the Whigs took the contest for mayor (52%) and carried the city in races for the congressional seat (52.7%), state representative (50.5%), state senator (50.7%), and governor (50.5%). In each race they carried seven of the twelve wards (wards one, two, five, six, seven, nine, and eleven). In 1843 the Whigs carried seven of the fourteen wards and won the mayoralty (51.1%), four of the five state Assembly seats (50.3%), and fifteen of the twenty-eight seats in the First Branch of the city council.[60]

In the rest of the elections between 1836 and 1850 Democratic victory followed Democratic victory with monotonous (for the Whigs) regularity. But the consistency did not depend on heavy Democratic majorities. Of the forty-two elections in this period for which actual votes were collected for analysis, in only three instances (only one before 1848) did the Democratic portion of the vote exceed 55% and only once was it greater than 57%. One-half of the time it was 52% or less.[61] Until 1841—while Baltimore was divided into twelve wards—the Democrats could normally expect to carry wards two, three, four, six, eight, ten, and twelve. This comprised all of the area east of Jones Falls except the extreme eastern first ward and the fifth (Old Town) ward, just north of the City Dock; the narrow strip just west of Jones Falls; Whetstone Point (the area south of the Basin); and the extreme western and northwestern wards. Much of the eighth, tenth, and twelfth wards lay beyond the limits of direct taxation. The Whigs, thus, controlled most of the central "city" wards, occasionally taking the second (Fells Point) or sixth wards, while the Democrats held much of the peripheral area. Changes in ward lines gave Baltimore fourteen wards in 1841 and twenty before the end of the decade, but though the numbers changed the areas of greatest Democratic and Whig strength shifted only slightly. The main difference was that the most easterly ward became intermittently Democratic by 1841, and more reliably so by 1847.[62]

Just as there was but a single Democratic city, so, too, there was but one metropolis—New York—in the "contested but leaning Democratic" category. True, the successful candidates for office in this period (1836–1850) were somewhat more likely to be Democratic than Whig or Native American, but in more than half of the fifteen years the anti-Democratic parties won some contests. Democratic victories in 1836, for example, were followed by Whig successes in 1837 and 1838. In the former year not only did the Van Buren electors carry the presidential poll with 51.6% of the vote, but Democrat Cornelius W. Lawrence took more than 60% of the mayoral ballots over Whig Seth Greer (23.3%), Equal Rights (old Workingmen and Loco-Foco) candidate Alexander Ming, Jr. (10.3%), and Nativist Samuel F. B. Morse (5.7%). At the same time, the city council was evenly divided among Democrats and Whigs. Morse, incidentally, was an ardent Jacksonian but violently antiforeign and anti-Catholic—beliefs that it was becoming increasingly difficult to harmonize within a New York Democratic party leaning more and more heavily on the immigrant Catholic vote. In the mayoral election the Whigs took the first three wards, at the lower tip of Manhattan, while the other thirteen wards went to the Democrats. Margins varied from pluralities in one Whig and one Democratic ward to a 96.4% Democratic vote in ward twelve. In the next year the Whig mayoral candidate, Aaron Clark, took a plurality victory (48.7%) over Democrat John I. Morgan (39.2%) and Equal Rights nominee Moses Jacque (12.1%). The Whigs carried twelve wards, five by pluralities, and garnered over 70% of the vote in each of the first three wards, which they had carried with 50.7%, 51.7%, and 46.7% of the vote the year before. These ward victories carried over to the council elections, resulting in a twenty-four–to–ten Whig margin in that body. In 1838 the Whigs' percentage of the vote increased but they carried fewer wards. Mayor Clark was reelected (50.2%) and Whigs were also victorious in the gubernatorial (50.6%), congressional (51.6%), and state Assembly (51.4%) races. They carried nine of the seventeen wards, giving them an eighteen-to-sixteen edge in the city council.[63]

The 1838 victories, in particular, may have been influenced by the 1837 panic. Certainly the disappearance of the Loco-Foco/Equal Rights/Workingmen's movement coincided with that economic upheaval, and, whatever the stance or rhetoric of their leaders, Workingmen in most cities eventually gravitated to the anti-Democratic ranks. In fact, as a sort of dying gasp, the Loco-Focos endorsed some of the Whig council nominees in 1837. In any event, 1839 saw a Democratic resurgence. Whig Mayor Clark, running for reelection, increased his vote by over 300, but the Democratic total—for Isaac L. Varian, whom Clark had defeated in 1838—rose by 1,850, giving that party 51.2% of the vote. The Democrats also garnered 52% of the vote in the state Senate race and carried twelve wards to give them a twenty-four–to–ten edge in the city council.[64]

There then followed a number of successive Democratic victories. Except for the Whig capture of twenty aldermanic and assistant aldermanic seats and control of the city council in 1842, the next four years were times of Democratic triumph, though never (except in 1843) by very large majorities. Van Buren electors took 50.7% of the vote in the 1840 presidential election, and Democrat William C. Bouck polled 52.2% of the city vote in the gubernatorial election of the same year. Two years later Bouck collected an almost identical percentage (52.4%) of the vote in his bid for reelection. The Democrats also emerged victorious in successive mayoral races, starting with Isaac L. Varian's win with 51.9% of the vote in his reelection bid in 1840. Varian was followed by Robert H. Morris, who polled 50.4% of the vote in 1841, 52.1% in 1842, and 56.5% in 1843. Democrats won twenty-four of thirty-six seats on the city council in 1840, twenty in 1841, and twenty-six in 1843. Indeed, the April election in this latter year seemed to promise great things for the Democrats; not since 1832 had any candidate for a major office polled as much as 56% of the vote, nor had any party had a majority of as many as eighteen seats on the council.[65]

Actually, the fall elections of 1843 ushered in a period of instability in New York City local politics. Although the Democrats continued to secure narrow majorities in the presidential and gubernatorial contests, not until 1848 would a Democratic mayoral candidate receive a majority of the vote, and even then the

figure was only 50.1%. The new ingredient in the political pot was the ree-
mergence of the nativist movement, in the form of the American Republican
party. Mangle M. Quackenbos, the ARP candidate for state senator in November
1843, polled 22.3% of the vote, while Democrat David R. Floyd Jones took
38.1% and won the election by a thirty-five-vote margin (out of more than
35,000 votes cast) over Whig Morris Franklin.[66]

The immediate, but temporary, effect of the surfacing of political nativism
was an increase in voter participation. The votes cast in the mayoral election of
1844 exceeded 50,000, compared to just under 45,000 in 1843. Many—probably
most—of these new voters gave their suffrage to the American Republican party,
but the surge was short-lived, with voter turnout in mayoral elections slipping
to just under 49,000 in 1845, less than 47,000 in 1846, and something over
43,000 in 1847 before rebounding to barely over 46,000 in 1848 and then declining again to a bit over 39,000 in 1849 and almost 41,000 in 1851. More
significant was the impact of nativism on the Whig and Democratic parties. The
Whigs, of course, had long counted among their numbers persons who were
disturbed by the potential impact on the American society and body politic of
non-British, non-Protestant populations. And although the Whig party maintained a presence on the ballots even in the worst of times, it is clear that most
of its members initially stampeded into the ranks of the American Republican
party—the Whig mayoral vote dropped from 19,507 in 1843 to 5,297 in 1844.
But the Democrats, too, had nativists among their adherents; Jacksonian nativist
Samuel F. B. Morse, after all, had taken 6% of the mayoral vote in 1836, and
since that date the continuing influx of Irish and Germans had doubtless nudged
many more Democrats toward Morse's position. The Democratic mayoral vote
dropped by almost 5,000 between 1842 and 1844 while the total vote rose more
than 5,000. The Democratic share of the whole vote dropped by almost 16
percentage points as nativist James Harper won the mayoralty with 48.7% of
the vote. In every ward the Democrats' share of the vote dropped between the
1843 and 1844 elections. The heaviest decline (from 20 to 33 percentage points)
came in the ninth ward, on the (then) upper west side, south of Fifteenth Street,
and an unbroken chain of five wards (the seventh, tenth, thirteenth, seventeenth,
and nineteenth) stretching from the East River across from Brooklyn north to
Fourteenth Street. In the eleventh ward the Democratic percentage declined from
76 to 43.[67]

In 1845 the Democrats rebounded and William F. Havemeyer won the mayoralty with 49.5% of the vote. Another plurality victory followed in 1846 when
Andrew H. Mickle garnered a 47.7% margin. In each case there were Whig and
ARP candidates who together polled a little more than half the vote. Additionally, there were representatives of the National Reformers (calling for the free
distribution of public lands) and the Abolitionists, who jointly took 0.5% of the
vote in 1845 and 1.4% in 1846. The ARP vote shrank to 31.1% in the former
year and to 18%, and third place, in the latter.[68]

As previously noted, the Democrats managed to maintain their majorities in the gubernatorial and presidential races even as their mayoral margins deteriorated. Not only did the Democratic presidential electors carry the city in 1844 with a clear majority (51.1%) but Democratic gubernatorial nominee Silas Wright carried the city vote in 1844 (53%) and 1846 (50.5%). In part this resulted from the absence of third-party competition on the ticket in 1844 and probably also reflected a diminished willingness to defect from the Democratic party in nonlocal contests. Moreover, the Democrats managed to hold onto majorities in most of the wards in 1844 and to parlay pluralities in a majority of the wards in 1845 into control of the city council with thirty seats in each of those years.[69]

The closing years of the half century were not golden ones for New York Democrats. Between 1847 and 1851 they were able to claim only two victories in major races—in 1848 William F. Havemeyer eked out (50.1%) a victory in the mayoral race, and two years later Horatio Seymour barely carried (50.8%) the city in the gubernatorial race. Otherwise, the Whigs were everywhere victorious. Hamilton Fish took 54.8% of the vote in the lieutenant gubernatorial race in 1847 and 53% in the gubernatorial contest the following year. The Whig presidential electors polled 54.3% of the ballots in 1848—almost 10,000 more than the Democrats. In the mayoral races, William V. Brady won (49%) in a four-way race in 1847, finishing 1,600 votes ahead of Democrat T. Sherman Brownell. After losing to Havemeyer in 1848, the Whigs came back to outpoll the Democrats by 4,100 votes and sweep Caleb S. Woodhull (55.1%) into office in 1849; and two years later Ambrose C. Kingsland defeated Democrat Fernando Wood by a slightly larger margin. And in 1850, in a much tighter race, the Whigs (50.5%) elected three congressmen to the Democrats' (49.5%) one. Finally, in part because of many Democratic splits, the Whigs controlled the city council throughout this period.[70]

As might be expected, changes in party dominance in the various wards occurred during this period. Though several ward modifications took place, the boundaries of thirteen of the wards (one through ten and thirteen through fifteen) remained unchanged, and wards eleven and seventeen had the same boundaries from 1837 on. In the mid-1830s the lower wards (first, second, and third) and the adjoining fourth ward on the lower east side were Whig, as were the lower west side wards (fifth and eighth) on either side of Canal Street, and the north central (Washington Square) fifteenth ward. The sixth (City Hall) ward and the two northern out wards (twelfth and sixteenth) were solidly Democratic, as were the upper west side ninth and upper east side eleventh wards. The lower east side seventh and thirteenth wards, separated by Grand Street, were mixed, as were the adjoining central tenth and fourteenth wards, though the latter tended to lean toward the Whigs. The Democratic rebound after the 1837–1838 Whig victories pulled the whole east side (wards four, seven, and thirteen, as well as the already Democratic eleventh) into that party's orbit (though the seventh ward was not entirely dependable), and also captured the eighth and fourteenth wards. This left the Whigs (in 1843) in firm control of only the first, second, third,

fifth, and fifteenth wards. The impact of the 1844 nativist victories has already
been traced (see above), but initially (1845–1846) these changes appeared to be
temporary as the Democratic pluralities and narrow majorities enabled them to
take every ward except the third and fifteenth, despite that party's inability to
capture a majority of the city vote. But with the return to more nearly normal
political patterns in New York in the late 1840s (i.e., basic two-party contests
with continuing splits in Democratic party ranks) the effects of the nativist
movement became clear; the Democrats found themselves, in 1847–1850, with
dependable majorities only in wards four, six, and fourteen, and an additional
likelihood of victory in wards eleven, twelve, thirteen, and sixteen. These were
the two out wards north of Fourteenth Street, the two upper east side wards
south of Fourteenth Street, and a rank of three wards stretching up the center
of lower Manhattan east of Broadway from the East River to Houston Street.[71]

Because of its large population, rapid and continuing growth, and an apparent
unwillingness to create a large number of new wards, New York had severe
problems regarding access to the polls. As long as there was only one polling
place per ward it was imperative that New Yorkers retain the three-day election
periods that had been common in the eighteenth and early nineteenth centuries,
but which many urban centers abandoned. This practice was retained in New
York throughout the 1830s despite (or because of) the fact that it facilitated
fraudulent multiple voting and contributed to political riots. By 1837 it was
patently impossible for existing conditions to continue; assuming that election
officers could accept sixty votes per hour (which a contemporary characterized
as a very high rate) and that the polls were open twelve hours a day, less than
37,000 votes could be cast in all seventeen wards over a three-day period. As
a practical matter, the populations of the various wards were very unequal (in
1840 the range was from 6,394 in ward two to 29,073 in ward eight), and in a
given ward (based on these assumptions) only 2,160 votes could be cast in any
election. By 1834 almost 36,000 votes were being cast (or, at least, recorded)
in elections and by 1838 the figure exceeded 40,000. In addition, the size of the
electorate voting at a given poll made it impossible for the election officals to
know personally all the voters and, thus, to prevent unqualified persons from
voting if they, in fact, had any interest in doing so.[72]

As early as 1838 nativist groups began to petition the state Senate to adopt
voter registration for New York City, and in 1840 a new election law addressed
both problems. It divided the city's seventeen wards into seventy-three election
districts (increased to eighty in 1842), ranging from two in the second and
twelfth wards to eight in the eighth. It also required prior registration of all
voters, and in the fall of 1840 officials registered 43,711 voters, a considerably
larger number than had ever voted in the city to that date. By common consent
the succeeding elections were remarkably free from violence at the polls. New
York political leaders, however, apparently found voter registration too restrictive and secured its repeal in 1842.[73]

Among these cities there were two—Cincinnati and New Orleans—in which the major parties closely contended, with the Whigs having a very slight advantage. In the former city, it will be remembered, the transition period had ended with consecutive, substantial Whig victories in 1834 and 1835. This momentum carried forward into the period of the "second American party system" and for a decade the Whigs took almost every election. In 1836 the Harrison presidential electors piled up a 912-vote margin in the city, losing only the third ward, and in a variety of other races the results were similar. The Cincinnati Whigs recorded majorities for their nominees for governor (Joseph Vance, 61.6%), congressman (Bellamay Storer, 61%), state senator (Henry Morse, 60.3%), and sheriff (Charles Mills, 57.7%), and carried the state Assembly ticket in like fashion (60.3%). They also elected thirteen of fifteen members of the city council. It should, perhaps, be noted that the Whig influence largely stopped at the city boundaries; with the exception of three townships, Hamilton County outside of Cincinnati was Democratic country. Vance's opponent, Eli Baldwin, for example, took more than two-thirds of the suburban and exurban ballots— enough to carry the whole county with 53.8% of the vote. Home state Whig presidential candidate William Henry Harrison did even less well, taking only 45.3% of the whole county vote, compared to 46.9% for Vance.[74]

Whig Samuel W. Davis defeated (53.6%) Democrat Elisha Hotchkiss for the mayoralty in 1837 and won reelection (47.7%) in the spring of 1839 over Hotchkiss and another Whig candidate, John A. Wiseman. Davis had majorities in wards one and three and pluralities in wards four, five, and seven (by only two votes), while Wiseman took pluralities in wards two (by a single vote) and six; the best that Hotchkiss could manage was a second-place finish in three wards (three, four, and seven). But despite Hotchkiss' dismal showing (25.1%), the Democrats were victorious in the 1839 fall elections, carrying the county vote in the state senate (58%), state Assembly (56.8%), treasurer (55.6%), county commissioner (57.1%), and prosecuting attorney (56.7%) races.[75]

In 1840, perhaps as a "rub-off" of the presidential campaign, Cincinnati voters stampeded back to the Whig camp. Not only did the Harrison electors carry the city that fall, taking all seven wards and 61.5% of the vote, but the Whigs swept the other races as well. In the gubernatorial, congressional, state Senate, and state Assembly contests the results were almost identical—the Whig candidates carried all seven wards and polled between 60.6% and 62.9% of the vote. In the spring a similar sweep had given the council seats in all seven wards to the Whigs.[76] In the following year the Whigs found themselves engaged in a number of three-way races against Democrats and Free Soilers, from which they emerged with plurality victories. They took the mayoralty in 1843 (44.9%), won nineteen of twenty-seven council seats in 1844, and in April 1845 added another mayoral victory when Henry E. Spencer collected 48.4% of the vote for a close win, despite the fact that his Democratic opponent, Henry Morse, won six of the ten wards.[77]

The narrowness of the Democratic loss boded ill for Whig hopes. In the fall of that year the Democrats gained the pluralities that seemed to constitute, at least temporarily, the measure of political success in Cincinnati, and swept the state Senate (49.4%) and state Assembly (49.7%) elections. They even managed to garner a majority (53.5%) in the county commissioner's race. The Democrats took six of ten wards in the state Senate election, and the two major parties split the wards five to five in the other contest.[78]

The closing years of the half century constituted a period of shifting strengths in Cincinnati between the two major parties but with greater success to the Whigs. The Democrats carried the city in the 1846 gubernatorial race by a margin of only sixty-one votes, taking five of ten wards, and in 1847 carried the state Senate (51% and four wards) and Assembly (51.5% and five wards) contests in the city. The Whigs, on the other hand, elected their mayoral candidate, Henry E. Spencer, in 1847 (53.9% and six wards) and 1849 (58.6% and eight wards), the latter in a three-way race. In 1848 the Whig gubernatorial candidate, Seabury Ford, won a plurality (46.9%) of the city vote and six of ten wards over Democratic and Free Soil opponents, and the Taylor presidential electors were also victorious, with pluralities or majorities in seven wards. The Whigs also controlled the city council in 1847 (twenty of thirty seats), 1848 (eighteen seats), and 1849 (seventeen seats). The Democrats closed out the decade with a substantial victory (59.4% and eight of twelve wards) in the 1850 gubernatorial race.[79]

Just before midcentury the Cincinnati Democrats tended to control the riverfront wards (third and fourth) and always carried the north central (tenth) and northeastern (ninth) wards. The Whigs were uniformly successful in the wards (first, second, fifth, and seventh) lying between the riverfront wards and the out wards. They almost never lost the sixth ward, which had some river frontage, well downstream from the public landing, and much of the area of which, like wards one and two, lay along the major commercial thoroughfare, Fifth Street. The far western eighth ward was a swing ward.[80]

Hundreds of miles downstream, almost to the mouth of the Mississippi, sat a city of similar party proclivities—New Orleans. To an even greater degree than Cincinnati, the Crescent City had been firmly Republican and then Jacksonian until the very end of the transitional decades (1815–1835). Doubtless one thing that contributed to keeping both parties viable in New Orleans was its unique "municipality" system of government, by which the city was divided into almost wholly independent political entities. Thus, even a minority party had a good chance of gaining some local victories—and, thus, patronage. But it must also be added that the New Orleans electorate (though much restricted before 1845) was unusually volatile, swinging (even in a single year) from narrow divisions to one-sided victories. The 1836 presidential election illuminates the narrow divisions. The Whig—in this case, Hugh Lawson White—electors carried only the Second (American) Municipality, while the First and Third Municipalities went to the Democrats. But the Whigs had a large margin in the Second Municipality (60.9%) and a substantial minority in the First (47.8%), which offset the enormous Democratic percentage (71.6%) in the much smaller

Third and gave the city to the Whigs with 50.4% of the vote. Two years later the extreme volatility of the voters was well illustrated as the Democrats took 50.1% of the city vote in the gubernatorial race and Democrat Albert Hoa won the state Senate contest with 54.4% of the vote; while Whig congressional nominee E. D. White took three-fifths of the vote to defeat John Slidell, and Charles Genois (Whig) polled 52.3% of the vote to defeat L. U. Gaienne (Democrat) for the mayoralty. To further complicate the matter, it has been pointed out that Genois attracted considerable suport from Democrats alienated by that party's leaders' forcing Gaienne's nomination through a reluctant convention.[81]

In the early 1840s the Democrats suffered some decline in strength, and 1840 was clearly not a Democratic year. In April the mayoral contest pitted a Native American candidate, William Feret, against Whig Charles Genois and four lesser candidates, mostly (perhaps entirely) Democrats. This particular nativist movement had at least some of its roots in resentment among some Democrats of the visible support given by some of the normally Democratic Irish to the 1834 gubernatorial candidacy of Irish-born Whig E. D. White, and it is clear that the Democratic Party mounted no organized opposition to Feret in this race. The nativists took 42.7% of the vote to Genois' 38.3%, as the other candidates split the remainder. Feret took a majority in the Second Municipality and the first district of the First Municipality; Genois had majorities in the other First Municipality districts and majorities or pluralities in three of the four districts in the Third Municipality. In July the Whigs took the Assembly races with 73.5% of the vote, and White took almost as much (72.7%) of the city vote in his congressional race. The Whigs rounded off a very satisfactory year by carrying all three municipalities and 60.6% of the vote in the November presidential election. In 1842 the Whigs' gubernatorial candidate took 55.7% of the New Orleans vote and carried all three municipalities, while their state senatorial candidate, Albert Hoa, did a percentage point better. Whig Judah P. Benjamin carried only the Second Municipality in his race for a state Assembly seat but still garnered 54% of the city vote. The mayoral contest, however, went to Democrat Denis Prieur, who amassed 55.5% of the ballots and swept all three municipalities.[82]

The next two years—1843 and 1844—demonstrated the transitory nature of voter loyalties in the Crescent City. Whig (and ex-Native) William Feret won the mayoralty with 56.9% of the vote in 1843 only to lose it the following year to Democrat Edgar Montegut, who polled 54.5% of the ballots. It is tempting to attribute this shift to the 60% increase in the vote, but unlike the situation in some other cities, more extensive analysis does not reveal a correlation between larger voter participation and Democratic victories. In 1843 the three municipal councils—contrary to all precedent—all had Whig majorities, but in 1844 returned to their more usual alignment—Whig in the Second Municipality (ten-to-two) and Democratic in the First (eight-to-four) and Third (six-to-one). In the July election in 1843 the Democratic congressional candidates carried the First and Third Municipalities and garnered 51.4% of the city vote, while the Whig state senatorial candidate amassed a slender majority (50.6%) of the total vote although carrying only the Second Municipality. In November of the next year Clay electors carried the Second and Third Municipalities and lost the First by only seventeen votes, and took 53.7% of the city vote.[83]

Such narrow division and volatility encouraged (or, perhaps, resulted from) dubious methods on the part of party managers. The July election in 1844 was marked by much controversy, as Whig inspectors refused to accept ballots offered by persons holding naturalization certificates from a former judge accused of issuing such documents fraudulently, and Democratic inspectors refused to accept *any* votes subsequently offered at those polls. The nominal result of these elections was the choice of a Democratic constitutional convention delegate to represent the state senatorial district and six Whigs and four Democrats to represent the Assembly districts (which were, combined, identical to the senatorial district in New Orleans), while seven Whigs and three Democrats were sent to the assembly. To a lesser extent some of these circumstances had prevailed the previous April, when the Democrats gained a two-to-one margin in the general city council.[84]

In 1845 Louisianians adopted a new constitution that provided for universal white manhood suffrage. In November New Orleans voters gave solid approval to the new document, with the strongest support coming from the Second Municipality, where the ratio of affirmative to negative votes was almost sixteen-to-one. The impact of this change was immediately apparent in the size of the vote cast, but not in the matter of party preference. Whig A. D. Crossman managed to win the mayoralty in 1846, carrying the First and Second Municipalities, but with only 40% of the total vote, the remainder being split between the regular Democratic nominee, A. J. Guirot (37.3%) and Democratic incumbent Edgar Montegut (22%). The membership of the general council of the city stood at six Whigs and six Democrats. In January, however, Democrat Isaac Johnson carried the First and Second Municipalities and won 49.5% of the vote in a three-way race for governor, losing the normally Democratic Third Municipality to the Whig candidate, William DeBuys. The Second Municipality had, of course, long been the Whig stronghold in New Orleans. Additionally, the Democratic state Senate slate had carried all three municipalities and 49.9% of the vote. The Native candidates polled less than 7.5% of the senatorial vote and less than 6% of the gubernatorial ballots. The lack of pattern prevailed in the next year as well. The general council stood at seven Whigs and five Democrats; the Democratic state senatorial slate carried the Second and Third Municipalities and polled 51.6% of the vote; and the state Assembly delegation was equally divided.[85]

In 1846 and 1847 the total vote (6,925 and 7,644) had been roughly three times the usual presidential vote in the first half of the decade (the presidential vote in 1840 and 1844 had been almost double the other votes). In 1848 the vote total again escalated, to 8,076 in the mayoral contest and 9,849 in the presidential election. The Whigs won both races, the mayoralty with 63% of the vote and victories in the First and Second Municipalities, and the presidential contest with 55.5% of the ballots and majorities in all three municipalities. The fact that Taylor owned a Louisiana plantation doubtless aided the Whig cause in the latter race. The next year the vote totals rose again, to 9,896 in the congressional election and 10,092 in the gubernatorial race. This time the Democrats benefited, winning both contests, the congressional race with 53.6% of the vote and victories in all three municipalities and the gubernatorial election more narrowly, with 50.8% of the ballots and majorities in the First and Third Municipalities. In both races the Whig vote declined significantly from the elections of the previous year. The Whigs did manage to gain a narrow margin (seven to five) in the general council of the city. The electoral volatility continued to the very end of the half century, with the Whigs taking a 53.8% victory in the 1850 mayoral race and the Democrats winning the 1851 congressional election with 52.9% of the vote.[86]

The general assumption—doubtless broadly correct—is that the First Municipality (*Vieux Carré*) was largely peopled by the Creole French population, and that the residents of the Second Municipality (the "American" sector) were Anglo-Americans in culture and identified by birth or parentage with the northerly and easterly sections of the United States. The Third Municipality housed some Old Spanish elements and later arrivals, especially the Irish and Germans. It is, moreover, commonly asserted that before 1852 the "Americans" (i.e., the Second Municipality voters) were strongly inclined toward the Whig party, while the Creoles and immigrants were largely Democratic. To test this assumption I have analyzed twenty-six elections in each of the first two municipalities and twenty-four in the Third between 1836 and 1851. The Second Municipality was, indeed, heavily Whig. In only seven of the electoral contests examined did the Democrats capture this municipality, and six of those cases occurred in only two years—1846 and 1849. It was also true that the Third Municipality was overwhelmingly Democratic, with the Whigs carrying only five of the twenty-four elections, three of them in presidential contests. In the First Municipality, on the other hand, the political performance did not conform to accepted generalizations. In more than half the elections examined it was the Whigs, not the Democrats, that emerged victorious in this sector. In all three municipalities political performance was most consistent in local (i.e., mayoral and council) contests. In all ten local races examined for the Third Municipality the Democrats were successful; of the twelve local contests checked for each of the First and Second Municipalities, the Whigs won ten in each subdivision. The tendency to vote Whig in the presidential races (1836, 1840, 1844, and 1848) was very strong—always in the Second Municipality, three of four times in the Third, and half of the time in the First. In congressional races, on the other hand, the tendency was strongly Democratic—all four times in each of the First and Third Municipalities and two of four times in the Second. The state elections (for governor, Senate, and Assembly) were least predictable, splitting between Whigs and Democrats three-to-three in the First, two-to-three in

the Second, and two-to-four in the Third Municipality. In short, political performance was somewhat more complex and subtle than the common generalizations would lead us to believe.[87]

In three of the cities under discussion—all growing rapidly during these years
(1836–1850)—though the Whigs were clearly predominant, the Democrats were
occasionally successful. These cities were Brooklyn, Buffalo, and St. Louis. The
first of these, it will be recalled, ended the transitional period with the emergence
of a Native American movement and victory by its candidate over a Democratic
opponent in the 1835 Assembly race. Led by some prominent political figures,
including George Hall (the son of Irish immigrants) and Edward Copeland—
both candidates for the village presidency in 1833—the party enjoyed some
slight success in the mid-1830s. The Democrats rebounded to take a majority
in the city council in 1836 and split the council nine to nine with the Natives
the next year. In the latter year the Democrats took the two northernmost wards
(the second and fifth) on the east (''democratic'') side of Fulton Street, stretching east to the Navy Yard, and the two far eastern out wards, the eighth and
ninth. The Natives carried the southern wards on the west (''aristocratic'') side
of Fulton Street—the first, third, and sixth—and the adjoining fourth to the east
of that street. The seventh ward, south of Wallabout Bay, was split.[88]

Although nativist sentiment doubtless persisted, the political movement
proved to be short-lived. By 1838 the Whigs (who had always been the primary
supporters of the Native American party) had resumed their earlier party name,
probably at least in part, fearing that open support for nativism might damage
the party's electoral chances on the state and national levels. In that year they
took eleven of the eighteen council seats (with a third of the Native councilmen
of 1837 being reelected as Whigs) and carried 50.3% of the city's ballots for
their gubernatorial candidate, William H. Seward. In both contests they carried
six of the nine wards, leaving only the second, fifth, and eighth for the Democrats. This pattern persisted for the next three years. In 1839 the parties each
took one Assembly seat, but the Whigs carried the same six wards. The Democrats took 50.3% of the votes in one race and the Whigs 50.2% in the other.
In 1840 the Whigs swept a number of races, reelecting the sitting Whig mayor,
Cyrus P. Smith (in the first popular election of that officer), taking twelve seats
in the council, and carrying the city for Harrison in the presidential election and
Seward in the gubernatorial contest. In each case the Whigs carried the same
six wards, though they increased their share of the vote slightly (e.g., to 52.3%
and 51.2% in the latter two races).[89]

The early 1840s constituted the most successful years of this period for
Brooklyn's Democrats. The run began with a split in the 1841 state legislative
races. The Whigs took 51.5% in the state Senate race, and the Democrats polled
the same percentage in the Assembly contests. In both elections the Democrats
carried the second, fifth, and eighth wards. Beginning in 1842 the Democrats
took four successive mayoral races, electing Henry C. Murphy in 1842 with
51.5% of the vote and carrying four wards, Joseph Sprague in 1843 (52.9% and

five wards) and in a three-way race in 1844 (40.9% and six wards), and Thomas
G. Talmage, also in a three-way contest, in 1845 (41.9% and six wards). During
the same period the Democrats controlled the council in 1842 and 1845 (eleven
to seven in each case) and carried the city in the 1842 gubernatorial race (51.4%
and five wards) and state Senate contests in 1843 (52.1% and five wards) and
in 1845 (44.2% and six wards) in a three-way race. The state Assembly seats
also went Democratic, by a somewhat smaller percentage (50.5%) in 1843 and
a slightly larger margin (45.3%) in 1845.[90] But even during this period of Democratic predominance the Whigs controlled the city council in 1843 (ten to eight)
and elected eight aldermen to the Democrats' six and the Natives' four in 1844.
In addition, they carried the city in both the presidential (53.1%) and gubernatorial (52.2%) elections in 1844.[91]

It was notable that the Democratic victories in 1844 and 1845 had occurred
when Native American candidates had taken up to a quarter or more of the vote.
But after 1845 the Native challenge was reduced or absent and the Whigs carried
almost everything before them. In the 1846 mayoral election nativist Thomas
C. Pinckney polled only 4.1% of the vote and Whig Francis B. Stryker (a former
Native) took an easy victory with 56.3% of the ballots. Stryker was reelected
in 1847 and 1848 with 60.3% and 57.2% of the vote. The Whigs even managed
to elect Edward Copeland (another ex-Native) to the mayoral office in 1849
(44%) despite the presence of an independent candidate (George Hall) in the
field. Because of a charter change, Brooklyn held two mayoral elections in 1850.
The Democrats emerged victorious from the April contest, carrying six wards
and 52% of the vote to elect Samuel Smith over Whig James S. T. Stranahan.
The November election saw the perennial independent candidate, George Hall,
back in the lists, to the detriment of the Democratic candidate, John Rice. Whig
Conklin Brush carried five wards, as Stranahan had in April. In a much larger
poll (10,148 compared to 8,865 in April) the Whig portion of the vote dropped
to 42%, but that was enough to take a plurality over Rice (38.3%) and Hall
(19.6%) for the victory.[92]

Only once during the last years of the half century were the Democrats able
to muster a majority in the city council and that was for the short (April–
November) term in 1850. Then the Democrats elected fifteen of the twenty-two
members (the number of wards had been increased from nine to eleven in that
year). Additionally, in 1846 each of the major parties carried nine seats in the
council. The Whigs commanded substantial majorities in the councils of 1847
(thirteen-to-five), 1848 (thirteen-to-five), and 1849 (twelve-to-six), and in November of 1850 elected fourteen members to the Democrats' seven, with one
election terminating in a tie.[93]

In the contests for state and national office the Whigs were almost universally
successful during these years. The Democrats did carry the city (53.5%, six
wards) for Silas Wright in the 1846 gubernatorial election but that was the extent
of their success. Whig Hamilton Fish took 57% of the vote in the 1848 gubernatorial race; the Taylor electoral slate garnered over 58% in the 1848 presi-

dential contest; and Whig majorities in the various state Senate and congressional races usually exceeded 55%. Thus, Brooklyn Whigs ended the half century in firm control of the city, and this despite a continuing intraparty squabble between Francis B. Stryker and Francis Spinola, and the occasional candidacy of the Temperance/Whig/Native former mayor George Hall. Until the changing of the ward lines in 1850 this Whig dominance rested on solid— frequently substantial—majorities in wards one, three, four, and seven, south of a line extended directly east from the Fulton Steam Ferry slip. The Democratic strength, on the other hand, was to be found in wards two and five, adjoining the Navy Yard and the dock district, and the two eastern out wards, eight and nine. The southern out ward (six) fluctuated, and was somewhat more likely to be Whig than Democratic.[94]

Except for the first half of the 1840s and the very end of the half century, Buffalo was a reliably anti-Democratic city. Its early Federalist tendencies and strong Anti-Masonic influence in the 1830s had laid down a solid base for the building of the Whig party in the period of the "second American party system." While local elections were often not contested on a national party basis until the end of the 1830s, only one person not clearly a Whig was elected mayor by the city council before it ceased to exercise that power. Meanwhile, Whig William H. Seward carried the city by comfortable majorities in the gubernatorial races of 1838 (62.5%) and 1840 (55.8%), and the Harrison presidential electors polled 56.5% of the vote in the latter year. Only one discordant note was to be heard in this Whig symphony at the end of the 1830s: Whig Sheldon Thompson, in the first popular mayoral election, eked out only a ten-vote victory over Democrat George Barker.[95]

And, indeed, 1841 ushered in five years of Democratic dominance in Buffalo. Democrat Isaac Harrington won the mayoral elections in 1841 and 1842 and Joseph G. Master defeated Whig Walker Joy for the mayoralty in 1843, polling almost 58% of the vote. While Whig William Ketchum won (53.6%) the mayoral race in 1844, the Democrats came back strongly in 1845 when Master regained the mayoral office with 54.4% of the ballots. Moreover, Democrat William C. Bouck carried almost 54% of the Buffalo vote over Luther Brandish in the 1842 gubernatorial election, and, in a closer race, Silas Wright took just under 51% of the vote over Whig Millard Fillmore two years later in another gubernatorial contest. Finally, the Polk electors garnered just under half the vote in the 1844 presidential election, taking a plurality victory over those for Henry Clay and James G. Birney.[96]

The Whigs made a strong comeback in the late 1840s, however, as they took four straight mayoral contests, electing Soloman G. Haven in 1846, Elbridge G. Spaulding in 1847, and Hiram K. Barton in 1849, by votes ranging from 52.1% to 57.5%. Whig Orlando Allen also took a plurality victory (43%) over Democratic and Workingmen's candidates in 1848. In addition, Zachary Taylor carried the city in the presidential contest of that year with 55.1% of the vote. At midcentury the Democrats won successive mayoral elections in 1850 and 1851 with 53.8% and 55.2% of the ballots. This partisan switch was accompanied by an abrupt increase in the total vote cast in mayoral elections and probably resulted from demographic changes in the rapidly growing city. Erie County as a whole remained very solidly Whig, and throughout the period 1835–1850 Buffalo was primarily a Whig city.[97]

St. Louis' anti-Jacksonian tendencies of the 1820s and early 1830s evolved into very solid Whig dominance in the late 1830s. But, like Brooklyn and Buffalo, St. Louis would see an upsurge of Democratic strength in the 1840s. Whig John F. Darby won the mayoral elections of 1836 and 1837 with about 80% of the vote in each contest. Darby was followed by another Whig—William Carr Lane—who took the 1838 and 1839 races with 57.6% and 54%, respectively, of the vote. In all of these races, Lane's and Darby's opponents were dissident Whigs. Darby then returned to carry the 1840 mayoral election with 58.7% of the ballots against primarily Democratic opposition (James T. Purdy), and Whig John D. Dagget followed the next year with a 56.3% victory over Democratic and Independent Whig opponents. During this same period the Whigs recorded victories in St. Louis County in various contests in which the city residents cast almost half of the vote. These included wins for the Harrison presidential electors in 1836 (55.3%) and 1840 (57.3%), victories in the 1838 (62.9%) and 1840 (59.4%) congresssional elections, and Whig control of the county delegation in the state legislature in 1840.[98]

Between 1842 and 1849 the Whigs of St. Louis fell upon evil times. The major reasons for this shift were divisions within the Whig ranks and the emergence of the Workingmen's and nativist political movements. Democrat George Maguire, for instance, won the 1842 mayoral contest over three oponents with 42.1% of the vote, and the next year John M. Wimer, running for mayor with the Democratic and Workingmen's nominations, managed to accumulate a majority of slightly over 100 votes over Whig ex-mayor John Darby. In 1844, when the Whigs were united and faced only Democratic opposition, their mayoral candidate, Bernard Pratte, garnered 54.4% of the vote, and they also elected the other city officers and thirteen of the eighteen members of the city council. It might also be noted, however, that in 1842 the Missouri legislature changed the voting procedures in St. Louis from a three-day *vive voce* election to a one-day contest using paper ballots. It is possible that this shift may have, at least temporarily, diminished the influence of Whig leaders on working-class voters at the very time that the Workingmen's party became active. One immediate effect was a tremendous increase in voter participation—the total vote cast in the 1844 mayoral election (4,154) was 85% greater than that polled in 1841 (2,345). Certainly the Workingmen—though disavowing connection with either major party—would appear to have given their votes primarily to the Whigs in 1841 (as was the more common practice in other cities). But in 1842 and 1843—enticed by some Democratic support for legislation establishing a mechanic's lien law, offended by merchants' hostility toward their demands in a period of mild depression, and, perhaps, emboldened by the protection granted by the use of paper ballots—the Workingmen's support would appear to have gone primarily to the Democrats.[99]

After 1843 the Workingmen's party faded from the political scene and, as has been noted, the Whigs reasserted their dominance in 1844. But in 1845 the slumbering nativist movement threw both Whigs and Democrats into confusion. Since nativist sentiment was well established and growing, the Democrats thought to capture this segment and gain political ascendancy in St. Louis. Abandoning an active role in the campaign, they threw their support to nativist mayoral candidate Peter G. Camden. This ploy proved unsuccessful, for Pratte won reelection on the Whig ticket with 48.1% of the vote to Camden's 45%, as the token Democratic candidate polled only 326 votes. But the more normal (and usual) course was for the Whigs (Camden was himself a Whig) to adopt the nativist rhetoric and program (and, in some cases, name); and just such coalescing obviously took place in 1845 and 1846. The Native Americans elected four of the six delegates to the constitutional convention in 1845; the Whig candidate (with no Native support) for Congress (to replace Sterling Price, who resigned) took 64.2% of the St. Louis vote in 1846; and Camden (still runnung as a Native American) defeated Democrat Samuel Hawken by 332 votes out of a total of 4,958 cast in the 1846 mayoral race.[100]

At least in the short run, this maneuver proved disastrous to the Whigs, probably because of the extensive native Catholic population in the city and, more significantly, the large and growing German element, not by any means all of whom were initially attached to the Democratic party. These circumstances led to a refusal on the part of a substantial number of Whigs to cooperate with the Natives and some accretion of uncommitted voters to the Democrats. In 1847, 1848, and 1849 the Democrats swept everything before them. In 1847 it was because of the breakdown of the Whig–Native American coalition. Democrat Bryan Mullanphy took 46.8% of the vote to defeat nativist William Campbell (34.9%) and Whig James H. Lucas (18.3%) in the mayoral race. Similar splits enabled the Democrats to carry four-fifths of the city council. And in the county recorder's race the city vote split 36.7% Democratic, 35.5% nativist, and 27.7% Whig. The Whigs frantically jettisoned their overt nativism, but for two more years the Democrats could actually command a majority in St. Louis. Democrats John M. Krum (54.9%) and James G. Barry (51.1%) defeated the Whig candidates in head-to-head mayoral races in 1848 and 1849; the Democrats' gubernatorial candidate rolled up a 346-vote margin in St. Louis in 1848; and the Cass presidential electors eked out a narrow victory (4,175 to 4,170) over the Taylor electors in 1848. But the epithet *nativist* (which the Democratic *St. Louis Daily Union* used against Whig mayoral candidate Joseph Festen in 1849) soon wore thin, and the normal Whig majorities reasserted themselves at the end of the half century as Whig Luther M. Kennett garnered comfortable majorities (54.9%, 54.6%, and 53.8%) in the mayoral races of 1850, 1851, and 1852.[101] Throughout the 1840s the central wards (the third and fourth), which normally cast 40% or more of the city vote, were the most solidly Whig, while the two southernmost wards (the first and second) were more variable. St. Louis' wards, incidentally, were divided by straight lines stretching from the Mississippi River to the western boundary of the city.[102]

In the remaining seven cities the Whigs were overwhelmingly dominant. In five of these cities—Boston, Louisville, Philadelphia, Providence, and Washington—the Whigs were so overpowering as to almost totally exclude the opposition parties from the victory column. Election data were collected and analyzed for a total of 142 electoral contests in these cities between 1836 and 1850. The Whigs were victorious in 137 of these. In no case did non-Whig candidates or slates obtain a citywide majority, though the Democrats did take plurality victories in Louisville in the 1841 mayoral race (46.5%) and in the 1849 legislative elections (36.8%), when the Whigs were split. Two additional Louisville races were not contested on party grounds. These were for the choice of delegates to the constitutional convention in 1849 and the approval of the new constitution in 1850. In the first of these the bipartisan proslavery slate defeated the bipartisan "emancipationist" ticket, with 54.3% of the vote. The proslavery slate contained two Whigs and one Democrat, but was probably supported by a larger percentage of the Democratic than the Whig voters. A careful analysis of the partisan, nonpartisan, and partially partisan votes cast in 1849 suggests that "emancipationist" candidates were supported by about one-fifth of the Democrats and two-fifths of the Whigs, but the success of the proslavery ticket of convention delegates could certainly not be viewed as a victory by either party. The second of the Louisville nonpartisan contests was the ratification election for the new (proslavery) constitution, on which there was no clear division of party opinion and which by no means turned wholly on the "emancipationist"/proslavery issue. The other non-Whig plurality was the second trial in the Boston mayoral race in 1844. In this instance nativist Thomas A. Davis garnered 39.4% of the vote against Whig (37.2%) and Democratic (22.5%) candidates.[103]

In Boston the Whig majority was greater than 60% in two-fifths of the elections examined, was reduced to a plurality only in the first trial in the three-way race for mayor in 1844, never otherwise dropped below 53%, and reached a high of 81.2% in the 1849 mayoral contest. The Whig share of the vote was not adversely affected by the presence of Free Soil candidates on the ballot, suggesting that the Native Americans in Boston drew primarily from the Whigs and the Free Soilers predominantly from the Democratic ranks. In Providence, too, similar situations prevailed; the Whig percentage exceeded 60% two-thirds of the time. The highest figure in a contested election was 90.8% in the 1850 mayoral race, when the Democrats mounted no opposition (but there were five elections in which there was *no* organized opposition); and the Whig share of the vote was below 53% only in the 1845 gubernatorial election, in the aftermath of the Dorr Rebellion. Whig dominance was not quite so pronounced in Louisville, where the Whig share of the vote exceeded 60% in only one-third of the elections that that party won and dropped to a plurality in the three-way legislative race of 1847 and the five-candidate mayoral contest of 1850. In Philadelphia during this period the Whig candidates polled over 60% of the vote half of the time, but, on the other hand, in one-quarter of the elections examined the Whigs could only muster a plurality victory. With a single exception these cases occurred in 1844, 1845, and 1846, when a nativist candidate was in the field. Finally, the nine mayoral or council contests examined in Washington included two plurality victories in multicandidate races (1844 and 1845), two unopposed victories, two races with Whig votes of over 60%, two contests (each involving three candidates) in which the Whig nominee polled between 55% and 57% of the vote, and one in which the vote data are not available (although the Whigs carried twenty-two of the twenty-four council seats).[104]

In Boston only the second ward—in the extreme northeastern section of the city, including the wharf area north of the market—consistently returned Democratic majorities during these years (1836–1850). Up until the mid-1840s the Democrats also ran well in two other north end wards—the first and third— opposite Charlestown and the eleventh and twelfth wards on the Neck and in South Boston; on rare occasions they carried one or two of these wards. But by the end of the 1840s the Democrats could count on only the second ward, and that last stronghold disappeared in the extensive redrawing of ward boundaries associated with the restriction of the second ward to East Boston (Noddle's Island) alone. In Providence only the extreme northeastern first ward was Democratic, though that party ran well in the sixth ward in the southwest and in a very few instances carried it. Only Philadephia's Upper Delaware ward in the far northeast, adjacent to Northern Liberties, returned Democratic majorities in that city. In Washington the opposition in the few elections that took place consisted so frequently of other Whigs or persons not identifiable by party that it is difficult to speak with authority about the geographic distribution of party strength. It would appear, however, that the Democrats had hopes of carrying only the lightly populated eastern sixth ward, lying mostly east of Eight Street, East. The situation in the fifth of these solidly Whig cities—Louisville—was a bit more complex. Louisville, like St. Louis, had long, thin wards running from the river to the city boundaries, cutting, in some measure, across the socioeconomic zones in the city. But at both ends of the city, which clung to the riverbank, the wards became more homogeneous—and as a rule, less affluent. Throughout this period the Democrats tended to be strongest in the east and west wards while the Whigs dominated the central area. With the popular James Guthrie as their candidate in 1839, the Democrats actually carried the fifth and sixth wards at the western end of the city. In the 1840s the Democrats also began to demonstrate strength in the far eastern wards (the first and second). With the changes in ward lines, the pattern emerged in which the Democrats frequently carried the first and eighth wards and usually ran well in the second and seventh as well. As the pork-packing houses, concentrated along the Beargrass Creek channel in the east end, increased in number and attracted more and more workers (including many immigrants) to their vicinity, the first ward became a Democratic preserve (with a majority frequently exceeding 60% and occasionally surpassing 70%), and the second ward, with some delay, followed at the end of the decade. Moreover, the Democrats remained competitive in the west end eighth ward, consistently carrying it by small margins in the last half of the 1840s.[105]

Thus, overall, the Whigs dominated the central areas of the cities, where the most affluent segments of the urban population tended to live and work. The Democrats, on the other hand, were strongest in the peripheral sections, where land values were lower, houses were smaller, and industrial activity was frequently concentrated.

The last two cities to be examined—Albany and Pittsburgh—were also strongly Whig in their political orientations, but the Democrats did manage to take an occasional victory, and the quantitative level of Whig support was, as might be expected, lower than in the five cities just discussed. Albany is almost a textbook example of such a situation. Data on twenty-six electoral contests in Albany between 1836 and 1850 have been collected and analyzed. In twenty-two of these the Whigs were victorious by any definition, winning the office or a majority of the offices at stake and taking a majority of the popular vote. In one instance—the 1845 council election—the Whigs were outpolled by the Democrats, 51.7% to 48.3%, but still took eleven of the twenty council seats because the winners were determined by the vote in each ward. In the case of one mayoral race, also in 1845, the Democrats eked out a narrow plurality—48.9% to the Whigs' 48.3%—as Native and Abolitionist candidates took 2.7% of the vote. And in the 1836 gubernatorial contest and the 1842 mayoral race the Democrats mustered clear majorities—53% and 54.1%, respectively. In the remainder of the races the Whigs amassed majorities of the vote but never by really dominating margins. The Whig share of the vote never reached 60% and in only six instances (four of them in 1838 and 1840) was it greater than 55%. In more than two-thirds of the contests the Whig vote was between 50% and 55% and in over a third of the elections was 52% or less.[106]

Through 1840 Albany was divided into five wards, and the Whigs almost always carried the first four. The Democrats could usually muster a small majority in the fifth ward—the northern out ward—and normally ran well (often more than 48%) in the fourth ward at the southeast extremity of the city. Beginning in 1841 the city consisted of ten wards, and the Democrats carried wards one, two, seven, and eight fairly consistently. The first and seventh were the south and north (respectively) out wards, the second was the next river ward to the north of the first, and the eighth the next "back" (west of Ten Broeck Street) ward south of the seventh. Thus, the basic pattern of the 1830s remained unchanged in the 1840s—the Democrats were strongest in the peripheral area and the Whigs most solidly entrenched in the central wards.[107]

In Pittsburgh the situation was considerably more volatile despite a high level of Whig electoral success. Of the twenty-nine races for which data have been analyzed the Whigs won twenty—five times as many as the Democrats. The remaining five elections were won by candidates running under various other labels, and it was this prevelance of what might be called "protest" candidates that contributed significantly to Pittsburgh's political volatility—almost a third of all the contests for which the actual votes have been located were decided by pluralities. In almost 45% of all these races there were three or more contenders before the electorate. This disorder was, at least in part, a result of the individualized nature of earlier Pittsburgh politics and the unnaturally lengthy survival of the Anti-Masonic movement. In 1835–1840 Matthew B. Lowrie and William W. Irwin were the Anti-Masonic candidates for mayor in six elections, all but one of which they lost. In the first Lowrie was defeated by Samuel Pettigrew (51.9%), who ran with both the Democratic and Workingmen's nomination. He and Irwin were then beaten three times in succession by Democrat Jonas R. McClintock. In 1836 McClintock ran as a Democrat, but received a great deal of Whig support and polled 58.7% of the vote. A year later he ran on the "city" ticket, and, although some Whigs openly supported Irwin, it was clear that many still adhered to McClintock, for he certainly could not otherwise have amassed the unbelievable 83.9% of the ballots reported by election officials. In 1838 most of the Whigs had apparently been weaned away from McClintock, who was presented as the "city improvement" candidate, for Irwin's support was much more extensive than earlier and McClintock's victory was much narrower than before (51.8%). In the meantime the city councils had Whig or Whig/Anti-Mason majorities, Harrison electors took 55.6% of the vote in 1836 and carried three of the four wards, and Whig gubernatorial candidate Joseph Ritner carried all four wards in the city in 1838 and garnered 59.2% of the vote. These results, taken together with the apparent unwillingness of McClintock to run as a Democrat, lent considerable credence to John M. Boucher's assertion that there was clearly a Whig (interpreting that term broadly) majority in Pittsburgh throughout these years despite McClintock's successes.[108]

Irwin's last two mayoral campaigns (1839 and 1840) continued to demonstrate the rapidly shifting political alignments in Pittsburgh. In the former year Irwin, running with support from regular Democrats, dissident Whigs, and Anti-Masons, lost his third straight race, this time to Whig (or, perhaps, ex-Whig) William Little, whose nomination by the "Firemen" was engineered by Van Buren (radical) Democrats and supported by conservative Whigs. Little took 55.2% of the vote. The next year saw Irwin (running with Whig and Anti-Masonic backing) finally winning the mayoralty, with almost two-thirds of the ballots, over Democrat John Birmingham, nominated on the "Citizens" ticket. Political fragmentation was again the rule in 1841 when Whig/Anti-Mason James Thompson (also supported by a revived Federalist element!) garnered 47% of the vote to defeat candidates of the Democratic (William McKelvy, 23.2%), Firemen and "Citizens" (William Graham, 24.7%), and Workingmen's (Hammond Marshall, 5.1%) parties. Alexander Hay then won three successive mayoral races by pluralities, first (1842) as a Whig and Anti-Mason against Democratic and "Citizens" and anti-Jacksonian Democratic opposition; then

(1843) as the "Volunteer" nominee over Democratic and Whig/Anti-Masonic candidates, and finally (1844), supported by both "Volunteer" and "Independent" elements in opposition to Democratic and Whig nominees.[109]

The Democrats made a strong, though unsuccessful, run at the mayoralty in 1845 when their candidate, Henry McGraw, polled 42.4% of the vote to Whig/Anti-Mason William Jordan Howard's 43.3%, while two minor candidates split the remaining 14.3%. In recent mayoral contests the Democratic vote had usually been between 32% and 35%, and occasionally less. Building on this momentum, Democrat William Kerr actually won the 1846 race, garnering 49.7% of the vote to incumbent Howard's 46.2%. Howard was doubtless damaged politically by allegations of fraud in the distribution of relief funds after the great fire of 1845, giving "the rich [including his partner] too much, the poor too little." But Kerr's victory was clearly an aberration; the city council was, as usual, heavily Whig.[110]

The Whigs and Anti-Masons rebounded in 1847, however, as Gabriel Adams carried every ward and polled a clear majority (54.2%) to defeat Democrat Andrew McIlwaine (34.3%) for the mayoralty. Two minor candidates, including Alexander Jaynes on the Native and "Citizens" tickets, split the remainder of the vote. The next year the Democrats brought former mayor William Kerr back into the lists and ran a much closer race, losing to Adams by only 46.8% to 44.3%. The Native vote for Samuel Stackhouse rose to almost 9%. In 1849, there was no Native candidate in the mayoral race, though anti-Catholicism and antiforeignism remained strong in the community, and Whig John S. Heron polled 48.9% of the vote over Democrat Calvin Adams (39.6%), Free Soiler Neville B. Craig (5.6%), and two other candidates.[111]

The half century ended with a mayoral election highly unusual, even by Pittsburgh standards. Joseph Barker was a petty Whig officeholder and, more recently, a violent street preacher notable for his denunciations of intemperance, slavery, prostitution, Masons, the economic elite, current political leadership, and, especially, foreigners and Roman Catholics. After numerous minor clashes with the local preservers of order, Barker was arrested in 1849 and charged with and convicted of obstructing the streets, using indecent language in public, and enciting to riot. Fined $250 and sentenced to a year in the county jail, Barker was perceived by many as a martyred reformer and was nominated by the "People's" party for the mayoralty. Meanwhile, a split in Whig ranks moved a number of the leaders of the majority party to approach Democrat John B. Guthrie and ask him to seek the mayor's office as a Whig. Subsequently nominated by the Democrats, he doubtless attracted some Whig support, but Robert McCutcheon was also in the field as the regular Whig/Anti-Masonic candidate. Barker won the election with 40.6% of the vote to 36% for Guthrie and 23.5% for McCutcheon. Released from jail by the sheriff in order to be sworn in as mayor, he was subsequently pardoned by the governor. The contemporary press, doubtless correctly, attributed his election to a combination of religious prejudice, opposition to his perceived mistreatment by local authorities, and a sizeable Whig support.[112]

These very fragmented mayoral races tend partially to obscure the strongly Whig predilection of the Pittsburgh electorate, which was clear in other electoral contests. The Taylor presidential electoral slate, for instance, carried every ward and polled 58.9% of the vote in 1848. In that same year gubernatorial candidate William F. Johnson rolled up a 59.9% majority, while Whig Moses Hampton's 53.3% victory in the congressional election was comfortable if not as pronounced. The next year the Whigs won victories in the races for state senator (52.7%) and sheriff (50.2%). Even in the turbulent year of 1850, when there were four candidates in each of the elections, the Whigs repeated their victories in the congressional (50.1%) and state Senate (49.0%) contests. The Native American vote, incidentally, was less than 6% in each of these latter cases.[113]

Thus, despite some appearance to the contrary, Pittsburgh—like Albany, Boston, Louisville, Philadelphia, Providence, and Washington—was a solidly Whig city. To be sure, the margins were much smaller than in the other Whig cities, the victories frequently being achieved by pluralities. But even so, the Whig candidates often carried all the wards in the city, and the persistant geographic concentration of party strength so obvious in many other cities was much less pronounced in Pittsburgh.

During the heart of the era of the "second American party system" (1836–1850), then, America's major cities were overwhelmingly Whig. Only Charleston (in its own peculiar way) and Baltimore were solidly Democratic, and New York was the only other city of Democratic inclination among these fifteen metropolises. In all of the cities except Charleston (and, to a lesser degree, Pittsburgh) national party alignments were reflected in local elections as well, though sometimes in a less pronounced fashion, as a multiplicity of candidates (some without announced national party affiliation) occasionally entered the electoral lists. There were, of course, political elements other than the Democratic and Whig parties that had an impact upon the political and electoral activities of these cities. The Native American movement attracted considerable support in more than half of these cities, mostly in the 1844–1848 period; and, usually in cooperation with elements of the Whig party, they often captured significant portions of the electorate and were occasionally victorious (e.g., Brooklyn in 1835, New Orleans in 1840, New York and Philadelphia in 1844, St. Louis in 1846, and Pittsburgh in 1850). An antislavery impulse, under various names, also surfaced in each of the northern cities, most extensively between 1844 and 1850. Its primary impact came in 1848 in Boston, Albany, Buffalo, and New York, where it drew its support mostly from the ranks of the Democratic party. Finally, in two cities political division shaped by local controversies—the Nullification/Unionist clash in Charleston and the Law and Order/Dorrite conflict in Providence in the 1840s—reshaped, superseded, subordinated, or supplemented the normal partisan physics of the "second American party system." With very rare exceptions the Democrats were strongest in the outer wards while the Whigs dominated the more centrally located areas. Even in the solidly Democratic city of Baltimore the Whigs held much of the center city.

About urban politics in the first half of the nineteenth century a few observations—basically restatements—can be made in summary. The city electorates clearly were more conservative (in the vague and shifting sense in which that term can be used in American politics) than those in the countryside. In the declining years of the "first American party system" Federalism survived longer (sometimes under other names) in urban areas, and even in heavily Republican western areas one finds a visible Federalist presence in such unlikely towns as Buffalo, Pittsburgh, and Cincinnati. In the transitional period (1815–1835) even some of the urban Jackson support can be seen as anti–Republican-establishment activity and included a fair number of Federalists. It is notable that a good deal of this urban Jacksonian support eroded with the emergence of the bank crisis. The clearest manifestation of political conservatism, of course, was the overwhelming Whig dominance in the urban centers in the era of the "second American party system."

One factor that may have contributed to this strong leaning toward the conservative end of the political spectrum was the pronounced tendency of political conservatives in the United States in the first half of the nineteenth century to be "interventionist" in attitude. That is, they frequently wished governmental bodies or societal organizations to intrude into individual lives or the social fabric for the purpose of "improving" society by restraining the undesirable impulses and appetites of its members—especially its lower classes. Thus, perceiving overindulgence in spirituous liquors (especially by the "working class") to be damaging to society, greater numbers of the persons aligning themselves with the more "conservative" political movements (e.g., the Whig party) than of those connected with "liberal" political organizations (e.g., the Democratic party) would be found engaged in temperance activities and espousing governmental restraints on the sale of liquor in small quantities. Similarly, it was not *just* because foreign-born Catholics (mostly of lower economic status) tended to vote Democratic that many Whigs held nativist opinions—though that partisan tendency confirmed their belief that the immigrants were ignorant and depraved—but also because the Whigs saw them as threats to the British, Protestant society that *was* the United States. Thus, their influences must be restrained if their presence could not be prevented.

The crucial factors, of course, were first, the certainty that many natural impulses of mankind are evil, undesirable, and harmful to society. Second, the belief that these inclinations could be suppressed in individuals by the closely linked influences of education and religion (i.e., Protestant Christianity), especially extending over several generations. Third, the conviction that in the meantime these impulses must be restrained by society as a matter of self-defense.

The key word here is restraint. Urbanites early learned that many things that were wholly acceptable—or at least not harmful—in a rural setting were inconvenient, annoying, or even dangerous in urban areas. Such activities, they quickly realized, must be restrained (i.e., prohibited or regulated) for the common urban good. In a rural setting a slothful householder might allow his chimney to go unswept and endanger only himself and his family. But if a soot-clogged chimney took fire in a densely packed city, hundreds of buildings—residential and commercial—might be destroyed and thousands of lives threatened. Hence, urbanites were, perhaps, much more predisposed than other Americans to embrace the interventionist methodology that was so deeply embedded in antebellum American political conservatism.

It should also be reiterated that it was not just the Whigs whose political strength lay in the center city, whose more affluent residents had more to lose (both of property and political power); the same had also been true, though in not so pronounced a fashion, for the Federalists and the more conservative elements in the transitional period. There were, of course, exceptions—both temporal and geographic—but in general the more "liberal" urban political movements found their strength in the poorer, less settled, more mobile population in the peripheral areas of the cities.

Finally, the diversity of population that has long been the hallmark of the urban condition doubtless contributed to the fragmentation and volatility of urban politics. This was, of course, especially true of the transitional period, but was also observable throughout the half century.

It may be argued that the nature of urban politics not only reflected the peculiarities of the urban condition but also epitomized the continuing search for urban order in an increasingly diverse era.

Chapter 4

Who Governed?

To deal with parties, voters, and elections is to address only the "process" part of the staffing of the city government. But doubtless more important to American urbanites of the first half of the nineteenth century were the "products" of all these activities—in short, who governed?

The first place to look for a part of the answer to this question—and the easiest place by far to find it—is the mayoralty. As has already been noted (see chapter 1) a number of these cities were not chartered until well into the antebellum era and, consequently, had no mayors (or the equivalents) for a portion of the period. During the half century, however, 202 persons—some appointed, some elected by the councils, and most directly elected—occupied the chief executive office in these fifteen cities. Some of these, of course, served on more than one occasion; they held 235 tenancies totaling 576 years.[1]

The average length of a tenancy was 2.45 years and the average length of service, 2.85 years. There were, of course, enormous variations in time of service. In Albany Philip Schuyler Van Rensselaer served nineteen of the twenty-two years between 1799 and 1821, while LeBreton Dorgenois and Paul Bertus, in 1812 and 1838, each served thirty-two days as acting mayor of New Orleans. Although twenty-eight of these chief executives served multiple tenancies— Robert Wharton of Philadelphia served four—lengthy periods of total service were relatively rare. Only seven of these mayors served as many as ten years, while more than ten times as many (seventy-four) served one year or less. In one-third of the fifteen cities—Boston, Brooklyn, Cincinnati, New Orleans, and Providence—multiple tenancies were unknown, while in Philadelphia more than a third of the mayors (six of seventeen) served more than once during this period. In nineteen years of chartered government each, seventeen Buffalo residents and only two citizens of Providence served as their city's chief execu-

Table 4.1
Average Length of Mayoral Service in Fifteen Cities (in Years)

City	Per Individual	Per Tenancy
Providence	9.50	9.50
Cincinnati	7.20	7.20
Louisville	4.71	4.13
Washington	3.77	3.50
New Orleans	3.62	3.62
Baltimore	3.40	2.83
Albany	3.19	2.55
Philadelphia	3.00	2.04
Pittsburgh	2.81	2.65
New York	2.50	2.00
Boston	2.42	2.42
St. Louis	2.15	1.87
Charleston	1.96	1.65
Brooklyn	1.70	1.70
Buffalo	1.12	0.95

tive—an average period of service of less than fourteen months in the former city and nine and half years in the latter. But the average length of service in the individual cities tended to fall much closer to the lower extreme than to the higher. With three exceptions (see Table 4.1) the average length of both individual service and of the extent of tenancy was less than four years—the length of a single term in most twentieth-century cities.

There would appear to have been no obvious reasons why mayoral tenancies varied among these fifteen cities. One might expect that there would be longer average tenancies in cities in which one party had achieved a position of dominance, and in some measure this would seem to be true. In the five cities in which the average mayoral tenancy was greater than 3.0 years, Whig dominance during the second quarter of the century (when the "second American party system" was established) was clearly observable in Cincinnati (where all the tenancies were filled by one National Republican and four Whigs), in Washington (where Whigs filled 86% of the tenancies), and in Louisville (where the figure was 75%, if the three mayors whose political affiliation is undetermined are excluded). In Providence the party connection of neither of the two mayors is known, but it is highly likely that they were Whigs. In the remaining city— New Orleans—Whigs held 60% of the tenancies if the five chief executives with undetermined party connection are excluded—hardly a figure associated with a position of dominance. At the other end of the scale, three of the four cities in which the average length of tenancies was less than 2.0 years showed Whig tenancies by 60% (Buffalo), 53% (St. Louis), and 40% (Brooklyn). The remaining town was Charleston, whose unique political culture makes it difficult to draw any conclusions about party (or factional) dominance. The six cities in the middle range—with average lengths of tenancies between 2.0 and 2.99 years—have party strength figures not much different from cities at the lower end of the scale. At either end of this midrange group, New York (2.0 years) and Baltimore (2.83 years) each had 67% of their mayoral tenancies held by Democrats. The other four cities in this group showed Whig predominances, but at a low level—the figures were 58% for Philadelphia and Boston, 56% for Albany, and 44% for Pittsburgh. Thus, the average political dominance figures were 80% (excluding Providence) for the upper group (3.0 years and greater), 58% for the middle range (2.0–2.99 years), and 51% (excluding Charleston) for the lower group (less than 2.0 years).[2]

But the shorter periods of tenancy did not always—or even usually—result from a change of party control in the mayoral office. There were nineteen replacements of the sitting mayor in Buffalo between 1832 and 1850, but only seven of these (excluding those mayors with undetermined political affiliation) resulted in a change of party control of the office. In Boston only three of eleven shifts between 1822 and 1850 involved party changes, and in some other cities the figures were six of fourteen in St. Louis (1823–1850), six of thirteen in Pittsburgh (1825–1850), three of seven (excluding mayors with unknown party affiliation) in Brooklyn (1834–1850), four of eleven (excluding one mayor of undetermined party inclination) in Philadelphia (1824–1850), and six of twelve (excluding three whose party connection is unknown) in Albany (1825–1850). Among the cities with average lengths of tenancy under 3.0 years only in New York did the connection between mayoral victory and change of party control approach the levels that might have been anticipated, such linkage occurring in nine of fourteen cases in the second quarter of the nineteenth century.

One of the factors contributing to this lack of relationship was the tendency for city elections to attract multiple candidates from the same party (as well as candidates of minor, and often temporary, political groups) long after the parties developed sufficient discipline to insure (usually) that only one candidate was presented for state and national offices. Throughout the entire antebellum period there was a persistent reluctance to concede the relevance of national party issues (or party discipline) to the urban political scene.

As might be expected, most of the mayors in the older or eastern cities were natives of the state in which their towns were located. This was the case for all of the Boston and Providence mayors and roughly two-thirds of those in Pittsburgh (69%) and New York (65%). These latter figure rise to 73% and 87% respectively when the mayors of unknown nativity are excluded.[3] With similar exclusions the figures were 70% for Baltimore, 60% for Brooklyn, 53% in Albany, and 50% in New Orleans, Philadelphia, and Buffalo. In the case of Washington, 62% of the mayors were born in either the District of Columbia, or Maryland, or Virginia, the two states from which the territory making up the District was taken. In each of the two younger western cities of Cincinnati and St. Louis, on the other hand, only a single mayor in this period was born in Ohio and Missouri, respectively; in each case the term began in the mid-1840s.

All in all, well over one-half (81) of the 146 mayors whose nativity has been established were ''native sons'' of the states in which they served as urban executives, and almost half of these (40) were born in the cities they would later administer. Another 51—rather more than a third—were born in other states. Thirty-three (64.7%) of these were born in free states and 18 (35.3%) in slave states. Among these "out-of-staters" 13 were "crossovers"—northern natives serving as mayors of southern cities, and *vice versa*. Ten of these were northern "crossovers" (almost a third of the northern "out-of-staters"), while only a sixth (3) of the southern "crossovers" headed northern towns, and two of these were Delaware natives serving as mayors of Pennsylvania cities. This means that almost a quarter (10 of 44) of the mayors of slave state cities whose nativities have been established were "crossovers," compared to less than 3% (3 of 102) for northern cities.

Almost a ninth (16 of 148) of these mayors were born abroad—7 in England, 4 in Ireland, 3 in France, and 1 each in Scotland and the Virgin Islands. Rather more than a seventh (7 of 46) of the chief executives of southern cities and a little over one-eleventh (9 of 102) of the northern mayors were immigrants.

It would appear that southern cities were likely to have mayors of more diverse nativities—a higher percentage of northern-born "crossovers" and of foreign-born—than was the case among northern city executives. But appearances may be deceiving in this instance because of the very large number of southern mayors (39 of 85) for whom no nativity data have been located. It is entirely possible that these missing mayors would not conform to the nativity patterns observable in the 46 here analyzed.

Of the 202 persons who served as mayors of these cities, occupations have been established for 195. Well over half of all these were merchants (26%) or attorneys (29%). For individual cities the figures ranged from 100% in Providence and Cincinnati to 8% in Washington. In all of the northern cities except Pittsburgh one-half or more of the mayors were lawyers or merchants, as was also the case in St. Louis (67%). In Pittsburgh (44%) and all the southern towns except St. Louis (8% to 47%) the figure was less than a half. Among these cities with half or more of their mayors following these two occupations, attorneys predominated in Albany (38%), Boston (50%), Buffalo (47%), Cincinnati (80%), Philadelphia (41%), and Providence (100%). Merchants were more numerous in Brooklyn (30%) and St. Louis (38%), while there were 30% of each occupation reported among New York's mayors.

Almost a tenth of the cities' executives were artisans or shopkeepers, and another 3% were grocers.[4] Included in this category were such occupations as stonecutter, tanner, locksmith, carpenter, saddler, mason, hatter, tobacconist, baker, druggist, steam engine builder, silversmith, painter, and jeweler. Two-thirds of the cities—all of the slave state cities, but less than one-half of the northern towns—had mayors following these occupations. A quarter or more of the mayors were drawn from these three employments (artisan, shopkeeper, and grocer) in Baltimore (27%), Brooklyn (30%), Louisville (29%), and Pittsburgh (25%). While it is likely that at least some of the mayors following these working-class or typically *petit bourgeois* occupations amassed a fair amount of capital, it is perhaps significant that neither of the two New York mayors in this category—tobacconist Andrew Mickle (1846–1847) and silversmith William V. Brady (1847–1848)—was listed in either of the two 1846 compilations (one contemporary and the other historical) of the wealthy men of New York.[5]

Exactly a third (65 of 195) of the cities' mayors whose occupations are known followed a variety of employments other than those previously mentioned. The eleven physicians served in seven of the cities, constituting an eighth to a ninth of the chief executives in Buffalo, Charleston, and Pittsburgh. But at least two of these—Ebenezer Johnson and Josiah Trowbridge of Buffalo—pursued other activities, probably to the exclusion of their professional pursuits; Johnson was deeply involved in banking and mercantile activities, while Trowbridge managed his extensive landholdings and was the proprietor of the U.S. Hotel. Another eleven were officers or employees of the federal, state, or local governments. More than half of these were mayors of Louisville or New Orleans, where they constituted 43% and 23% of all of the mayors who served during this period; the others were scattered widely, with one each in Charleston, New York, Philadelphia, St. Louis, and Washington. Doubtless several of these had sources of income from other occupations or from capital holdings which they managed. Another eleven mayors were printers, publishers, or editors. Five of these (38.5% of all the city's mayors) headed the government of Washington, among whom were the proprietor and the publisher of the national Whig organ, *The National Intelligencer*, Joseph Gales, Jr., and William W. Seaton. The other six were to be found in Baltimore (Sheppard C. Leakin, editor of the *Baltimore Chronicle and Daily Advertiser*), Boston, Charleston (Henry L. Pinckney, proprietor of the *Charleston Mercury*), New York (James Harper, founder of the Harper and Brothers publishing house), Philadelphia, and Pittsburgh (John M. Snowden, proprietor of the *Mercury*). Of the eight mayors who were engaged in manufacturing, four (including Erastus Corning, president of the Iron Works of Troy) headed the government of Albany, where they made up a quarter of all the chief executives of that city. The other four held office in Baltimore, Louisville, New York (wealthy sugar refiner William F. Havemeyer), and Pittsburgh. Four chief executives—one each in Albany, Baltimore, Buffalo, and Washington—were identified primarily as banking or insurance executives, though a number of other mayors following other occupations were also engaged in these financial enterprises. Nine of the mayors somewhat incongruously followed agricultural occupations, eight Charlestonians (31% of all mayors) as planters and one Brooklyn chief executive (Jeremiah Johnson) as a farmer.

Among the remaining eleven mayors for whom occupational data have been located, three (one each in New Orleans, New York, and Washington) appear to have derived their income primarily from extensive family real estate holdings, and one other (in Brooklyn) was a real estate speculator and broker. Two others (in Philadelphia and Washington) were "entrepreneurs," two (in Boston and Philadelphia) were engaged in literary pursuits, and one each was an architect (Albany), a hotel proprietor (Buffalo), and a street preacher (Pittsburgh).

As might be expected, the mayors of these cities tended to be drawn from the economic elites of their communities. Unfortunately, the necessary data to establish precisely the extent of this elite status are not routinely available for all cities. Nevertheless, some evidence that is at least suggestive might be examined. In 1852 Abner Forbes published *The Rich Men of Massachusetts*, intended to list the most affluent citizens of that state and the extent of their wealth.[6] Of the five mayors of Boston of this era who were still alive, three (Josiah Quincy, Josiah Quincy, Jr., and Samuel A. Eliot) were listed in Forbes' compilation, where they were credited with a total wealth of $1 million dollars. The other two (Charles Wells and James P. Bigelow) were assessed on property valued at $26,000 and $20,500, respectively, in 1850—sums quite modest in comparison to their fellow urban executives—but an analysis of a 5% sample of the 1850 Boston tax list reveals that fewer than two-fifths of the property holders assessed at $6,000 or more owned as much as $20,000 worth of property.[7]

Five years earlier, in 1847, John Lomis and Alfred S. Peace published a similar volume on Brooklyn's economic elite.[8] Nine of the ten men who served as mayor of that city before 1851 were listed in this compendium, though the threshold for inclusion was admittedly much lower than for Forbes' Boston compilation—the wealth of Francis B. Stryker, the current chief executive, was listed as only $10,000, the minimum required for inclusion in the volume. Stryker was, thus, in the bottom 100 or so Brooklynites in the economic elite—but, still, in that elite. The wealth of these nine mayors totaled $525,000, less than the individual wealth of fellow Brooklynite John Rankin. But the important element is inclusion in the local elite, not the relative wealth in that elite in comparison to those of other cities.

The most famous of the "wealthy men" publications were those of Moses Beach. In his 1846 issue[9] Beach included ten of the thirteen living mayors of New York during the period 1800–1850,[10] estimating their (or their firms') combined wealth at $2,200,000. Two of the omitted mayors served after the publication of Beach's compilation.

In other cities the mayoral property holdings were clearly more modest. In Philadelphia, for example, only three of the nine pre-1851 mayors alive at the time of its printing (1846) were listed in the comparable publication for that city, which included persons with estimated estates of $50,000 and up.[11] Moreover, these three just barely made the cutoff, being credited with a combined wealth of $175,000. And in Providence the 1850 tax list showed Thomas A. Burgess (mayor, 1841–1852) with $75,800 in taxable property and the heirs of Samuel W. Bridgham (mayor, 1832–1840) holding property valued at $8,500. Finally, an 1851 list of sixty-two wealthy taxpayers of St. Louis included three of eleven living mayors of that city and the estate of a fourth, recently deceased. The total valuation of the four estates was $853,000.[12]

Another measure of involvement with the urban economic elite was service as an officer or a trustee or director of a bank or insurance company. Since those officers and directors were frequently (but not always) listed in city directories, it is possible to gauge such involvement by the mayors of several of the cities. For instance, between 1813 and 1850 every Albany mayor serving in the first half of the nineteenth century except William Parmalee (1846–1847) held such offices. Usually they served more than one corporation; only Ambrose Spencer (1826–1829), John Keyes Paige (1845–1846), and Franklin Townsend (1850–1851) were connected with a single institution. Twelve of Albany's chief executives, on the other hand, served two or more, with John Townsend, Erastus Corning, and Friend Humphrey being attached to four companies each. Humphrey was a trustee of the Merchants Insurance Company, the Mechanics and Farmers Bank, and the Albany Mutual Insurance Company, and vice president of the Albany Savings Bank.[13] The only one of these cities with a higher rate of mayoral connection with financial institutions was Providence, where both mayors served as directors of multiple institutions—two in the case of Samuel M. Bridgham and four with Thomas M. Burgess as director.[14] In three other cities, also in the northeast, three-fifths of the mayors held such positions— Brooklyn (six of ten), New York (twelve of twenty), and Boston (seven of twelve).[15] These five towns were the only ones examined in which more than one-half of the mayors served as directors, trustees, or executive officers of such financial institutions.

In five of the other cities, however, between two-fifths and one-half of the chief executives held such offices. The proportion was identical for Buffalo and Philadelphia (seven of seventeen), slightly higher for Washington (six of thirteen), and exactly 40% in Cincinnati (two of five) and Baltimore (six of fifteen).[16]

At the lower end of the scale, St. Louis and New Orleans each had thirteen mayors in the first half of the nineteenth century, but only two of the Crescent City's executives and none of those from St. Louis held bank or insurance company directorships or executive positions.[17] The figure for the remaining three cities cluster tightly around three-tenths—five of sixteen in Pittsburgh, eight of twenty-six in Charleston, and two of seven in Louisville.[18]

In seven cities half or more of the mayors who held these positions with financial institutions were connected with more than one such company. As has been indicated, all of the Providence mayors and four-fifths of the affected Albany executives fell into this category. The figures for the other five cities were 75% in New York, 71.43% in Boston, 60.67% in Brooklyn, 57.14% in Buffalo, and 50% in Cincinnati. Mayors in these cities serving four or more institutions (not necesarily simultaneously) were Jonathan Chapman in Boston, Samuel Smith in Brooklyn, Isaac G. Burnet in Cincinnati, and Isaac L. Varian, Walter Browne, Phillip Hone, and Cornelius W. Lawrence in New York. Lawrence was the most active in this area of any mayor, serving as director or president of eight institutions (one bank, two savings banks, and five insurance companies), six of them simultaneously.

Lower levels of multiple engagement were found among the mayors of the other cities—40% in Pittsburgh, one-third each in Baltimore and Washington,

28.57% in Philadelphia, one-quarter in Charleston, and none in New Orleans, Louisville, and, of course, St. Louis.[19] Among the 202 mayors, 87 (43.07%) had some official connection with these financial institutions and 47 of those (54.02%) held positions in multiple companies.

These figures clearly indicate that the mayors were heavily drawn from the economic elite of the urban populations. But it is also clear that the degree to which that was true varied from city to city and, indeed, from region to region. All five of those cities in which more than half of the mayors held offices with banks and insurance companies were located north of the Mason and Dixon line and east of the Hudson and Susquehanna river valleys. Four of the five cities for which the figure was less than one-third were located in the slave area— more specifically, either the lower south or southwest—and the fifth was the trans-Appalachian city of Pittsburgh. In the middle range (40%–50%) were two from the upper southeast, two from the trans-Appalachian north, and Philadelphia.

Thus, by this admittedly crude, but more nearly universally available measure, mayors of the cities in the northeastern section of the country were much more heavily drawn from the urban economic elite than were those of the cities of the south and west.[20] It is tempting to suggest that this regional concentration of higher levels of mayoral participation in financial corporations was a simple reflection of the presence of larger numbers of such institutions in the northeast. But this assumption is not, in every case, correct, and, more significantly, statistical analysis of the correlation between the percentage of mayors holding such positions and the number of banks and insurance companies for whom directors and officers were published in directories yields indices of .3000 for Spearman's rho and .3217 for Pearson's r—both indications of insignificant levels of correlation. There is, additionally, an observable negative relationship between the percentage of mayors holding such offices and the selection of artisans and shopkeepers to the mayoral office. When the cities are rank ordered by percentage of chief executives holding bank and insurance company officers, the top three-fifths of those cities include only one-third of those with artisan/ shopkeeper mayors; the bottom two-fifths of the cities *all* had chief executives who were artisans or shopkeepers. The conclusion seems almost inescapable that southern and western mayors were significantly less likely to be drawn from the narrowest upper segment of the economic elite.

The problems posed by carrying out even a modest analysis of more than 200 urban chief executives—and they are substantial—seem inconsiderable when compared to the difficulties encountered in attempting even the most superficial examination of several thousand members of city councils, town councils, and boards of selectmen and trustees. Even the names of these urban officials are not always discoverable, and any personal characteristics—political, economic, occupational, or other—are, except in rare instances, difficult or, more frequently, impossible to obtain.

For thirteen of these cities (all except New Orleans and Pittsburgh) substantial numbers of councilmen have been identified, and for twelve of the towns (Cincinnati is the exception) the listings are substantially continuous. The listings for eight of the cities begin in 1800, while those for Washington, Albany, Buffalo, and St. Louis commence in 1802, 1812, 1816, and 1823, respectively.[21]

In the thirteen cities a total of 4,416 councilmen were identified. It proved impossible to establish an occupation for 421 of these (9.5% of the whole number). Some were not listed in the city directories; some were listed without occupation or identified as "gentlemen"; and some had names common to a number of other residents (and, where relevant, located in the same ward), making it impossible to establish a relationship between the councilman and an occupation with any acceptable degree of probability. The proportion of those not identified by occupation varied greatly in the different cities, however. In Louisville and Washington, for example, the figures were almost a third (31.22%) and a quarter (22.92%), respectively, while in Charleston the proportion was less than 3% and in Cincinnati just over 5%. In eight (including Charleston and Cincinnati) of thirteen cities the occupationally unidentified amounted to less than 8.5% of the total, and in three others the figures were 10.84%, 11.81%, and 12.63%. These figures, of course, reflect the inadequacy or nonexistence of city directories in some of the cities. In Louisville and Washington, where the figures were highest, the first directories were published in 1832 and 1822, respectively, while the lists of councilmen (or trustees) begin in 1800 and 1802. Consequently, thirty-eight of the first forty-seven trustees listed in Louisville (all before 1820) and forty-eight of the first seventy-nine councilmen in Washington (all before 1811) could not be assigned an occupation, thus accounting for 60% or more of all occupationally unidentifiable councilmen in each city. In six other of these towns the first directories appeared in the second (two), third (three), and fourth (one) decades of the nineteenth century. In four of the five cities with higher than average percentages of councilmen with unknown occupations, the first city directory appeared in the third or fourth decade and an average of twenty-two years after the earliest council listings.

Occupations were at least presumptively located for 3,995 councilmen in these cities;[22] the number ranged from 130 in Louisville to 683 in Boston. For occupational analysis these were grouped into ten categories: mercantile employments; attorneys; grocers;[23] artisans and shopkeepers; physicians; government officials and employees (city, county, state, and federal); editors, printers, and publishers; bank and insurance company officers and employees; manufacturers; and "other."[24] In these thirteen cities the most heavily represented occupational category, by a substantial margin, was artisan and shopkeeper. A total of 1,468—more than a third (36.75%) of the councilmen—followed these occupations. Not only did this category constitute the largest single occupational block in the full universe of thirteen cities, but such individuals also formed an occupational plurality among the councilmen in each of the towns except Philadelphia (33.26%) and Charleston (11.79%). In addition to Charleston, it was only in Buffalo (29.80%) that the proportion of artisans and shopkeepers fell below 30% of the councilmen, and there it still was in the plurality category. In five of the cities artisans and shopkeepers made up 40% or more of the councilmen—Boston (43.78%), Baltimore (41.96%), Providence (41.27%), Cincinnati (40.89%), and New York (40.53%). There was, it will be noted, a certain amount of concentration (60%) of these cities in the northeastern section of the country, but little more than might be expected in a universe in which seven of the thirteen towns were located in that area. The five southern cities in the thirteen—Baltimore, St. Louis (36.94%), Washington (32.72%), Louisville (32.23%), and Charleston—ranked second, sixth, tenth, eleventh and thirteenth in the proportional size of the artisan/shopkeeper component.

The only other occupational group to achieve a plurality in any of the cities was the mercantile segment, which made up more than a third of the councilmen in Charleston (37.59%) and Philadelphia (35.07%). The proportion dropped below a fifth in New York (19.89%), Cincinnati (19.56%), Providence (19.05%), Louisville (15.70%), and Washington (6.69%). In all thirteen cities, just under a quarter (24.23%) of the councilmen followed mercantile pursuits—almost precisely two-thirds of the artisan/shopkeeper figure. The disproportionately low mercantile percentage among the councilmen in New York, Cincinnati, and Providence were, at least in part, the simple obverse of the high (above 40% in every case) figure in the artisan/shopkeeper area. Washington's extraordinarily low mercantile proportion reflects the scarcity of mercantile activity in the nation's capital—the only major city in the country without a significant commercial economic base. In the case of Louisville, the low mercantile figure was probably the product of both a higher level of manufacturing activity in the Falls City and a high level of councilmen for whom no occupation has been established in the early years of the century, when mercantile interests were probably more influential.

The mercantile and artisan/shopkeeper occupational groupings combined accounted for more than three-fifths of the councilmen in eight of the thirteen cities: Boston (71.95%), Philadelphia (68.33%), Baltimore (64.28%), Albany (62.32%), St. Louis (61.71%), Cincinnati (60.45%), New York (60.42%), and Providence (60.32%). The proportion was rather above one-half in Brooklyn (54.34%) and Buffalo (54.30%) and just below that figure in Charleston (49.78%) and Louisville (47.93%). The low outlier was, of course, Washington, where the proportion was only 39.41%.

The third-ranking occupational category, which constituted rather more than a tenth (10.61%) of the councilmen in these cities, was composed of lawyers. The figure was more than twice that large (21.40%) in Charleston. Other cities in which legal practitioners formed more than a tenth of the council members were Philadelphia (14.25%), Buffalo (13.91%), New York (13.07%), and Albany (11.76%), while the figure was a little below that level in Brooklyn (9.25%), Louisville (9.09%), and Boston (9.08%). At the low end of the range were Providence and Washington, with 4.76% each, while Baltimore (8.71%), St. Louis (8.11%), and Cincinnati (7.56%) lay in between.

No other occupational component accounted for as much as 10% of the 3,995 councilmen and in only a few instances did another component exceed a tenth in an individual city. The most notable exception was to be found in Washington, where governmental employees and officials accounted for almost a third (32.34%) of the council occupations. This circumstance, of course, was a direct result of the presence of the federal government in that city, for most (seventy-one of eighty-six) of these people were employees of the government of the United States. Forty-four, for instance, held clerkships in various executive offices and sixteen were congressional employees. Among the councilmen in all these towns only about 5.25% were government employees or officials, and in no other city did the proportion reach as much as one-twelfth.

With considerably less deviation from the norm, three cities recorded a tenth or more of their councilmen as grocers—Providence (13.23%), Buffalo (10.60%), and New York (10.23%)—as compared to 6.06% for the thirteen cities as a whole. In both Providence and New York the mercantile percentages were unusually low, and the high proportion of grocers *may* result from a tendency on the part of directory compilers not to identify grocers engaged in the wholesale trade as merchants or wholesalers. In Buffalo, on the other hand, no such anomaly is observable. In the other ten towns the proportion of grocers among the councilmen ranged from 1.75% in Charleston to 8.0% in Cincinnati.

In two cities—Louisville (13.22%) and Providence (10.05%)—more than a tenth of the council members were engaged in manufacturing. This classification included founders, millers, brewers, distillers, and rectifiers in addition to the directory entries that specify manufacturing. In the remaining towns the figure ranged from 9.01% in St. Louis and 8.0% in Cincinnati to 0.44% in Charleston and 0.37% in Washington. In just over one-half of the cities (seven) the proportion of manufacturers among the councilmen was less than a twentieth.

Finally, the "other" category accounted for more than a tenth of the council members in Brooklyn (15.03%) and Charleston (11.35%). These levels are clearly the result of a decision not to set up an agricultural occupational category, for if the fifteen farmers in Brooklyn and the twenty-three planters in Charleston are removed, the proportion of "others" drops to 6.36% and 1.31%, respectively, the latter the lowest percentage in any of the thirteen cities. Once these adjustments are made the highest remaining "other" proportion is Louisville's 8.26%, which consists of only ten individuals, three of whom were steamboat captains and three others proprietors of hotels or "resorts." In no other town was the proportion as high as one-fifteenth.

In the other three categories, Louisville ranked first in the proportion of physicans (as it did in manufacturing) with 6.61%, and Washington had the highest proportion of bank and insurance officers and employees and of editors, printers, and publishers, with 4.09% each. The lowest levels were 0.53% physicians in

Providence, 0.65% bank and insurance employees in Albany, and *no* editors, printers, and publishers in Brooklyn and Louisville.

The overall analysis of these 3,955 councilmen does, however, leave one question unanswered: in what way, if at all, did the occupational pattern of the councils change over time? To address this question I have created three subsets of the 4,416 councilmen identified for analysis. These consist of all council members serving in each of the cities during the time periods 1816–1820, 1828–1832, and 1840–1844. These three subsets contain 2,061 "nominal" councilmen—that is, councilmen serving in one of the subsets. A number of individuals served in more than one time block, and, since our concern here is with the changing occupational pattern (if any) over time, such persons would be counted in each block in which they served.

The most cursory examination of the data reveals a striking anomaly—in several of the cities the number of councilmen serving in the period 1816–1820 was very small indeed. This is especially notable in those towns that received city charters after 1820 and which were, consequently, governed before that date by boards of trustees or town councils, which tended to be much smaller than the councils authorized by the city charters. When the councils numbered only five, as they did in Brooklyn, Buffalo, and Providence, or seven, as in Louisville, and when individuals tended to serve successive terms, the result was a small number of persons in office during a five-year period—thirteen in Buffalo, eleven in Brooklyn, and nine in Providence, for instance. Comparative analysis by occupation is rendered even more difficult by the high proportion of these early council members whose occupations cannot be determined. Since the comparative figure sought is the proportion of council members following different types of employments, stated as a percent of the number for which occupations are known, the very small number of councilmen with known occupations significantly distorts the analysis. In Louisville, for instance, twenty persons served as trustees between 1816 and 1820, but the employment of only two is known; the statement that 50% of Louisville councilmen in this period were merchants is, thus, grossly misleading when the number of such merchant councilmen is one. Consequently, I have excluded from this analysis all towns in which there were fewer than twenty councilmen whose occupations were known in each of the three time blocks. This left seven cities—Albany, Baltimore, Boston, Charleston, New York, Philadelphia, and Washington. These cities had 351 councilmen with known occupations in 1816–1820, 515 in 1828–1832, and 602 in 1840–1844. The number of "nominal" councilmen whose occupations were known in all three time blocks ranged, among the towns, from 79 in Charleston to 331 in Boston.

Any major shifts in occupational patterns will be seen, obviously, only in the occupations followed by a significant number of councilmen. The changes in the average proportion of physicians serving as councilmen in the seven cities from 0.57% in 1816–1820 to 4.64% in 1828–1832 and 3.53% in 1840–1844 is proportionately large when viewed from the 1816–1820 base, the 1828–1832

figure being more than eight times as large and that in 1840–1844 more than
six times as great. But in the broader context, these shifts are insignificant. In
only three categories—mercantile, artisan/shopkeeper, and attorney—did the average proportion of councilmen in the seven towns consistently exceed a tenth,
and in one other—government employees and officials—the average of the
seven cities exceeded a tenth on one occasion. In a handful of other cases the
figure reached a tenth in individual cities.

By far the most significant shifts came in the mercantile and the artisan/
shopkeeper categories. The average proportion of councilmen engaged in mercantile activities declined by rather more than a third during the period, from
32.39% in 1816–1820 to 23.17% in 1828–1832 and to 21.19% in 1840–1844.
This pattern, though not identical in magnitude, was matched in six of the seven
towns, with Washington being the only exception. In that city, which had a
much smaller proportion of merchants in its councils than any other, the figure
rose from 4.44% to 6.06% to 8.14%, but the actual numbers were only two,
four, and four, respectively. But in the cities where more than three-tenths of
the councilmen had engaged in mercantile pursuits in 1816–1820, the decline
was everywhere apparent. The reduction was more than a quarter in Albany
(from 31.25% to 23.68%), Philadelphia (from 37.33% to 27.54%), and Boston
(from 40.00% to 25.63%), and a little more than one-half in Baltimore (from
33.72% to 16.36%), between 1816–1820 and 1840–1844. The most precipitous
decline was in New York, where the drop was well over two-thirds (from
35.42% to 10.09%). In Charleston the figure fluctuated wildly, from 44.44% in
1816–1820, to 21.43% in 1828–1830, to 37.50% in 1840–1844, but the swings
were exaggerated by the fact that there were fewer councilmen in Charleston
than in any other of the cities.[25]

As the proportion of merchants in the councils of the seven towns declined,
that of artisans and shopkeepers rose, and by about the same ratio. The average
percentage of artisans and shopkeepers increased by a little more than a third,
from 26.67% in 1816–1820 to 32.40% in 1828–1832 and to 35.83% in 1840–
1844. As in the case of the changes in the mercantile component, this shift was
mirrored generally, though not in identical degrees, in almost all of these towns.
Only in Charleston did the proportion of artisans/shopkeepers actually decline;
the drop was almost exactly a quarter, from 11.11% to 10.71% to 8.33%.[26] The
increase in Washington was only about one-fourteenth over the whole period
after a rather erratic fluctuation—from 31.11% in 1816–1820 to 27.27% in
1828–1832 to 33.33% in 1840–1844. In Philadelphia the growth was only a
little greater—by about one-twelfth—and the figures were more volatile, rising
from 24.00% in 1816–1820 to 40.47% in 1828–1832 before declining to 26.09%
in 1840–1844. The growth in Albany was just under a tenth and occurred wholly
at the end of the period, when (in 1840–1844) the proportion of artisans/shop-
keepers rose to 43.42% from the 1828–1832 figure of 38.78%, which represented a small drop from 39.58% in 1816–1820.

In the other three cities the increase was both greater and more consistent. In

Boston the seventy artisans and shopkeepers in 1840–1844 constituted 43.75% of the councilmen and represented an increase of more than one-half over the 28% in 1816–1820. The growth was even greater in Baltimore, where the proportion of artisans and shopkeepers on the council increased by almost two-thirds, from 27.91% in 1816–1820 to 33.23% in 1828–1832 to 46.36% in 1840–1844. But it was in New York, where the proportion of artisans and shopkeepers was greatest among all the cities—49.54% in 1840–1844—that the growth was also most pronounced, with the figures almost doubling from the 1816–1820 level of 25%.

These contrary shifts in the mercantile and artisan/shopkeeper components among council members probably reflect the changes (already discussed in chapter 1) in the property qualifications for voting and office holding, with the decline in such requirements resulting in a lower elite representation (merchants) in the councils and a rise in the number drawn from the "middling sort" (artisans and shopkeepers). It is worth noting that the shift was most dramatic in such cities as New York and Albany, where the modification in suffrage requirements was most pronounced.

The lawyers' component of the councils did not change greatly over the whole period but did fluctuate pronouncedly. The average for the seven cities stood at 10.92% in 1816–1820 and at 11.52% in 1840–1844—a gain of just over one-twentieth. But in 1828–1832 the proportion had risen to 14.85%, a growth of rather more than a third, before declining almost as much to the next time block.

Similar irregularities are to be found in the individual cities. In three, the 1840–1844 proportion of attorneys in the council was lower than that for 1816–1820. The 6.12% figure for Albany in 1828–1832 represented a decline of almost three-fifths from the earlier level of 14.58% but was followed by an increase of more than two-thirds to the 1840–1844 level of 10.53%—a decline of more than a quarter from the 1816–1820 proportion. The fluctuation was even more pronounced in Boston, where the 8% in 1816–1820 was followed by an increase of over one-half to 12.08% and then by a drop of more than seven-twelfths to 5%—three-eighths below the 1816–1820 level. In Philadelphia the shifts were more extreme still. By 1828–1832 the proportion of lawyers in the Quaker City councils had dropped to 8.33%, considerably less than one-half of the 1816–1820 figure of 18.67%. But by the next time period the proportion had increased by almost three-quarters to 14.49%—a figure that was, nevertheless, well over a fifth below the earliest level.

Washington had the lowest proportion of attorneys in its council of any of the seven towns. There had been none in 1816–1820, 6.06% in 1828–1832, and 3.07% in 1840–1844. The volatility seen in the nation's capital was matched in Charleston, where the successive figures were 14.81%, 46.43%, and 25%. Less observable in Baltimore (5.81%, 9.33%, and 7.27%), the variations were scarcely noticeable in New York, where the levels in successive time blocks were 14.84%, 15.63%, and 14.68%.

These patternless shifts were notable in other occupational groupings as well.

In three cities there was an increase in the proportion of grocers in the councils, in four, a decline; and in six of the seven towns the shifts were erratic (i.e., both increases and decreases across the period). And the average of the percentages in the seven cities was almost unchanged in the earliest (5.88%) and the latest (5.73%) periods. The apparent upward movement of six of the seven cities in percentage of physicians in the councils and the growth in the average of the city percentages (from 0.57% to 3.53%) between 1816–1820 and 1840–1844 were alike the result of zero percentgage bases in the six towns in 1816–1820. A similar situation existed in the editor/printer/publisher category. The average of the percentages for the seven cities rose from 0.86% to 2.44% between 1816–1820 and 1840–1844, and the individual city percentages were higher in five of the seven in 1840–1844 than in 1816–1820 and unchanged in the sixth. But four of the cities with increasing percentages and the one that was unchanged all operated from a 0% 1816–1820 base figure. The Philadelphia data are very stable (2.67%, 2.38%, 2.90%) and the high percentage/low gross increase in Washington included volatile shifts (2.22%, 6.06%, 3.70%). The decline of rather more than a quarter in the average percentage of government officials and employees serving as councilmen in the seven towns from 10.62% (1816–1820) to 7.82% (1840–1844) was primarily the product of declines of about 9 percentage points each in the figures in the two cities with the highest proportion of this occupational category in 1816–1820—Albany (from 10.42% to 1.32%) and Washington (from 46.67% to 37.04%). The average percentage of manufacturers on the councils remained essentially unchanged, moving from 3.89% to 3.12% to 3.78% though there was a good deal of erratic fluctuation in the individual cities.

Finally, there was an increase of almost one-half in the average number of councilmen in the "other" occupational category; five towns showed individual increases, some substantial. The Boston proportions went from none in 1816–1820 to 3% in 1828–1832 to 11.25% in 1840–1844; the Albany figures more than quadrupled from 2.05% to 4.08% to 9.21%; and in Philadelphia this category rose from 3.67% in 1816–1820 to 10.14% in 1840–1844, only slightly less than Albany. The growth was slighter in New York, where the 1840–1844 figure (5.50%) was almost four-fifths greater than that for 1816–1820 (3.08%), and in Baltimore, where the increase was less than a twentieth between the second and fifth decades of the nineteenth century (10.47% to 10.91%). There were decreases in Washington—a modest drop of a little less than an eighth (from 8.89% to 7.41%)—and Charleston—a more pronounced decline of rather more than two-fifths (from 22.22% to 12.50%). The Charleston reduction was entirely due to the drop in the number of planters; if the planters were removed from the calculations in both 1816–1820 and 1840–1844 the "other" percentage would be substantially identical. The growth in this category was probably a simple reflection of the increasing economic and employment complexity of urban life as the cities became larger.

There were, as might be expected, very considerable diversities in the years served in the councils by these 4,416 men. A total of six (0.13%), in four cities, served for twenty years or more during the half century. The leader in this area was William Rust, a carver of Philadelphia, who was a member of the Common and Select Councils for a total of twenty-four years in four periods of consecutive service between 1801 and 1829. Baltimore merchant Baltzer Schaeffer, who served two successive periods of nine and thirteen years, respectively, on the First and Second Branches of the council between 1800 and 1838, actually had the same longevity as Rust, if you count his earlier service in 1798 and 1799. Two other Baltimoreans—brick maker Alexander Russell and merchant Henry S. Stouffer—served twenty years (two less than Schaeffer in the 1800–1850 period), each in five separate periods. Russell's service was entirely in the First Branch; Stouffer's in both. The fifth twenty-year veteran was butcher James Gibbons of Albany, who served for nineteen straight years (1816–1834) as alderman and assistant alderman and added a valedictory year in 1837. Boston distiller Ebenezer Oliver served his twenty years entirely as a selectman (1800–1819) before Boston was chartered as a city.

At the other end of the spectrum there were literally hundreds of councilmen who served only for a single year—1,819 in the thirteen cities, 1,690 if Cincinnati is excluded.[27] As a matter of fact, more than two-fifths of all councilmen served for but a single year. There were, however, very great differences among the cities. In Providence the proportion of single-year councilmen was less than three-tenths (29.90%), while in Buffalo the figure was almost double that (58.13%). In five other cities more than two-fifths of the council members served but a single year—St. Louis (53.41%), Brooklyn (46.97%), Albany (44.79%), Louisville (44.44%), and New York (41.20%). Another five cities, on the other hand, had *fewer* than two-fifths of the councilmen with single-year tenancies—Boston (36.06%), Washington (36.39%), Philadelphia (36.44%), Baltimore (37.99%), and Charleston (39.93%).

There were also wide variations by occupation. More than one-half (50.46%) of all physicians who were councilmen in the twelve towns, for instance, served for but a single year. At the other extreme, just barely over a third (33.85%) of the editors, printers, and publishers had one-year tenancies. The proportion of artisans and shopkeepers (40.70%) who served single-year terms was almost exactly the all-occupations figure in all the cities (40.44%) There were five other categories in which the proportion of one-year councilmen exceded the overall percentage—planters and farmers (46.34%), "other" (45.51%), those with unknown occupations (42.79%), attorneys (41.77%), and grocers (41.52%). In four additional occupational groupings the proportion was less than two-fifths—merchants (36.90%), manufacturers (36.90%), government employees and officials (39.00%), and bank and insurance company officers and employees (39.19%).

There were, of course, some very wide variations in individual cities. An analysis of individual city/occupational grouping cells[28] shows seven in which single-year councilmen composed 60% or more of the total and three in which they constituted 20% or less. The two highest-proportion cells were those for

Table 4.2
Average Length of Service by Councilmen, 1800–1850

City	Number of Councilmen	Average Length of Service (years)
Albany	326	2.33
Baltimore	508	2.91
Boston	710	2.59
Brooklyn	198	2.42
Buffalo	160	1.76
Charleston	236	2.23
Louisville	189	2.64
New York	568	2.32
Philadelphia	483	3.20
Providence	203	3.46
St. Louis	249	1.90
Washington	349	3.51

grocers in Buffalo (81.25%) and Brooklyn (72.73%). These were followed by those for unknown occupations in St. Louis (70.37%), Albany physicians (70.00%), Baltimore physicians (61.11%), Louisville "others" (60.00%), and Buffalo artisans and shopkeepers (60.00%). The three with smallest proportion of single-year councilmen were those for Boston editors, printers, and publishers (15.38%), and for Philadelphia manufacturers and Baltimore bank and insurance company officers and employees (18.18% each). Thus, 87.95% of the nonexcluded cells (see note 28) were clustered between the twentieth and the sixtieth percentiles.

It was this great center block, of course, that most heavily influenced the average years of lifetime service of the councilmen in all of the various employment categories in the twelve cities. The average period of service for these 4,179 council members was 2.39 years. This average varied from city to city but rather less than the percentage of single-year terms. The lowest city average was that of Buffalo (1.76 years) and the highest was Washington's 3.51 years (see Table 4.2). One other city—St. Louis (1.90 years)—had an average below two years and two others—Providence (3.46 years) and Philadelphia (3.20 years)—had averages above three years. The other seven cities were rather tightly clustered between 2.23 years (Charleston) and 2.91 years (Baltimore).

The variations among the occupational groupings across the twelve cities were even smaller. The shortest average lifetime service in any occupational category was 2.10 years for physicans, and the longest was 3.70 years for officers and employees of banks and insurance companies. In only one other occupational category did the average exceed three years—editors, printers, and publishers at 3.49 years. The remaining nine categories had averages concentrated between 2.58 years and 2.94 years—eight between 2.50 and 2.73, a spread of less than three months.

There were, naturally, more pronounced variations among individual city/ occupation cells. Among the nonexcluded cells (see note 28, above) there were

Table 4.3
Average Length of Service, in Years, by Councilmen Serving in Three Time Blocks

City	(N)	1816-20	(N)	1828-32	(N)	1840-44
Albany	(55)	3.29	(52)	3.88	(79)	2.57
Baltimore	(92)	6.43	(84)	5.73	(121)	3.55
Boston	(25)	5.92	(155)	3.23	(162)	3.33
Brooklyn	(11)	3.36	(24)	4.58	(52)	3.02
Buffalo	(13)	3.38	(22)	3.37	(41)	1.62
Charleston	(28)	3.82	(29)	3.55	(25)	4.96
Louisville	(20)	5.00	(34)	3.84	(60)	3.53
New York	(53)	4.28	(67)	3.18	(114)	2.14
Philadelphia	(78)	4.68	(91)	4.57	(73)	4.99
Providence	(9)	8.56	(13)	5.62	(68)	4.65
Washington	(61)	5.44	(67)	6.06	(60)	6.63

six with average lifetime service figures in excess of 4 years and two with averages below 1.5 years. The longest average service was 6 years among Providence councilmen of unknown occupation, while manufacturers in the same city ranked second with 4.86 years. Next in order were two Washington occupational groups—editors, printers, and publishers (4.73 years) and bank and insurance officers and employees (4.45 years). These were followed by two groups of grocers in the councils of Philadelphia (4.21 years) and Washington (4.11 years). At the other end of the spectrum were Buffalo grocers (1.19 years) and Albany physicians (1.30 years). There were an additional twenty cells in seven cities with average lifetime service figures below 2 years. Naturally, these low-figure cells were concentrated in the cities with low overall average lifetime service—all four of the included cells in Buffalo and six of the seven in St. Louis.

Analyses of the average years of service in three time blocks (see pp. 150ff) shows a steady decline of about two-sevenths, from 4.97 years for those serving in 1816–1820 to 3.57 years in 1840–1844. Eight of the cities recorded declines in the length of service of council members by margins of a tenth to more than one-half (see Table 4.3). In five cities—Buffalo, New York, Providence, Baltimore, and Boston—the reductions were more than two-fifths; in the first two, one-half or more. Philadelphia, Washington, and Charleston, on the other hand, showed rather more modest increases of one-sixteenth, one-fifth, and a little under three-tenths, respectively.

Like the mayors, the members of the city councils were disproportionately drawn from the economic elite, though to a somewhat lesser degree. Rather more than a sixth of Boston councilmen, an eighth of those from New York, and almost a twelfth of Philadelphia council members were listed in contemporary compilations of wealthy residents as holding property valued at $100,000 or more.[29] But a better indicator of the degree of elite involvement is the broader test of service as officers or directors of financial institutions.[30]

Because of the great diversity in the size of city and town councils and boards

Table 4.4
Councilmen Connected with Financial Institutions

City	N	Percentage Councilmen Who Were Officials of Financial Institutions	Percentage Financial Institution Officials Who Were Councilmen
Albany	7	27.91	33.21
Baltimore	6	24.61	22.85
Boston	5	35.63	23.23
Brooklyn	8	25.76	32.09
Buffalo	5	22.50	40.00
Charleston	8	36.44	22.85
Cincinnati	5	24.47	22.89
Louisville	4	15.34	20.35
New York	5	25.88	11.05
Philadelphia	6	33.95	18.02
Providence	4	48.28	27.08
St. Louis	3	4.02	24.24
Washington	4	14.90	49.53

N = number of directory listings of institutional officers examined (not the number of institutions).

of trustees and the enormous differences in the number of banks and insurance companies in various cities and at different times, it is necessary to employ two different measures of involvement: (1) the percentage of all councilmen in each town with connections to financial institutions, and (2) the percentage of all officials and directors of such institutions who were councilmen. In all thirteen cities one or the other of these measures was greater than 20% and in eight cities both measures exceeded that figure (see Table 4.4). The highest levels of involvement were more than 48% of all Providence councilmen serving as financial institution officials and almost half of the Washington bank and insurance company officials being drawn from among the councilmen. At the other extreme, in St. Louis (where there were very few banks and insurance companies) barely over 4% of the councilmen held offices in these corporations, but almost a quarter of the financial institution officials were councilmen. In New York, on the other hand, such corporations were numerous; fewer than a ninth of the institutional officers were councilmen though more than a quarter of all councilmen held such offices.

An examination of council members' involvement with financial institutions across time revealed no consistent pattern, with the figures for most cities fluctuating both upward and downward. There was a slight upward trend in one city (Louisville) and stronger declines in Baltimore, Brooklyn, and Cincinnati.

These figures clearly indicate that the members of the city councils in the first half of the nineteenth century were disproportionately drawn from, or became attached to, the economic elite in their cities. This is hardly an unexpected conclusion. The analysis of council members' occupations revealed no unskilled (e.g., laborer, seaman) or semiskilled (e.g., wood sawyer, whitewasher) workers, no persons following personal service occupations (e.g., servant, waiter, barber), and almost none directly engaged in transportation-related occupations (e.g., porter, coachman, carter). It is not possible to compare the involvement in financial institutions of council members following a given occupation with all other city residents following the same occupation, but the impression derived from examining more than 4,000 councilmen—a very small percentage of the whole population or of any occupational segment thereof—is that, by any calculation, city council members would be found to be disproportionately connected with the economic elite.

One additional consideration related to urban governmental officials should be addressed. The analyses of the directorships and officers of urban financial institutions has shown that throughout the half century mayors and councilmen continued to be represented in the management of these corporations at levels disproportionate to their numbers. The relationship between government service and membership on these boards of trustees or directors may be more complex than it appears at first glance, however. Early in the century the councillors and executives were almost certainly drawn from the economic elite, which would normally be expected to invest in these institutions and, consequently, to supply them with their officers and directors. But as the occupational elitism of the councils, at least, was disturbed by the impact of declining franchise and office holding property requirements, the level of involvement in the financial institutions was largely unchanged. This circumstance raises the possibility that what was at work was not the politics of deference, as has been so often assumed— that is, that even as the electoral processes became more democratic the enlarged electorate still chose members of the economic elite as mayor and council members—but, rather, that the public financial institutions became more egalitarian in their management in response to the changes in the political process. It may well have been that the ballot box was a source not only of political prominence but also of preferment for financial influence—that the economic as well as the political institutions were affected by the democratization of the era and in a single, interconnected fashion.

Though it is clear that urban elected officials did not constitute a cross section of the electorate (except in regard to race and gender), such limited data as are available would seem to suggest that the voters generally found governmental actions representative of their views. Admittedly, the Boston town meeting did repudiate the council's plan to sell off the land that later became the Public Garden, but, on the other hand, in case after case the electorate approved council decisions (and associated tax levies) to purchase stock in private transportation corporations (see chapter 7). Even if there was no identity of economic, occupational, and social status between the electors and the elected, there would appear to have been an identity of perceived interest—the essence of representative government.

Chapter 5

The City and the Plan

The whole concept of urban planning in antebellum America was far less complex than later; conscious planning really embodied nothing more than sketching out on blank paper the relationship between putative streets and public places and such natural terrain factors as rivers, lakes, and (occasionally) hills. There was, in fact, little recent precedent in the seventeenth and eighteenth centuries for even that minimal advance conceptualization. But settlements in America offered unprecedented opportunities—indeed, almost unavoidable incentives—to envisage streets thrusting across a forested site, as the founders of the colonies strongly urged upon the settlers (sometimes futilely) the necessity of developing towns in the wilderness. Even by the nineteenth century, city planning meant little more than this—if a visitor had asked a native about the city plan of Philadelphia, Charleston, or Boston, he would almost certainly have been handed a city directory which contained a street map of (frequently entitled "A Plan of . . .") the city.

Despite these strong enticements to conceptualize great metropolitan futures for wilderness settlements, fully one-third of the fifteen cities we are here examining bore no discernible trace of significant structural forethought prior to settlement. These towns—Albany, Boston, Brooklyn, New York, and Providence—were those in which the first settlement antedated 1650. In Albany and New York the forts that preceded the establishment of the town proper influenced the form that the streets assumed. By the end of the eighteenth century there was no visible trace of any effect on the plan of Albany of the original Fort Orange, located near Lydius Street. This was hardly surprising, since the fort was almost entirely destroyed by a flood in 1656. The relocation of the fort some third of a mile farther north, however, did establish a container within which the earliest streets developed. Inside that irregular quadrangle—bounded

roughly by the later Steuben, Hudson, and Pearl streets and the Hudson River—
there emerged within the next twenty years the vague outline of what would be
State and Market streets and Maiden Lane. In the next two decades the lines of
fortification were somewhat further extended and a seven-sided (or eight-sided,
if one counts the small fort that by then constituted the western extremity)
enclosure with highly diverse angles emerged, with interior lines which clearly
displayed the street lines that would follow—the pronounced doglegs in Hudson
and Beaver streets (which followed the south wall), the offset and change of
width in Pearl Street as it crossed State Street, and the bowed lines and irregular
open space that would be the hallmark of Market Street (later Broadway) for at
least a century and a half.[1] (Maps follow p. 193.)

Over the next three-quarters of a century the plan of Albany changed hardly
at all. The west and north walls were extended to make better use of terrain
irregularities, and the south wall was somewhat straightened. The extensions did
bring the later Barracks, Division, and Hamilton streets within the laid-out area,
but the basic street lines remained unchanged. Then, in the closing years of the
eighteenth century, a dozen ranges of regular squares were added along the river
in the vacant space south of the built-up area and line after line of rectangular
blocks roughly 230 feet long were projected across the land north of Eighth
Street and between Patroon and Mink streets.[2]

In early New Amsterdam the street lines were determined by the shore lines
in south Manhattan and by the fort established very early on the southern tip of
that island. But while the settlement clustered within the fortification lines in
Beaverwyck (Albany), in New Amsterdam the settlement (and, hence, the developing streets) lay outside the fort. Two lines strongly influencing street development quickly emerged. The lots along both the Hudson and East rivers
were set back from the shore, leaving narrow spaces following the waterlines
on each side of the settlement. These were utilized as roadways and became
later Greenwich (along the Hudson) and Pearl (along the East River) Streets.
The latter of these, conforming to the much more irregular riverbank, established
a curving line that was roughly followed by the streets lying successively back
from the river—later Stone and Mill Streets.

The second influential line was that of the Great Highway (later Broadway),
which ran north-northeast from the fort in a surprisingly straight line through
lower Manhattan. The line of Broadway exerted control in two ways. First, its
importance tended to pull the north-south streets between it and the Hudson
River (e.g., Lumber, Church, and Chapel streets) to its line rather than allowing
them to follow the somewhat more "normal" pattern established by the river
shore and Greenwich Street.

The second effect of Broadway is seen at its southern extremity. The location
of the fort blocked direct access by Broadway to the shore, but such access for
carts and wagons carrying goods between the Great Highway and the early
wharf area in the Strand (Pearl Street) was considered essential for commercial
purposes. This connection was provided by a short street—Marketfield (later

Whitehall)—that passed to the east of the fort and joined the south end of Broadway along a gently curving line. It was clearly regarded as essentially an extension of Broadway and on the contemporary maps (e.g., 1729, 1730, 1755) usually was given no name. This curve through about forty-five degrees was then transmitted to successive north-south streets lying to the east of Broadway—New, Broad, and Smith streets.

Thus the two intersecting curves of the East River shore and the Broadway-Whitehall line created a series of oddly shaped blocks whose sides were almost never parallel. The diversity and irregularity thus produced was doubtless interesting and much later thought charming, but it was hardly ideal from the viewpoint of either merchants or land developers.[3]

In the middle of the seventeenth century (late in the Dutch period) another very influential line was laid down that would introduce very different patterns of development. An east-west wall was erected entirely across lower Manhattan about 1,200 feet north of the fort. This bastion was almost straight and along it developed a street that mirrored that regularity and took its name from the fortification—Wall Street. This street crossed Broadway at a right angle, and these two straight lines and the included angle gave form to the streets farther north, though some variations did exist (notably Maiden Lane and John Street).[4]

As the population moved north of Ann Street, however, the East River line began to assert its influence, bending the north-south King, George, Princes, and Vandewater streets through an arc and to an east-west orientation. The east-west cross streets rotated with this shift until those farthest from the fort (e.g., Roosevelt, St. James, Oliver, and Catherine) reached a north-south position.[5]

In this process, however, Broad/Nassau/Chatham Street had been twisted into Division Street, which reestablished a base for the future expansion of the rectilinear street system. From this point on, New York's streets moved up the length of Manhattan Island in regular rectilinear order, subject only to minor shifts of angle to accommodate preexisting roads.[6]

Three other of these fifteen cities—Boston, Brooklyn, and Providence—were both unplanned and uninfluenced by the presence of early fortifications. In Boston, the oldest and, in the eighteenth century, the largest, of these, there was little discernable pattern in the street development. As late as 1722, despite seven major fires which presented at least theoretical possibilities for widening and straightening public ways, the city's streets remained narrow and crooked. Essentially all of the laid-out area lay east of the Common Street/Tremont Street/Sudbury Street line, and the most notable feature was the line of streets (connected end to end) that followed the shore—Ferry Way/Lyn Street/Ship Street/Fish Street/Ann Street/Dock Square in the North End and Warehouse Lane/Crab Lane/Battery March/Belchers Lane/Flownder [sic] Lane/Sea Street in the South End. Inland from these a few streets paralleled the shore road (e.g., Cow Lane and Belchers Lane), but more commonly the lines diverged in unpredictable directions. The South End was traversed by an off-center roadway—Orange/Newbury/Marlboro/Cornhill—while a somewhat more centrally located Hannover [sic]/Middle/North road cut across the North End. The two did not connect. The winding lanes divided the ground into blocks of all sizes—adjacent blocks in the North End had area ratios of about five to one—and various shapes. The sides were frequently curved, often in opposite directions, and frequently no two sides were parallel. Most blocks had four sides, but three-and five-sided ones were not uncommon and six-sided parcels were not unknown.[7] By 1800 little had changed except that the same types of street layouts had been extended west of the Common/Tremont/Sudbury line, a number of street names had been changed and a few lanes straightened, and the blocks were sometimes further subdivided.[8]

The last of the unplanned towns—Brooklyn and Providence—extended themselves slowly along country lanes. Although a distribution of lots was made in Providence toward the middle of the seventeenth century, the location would appear merely to have followed the line of the Providence River and the Cove. The slow growth of the town left the pattern of occupancy largely unchanged; a century later Providence consisted of thirty-five houses strung out along the later Main Street east of the river, and five others on irregular tracks west of the river.[9] By the beginning of the nineteenth century Benefit Street had become fully established, paralleling Main Street to the east, and the beginnings of another parallel lane (Water Street) along the waterfront west of Main Street could be discerned.[10]

Although the earliest settlers within the later town of Brooklyn (Breuckelen) would appear to have been farmers at Gowanus Bay and Wallabout Bay—both far removed from the town center—the earliest concentrations of settlement were at the ferry and, more importantly, about a mile inland on the road to Flatbush. It was this latter settlement that was given municipal privileges by the Dutch West India Company in 1646. The Flatbush road snaked southeast from the ferry and then south and then southeast again—a line that Fulton Street would later follow almost exactly—to the settlement just beyond Red Hook Lane. By the end of the French and Indian War that settlement, as well as the one at the ferry, had grown, and a smaller settlement farther down the East River had grown up in the vicinity of Philip Livingston's estate and distillery at the foot of what would later be Joralemon Street. In 1760 several street lines had emerged that would persist beyond the middle of the nineteenth century— Fulton Street, Joralemon Street (slightly straightened from the 1760 line), and a then more sharply angled Boerum Street/Atlantic Street line.[11]

The first village map, which the trustees of the newly incorporated village were directed by the 1816 act of incorporation to cause to be prepared, showed the town developed within a crude triangle with the three earlier settlements at the apexes. East of Fulton Street the streets had been, with rare exceptions, laid out in a regular rectilinear pattern, with Poplar, Middagh, Cranberry, Orange, Pineapple, and Clarke marching in regular order from north to south, crossed at right angles by Clinton, Henry, Hicks, Willow, and Columbia streets from east to west.[12]

All of these wholly unplanned towns were founded before the middle of the seventeenth century and put down their roots when there were few town dwellers in the area and growth was slow. Randomness characterized their development, and terrain features and necessary fortifications pushed the streets into odd and twisted shapes.

The next two of these cities, founded in the last half of the seventeenth century, were the first planned towns in the English colonies in North America. One, indeed, was the exemplary planned city. Philadelphia's plan, according to one account, was originally designed to reproduce the form of ancient Babylon, but this concept was found to be too grandiose and was reduced to one-quarter of the size.[13] This conceit is obviously untrue, since no one then (or later) had any reliable knowledge about the plan of that celebrated metropolis. The concept is, however, revealing; this settlement was designed to be the equivalent in the New World to the preeminent urban center of antiquity—a city whose very name evoked visions of power, grandeur, opulence, and, above all, civilization in the midst of barbarism. However far short of that reality Philadelphia may have fallen (and the idea of a Quaker Babylon is admittedly startling!), it did become the model urban center in America. Its planning was spacious to a degree not even remotely approached in any older colonial town and (in its initial version) its streets crossed only at right angles—a circumstance virtually unknown among plans of major cities.

The regularity of the plan was unusual, but not unrelieved; the sizes of the squares created by the intersecting streets varied considerably, with the largest almost two and a quarter time the size of the smallest. The four smaller public squares (later Franklin, Washington, Rittenhouse, and Logan) were equally sized and placed at the corners of a large rectangular space with a more spacious square (Penn) in the center. But the entire rectangle was off center on the plan—one side identical with the north boundary but the other more than two squares removed from the south boundary.

Aside from the general regularity of the plan, there were several other notable features. Although the original drawing had no scale, it seems almost certain that the streets were intended to be unusually wide, and the city was cut into two unequal pairs of quadrants by crossing streets—later High (and then Market) and Broad—each of which would be 100 feet or more wide. Further, the five public squares and two open riverbanks constituted a remarkable assignment of land to nonprivate purposes.[14]

The original plan (as is frequently the case) was subject to some modification. But the remarkable circumstance was that the changes were so few. Any one looking casually at the original drawing and a map of the city in 1775 or even later would instantly recognize the substantial identity of the two documents. The changes that did take place were produced by accommodation to terrain or the demands of the mercantile economy. For instance, the Delaware riverfront (and that of the Schuylkill) were too valuable to expect private capitalists to acquiesce in their designation as public lands; they were occupied, heavily built over, and cut with many small streets. All across the city Penn's spacious squares were cut by alleys and even substantial streets to facilitate more dense occupation. Where the proprietor's plan had shown eight squares from north to south, the stroller down Eighth Street in 1775 would have counted thirteen. This was, on the eve of the Revolution, the extreme western edge of urban development; farther to the east even more extensive subdivision of blocks would have been observable. The contours of the riverbanks also produced some modifications. East of Second Street between Walnut and Pine streets, and lying directly athwart the line of Spruce Street and joined to the Delaware River by a channel, was a cove ("the Dock") which was targeted as the primary initial wharf area for the city. The need to secure adequate access to this mercantile center produced the only crooked street in Philadelphia—the double curved Dock Street following, first, the creek feeding the cove, and then the east side of the Dock, and almost as wide as High Street. As the entire Delaware riverfront was developed and wharves thrust into the river all across the east end of the city and beyond, the Dock was filled in and built over, but Dock Street remained. In addition, First Street angled east slightly north of High Street, diverging from the other north-south streets slightly, as though anticipating the bend in the river that lay north of the city. The Schuylkill riverfront was, in reality, not nearly as straight as indicated on Penn's drawing, and High Street (and adjoining parallel streets) had to be considerably shortened. Thus, the ratio of the length of High Street between Penn Square and the Schuylkill, on the one hand, and the Delaware, on the other, which had been one to one on the original plan, became, on the ground, more nearly two to three. Nevertheless, on the whole, what was surprising was not what was changed, but the extent to which the original plan substantially determined the major aspects of Philadelphia's physical development.[15]

In Charleston the situation differed considerably, in terms of both foresight and scope. There were, in 1673, three settlements in the southern portion of the Carolina proprietors' grant—Charles Town, James Town, and Oyster Point. The latter of these was located at the present site of Charleston. As early as 1692 the proprietary council ordered a concentration of the inhabitants at that point, where the Ashley and Cooper rivers joined, and caused a plan to be prepared for the "New Towne." Acting for the proprietors, Lord Ashley ordered that the city contain at least 120 squares, each of which should measure three hundred feet on each side. No street was to be less than 60 feet wide and the "great street" should be at least 100 feet broad. Lord Ashley, of course, wrote from England; the governor and council in South Carolina took a more modest and more realistic approach. Their plan envisaged a roughly trapezoidal fort enclosing approximately eight city blocks, with the longer side lying along the Cooper riverbank between two tidal creeks of considerable breadth. The "Grand Model," as the plan was known, contained more irregularities than Penn's outline; none of the four sides of the fort were parallel, and the "squares" were alike only in the sense that, with two exceptions, each had four sides.[16]

By 1680 the colonists began to occupy the "New Towne." The settlement was almost wholly contained within the fortified walls until the great Indian defeat of 1717, after which the walls were razed and the initial streets were extended toward, and, eventually, to, the Ashley River. The unconfined settlement began to expand to the southwest and northeast as well. The streets within the old fortification bounds were straightened somewhat, but a number of irregularities remained, especially betwen Tradd and Queen streets east of King Street. The south line of fortification was replaced by Water Street, which retained the wall's alignment and thus cut across the other streets at approximately a forty-five-degree angle. The eventual line of Hasel and Beaufain streets crudely, but by no means precisely, paralleled the north battlements, at roughly a 1,000-foot distance, crossing the north-south streets at about a sixty-degree angle. The old west rampart became the line of Meeting Street. The streets beyond the original fort bounds were more nearly rectilinear, but the originally skewed joining of the east-west streets to Bay (later East Bay) Street transmitted its perturbation, in some measure, across the city, so that right angles at street crossings were the exception, rather than the rule. The primary street line bases were Broad Street for about 4,500 feet north of the southern point and Hasel/Beaufain farther to the north.[17]

The "Grand Model" was clearly much less extensive and the product of much less social concern than was Penn's plan for his "Great Town." It was more like a root from which the city of Charleston grew than a framework of a great city to be filled in piece by piece. The Charleston plan was not, however, without influence on the future development of that city—even its flaws were transmitted in the process of growth. One of the most favorable of its legacies was the creation of three spacious streets, each more than sixty feet wide—Meeting and East Bay streets, which formed the west and east boundaries of the fort, and Broad, which cut through its center. The odd-angled streets and offsetting intersections were less praiseworthy initially, but would later appear picturesque.[18]

Two other of these cities had their foundations laid down in the first half of the eighteenth century—Baltimore and New Orleans. In 1729 certain "inhabitants of Baltimore County" petitioned the Maryland Assembly to establish the town of Baltimore, which that body did in the same year. The proprietors had originally intended to locate the town on the Middle Branch of the Patapsco River, but, the landowner at the selected site, John Moale, declining to sell the property, they settled on the Northwest Branch instead. On the whole, the change was probably for the good, for the "Bason," sheltered by Fells Point, constituted an admirable harbor. The original plat, completed in the same year, was unusual in that the boundaries were highly irregular—shaped rather like a clumsily made flint arrowhead—within which the streets were laid out in rigidly rectilinear fashion. The town was roughly six blocks long (east to west), about two-thirds as wide at the narrowest part (approximately 2,400 by 1,600 feet), and roughly one and a third as wide at the broadest point. The indentations on the north and south sides were created by conformity to the shore of the Basin (on the south) and the old course of Jones's Falls (on the north). The eastern edge abutted Harrison's Marsh. Two of the streets (later Baltimore and Calvert) were sixty-six feet wide and a third (later Charles) almost fifty feet.[19]

In 1732 the colonial legislature created Jones's Town to the northeast of Baltimore, separated from it by Jones's Falls, Harrison's Marsh, and, in the loop of the original course of the falls, Steiger's Meadow. The new town consisted of twenty half-acre lots on either side of a single street (Front Street) paralleling the falls and making about a thirty-degree bend to follow its course. This was cut at a right angle by a single cross street (Gay), which passed over the falls on a bridge and connected with Baltimore Street in that town via a winding causeway across Harrison's Marsh.[20]

Some minor irregularities were thus introduced both east and west of Jones's Falls. To the west the arrowhead shape was reflected in diagonal streets (Uhler's and McClellen's alleys) and by two additional streets (Liberty and North Sharp) running parallel to the latter alley. Additionally, Water Street snaked along the south edge of the original plat, tracing fairly closely the bank of the Basin. Finally, as Harrison's Marsh was filled and built over, the northern ends of Gay, Frederick, and Harrison streets were angled toward each other to accommodate the curve of the old and new courses of Jones's Falls and to channel them across the falls bridge. To the west the angle of the initial street (Short/Front) was transmitted to two (and later four other) additional streets (High and Green).[21]

Nevertheless, the rectilinear pattern initially established (although much cut up by alleys within the original platted area) prevailed with great regularity (though sometimes at altered angles) across the city. Jones's Town was incorporated into Baltimore in 1745, as was the settlement at Fells Point (southeast of Jones's Town) in 1781. In this latter area the rectilinear pattern was broken only by the Queen/Thomas/Fells/George/Pitt streets line following the harbor boundary at the southern tip of the town. By the end of the century the rectilinear pattern of streets had been extended by survey to cover (with rare exceptions) the entire city, including a great deal of land not yet occupied.[22]

New Orleans, founded by Bienville in the spring of 1718 under the auspices of John Law's Mississippi Company, was apparently precisely planned in advance of settlement. A detailed map of 1720 shows four ranges of regular squares along the riverbank, but not conforming to its curving course. In the middle of the riverfront (eastern) range was a public square (the Place d'Armes), and behind it the successive western squares were cut in half by the Rue d'Orleans—the only variation in the size of the squares formed by the uniform crossing of the streets at right angles. Within four years of its foundation New Orleans had (supposedly) 500 inhabitants and was made the capital of the province. As the city grew the same patterns were replicated. By 1728 there were six ranges of squares west of the river with each range an exact replica of the second (the first being different because of the Place d'Armes). The layout remained essentially unchanged when the French departed at the end of the

French and Indian War in 1763, except that the city had been surrounded by rather elaborate fortifications. By the end of the century additional blocks were being laid out south of the city and not yet directly connected to it, but these were still wholly unoccupied at this date.[23]

All nine of these towns were seaport cities—even Albany was served by oceangoing vessels—though Brooklyn's commercial activity was limited. The five founded in the last half of the eighteenth century included four interior river cities and the capital of the new nation. This is hardly surprising, since it was in this period that settlement began in the trans-Appalachian region. Pittsburgh, Cincinnati, Louisville, and St. Louis were all established between the end of the French and Indian War and the drafting of the Constitution of the United States.

Pittsburgh is somewhat like Charleston in being sited on a spit of land between two rivers. In the case of Charleston the rivers formed two convex sides to the triangular site; in Pittsburgh's case the southern (Monongahela) river traced a convex course and the northern (Allegheny), curving in the same fashion, cut a concave bank, shaping the spit into something approximating a rhinoceros horn. The city emerged in a series of halting steps. There were English settlers in the vicinity of Fort Pitt in the early 1760s, but "Pontiac's Rebellion" in 1763 sent a number of them fleeing eastward. Nevertheless, Colonel John Campbell laid out a half dozen small rectangular blocks (four of which he divided into lots) southeast of the fort along the Monongahela. The streets roughly paralleling the shoreline (Water, First, Second, and Third) ran from northwest to southeast and were cut at right angles by Ferry Street, Chancery Lane, and Market Street. This early survey established the baselines which a large number of Pittsburgh's streets would follow; the building sites would later be called the "military lots."[24]

In 1783 the current proprietors—John Penn and John Penn, Jr.—ordered a survey of the town site preparatory to selling off the land. This project was carried out by George Woods and Thomas Vickroy in the following year. They began their detailed survey at the southeast corner of the military lots, acceding to the pleas of the occupants to leave them undisturbed, and extended those earlier short lines to lay out a rectilinear web of streets stretching back from the Monongahela River. These formed a right triangle with Grand Street, to the southeast, and Water Street, to the southwest, as the including sides, each between 1,000 and 1,100 yards long (though not identical in length). The hypotenuse of this triangle was formed by Liberty Street, which, together with Penn Street, were laid out to conform more nearly to the course to the Allegheny River. The original plan of Pittsburgh, then, was roughly triangular, to fit the spit of land between the two rivers. It consisted of two sets of streets roughly oriented to the rivers, with the line of the rectangular plot containing the Allegheny-oriented streets (a little less than a mile long and a furlong wide) crossing the street lines of the larger Monongahela-oriented section at roughly a forty-five-degree angle.[25]

These streets, though surveyed, were by no means actually laid out, nor would be for some years. As late as the end of the eighteenth century Fort Pitt and its moat occupied the western tip of the triangle, four ponds sprawled across the streets on the Monongahela side, and the total population was less than 1,550. The plan, designed to facilitate land sales, thus far outstripped immediate demands for building lots.[26]

Like Pittsburgh, St. Louis owed its origins to the French and Indian War, though in very different circumstances. Unwilling to live under English rule after the French surrendered their claims to the area between the Ohio River and the Great Lakes, Pierre Laclede Linguest moved his trading operations from Fort du Chatres to the present site of St. Louis early in 1764. He laid out the town in the early spring of that year, in the form of a rectangle three by eleven blocks runnning north and south along the west bank of the Mississippi, with two four-by-three block wings slanting to the west at somewhat different angles from the center, following the river line. A battlement ran along three sides (the river marked the fourth) enclosing a plot of land some 5,000 feet long by about 1,200 feet wide at its broadest part. The blocks in this plat were separated by narrow streets—those paralleling the river about thirty feet wide and the cross streets somewhat narrower.[27]

In dividing the ground for occupancy, very few lots smaller than one-quarter of a square were laid off—that is, roughly 150 feet square. This resulted in very scattered construction of houses. By 1804 every square but seven within the original bulwarks was at least partially occupied, but well under twenty buildings (including churches, barns, warehouses, and other nonresidential structures) are known to have existed within those lines. By that date part of a fourth range of squares had been laid out west of the center rectangle and the southern wing.[28]

The Revolutionary era saw the establishment of two towns on the Ohio that developed simultaneously with the initial settlements of the region. Each grew up around the site of a fort, though not within the walls of the fort.

In the case of Louisville, the fort (or, more accurately, forts) served simply as a refuge and had no real permanent existence in the absence of the settlers on their holdings. Colonel George Rogers Clark, acting under authority of the government of Virginia, gathered military supplies and a force of 150 militia at Redstone on the Monongahela River in the spring of 1778 for the purpose of attacking the British settlements in the Illinois country. When Clark set out down the Ohio River in May he was accompanied, despite his opposition, by a number of persons—perhaps a score of families—intending to settle in the Kentucky region. The party landed in late May on Corn Island, a small (forty-three acres), densely forested bit of land close to the south bank of the river and a short distance above the falls (or rapids) of the Ohio. The Indian menace (further fomented by the British) was still very real in 1778; indeed, the attacks of the previous year—the "Year of the Bloody Sevens"—had been so severe as to raise the real possibility of the abandonment of all of the settlements in the Kentucky country. Consequently, as he trained his troops, Clark constructed a log fort (or "station") on Corn Island to house and protect his supplies and personnel, into which were incorporated houses for the settlers (who doubtless did most of the work on the structures). After Clark's success in the Illinois region in the summer of 1778, the settlers (apparently at Clark's instigation) began the building of another log fort (the ''Station-on-Shore'') above the flood plain slightly downstream from the island. To this location the settlers moved in late 1778 and early 1779. In early April of the latter year the court of Kentucky County of Virginia recommended that the residents in each of the settlements should elect trustees ''who shall be invested with authority to lay off such town with regularity.'' This the settlers did within three days of the court's action, and the trustees apparently completed a plat for the town within two weeks.[29]

Of the town as it was laid out in 1779, there were three contemporary plats. Two of these were clearly connected with the distribution by lottery of the lots to the original ''adventurers,'' each drawing a single lot. Both of these maps show a straight east-west street back from the riverbank, corresponding to the later Main Street, along which eighty-eight half-acre lots were laid out between what would later be First and Twelfth streets. Twenty-four other lots were shown between Main Street and the river, stretching as far west as the later Fourteenth Street. The placement of these latter lots would not appear to correspond to any street existing then or later, except for the area between Tenth and Fourteenth streets, where Monroe and Rowan would later be located.[30] A number of these lots would doubtless have been below flood level, and it is quite likely that they did not continue to be occupied and that no street emerged in that area. The third map, which is attributed to George Rogers Clark, was apparently drawn from observation or as a plan for further development and covers a broader area. This is generally accepted as the initial plan of the city of Louisville.[31]

The Clark plat shows a strict rectilinear plan with three east-west streets (corresponding to Main, Market, and Jefferson streets, in order from north to south) with twelve north-south streets cutting them at right angles (corresponding, from east to west, to First through Twelfth streets). The blocks between Main and Jefferson streets were, with two exceptions, divided into eight lots each; four facing each of the east-west streets. No lots were laid out north of Main Street, where the blocks were shown extending to the river and were, thus, of variable depth. The plat ended a half block south of Jefferson Street, and no lots were shown south of that street. There was a substantial parcel of land between Market Street and the south boundary of the plot, between Fifth and Seventh streets, through which Jefferson Street did not run, which was labeled ''Public Ground.'' How far to the south this parcel was intended to extend, and whether the unsubdivided blocks north of Main Street and south of Jefferson Street were also intended to be public as well, is uncertain. Much of the undivided land had to be sold off after the Revolution to secure undisputed title to the distributed lots. In any event, the plan of Louisville is unusual (but not unique) in setting aside ground for public use (undefined) in advance of settlement. The east-west streets were ninety feet wide and the north-south ones, sixty.[32]

The presence of Fort Washington at Cincinnati was even more incidental. The more substantial portion of this area was a part of the John Cleves Symmes patent, which, after some resales, came, by 1788, into the hands of Matthias Denman, Robert Patterson, and Israel Ludlow. In early 1789 Ludlow surveyed and laid out the first section of Cincinnati (then called Losantiville), and some thirty lots were drawn by the settlers who had arrived rather more than a week earlier from Limestone (Maysville), Kentucky, where they had reached an agreement with the proprietors. Ludlow doubtless continued his surveying, for in a very short time a rigorously rectilinear plat existed consisting of nine roughly north-south streets stretching back from the Ohio River across the lower level of the hill (a rise of some 50 feet) in absolutely straight lines. These were cut at right angles by seven cross streets, with one additional cross street between Main and Western Row (the Losantiville Purchase extended as far north as later Liberty Street, about a mile and three-eighths from the river). These streets were probably not plotted until later in the eastern section of the town away from the river, where Fort Washington was erected in the fall of 1789 in the vicinity of Eastern Row (later Broadway) and Third Street. All of these streets were 66 feet wide except the boundary streets—Eastern Row, Northern Row (Seventh), and Western Row—which were initially 33 feet wide. The basic block in Ludlow's plan was 384 feet square and there were few exceptions to the rule—none in the east-west dimensions. The blocks between Front and Water—the streets closest to the river—were only 165 feet from north to south, and those between Water Street and the river were less, but variable because of the irregularity of the riverbank. The blocks between Second and Third streets, where the terrain rose abruptly to the hill, were somewhat deeper than the standard—480 feet. There were no alleys, courts, or diagonal streets in the original plat. There were, however, a couple of parcels of public land; the area along the riverbank south of Front Street between Eastern Row and Main Street was designated as common land and would eventually be the public landing; and the square bounded by Fourth, Fifth, Main, and Walnut streets—rather more than two-tenths of a mile from the river—was also set aside for public purposes.[33]

Just to the east of Fort Washington, in an area later incorporated into the city, Symmes laid out a half dozen blocks at about the same time as Ludlow. Though clearly designed to mesh with the Ludlow survey—the blocks were of quite similar size, though the streets were slightly narrower (sixty feet wide)—the Symmes streets angled more sharply to the northeast to align them more closely to the riverbank, which swung more to the north at that point. These lots were quickly sold off (several to military officers or civilian officials connected with the fort), but the lines drawn by the town charter of 1802 still excluded the area, although the town extended west to Mill Creek, including, consequently, a great deal of unplotted, sparsely occupied area.[34]

The preeminent example of the planned city was, of course, Washington, D.C. A French engineer, Pierre Charles L'Enfant is—quite correctly—given credit for the general conceptualization of the, at this time, innovative plan for the nation's capital. The actual surveying and plotting, however, were done by Andrew Ellicott, assisted by Benjamin Bannaker. There are several things to be noted about the Washington plan. It consisted of two separate and distinct street systems: (1) a rigorously aligned (though the block sizes varied) north-south (1 through 27), east-west (A through W) rectilinear grid, and (2) a network of diagonal avenues named for the states. Secondly, this was not an abstract pattern transferred to the ground (as was the case in Philadelphia) with no consideration of any terrain features except riverbanks and shorelines. Such a process was, in fact, scrupulously avoided from the outset. In a section headed "Observations explanatory of the Plan," printed on an 1800 map of the city, the method of transferring the plan from the drawing board to the ground was specifically (if somewhat murkily) spelled out.

The positions for the different Edifices, and for the several Squares or Areas of different shapes, as they are laid down, were first determined on the most advantageous ground, command the most extensive prospects, and the better susceptible of such improvements, as either use or Ornament may hereafter call for.

... Avenues of direct communication have been devised to connect the separate and most distant Objects with the principal, and to preserve through the whole a reciprocity of sight at the same time. Attention has been paid to the passing of those leading Avenues over the most favorable ground for prospect and convenience.

North and South lines, intersected by others running East and West ... have been so combined as to meet at certain given points with those divergent Avenues, so as to form on the spaces first determined, the different Squares or Areas.[35]

Moreover, these considerations deliberately introduced certain irregularities into the Washington plan. The reference here is not to the creation of a large number of nonrectilinear three-, four-, and five-sided plots produced by the overlaying of the two different street systems. These are inherent in the type of design and would occur regardless of the flexibility or rigidity with which the plan was platted. The city was divided into four unequal quadrants by north-south and east-west lines crossing at the Capitol. The lettered (east-west) streets were arranged in orderly progression north and south of the east-west baseline and the numbered (north-south) streets on either side of the north-south dividing line. These streets varied considerably in width, though they were usually comparatively wide; only one of the forty-four lettered streets (W, south) and six of the fifty-six numbered streets (1/2 and 1, east and west and 4 1/2 and 13 1/2, west) were less than 70 feet wide, and 60% of the streets were 90 feet or more wide. The avenues and North, South, and East Capital streets were all well over 100 feet (usually 160 feet) wide. Very considerable diversity is also to be seen in the distance between the streets (excluding the effects of the diagonal avenues). In the northwest quadrant, for example, the blocks between Thirteenth and Fourteenth streets were three times as wide as those between Eleventh and Twelfth and half again as wide as those between Eighteenth and Nineteenth.

The same ratios existed among the blocks between M and N streets and those between F and G (three times) and N and O (one and a half times). Nor was the pattern replicated in other quadrants; the width of the P–Q street blocks in the northeast was half again as great as the same squares in the southwest, and the width of the Seventh–Eighth street blocks in the northeast was a third larger than that in the northwest. Five-hundred rods north of the east-west baseline was found T Street; the same distance south of that line brought one only to R Street. Nor were the street lines always straight. Not only were H and I streets, northwest, shifted a half block north between Twelfth and Thirteenth steets, to accommodate the later Lafayette Square, but the diagonal avenues sometimes changed direction as they passed through squares and circles. Pennsylvania Avenue, for example, followed three different compass headings on its route from Rock Creek to the Eastern Branch (Anacostia).[36]

Finally, as might be expected, exceptional amounts of land were set aside for public use. In this case, of course, public meant primarily governmental. There were "government reservations" scattered all over the map—to accommodate the Capitol, the presidential mansion, a marine hospital, the Navy Yard, a jail, judicial offices—but the only one that had any possibility of significant use for a park or common purposes was the Mall, lying to the west of the Capitol; and no one had really reached a decision of exactly what use would be made of that area.[37] Thus, by locating governmental facilities at specific points this was the first urban plan in the English colonies or the United States to incorporate the concept of assignment of specific geographical areas to house certain functions. The closest that previous plans had come to this position were the casual assumption that commercial activities would be concentrated in waterfront areas and the occasional designation of some portion of that area as a public landing. In this aspect as well, then, the Washington plan marked a new era in American urban planning.

The last of these fifteen cities for which a plan was developed was Buffalo, New York. By an involved series of transfers in the 1790s a large block of land in western New York (including the site of Buffalo) came into the hands of a group of Dutch capitalists, organized as the Holland Land Company. The agents of the company extinguished (as a practical matter) the Indian title to the land in 1797, and in that same year Theophilus Cazenove, the company's principal agent, employed Joseph Ellicott to survey the area. This Ellicott did, picking a site where Buffalo Creek flowed into Lake Erie as the location of the town. In 1803 and 1804 Ellicott and his assistant, William Peacock, laid out the plan for the village that was designated by the company as New Amsterdam, but which the settlers persisted in calling Buffalo.[38]

Joseph Ellicott probably came as close as any one person could to being personally responsible for the foundation of a city. He not only picked the site and laid out the city plan, he also urged the representatives of the Holland Land Company to acquire the site and apparently induced the Indians to leave it outside the boundaries of their reserved lands. Ellicott had assisted his brother,

Andrew, in surveying and plotting Washington, and the influence of that experience is obvious in his plan for Buffalo, most notably in the use of diagonal avenues converging at open spaces. In the village proper (i.e., excluding the "out lots") the basic street plan is rectilinear within the irregular plot bounded by Chippawa, Oneida, Seneca, and Onondaga streets, Little Buffalo Creek, Van Slaphorst Street, Casenovia and Busti terraces, and the curving New York State reservation line. But within this relatively small area (seven by nine blocks at maximum extent) Ellicott introduced three diagonal avenues cutting boldly across the interior streets, and two others (the "terraces") formed parts of the boundary. There were two open spaces with which these diagonals connected. One was identified as "Public Square" on the plat and was cut from side to side by Delaware Street (north-south) and Casenovia Avenue (east-west) and from corner to corner by Busti (southwest to northeast) and Schimmelpeninck (variously spelled) avenues. Three blocks to the southeast was an unlabeled semicircular protrusion on the west side of Van Slaphorst Avenue (north-south). Schimmelpeninck Avenue, after passing through the Public Square, ran into this semicircle from the northwest, as did Stadnitski Avenue from the west and Vollenhovens Avenue from the southwest. This layout was distinctly reminiscent of the street pattern to the east and southeast of the Capitol grounds in Washington, a similarity further reinforced by the platting of out lot number 104 (sometimes referred to as Ellicott's Reservation) two city blocks wide, stretching more than a mile in length just east of the semicircular space on Van Slaphorst, which invites comparison with the Mall in the nation's capital.[39]

In addition to laying out the village lots, Ellicott also surveyed the "out lots." These were much larger than those in the village, ranging from less than five acres to more than thirty acres (excluding Ellicott's Reservation, which was more than a hundred acres in extent). Ellicott and Peacock laid these out in four fairly distinct segments. One was directly north of the village, where the lots were platted on either side of the extensions of Delaware Street and Van Slaphorst Avenue. A second section, also aligned with the village's rectilinear street plan, lay east of the southern portion of the town, where the east-west streets of Eagle, Swan, and Seneca were extended and lots were laid out along them and also in tiers extending southwest to Big Buffalo Creek. A third group of out lots lay southwest of the village and took their alignment primarily from the diagonal Busti Terrace; the same basic lines were transmitted to a tier of out lots farther to the southwest between Big Buffalo Creek and Lake Erie. The final block of out lots was located east and northeast of the town and took their shifting alignments from the extension of the diagonal Busti Avenue after its passage through the Public Square; from a second diagonal street further to the southeast, Batavia Street, whose lines were not parallel to any other street; and, farther to the south, from the extension of the east-west Eagle Street, thus aligning these last lots with the village's rectilinear grid. The product of this survey was a number of angled lots having the general appearance of segments in a radial spider web.[40]

The result of Joseph Ellicott's labors was a complex and diverse survey of an extensive area (a little less than three miles from southwest to northeast and a mile and seven-eighths along the full extent of Busti Avenue), in which the out lots took their lines much more heavily from the diagonal, radial streets than was true anywhere in Washington. The Buffalo plan, thus, represented a conscious rejection of purely rectilinear patterns by refusing to treat the diagonal streets as merely an overlay.[41]

As we have seen, although two-thirds of the cities were planned in advance of significant settlement, in only three of them—Philadelphia, Washington, and Buffalo—did the plan extend for considerable distances beyond the area that appeared to be needed to accommodate residents in the near future. In the cases of Cincinnati, Louisville, New Orleans, and Pittsburgh the platted areas were certainly greater than was immediately settled, but the plans of none of these were marked by the optimistic spaciousness of the three cities first mentioned.

It was only to be expected that those cities whose plans extended farthest beyond the early settled area should experience the fewest significant changes in their geographic structures. The Washington of 1850, for instance, was, in terms of street lines and public places, very much like the Washington of 1801; that is, the growth that had taken place had resulted primarily in the implementation of, rather than the modification of, the L'Enfant/Ellicott plan. Indeed, by 1851 the map of the nation's capital showed few changes from that of a half century before aside from an expansion of the built-up area and the erection of various public buildings. The few exceptions were the routing of the Chesapeake and Ohio Canal through the lower northwest between Georgetown and the western edge of the Mall; the naming of three previously undesignated avenues— Ohio, Louisiana, and Indiana—between D Street, northwest, and the Mall; the opening of two short diagonal avenues at the east end of the Mall—Maine and Missouri; and the Baltimore railroad snaking in from the northeast. This absence of change, to be sure, was not solely because of the detail and extent (or even excellence) of the original plan. There was really not much of an alternative; the corporation of Washington had not been empowered to alter the plan, and in 1806 Attorney General John Breckenridge gave it as his opinion that the Congress itself lacked that power.[42]

The development in Buffalo differed from that in Washington primarily in the further extension of the bounds of the city, the opening of streets through the out lots, and extensive street name changes. In the old village center there was a strong tendency to abandon the names associated with the Holland Land Company. Busti Avenue became Genesee; Van Slaphorst became Main; Schimmelpeninck, Niagara; Casenovia, Court; Stadnitski, Church; Vollenhoven, Erie; and Casenovia and Busti terraces became Court Terrace. They all retained, however, their basic street lines. As the city grew (overspilling the old New York State reservation lines that hemmed it in to the northwest, for instance) and the out lots were divided, new streets came into existence; but to a remarkable degree they followed the old Ellicott plot baselines. All of the area south of

Eagle Street, for example, took its street lines from Eagle and Main (Van Slaphorst) streets, except for a few irregularities near the southeastern boundary
created by preexisting roads entering from the countryside. To the northwest the
diagonal line of Niagara (Schimmelpeninck) largely prevailed; the pie-shaped
quadrant between Eagle and Main retained the old spider web appearance as
new streets were added; and Delaware and Chippawa streets gave their lines to
the area north of the old village. There were, of course, some irregularities
created as the streets in the various blocks merged and as new streets were
introduced. And as the streets toward the northern and eastern boundaries were
laid out, those bounds, which were accurately aligned with the township lines,
shifted the angles of some of the streets in the northeastern corner of the city.[43]
On the whole, however, the 1803–1804 survey pretty well determined the plan
of the city of Buffalo.

In broad outline, the development of Philadelphia's plan closely conformed
to that of Washington. The basic street layout remained unchanged, primarily
because all available space was taken up by the original plat. To be sure, the
built-up area expanded beyond the northern and southern boundaries of the city,
but, unlike the situation in Buffalo, the city did not (until 1854) expand to
encompass those areas. Instead, the areas outside Philadelphia's boundaries were
organized into separate political entities. Though the north-south streets in the
suburbs of Northern Liberties, Southwark, Moyamensing, and Spring Garden,
almost without exception, were straight-line extensions of Philadelphia's numbered streets, the east-west streets were much more irregular. But within the city
the changes consisted entirely of continuing to split Penn's generous squares
with additional streets and alleys, making more building lots available but leading to greatly increased congestion. Between the Delaware and the Schuylkill
twenty-eight streets crossed or opened onto Spruce Street in 1802, compared to
twenty-one in Penn's original plan; by 1849 the number had risen to forty—
almost twice as many as platted in 1683. The north-south streets presented the
same picture; the number of openings onto Fifth Street increased from sixteen
in 1802 to twenth-six in 1849. The actual subdivisions were even more extensive. Alleys ten or twelve feet wide and diminutive interior squares and courts
appeared and disappeared in rapid sucession; the square bounded by Race, Vine,
Fifth, and Sixth streets had eight such openings in the 1830s and 1840s, and
the same was true of the block enclosed by Ninth, Tenth, Locust, and Spruce
streets.[44]

During the half century the city added only one public square to the four in
Penn's original plan. Several years after the capital was moved to Harrisburg
(1812) the city obtained the old State House and its grounds, which it developed
into Independence Square. In addition, the corporation, between 1812 and 1844,
acquired all of the land to form the initial Fairmont Park, which was opened in
1855.[45]

In broad terms, therefore, the original city plan prevailed absolutely. But a
closer look inside the skeleton of the plan shows a significant erosion of one of

the most important aspects of Penn's vision—a certain spaciousness in the distribution of people and function in the urban environment.

Baltimore, of course, was a different matter entirely. The original plat and subsequent annexations of Old Town and Fells Point and the expansion of the initial plat westward and southward had, by 1800, produced an irregular, sprawling parcel of land surrounding the Basin, or harbor area. The city stretched east and west something less than two miles, and at its greatest extent, rather less than a mile and a half north and south. While there was a sizeable area within the city that was not built over in 1800, it was, nevertheless, apparent that the burgeoning population of Baltimore would quickly overspread these boundaries. Additional segments were added to the city from time to time, but the major enlargement came when, by an act of the state legislature on February 3, 1817, the boundaries of the city were extended to include all of the old "precincts"— areas lying outside the taxing or ordinance authority of the mayor and councils. According to Hezekiah Niles, the Baltimorean who published *Niles' Weekly Register*, the annexation was "against the consent of nine-tenths, perhaps, of the people of both" the city and the precincts, and was politically inspired. In any event, the actions of the Maryland legislature had made Baltimore more than five times as large as before (containing roughly 10,000 acres of land and water), for some four-fifths of which no street plan existed. Recognizing the difficulties that were certain to arise for both the corporation and the landholders from unregulated building throughout the area, the legislature, a little over a year later, as a part of a general charter amendment act, created a commission to survey and plat streets. This arduous task was not completed until 1822, when the commissioners employed one T. Poppleton to prepare and publish a plan of the entire city reflecting the work done by the commissioners. This was the renowned Poppleton Plat, which governed street development in Baltimore for years to come and which, until 1839, could be modified only by action of the state legislature.[46]

It is obvious that the survey took five years not because the commissioners were developing some innovative approach to city planning, but simply because there was a lot of ground to cover. Clearly, the commissioners took their cue from what had already been done. The additions that had been made to Baltimore before 1800, with the exception of Old Town, had emphasized regularity, right angles, and a concern for alignment with preexisting streets. Even the initial Baltimore plat, within its arrowhead shape, had a street layout that was vaguely rectilinear, and the platting of the additions had been much more decidedly so. Fells Point, aside from some irregularity around the harbor area, had a strict gridiron plan that had been extended both to the north (in the area bounded by Hartford, Hampstead, and Chester streets) and westward, south of Old Town. At the other end of the city, everything west of Howard Street and south of Pratt was unrelievedly rectilinear, even as the plan swept around the Basin and eastward to Federal Hill.[47]

In any event, it seems unlikely that the commissioners considered any other alternative. There were, to be sure, seven major roads ending in Baltimore whose routes could not be precisely accommodated by a rigid adherence to rectilinear street patterns and which, thus, introduced diagonal streets into the plat—Washington Turnpike from the southwest; Frederick Road from the west-southwest; Reistertown Turnpike, northwest (Pennsylvania and Cove streets); the Falls Turnpike, north-northwest (Cathedral Street); York Road, north; Harford Road, north-northeast; and Belle Air Road, northeast. But basically, the new portions of the Baltimore plan consisted of blocks of right angle grids. The entire northern and eastern segment of the city was a single grid taking the Fells Point streets (e.g., Market and Baltimore) as bases, cut by the Belle Air, Harford, and York streets diagonals, and bounded on the northwest by Cathedral Street. A second large triangular block of streets took the old western Baltimore grid (e.g., Baltimore and Greene streets) as bases and extended from Cove Street to James Street (one block northwest of Washington Turnpike). The third segment attached to this grid lay directly south of Old Baltimore on the peninsula between the Middle and Main branches of the Patapsco. Interspersed among these three major components were four smaller right angle grids tilted away from the major compass points. Two of these—between Cathedral and Cove streets and southeast of James Street—took their main lines from Pennsylvania Avenue and the Washington Turnpike. The other two lay south of old western Baltimore and along Whetstone Point, and each was tilted about thirty degrees eastward from the north-south lines. As was to be expected, a few irregularities developed, especially at juncture points. Nothing in the way of park or common land was provided for, though there was a "Public Square" designated on earlier maps at Baltimore and Paca streets. The city boundaries on the north, east, and west were to consist of straight spacious avenues 100 feet in breadth.[48]

New Orleans, like Baltimore, began with a relatively small—but larger than was immediately occupied—gridiron plan. Confined by the fortification, the crumbling, overgrown ruins of which still survived at the beginning of the nineteenth century, the New Orleans plan was even more decidedly rectilinear in form. By that date, however, the increasing population had already stimulated the laying out of another section of streets—the later "American" district—upstream (south) from the *Vieux Carré*. This new addition was right angled gridiron in form except for two slanted streets as it approached, but did not touch, the older section. These new north-south streets roughly paralleled the riverbank in that locality. This accretion to the street plan established a pattern that would be followed as the city expanded throughout the first half of the nineteenth century. The 1805 charter of New Orleans drew boundaries for the city that enclosed an enormous block of land (perhaps as much as 400 square miles) on both sides of the river and stretching north to Lake Pontchartrain, and south beyond Lake Cataoucha and east to Lake Borgne. The sheer size of this area—which was subsequently much reduced—militated against any action such as that taken by Baltimore in laying out a plan for the whole city in advance of need. Instead, blocks of streets were laid out as needed in a series of gridiron plans. The streets closest to the river were roughly aligned with the riverbank at that point—the river below the city flowed first north, then northeast, and then east—and the parallel streets lying back from the river and the crossing streets constituted a rectilinear grid of squares with the streets at the edges necessarily angled to achieve a meeting with the adjacent grid. Once the river-aligned baselines were established these were transmitted (with some slight variations) to the new streets added to the "rear" (i.e., away from the river) of the city. Only in the Second (American) Municipality between Felicity and Common streets, was there an intermixture of smaller gridirons. Thus, by shortly after the end of the first half of the nineteenth century, after the annexation of Lafayette, a series of gridiron segments more than two miles deep snaked for more than six miles along the riverfront. Scattered through these districts were a half dozen public places: two—Place d'Armes and Circus Square—in or at the edge of the Vieux Carré, one—Washington Square—in the Third Municipality, and three—Lafayette Square, Annunciation Square, and Tivoli Circle—in the American sector. Of these, only Lafayette Square had been significantly improved by walks and plantings.[49]

Pittsburgh, it will be remembered, had been laid out in two connected grids. Early in the nineteenth century modest additions to the city were made along both rivers. The Monongahela extension replicated the street lines on that side of Pittsburgh except for one curving street that skirted the southern flank of Grants Hill. On the Allegheny side Penn and Liberty streets were turned northward at roughly a thirty-degree angle and became the baselines for a twenty-block grid. The annexation of the Northern Liberties in 1837 led to the transmitting of this grid up the Allegheny River plain to include Lawrenceville, almost two miles northeast of the original boundary. In the other areas east of Pittsburgh the terrain was much more broken, but so strong was the predilection for rectilinear surveys that the primary effect on the street plan was a slight shift of grid angles—a forty-five-degree northern tilt from the Monongahela street pattern in the Grants Hill area and roughly thirty degrees on Ayres Hill—and a few curving streets reflecting the bend in the riverbank or the course of Sykes Run. Throughout the entire half century the only public grounds were those dedicated to such utilitarian purposes as the courthouse and markets.[50]

There are some obvious similarities between the Pittsburgh and the Louisville experiences. Louisville's original plan was more unrelievedly rectilinear than that of Pittsburgh, and both had plats considerably larger than initially needed. Louisville, indeed, had a substantial amount of land unplotted—the so-called five-acre, ten-acre, and twenty-acre lots (the equivalent of Buffalo's out lots) within its original boundaries. The extension of the gridiron was highly likely, and that probability was guaranteed when the Kentucky legislature, in 1818, authorized the trustees to "extend the cross streets" through those lots which lay south of Green Street. Thus, the rectilinear pattern spread south to Prather Street (Broadway), the slightly angled southern edge of the town plat. The proprietors of "Preston's Enlargement," which was annexed to Louisville in 1827, had apparently already laid out at least some streets following the city pattern, and this process was completed after annexation. It would appear that this practice was also followed by other holders of substantial blocks of land east of the city, doubtless anticipating eventual annexation, which was, in part, accomplished in 1828 and 1833. To the south, the jurisdiction of the city (except for purposes of taxation) was extended a half mile beyond Prather in 1833, and that area was annexed three years later. Quite naturally, the existing street plan was extended in this region, except for the Elizabethtown Turnpike and Pope Street, which followed the line of preexisting roads.

On the west, the original town line at Twelfth Street was shifted by the first city charter in 1828 to include the town of Shippingport, northwest of Louisville, and all of the territory south of that town as far as the Shippingport–Salt River Turnpike. Shippingport had its own right-angled street grid already established, and the initial Louisivlle grid was extended due west to fill the area between Main and Prather streets, and some of the land north of Main Street. In the small section running northwest from Twelfth and Main streets (but south of Shippingport) the streets took their lines from two eastern roads—High Street and Portland Avenue—which roughly followed the lines of the Louisville and Portland Canal; this gave the streets in this area a somewhat more irregular (though still primarily rectilinear) pattern. In 1837 Portland, beyond Shipping-port to the northwest, with its separate regular gridiron of streets, tilted slightly from the Louisville grid, was added to the city.

By the early 1850s Louisville's boundaries had been extended to the east to include the newly established Cave Hill Cemetery and the areas to its southwest and northwest. These—aside from the Portland Avenue section, Shippingport, and Portland—were the only parts of the city in which the lines of the original town plat did not prevail. Southwest of the cemetery was a small rectilinear grid lying at a forty-five-degree angle to the older Louisville streets, which took its orientation from the Louisville and Bardstown Turnpike. Northwest of the cemetery—the extension of the northeastern part of the city—was the only truly irregular street layout in Louisville. There the streets took their line roughly from the riverbank but were not always parallel, and frequently right angles at crossings did not prevail.

Thus, with few terrain difficulties to be accommodated or overcome, Louisville's street plan was almost entirely an extension of the original plat. One concept in that plat that did not prevail, however, was the setting aside of public lands. A combination of unfortunate circumstances and routine greed had produced a plan that, by the middle of the nineteenth century, made no provision for public areas except those dedicated to specific uses—the courthouse square, the city graveyard, the public landing, and the marine hospital grounds.[51]

Cincinnati, of course, began its existence as a town with an almost completely rectilinear plan and a good deal of undeveloped land within its boundaries. By the first city charter in 1819 its boundaries were greatly expanded to include all the territory south of Liberty Street and east of Mill Creek—approximately three square miles, much of it undeveloped; in very little of the area contiguous to the city were any streets laid out. Until the middle of the nineteenth century the boundaries of the corporation did not change.

Then, in 1849 and 1850 occurred two annexations, by which Cincinnati's area was doubled, reaching north to McMillan Street and east to the Fulton town line. It might be expected that under these circumstances the regular extension of the original plat lines would be almost automatic, but two other factors, one natural and one man-made, influenced the development of the Cincinnati city plan. Ohio was, of course, one of the many states in which federal lands were surveyed under the terms laid down in the Ordinance of 1786. The land was, consequently, divided into townships and section squares by lines that were carefully aligned with the cardinal points of the compass. The original Cincinnati grid was not so aligned; rather, the streets ran (roughly) from west-southwest to east-northeast and south-southeast to north-northwest. This pattern did prevail between Broadway and Western Row as far north as Liberty Street to the east and Findley Street to the west, with some overlap to the west along John and Smith streets. But west of John Street and north of Liberty between Price and Main streets, the streets took their lines from the section boundary lines.

The other (natural) factor was terrain. Directly to the east of the original plat, 100 to 300 yards back from the river and beyond the earlier Symmes plat, lay a steep hill that threw the streets in this area into considerable disarray, though there were a few rectilinear blocks on either side of the Miami Canal not aligned with either of the major Cincinnati grids. Finally, north of Liberty four parallel streets ran from Main northwest and then west-northwest to the Miami Canal north of Linn Street. This segment was not aligned with any other part of the Cincinnati street plan and appeared to have been shaped partially to conform roughly to (though at some distance from) the bend in the canal and partially to avoid limestone quarries to the northeast.

Late in this period additions were apparently made to the limited public grounds provided for in the Ludlow plat. In the 1840s the council passed ordinances to protect the fence and plantings of "the ground on Eighth Street, between Vine and Elm streets, known as the park" and to prevent the placing of encumbrances on "either of the public squares laid out by James Ferguson" within the block bounded by Vine, Elm, Twelfth, and North Canal streets. These do not appear on the contemporary maps, and Ferguson later gave the latter squares to the lot holders in those blocks when the city refused to accept them as a gift because of the expense of enclosing them. Surely, little evidence of interest in public places appears in the emerging city plan of Cincinnati. This plan does demonstrate the effect of several common influences: precedent (i.e., the expansion of the initial plat lines), terrain difficulties, and the impact of other artificial boundaries. One might even add caprice. But even with the modifications produced by all of these influences, the predominance of the rectilinear conceptualization of city plans is obvious.[52]

In Charleston, as has been noted, the basic street layout in the area south and southeast of Boundary Street and east of the line of Coming Street—that is, almost all of Charleston before 1849 (a slight addition was made in 1822)— was established by 1790. It reproduced both the regularities and the irregularities of the original plan, as modified by the shift of the center line of the peninsula from roughly north-south to approximately northwest-southeast in the vicinity of Beaufain/Hasell streets. The only additions made to Charleston south of Boundary Street were occasioned by the filling of the shallow and swampy area along the east bank of the Ashley River west of Coming Street to the north of Beaufain and Logan. These segments were covered by extensions of the fairly regular grid pattern lying to their east, except for the short parallel diagonal Savage and New streets between Broad and Tradd.

Within the entire plat, as the population grew, larger blocks of land were subdivided by new streets and alleys; between Beaufain and South Battery streets King Street was entered or crossed by thirteen streets in 1790 and by nineteen in 1849. In addition, streets were laid out beyond the city boundary on the northwest—an area denominated Charleston Neck. The main lines for these were the extension of Meeting, King, and St. Phillips streets directly across Boundary. The other northwest-southeast streets on the Neck were roughly (but not precisely) parallel to these, while the cross streets took a greater variety of angles. This area was annexed to the city in December 1849.

Although there frequently seemed to be a shortage of right angles in the Charleston plan and some streets shifted direction in midcourse (e.g., Meeting, King, Coming), straight lines were almost universal. Even East Bay Street pursued its devious path along the Cooper River in a series of straight increments. The only deviations were Church Street's abrupt semicircular path around St. Phillip's Church and the curving course of College and Glere streets between Boundary and Wentworth streets. Only two public spaces emerged—a "Public Square" at Columbus and America streets in the extreme northeast corner of the expanded city, and the Battery on the southern tip of the peninsula, improved as White Point Gardens in the 1830s and 1840s. This latter clearly served as a park and was rare among American cities in that it occupied potentially prime commercial property. Lurking behind the Charleston street plan was the concept of rectilinear organization, but the execution was significantly short of perfect.[53]

The St. Louis of 1804 was somewhat enlarged by the first city charter of 1822. The western boundary was extended by three blocks (to Seventh Street), the southern by two blocks on the river and four at Seventh Street, and the northern by about four blocks. The only really significant shift was that the attenuation of Third and Fourth streets made it possible for Fifth and succeeding streets to follow an almost straight (roughly) north-south course from boundary to boundary, eliminating the angled bow built into the earlier plat. But the rectilinear regularity of development that this change seemed to portend was not to be wholly realized. As the city expanded by additions in 1839 and 1841 from 385 to 2,865 acres, the pattern established in 1822 was quite consistent (though the squares were of varying sizes) between Chouteau and Howard streets west of Fourth Street/Carondelet Avenue in the south and Third Street/Broadway to the north. East of the latter line and north of Hasel Street the longitudinal streets tended to follow the river line, and the crossing streets carved out irregularly shaped blocks. North of Howard Street this riverbank pattern, straightened by First Street (the second street from the river) was replicated to the city's western boundary. South of Chouteau no consistent baselines can be extracted from the eight street grids that filled the area; right angle grids of various orientation were most common, but diagonal crossings were not rare. The western edge of the city was delineated by two straight lines—one south-north and one north-northeast-south-southwest) which met at Chouteau Street. It is clear that a number of streets had been laid out before the area's incorporation into the city. Except for the riverbanks, terrain features appear to have had no influence on the street patterns of St. Louis; the major natural features of the area—the "bluff," Chouteau's Pond, and Mill Creek—were completely ignored by the street surveyors. The developed plan of St. Louis was quite unusual in the number of public reservations that it included. There were two waterfront parks—the "Public Ground" in the south and Exchange Place in the north—and Washington and Carr squares in the central section of the city. Three lay west of the city bounds—Lafayette Park (the largest of the reservations at thirty acres) to the south and St. Louis Place (about half that size) to the north, and the much smaller Gravois Park, which, like Lafayette Park, had been salvaged when the state had authorized the sale of the old commons in 1835. In addition, three developers in the northern area, who had also given Exchange Place to the city, set aside three circles between Eleventh and Twelfth and Benton and Madison streets—Jackson Place for public use, Clinton Place for a school, and Marion Place as a church site. These circles, wholly enclosed within grid squares, were the most unusual aspect of the city plan, which was shaped primarily by a predilection for rectilinear street layout, with considerable turbulence introduced by developers and an occasional rare flash of aesthetic foresight on the part of the political leadership.[54]

It will be remembered that by the time of the first Brooklyn village map in 1816 the town had developed a slightly modified grid street plan west of Fulton Street. This formed the general—but not the specific—pattern for the future development of the city's streets. Within a decade the area east of Fulton and north of Red Hook Lane was filled with an almost unrelievedly rectilinear street pattern aligned with the East River line west of the Navy Yard. The only variations were some slight shifts of angle as the cross streets met Fulton, a couple of streets beside the Navy Yard, and the forty-five-degree angled line of James Street roughly paralleling Fulton between Front and Prospect streets. Within another decade the grid west of Fulton had spread south of State Street and west of Court Street and, with a slight shift of angle, further east to the Gowanus Road. East of Fulton Street that grid was also extended to Flatbush Turnpike.[55]

In 1835, the year after the incorporation of Brooklyn, the state authorized the laying out of streets and squares throughout the city, which now extended to the boundaries of the adjoining towns of Bushwick, Flatbush, and New Utrecht. This task was completed in 1839, and the existing grids were extended in all directions to the boundaries, with some irregularities as the grids merged. There were, as might be expected, a number of preexisting roads that continued in use for a greater or lesser period of time. Also in 1835 landowners in the Wallabout Bay area obtained permission to take earth from Fort Greene and use it to fill the low-lying lands in that region, with the requirement that the proprietors sell land to the city for park purposes. This was done and City Park was created. The Fort Greene site was also converted into Washington Park, though that title had been assigned by the commissioners to a site two blocks to the southwest, not subsequently laid out. Of the eleven public areas shown on the commissioners' 1839 plat, only these two had been developed thirty years later.[56]

By the end of the eighteenth century Albany had overspread the cluster of irregularly aligned streets east of Eagle Street, and two rectilinear strips now stretched out a half mile to the southwest and considerably farther to the northwest. This plat extended far beyond the built-up area, and, perhaps in consequence of this, there had been relatively slight further expansion of the plat by the middle of the nineteenth century. There was essentially no extension to the southwest along the river but a considerable (perhaps a half mile) growth of this grid in the area away from the river. There was also little expansion of the grid northwest along the Washington (earlier, Lion) Street line, but substantial (perhaps a quarter of a mile) expansion of that grid to the southwest. Also new, by midcentury, was the splitting of Washington Street into two turnpikes about two-thirds of a mile from the riverbank. Finally, the irregular street pattern along the riverbank was extended another third of a mile to the northeast, as was the regular grid back from the river. A most notable difference between the plan in 1800 and in 1850 was the creation of five small or medium-sized parks—Clinton Park, on North Pearl Street; Capital and Academy parks, at the lower end of Washington Street; Delaware Park, at Lark at the Delaware Turnpike; and the largest of the five, Washington Square, on Knox between State and Lydius. The "new" plat also far outstripped the population growth, leaving large areas undeveloped.[57]

Before 1800 New York's irregular street pattern, which extended northward from the Battery east of Broadway, had been encapsulated by a series of slightly divergent rectilinear street grids. The outer edge of the built-up area was marked by five such blocks, and contemporary maps showed street lines (in divergent versions) well beyond the settled area. The city already contained the whole of Manhattan Island within its bounds, and in 1807 the state legislature created a commission of three persons, appointed by the governor, to lay out streets in all of the island north of a line from the Hudson River to the East River, via Fitzroy Road, Greenwich Lane, Art Street, Bowery Road, and North Street. On April 1, 1811, John Randel, Jr., who had been employed by the commissioners to execute the survey, filed the requisite map. This new survey was unreservedly rectilinear—taking the grid of the Broadway corridor as its base, but making the individual rectangular blocks run east and west rather than north and south. The only exceptions were the retention of a few preexisting roads. The commissioners justified their reliance on this pattern by observing that the city was and would be "composed principally of habitations of man and that strait [*sic*] sided and right-angled houses are the most cheap to build, and the most convenient to live in." Then Chief Justice of the New York Supreme Court James Kent asssserted that the plan "laid out the highways on the island upon so magnificent a scale, and with so bold a hand, and with such prophetic views, in respect to the future growth and extension of the city, that it will form an everlasting monument of the stability and wisdom of the measure." More than a century later I. N. Phelps Stokes would counter sourly that "as a matter of fact it destroyed most of the natural beauty and interest of the island which, but for the commission of 1807, might have possessed the charm and variety of London"; but contemporary opinion would seem to have been less concerned with "charm and variety" and more with utility and financial reward. It is true that the grid—which ran north to One Hundred Fifty-fifth Street—came under immediate and continuing pressure for change, but the purpose of these changes was not to introduce variety.[58]

The Randel map showed eleven primary longitudinal avenues (five others appeared briefly or intermittently) 100 feet in width with cross streets generally 60 feet wide, though more than a dozen of those were also 100 feet in breadth. In addition, eight parcels of public land appeared on the plat, ranging in size from only a few acres (Union Place) to almost 280 acres (the Parade). Though the commissioners felt compelled to justify the fact that "so few vacant spaces have been left, and those so small" by citing the healthful effects of "those large arms of the sea which embrace Manhattan Island," the city authorities (and the landed proprietors) quickly began to shift significant blocks of land from public to private use. In 1814 the corporation successfully petitioned the state legislature to reduce the largest of these reservations—the Parade (Twenty-fourth Street and Seventh Avenue)—to roughly one-third of its original extent. A decade later the city found the Market Place (Seventh Street and First Avenue) "not an advantageous or convenient position for the purpose contemplated," and secured its return to private owners, together with several small gores of land created by the merging of the old and new street grids at North Street. The same petition complained of the "unnecessary breadth" of Avenues A, B, C, and D, and secured the reduction of the size of these streets from 100 feet to 80 feet, in the first instance, and to 60 feet for the latter three avenues. Another five years saw the elimination of the remnants of the Parade.[59]

The commissioners' plan resulted in the elimination of a great many streets already named and entered on maps before 1807—four ranges of blocks above North Street in the same grid and still more in the next grid to the north, in which the streets were, for the first time, aligned with the central points of the compass. This latter pattern—however logical—was rejected and displaced by the commissioners in favor of an alignment with Broadway, which line was then extended throughout the plan. These streets, however, were not actually laid out on the ground, and the change, in most instances, involved nothing more traumatic than changing one set of lines on a map for another. But the post-Revolutionary and antebellum years also saw a number of actions designed to rationalize the developed street plan farther south on the island—that is, to strive for straighter lines and wider streets. Certainly lower Manhattan offered abundant opportunity for such actions. "The streets of the old part, at the South end of the island," wrote James Hardie in 1827,

> are in general irregular, narrow, crooked, and badly adapted to the comfort of the inhabitants or the elegance of the city. Our Common Council have of late years, done much to obviate these inconveniences, by straightening a number of crooked streets, and widening several that were narrow. The improvements have been attended with heavy expenses; but those who have to pay for them, do not complain, as the value of their property has been greatly enhanced.

Hardie clearly revealed his model when he observed that "the northern part" had been "laid out in a judicious manner . . . by the commissioners." The state legislature provided for the widening of lower John Street in 1793 and Beaver Lane two years later—these streets were slightly more than thirteen feet wide. In the first quarter of the nineteenth century a number of changes were made in the area south of the Park: two Pearl Street intersections were eased by the creation of Franklin and Hanover squares (paved triangles, actually); Beekman Street was extended to the East River; South Street (wide and straight) was laid out along the waterfront; Fulton Street was created from Partition and Fair streets, straightened, widened, and extended to the East River; and Front Street was straightened and Cliff/Jacob/Skinner joined and straightened. During the next two decades Beaver and Cliff streets were further straightened.[60]

Thus, New Yorkers of the first half of the nineteenth century tended to turn their backs on the "aesthetic" aspects (a highly subjective concept) of city planning, whether it was represented by Stokes' nostalgic "charm and variety of London" or the commissioners' modest public places. They favored instead the utilitarian concepts (another subjective characterization) of regularity and economic advantage. This meant that they embraced straight streets, maximum front footage, wide streets in the commercial areas, narrower streets where the sacrifice of marketable land seemed excessive, and open spaces primarily where the immediate economic gain would seem to warrant them. Perhaps the commissioners spoke more wisely than they knew when they observed, "If it should be asked, why was the present plan adopted in preference to any other? the answer is, because after taking all circumstances into consideration, it appeared to be the best; or in other and more proper terms, attended with the least inconvenience."[61]

Providence and Boston not only were established with no prior plan, they also were not chartered as urban corporations until almost 200 years after their founding. The absence of such chartered authority made it difficult, if not impossible, to develop comprehensive plans for these cities. The layouts of the towns, thus, were much more at the mercy of private interests (an influence not absent in other cities). Providence, in particular, appeared to have expanded with little conscious guidance. East of Providence River the filling and development of the riverbank had, early in the nineteenth century, made room for another street—Water—following the riverfront as the earlier Main and Benefit streets to the east generally did; and farther to the east the number of roughly north-south streets within a mile of the "Great Bridge" (Westminster Street) more than doubled (from five to eleven) in the half century. The cross streets—some straight and some crooked and at various angles—grew from seven between Williams and Olney streets in 1803, to twelve in 1823, and to nineteen in 1849. Some vague suggestion of a rectilinear pattern could occasionally be discerned. West of the river even less regularity was to be seen. North of the Cove, streets thrust out wildly in all directions, and the situation was little different south of the Cove. The major streets headed from the southern and western extremities of the town vaguely toward the "Great Bridge" but they frequently joined others short of that goal, changed direction several times, and arrived in the vicinity of the bridge (if at all) at a variety of angles. Broad Street, emerging from Westminster Street two blocks southwest of the bridge, changed direction nine times before reaching the city's southern boundary and, in the process, took a number of headings between south and west. Even when a major street was straight for a considerable distance, it rarely influenced streets alongside. Broadway, beginning about a half mile from the bridge, lay in a straight line for more than a mile, but only for a space of about a quarter of a mile did *any* adjacent street follow a parallel course. From time to time a few streets were found (especially in the outer, underdeveloped areas of the town) that formed a small rectilinear grid, but these were exceptions to the general irregularity. In 1837 Asa Greene referred to the streets of southern Manhattan as "running into and crossing each other at all sorts of angles except a right angle," and that observation was at least as accurate a description of the situation in Providence as of that in New York.[62]

Public lands were not numerous in antebellum Providence. In the years after the incorporation of the city (1832) the east end of the Cove was piled and filled into an oval form and a public walk was built around its edge. This primarily provided space for the railroad station, tracks, and various railway buildings, but it also gave the citizens a pleasant promenade. A major history of the city asserts (apparently correctly) that there was no park development in Providence before the Civil War. It would appear that the public (probably only the "respectable" elements) had access to walks and improved grounds in a park associated with the hospital in the extreme southern portion of the city and that the corporation was associated with this to a limited degree. With this exception, the city of Providence would seem to have given no more attention to public grounds than it did to its street plan.[63]

And then there was Boston—the supreme example of nonplanning, planning by bits and pieces, and the surrender of the planning function to the private sector. However much they might admire its cultural development, acknowledge its political leadership, or envy its financial dominance, no one had anything good to say about the urban plan of New England's preeminent city. Even Providence had a greater semblance of regularity. "The streets are narrow," wrote Carl Arfwedson, in the mid-1830s; "not one can be compared to Broadway in New York. In the old part of the town particularly, there are some so confined and crooked, that it is really impossible to distinguish an object fifty yards ahead." Timothy Dwight, writing from a perspective of four decades earlier, would have agreed:

The streets, if we except a small number, are narrow, crooked, and disagreeable. . . . The streets strike the eye of the traveller as if intended to be mere passages from one neighborhood to another, and not as the open, handsome divisions of a great town; as the result of casualty, and not contrivance.

Nor was this circumstance rendered necessary by physical features, Dwight insisted. "No spot of ground," he observed, "is a happier site for a large city." Indeed, Dwight asserted,

had the main street been carried with a breadth of one hundred and twenty feet from the southern limit to the northern, and accompanied by others running parallel to it, ninety feet wide, and sufficiently numerous to occupy the whole ground; had these been crossed at right angles by others of a corresponding breadth; had ten open squares been formed at the proper intersections of the principal streets, . . . or had some other plan, substantially resembling this and directed by the nature of the ground, been completed,—Boston would even now have been the most beautiful town the world has ever seen.

But no such comprehensive or rational view of the city had been taken or would be taken in antebellum Boston. It is true that the city councils established a joint committee in 1824 to inquire into the expediency of creating a general survey and plan of all streets and concluded that "the tendency of the present system is as little calculated to give satisfaction to the owners of estates, as to promote the improvement of the public streets." The surveys were begun in 1825 and extensive expenditures followed, but by 1850 the map of the older section of the city showed limited improvement. From the old Market Square curving tentacles of streets sprawled out octopus-like, perhaps even more erratically than a half century earlier; Ann Street (formerly Ann/Fish) snaked with even broader swings through the North End, transmitting its curves to smaller streets formerly straight (e.g., Noon); and the North End streets of Hanover (formerly Hanover/ Middle/North), Salem (formerly Salem/Back), and Prince retained their shifting courses of 1800. Washington Street (formerly Cornhill/Marlborough/Newberry/ Orange) pursued its serpentine course from the old Market Square for more than two miles to the southern boundary of the city. To be sure, some few of the streets in the older part of Boston were straighter in 1850 than in 1800—Charles Street was not quite so pronouncedly angled and the new streets of Commercial and Fulton on the east side of the North End were straighter than the old streets behind them—but most changes in these areas apparently consisted of street widening.[64]

In the area around Fort Hill a great deal of redesign and rebuilding took place under the auspices of the Broad Street Association after its incorporation in 1805. The major achievements here were the constuction of two commodious wharves (Central and India) with magnificent warehouses. But streets were changed as well; two new wide avenues—Broad and India—were laid out close to the harbor, and some of the other streets behind them were also modified.[65]

While complaining of the older streets of Boston, Arfwedson added, "The new part, however, is very different, but still I cannot say that there is any street particularly fine." One of the older of the "new parts" was the north and northwest side of Beacon Hill, where, in the eighteenth century, the area on either side of Cambridge Street had been platted in a crude approximation of a gridiron pattern. But it was, indeed, in the sections where activity took place in the nineteenth century (though sometimes in areas of older occupation) that more regular street patterns sometimes (but not always) could be found. In 1801 the selectmen caused the lands on the Neck to be laid out in rectilinear form embellished by a grass oval—Columbia Square—through which ran Washington (Orange) Street, the most important thoroughfare on the Neck. Although there was little immediate demand for lots in this area and Columbia Square (later Blackstone and Franklin squares) "was chiefly apparent on paper for many years," the grid pattern here established generally prevailed—there were a few exceptions—when the area was developed, despite the fact that filling created additional unplatted acreage for subdivision. Action in 1804 set in train further use of the gridiron plan. Just a few hundred yards east of Boston Neck lay a pennisula only a little smaller than the town of Boston north of the Neck. This piece of land—a part of the town of Dorchester, most of which lay south of Boston—was sparsely populated: there were only ten families in 1803. Its proximity to Boston led several entrepreneurs of that town—Gardiner Green, Harrison G. Otis, William Tudor, and Jonathan Mason—to invest heavily in land on the Dorchester Neck, as the pennisula was called. For these capitalists and other Dorchester Neck landholders to realize maximum appreciation on their property, two actions were desirable—easy communication with Boston must be established and the area incorporated into Boston town. As a result of a petition of the Dorchester Neck residents and proprietors (and, it would seem, a certain amount of bribery) three legislative actions were taken in 1804: Dorchester Neck was transferred to the town of Boston; the Front Street Proprietors were incorporated to improve lands along the east side of Boston Neck (across a narrow strait from Dorchester Neck); and the Boston South Bridge Company was chartered to build a bridge to what now came to be known as South Boston.

These actions, in turn, resulted in the building of the bridge provided for; the piling and filling of a portion of Boston Neck and the laying out of a long, straight (except for one angle) street (Front, later Harrison, Street) with right angled crossing streets; the platting of the whole of South Boston in two joined rectilinear grids, with the east-west streets (except Broadway) numbered and the north-south streets designated by letters; and, finally, a tenfold increase in property values in South Boston.[66]

On March 9, 1804, just three days after the three acts mentioned above were passed, the Massachusetts legislature incorporated the Boston Mill Corporation (more commonly known as the Mill Pond Corporation), which would lead to the creation of new land—and a new rectilinear street segment—at the other end of the town. More than a century and a half earlier (in 1643) the marshy area west of Copps Hill had been dammed and converted into a millpond; but by the early nineteenth century the pressing need was for land, not mills. What the incorporators—who claimed to be the successors of the builders of the dam, and were referred to by the selectmen as "the supposed Proprietors"—proposed was to take earth from Beacon Hill and use it to fill the millpond. An agreement was eventually reached between the selectmen and the proprietors; the latter were to fill the pond at their own expense, one-eighth of the land created was to become the property of the town, and streets were to be laid out in accordance with a plan prepared by Charles Bulfinch, the chairman of the selectmen. This was done over the next twenty years. The plan consisted of a triangle of enclosing streets (Merrimack, Charlestown, and Causeway) with seven parallel north-south streets crossed at right angles by two intersecting streets. To the east of the triangle two additional streets (Pond and Margot) were added parallel to the eastern boundary. The work was completed by 1825.[67]

Similar actions took place on either side of Boston Neck—the Back Bay on the west and South Cove on the east. The train of events leading to the former was set in motion in 1813 when a group of Bostonians proposed a complex of dams on both sides of the Neck. Incorporated in 1814 as the Boston and Roxbury Mill Corporation, the company completed in 1821 a dam a mile and a half long from the west end of Beacon Street to Sewell's Point, south of Cambridge, across the top of which ran a toll road called Western Avenue. This massive work (the South Cove proposals were dropped) cut off half of the Great Bay between Boston and Cambridge and created, with a much shorter cross dam, two basins—a smaller one to collect the water and the other to receive if after it passed through the millrace. One of the proprietors, Uriah Cotting, who had been the leading light of the Broad Street development, asserted that the project would accommodate eighty-one mills. What this ambitious construction produced was not, in fact, a thriving industrial complex, but, instead, an intolerable nuisance of malodorous mudflats. But the situation did offer the possibility for a substantial addition of new land—the Back Bay area—to be added to the city in the 1850s with the more regular street plans typical of the newer developments (and particularly, the Neck). Even earlier, by the 1830s, some portions of the Back Bay had already been filled and streets laid out in rectilinear form. An 1824 map shows only one north-south road along the Neck—Washington (Orange) Street, which hugged the Back Bay shore—while on an 1833 map there appear three ranges of blocks west of Washington and two additional parallel streets, Suffolk and Tremont.[68]

In the 1830s two other projects were undertaken that were roughly analogous to the millpond conversion. In 1835 and 1836 the top sixty-five feet of Pemberton Hill were removed and dumped into the Charles River northwest of the old millpond. On the eight acres of filled land were laid out the parallel streets of Lowell, Billerica, Nashua, and Andover, while the reshaped hill was platted in a less regular fashion (a crescent later denominated Pemberton Square) for more elegant, elite housing. All of this was done as a private venture. But an even more extensive land reclamation activity was in process in the South Cove area, which was bounded by Front (Harrison) Street on the west and Essex on the north in 1833 when the South Cove Associates was incorporated. The company had a contract with the Boston and Worcester Railroad to provide that corporation with space for railway terminal facilities. The Associates purchased more than 3 million square feet of land, mostly in the form of mudflats in the South Cove. Filling was completed by 1839, and the corporation ended up with almost eighty acres of mostly new land on which they laid out eight north-south and seven east-west streets in almost strict rectilinear fashion.[69]

There was one built-up area in the old city that was wholly reconstructed during this era—the region around Town Dock, north of the Long Wharf. In 1825 and 1826 the city of Boston under the leadership of Mayor Josiah Quincy filled in the Town Dock and built over the wharves between Long Wharf and Blackstone Street, creating a substantial open space east of Faneuil Hall. Here were erected a handsome Market House and two flanking warehouses and, in the process, the straight, parallel east-west streets of Clinton, North Market, South Market, and Chatham, with two short parallel crossing streets, were produced. Thus was created a small island of rectilinearity in the wilderness of old Boston's "narrow, crooked, and disagreeable" streets.[70]

Timothy Dwight observed in the late eighteenth century that Boston contained, in addition to 135 streets, 21 lanes, and 18 courts, "it is said, a few squares; although I confess, I have never seen anything in it to which I should give that name." It was certainly true that the public squares of Boston were, in the early nineteenth century, nothing more than unembellished street widenings (e.g., Garden Square) or streets around public buildings (e.g., Market Square, Church Square), and that private squares and places were (except for Charles Bulfinch's Franklin Place) a development of the future (e.g., Louisburg Square [1834] and Pemberton Square [1835]). But there was, of course, the Common—Boston's major piece of public land. Though used for grazing as late as 1830, a tree-lined walk along Tremont Street dated from the eighteenth century and a second would be added adjacent to Beacon Street in 1816. This tract of some fifty acres was periodically further improved throughout the first half of the nineteenth century. Directly west of the Common lay another block of land about half the size of the Common that the city government was, much against its inclination, required by a town meeting in 1824 to retain for public purposes. It lay deserted for more than a decade before Horace Gray and his associates, with the approval of the council, began to improve it with plantings; it came to be called the Public Garden, but the city spent no money for its development in the first half of the century. There was also land open to the public on Fort Hill in the eighteenth century. This circular plot was not laid out until the operations of the Broad Street Association in 1803 nor fenced for more than a decade thereafter; it was a well-established public plot by the 1830s or earlier. There were, of course, other public spaces, as has previously been noted, on the Neck, and in East Boston, that were largely undeveloped until the end of this period; and there was a rash of park establishments in the Neck, South Boston, and East Boston in 1850–1851. But, as a practical matter, the used public plots in Boston in the first half of the nineteenth century were Fort Hill, the Common, and the Public Gardens—neither sufficient for the population nor well distributed to serve it.[71]

It would have been, one supposes, unrealistic to expect that a handful of settlers—of whom some came as traders expecting to return to their homeland in a few years and others hoped that they might survive long enough to be counted among the few dozen or few hundred Europeans to be found along 2,000 miles of coast line—would pause to conceptualize a structure for a city of 100 or 1,000 times their numbers. Such an action was rendered even less likely by the absence of any such approach in their English or Dutch heritage. But once the haphazard alignment of houses and lanes are spread on the ground and occupants acquire title to their domiciles, changes become difficult and that difficulty becomes greater with each passing year. These circumstances illustrate one of the primary realities of urban planning in all eras—few things are more resistant to change than private real estate capital in place.

By the 1680s both investors and settlers demonstrated greater confidence in the survival of American settlements, in part because a number of efforts had resulted in communities that had not only persisted but flourished, and in part because of special circumstances in individual cases. The Charlestonians were already established in the region before their move to the permanent site, and Penn and at least some of his followers believed they acted under divine guidance and protection—a view doubtless held by many of the Bostonians a half century earlier. The Charleston plan might be seen as transitional: rectilinear in conception but rather irregular in execution. The plat of Philadelphia, on the other hand, was bold, venturesome, and a century ahead of its time in incorporating complete regularity, spaciousness, and foresight, extending the street plan well beyond the area of likely occupation for decades to come.

In the early eighteenth century the New Orleans plan, which preceded any settlement, mirrored the regularity and foresightedness of Penn's vision of his Great Town, but lacked its spaciousness. The Baltimore platters, on the other hand, while having regularity as their goal, were inhibited by prior occupation and intransigent physical features, which left the plat inadequate for the needs of the immediate future. The later foundations benefited from an absence of on-site settlement (St. Louis and Louisville), or from proprietary control of the land and plan (Pittsburgh, Cincinnati, and Buffalo), or both. All of these shared the rectilinear vision, though, as has been noted, with some variations in application. All of these post-Philadelphia cities illustrated consistently a second major premise of urban planning in the era—in every case where planning precedes occupation (and in a few cases where it does not) the model is rectilinear, which satisfies both material concerns and contemporary aesthetics.

Washington, of course, was a case apart. Although all of the land it occupied was owned by individuals, the proprietors ceded their claims to the central government in return for receiving a portion of their original holdings back in the form of city lots. This freed L'Enfant from any significant restraints imposed by capital in place. Although the plan was registered at crucial points to terrain features, only the river modified L'Enfant's design, which combined a rationalistic rectilinear grid with an orderly baroque overlay of diagonal avenues, squares, and circles.

All of the post-1680 city plans, with their strong commitment to at least aspects of the Philadelphia model (preeminently, of course, to the rectilinear grid), can be seen as embodying a search for order. Clearly that circumstance produced (or at least suggested) a more orderly urban life—destinations were more certainly located, routes more clearly plotted, buildings more easily planned and constructed. To some this doubtless implied a step toward social order as well; was it accidental that Boston, in the last half of the eighteenth century, had a reputation (not necessarily deserved) for hotheaded radicalism while the Philadelphia image was one of solid, prosperous conservatism? The events of the nineteenth century, of course, proved these assumptions untenable. But most obviously the order that was sought was that of disciplining—even subduing—character. For nature is, at least apparently, disorderly, abhorring a straight line; and its subjugation is a necessity for the establishment of civilization—an urban condition.

In the nineteenth century as the urban population grew and the cities expanded, there were excellent opportunities to develop the street plans in advance of occupation by city residents, though not in advance of land acquisition. The best examples of such operations on a large scale were in New York and Baltimore, though they, like most cities, accomplished some of the platting on a piecemeal basis. Providence never addressed the challenge in any organized fashion, and the response of Boston was spotty and more in the hands of private developers than elsewhere. Washington and Philadelphia were atypical cases; the former still had much vacant space within its original boundaries at the end of the half century, and the initial Philadelphia plan covered all of the ground within the jurisdiction of the city at any time before the 1854 consolidation. Thus, in the Philadelphia metropolitan area the expansion plans were in the hands of suburban jurisdictions. In all of the cities in which advanced planning took place the rectilinar approach prevailed, though often with less than perfect execution.

Many of the cities also found it desirable to modify existing street plans to approach more closely the Philadelphia ideal. There were some instances of widening and straightening streets in such cities as New York and Boston, especially taking advantage of destructive fires to diminish the inertial force of capital in place; the changes of this sort ranged from minimal to modest.

Concurrently, less advantageous changes were occurring in cities with rectilinear plans. Philadelphia's spacious blocks were sliced up into congested sections by streets, alleys, places, and courts. New York landowners complained that platted streets were too broad and secured their reduction in width. There and elsewhere (e.g., Philadelphia, St. Louis, and Louisville) developers nibbled away at the public places, and only the stubborn resistance of the Boston citizenry prevented the councils from platting and selling the Public Garden. It is likely that only the fact that Washington's unique and remarkable street plan was not subject to local control prevented similar occurrences in the nation's capital. In almost all of these cases potential profit undermined the aesthetic aspects of the city plan—not just the aesthetic concepts of the nineteenth century, but also those of the seventeenth and eighteenth centuries built into the initial plats. Thus was illustrated another premise of nineteenth-century urban planning—short-term profit has, as a rule, more influence on planning than aesthetics or even the search for order.

Yet out of it all came genuine advances in the urban vision that motivates city planning. The Philadelphia model, without its degradations, and the Washington aspiration, which exceeded its achievement, were the primary themes. With rectilinearity achieved as a base, experimentation and venturesomeness could be adopted without risking degeneration into disorder. Spaciousness came to be perceived as having at least long-range developmental (hence, financial) benefits that might outweigh the immediate profitability of cramming more buildings and more people onto a given parcel of urban space; and even capital in place sometimes weighed in on the side of broader avenues (to carry traffic more expeditiously) and more and larger public places (to improve the image, healthfulness, and, hence, attractiveness of the city). And the lion of developmental profits and the lamb of aesthetics found common cause in the support of a vision that emerged from a half-century of urban experience.

Figure 1. Albany—1695

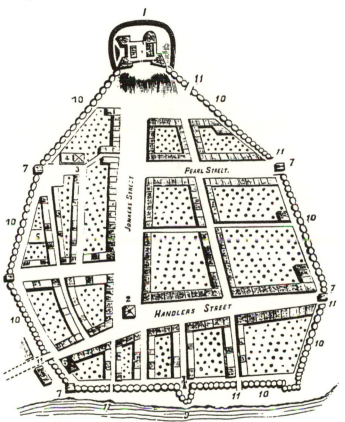

PLAN OF ALBANY, 1695.

1. The Fort.
2. Dutch Calvinist Church.
3. German Lutheran.
4. Its Burying Place.
5. Dutch Calvinist Burying Place.
6. Stadt House.
7. Block Houses.
9. Great Guns to clear a Gully.
10. Stockades.
11. City Gates, six in all.

Source: George R. Howell and Jonathan Tenney, eds., *History of the County of Albany, N.Y., from 1609 to 1886* (New York: W. W. Munsell and Company, 1885), 505.

Figure 2. Albany—1770

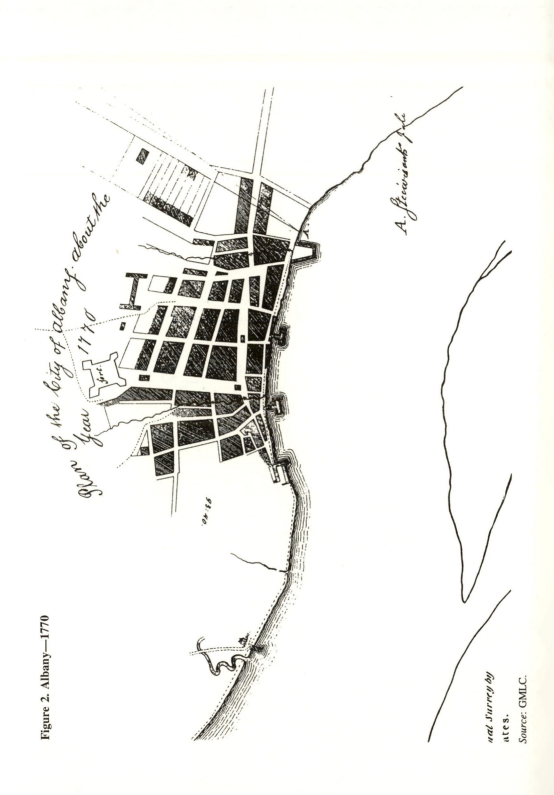

Plan of the City of Albany. about the Year 1770

A. Stevison fct.

nal Survey by
ates.
Source: GMLC.

Figure 3. Albany—1794

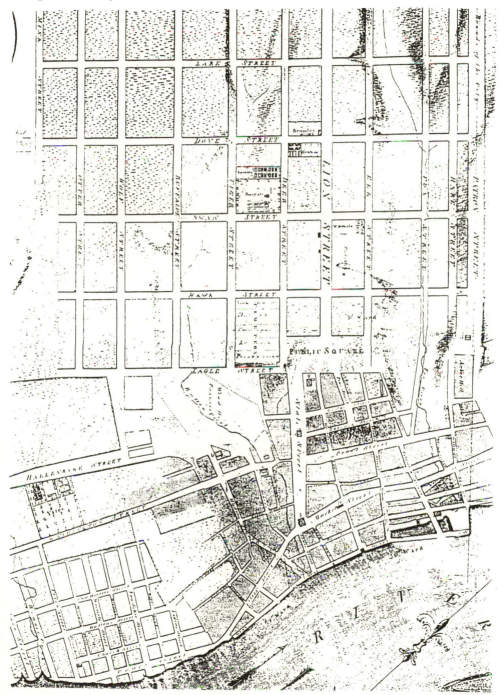

Source: GMLC.

Figure 4. Albany—1833

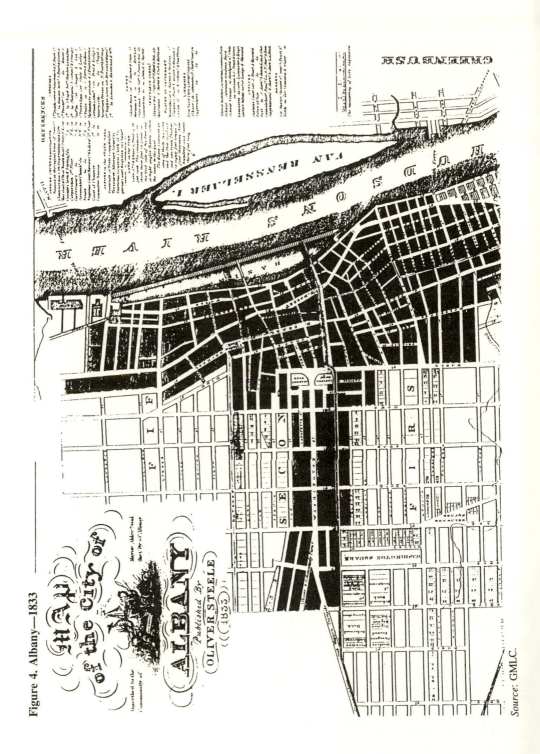

Figure 5. Albany—1841

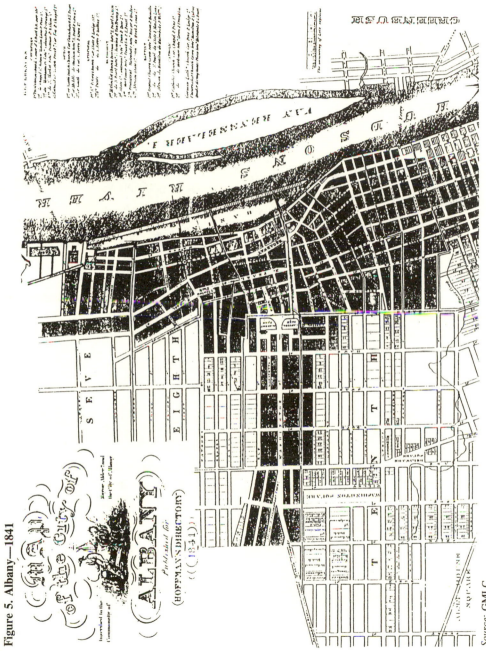

Figure 6. Baltimore—1732

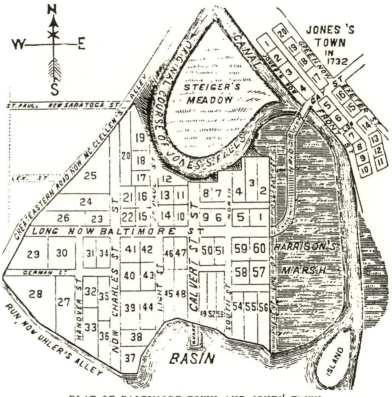

PLAT OF BALTIMORE TOWN AND JONES' TOWN.

Source: J. Thomas Scharf, *History of Baltimore City and County* (Philadelphia: Louis H. Everts, 1881), 1:52.

Figure 7. Baltimore—1804

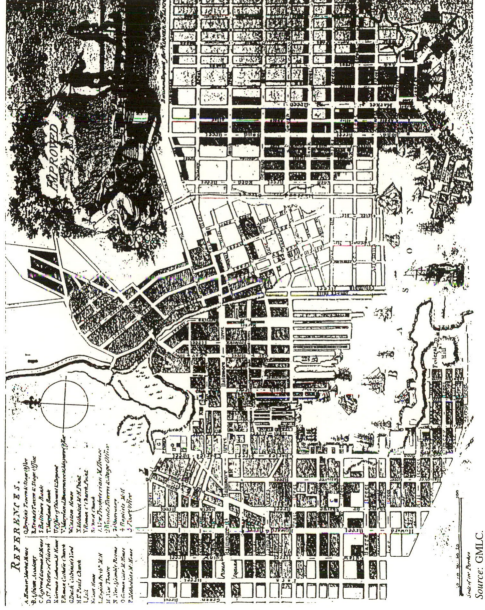

Figure 8. Baltimore—1838

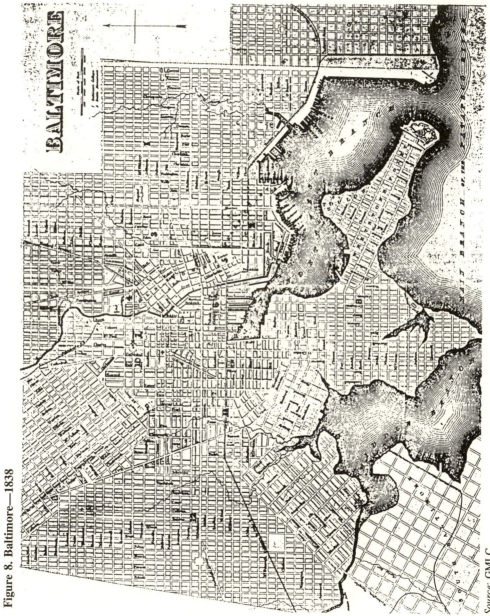

Source: GMLC.

Figure 9. Baltimore—1846

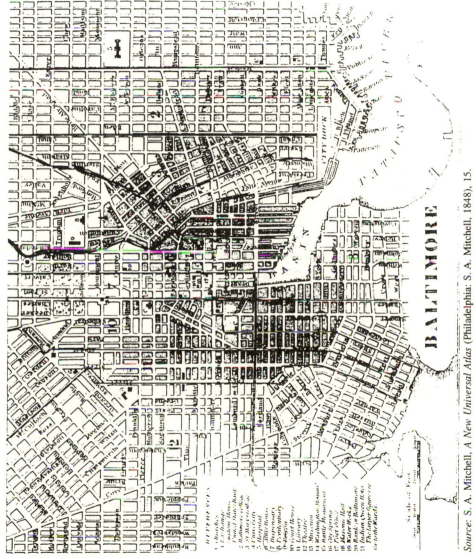

Source: S. A. Mitchell, *A New Universal Atlas* (Philadelphia: S. A. Mitchell, 1848), 15.

Figure 10. Boston—1728

Source: GMLC.

Figure 11. Boston—1800

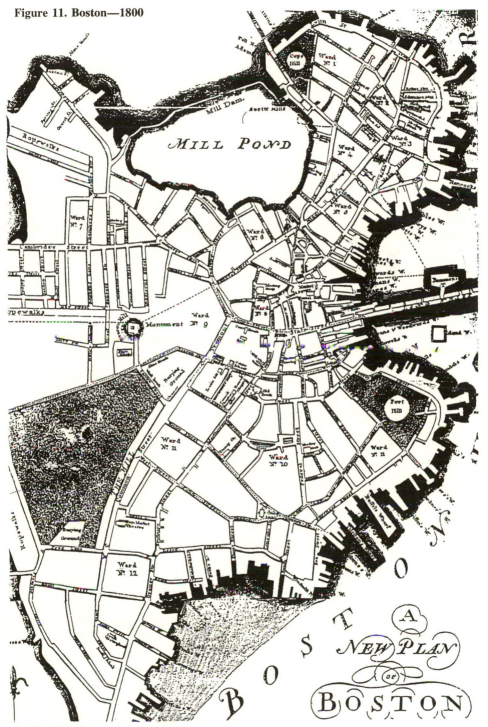

Source: GMLC.

Figure 12. Boston—1833

Figure 13. Boston—1851

Source: GMLC.

Figure 14. Brooklyn—1766

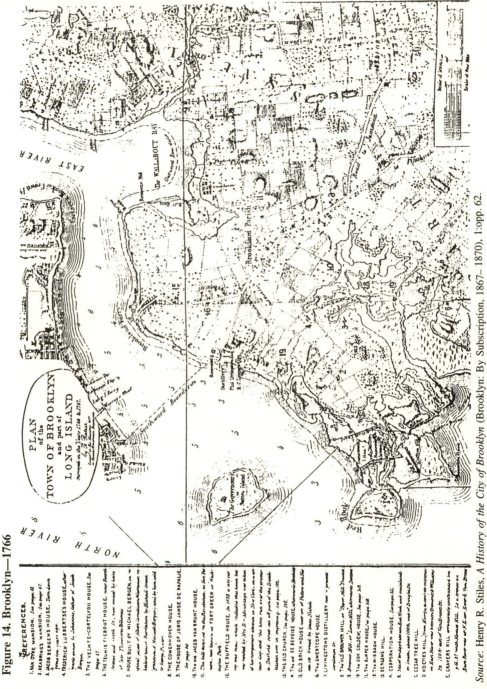

Source: Henry R. Stiles, *A History of the City of Brooklyn* (Brooklyn: By Subscription, 1867–1870), 1:opp. 62.

Figure 15. Brooklyn—1816

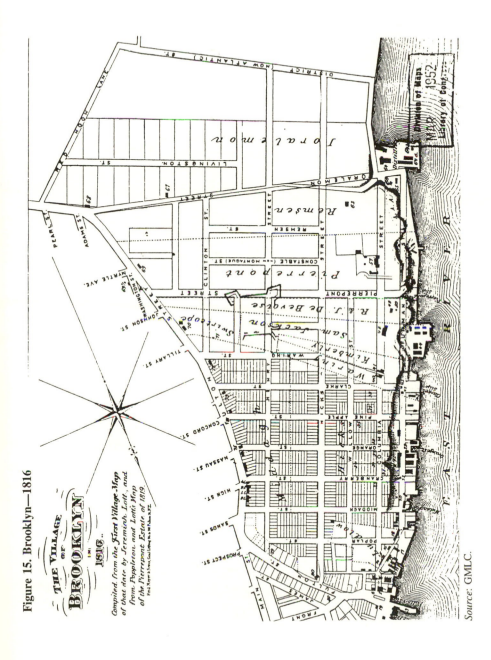

Figure 16. Brooklyn—1835

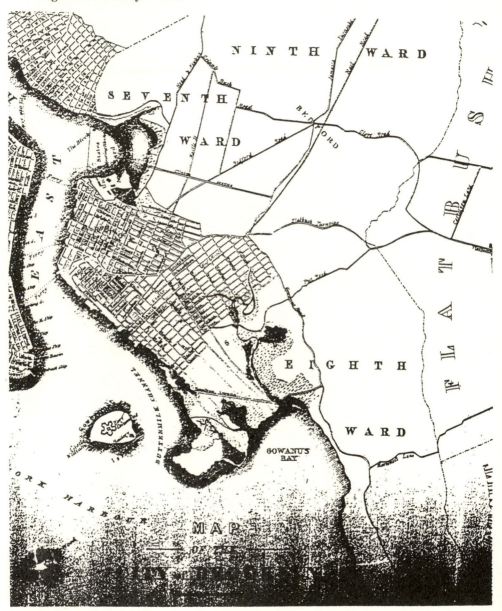

Source: GMLC.

Figure 17. Brooklyn—1852

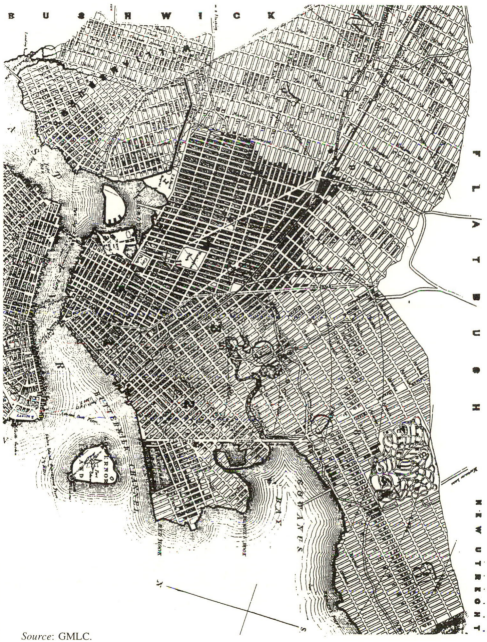

Source: GMLC.

Figure 18. Buffalo—1804

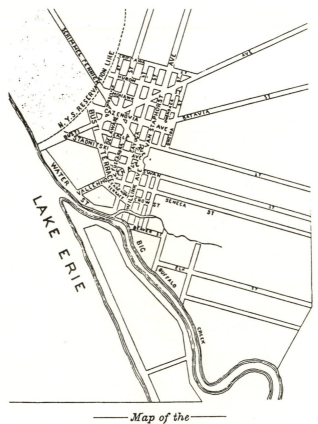

—— *Map of the*——
Village of New Amsterdam
—— *(now the City of Buffalo)*——
Made for the Holland Land Company
—— *by*——
JOSEPH ELLICOTT, Surveyor.
1804

Source: H. Perry Smith, ed., *History of Buffalo and Erie County* (Syracuse: D. Mason and Company, 1884), 2:27.

Figure 19. Buffalo—1810

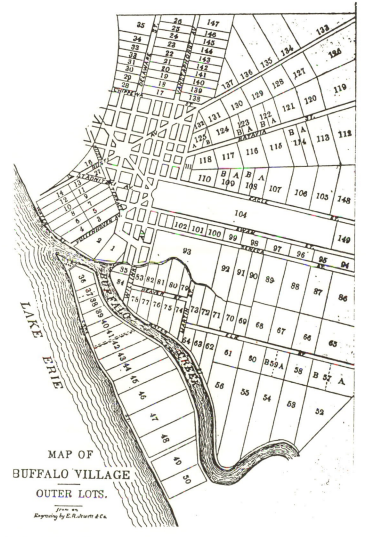

Source: Smith, *Buffalo*, 2:30.

Figure 20. Buffalo—1825

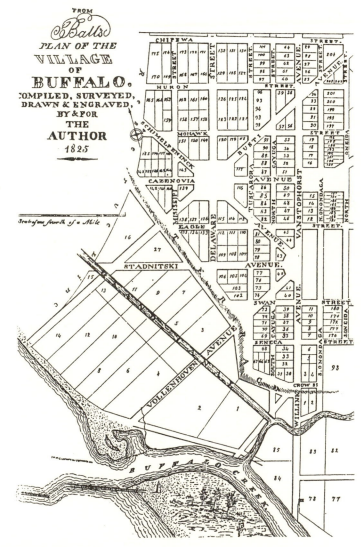

Source: Smith, *Buffalo*, 2:101.

Figure 21. Buffalo—1847

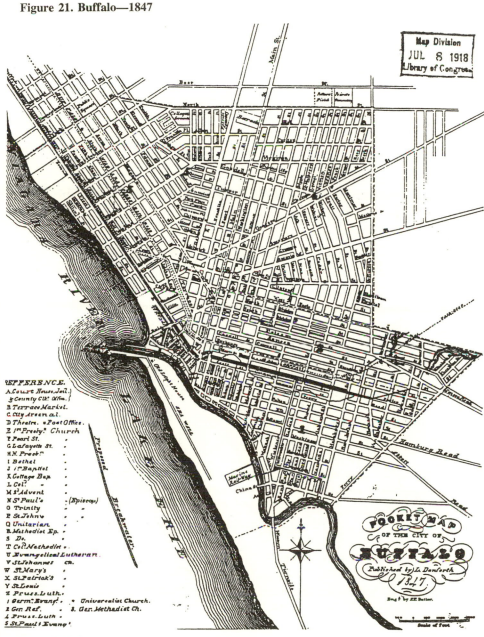

Source: GMLC.

Figure 22. Buffalo—1853

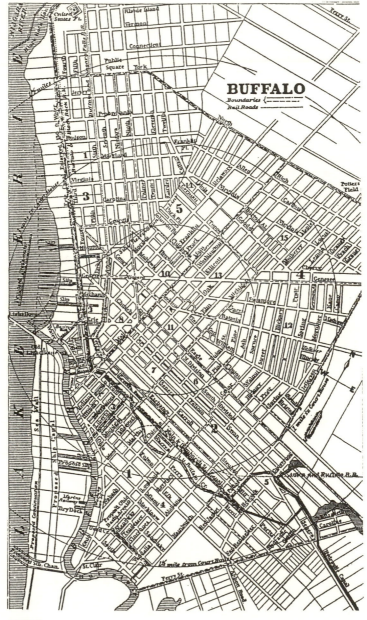

Source: GMLC.

Figure 23. Charleston—1704

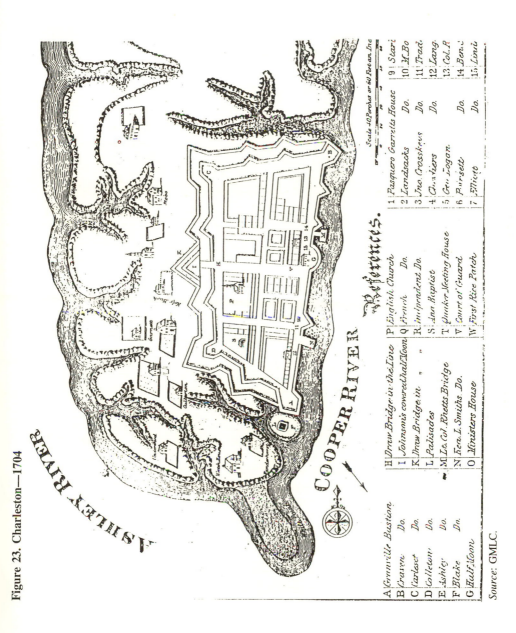

Source: GMLC.

Figure 24. Charleston—1770

Source: GMLC.

Figure 25. Charleston—1843

Source: H. S. Tanner, *A New Universal Atlas* (Philadelphia: Carey and Hart, [1843]), 15.

Figure 26. Charleston—1853

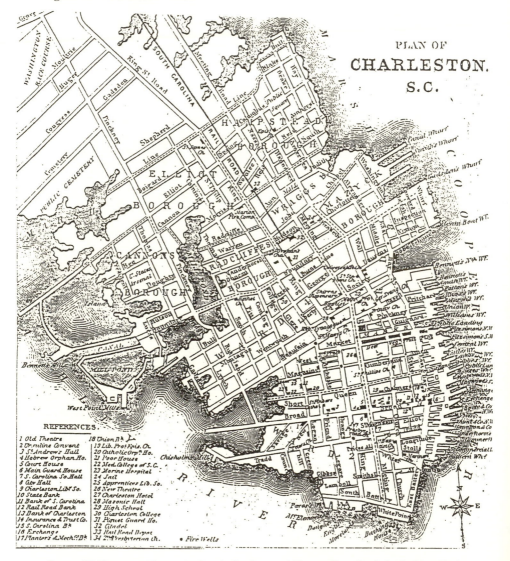

Source: Wellington Williams, *Appleton's Southern and Western Travellers' Guide* (New York: D. Appleton and Company, 1853), opp. 105.

Figure 27. Cincinnati—1792

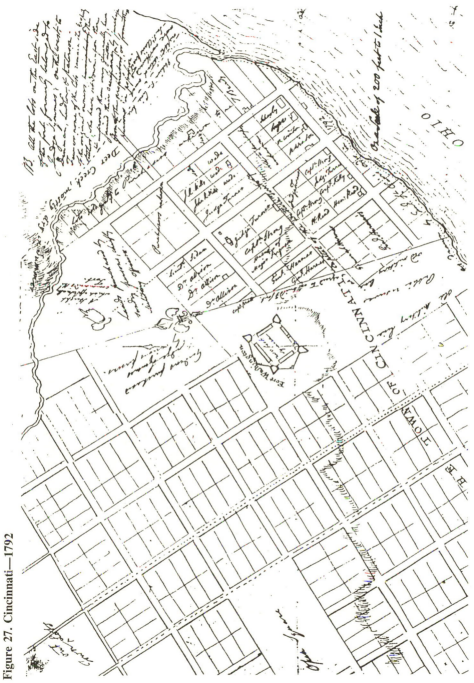

Source: GMLC.

Figure 28. Cincinnati—1819

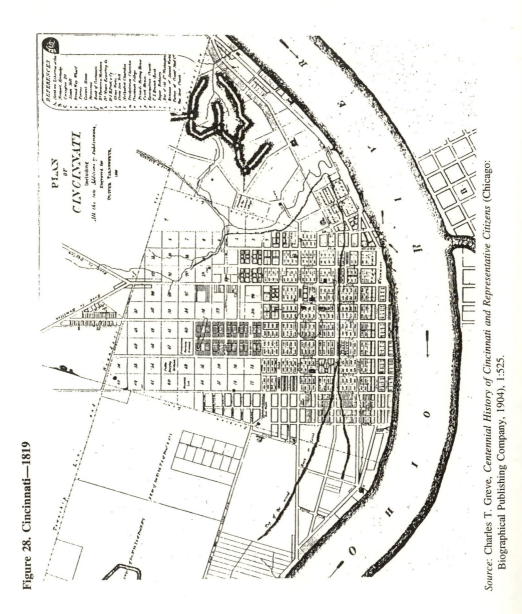

Source: Charles T. Greve, *Centennial History of Cincinnati and Representative Citizens* (Chicago: Biographical Publishing Company, 1904), 1:525.

Figure 29. Cincinnati—1839

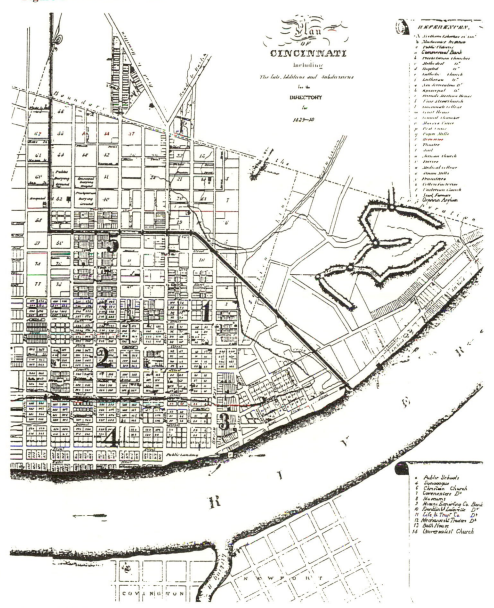

Source: GMLC.

Figure 30. Cincinnati—1848

Source: Williams, *Southern and Western Guide* (1853), opp. 19.

Figure 31. Louisville—1779

Source: Raymond C. Riebel, *Louisville Panorama* (Louisville: Liberty National Bank and Trust Company, 1954), 10.

Figure 32. Louisville—1819

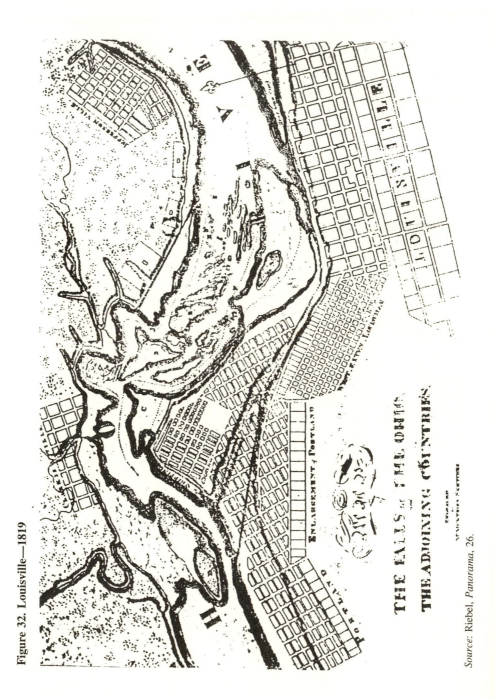

THE FALLS OF THE OHIO,
THE ADJOINING COUNTRIES.

Source: Riebel, *Panorama*, 26.

Figure 33. Louisville—1832

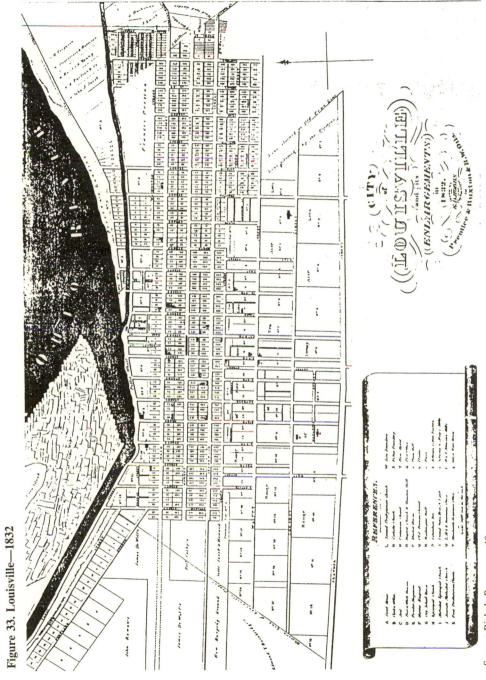

Source: Riebel, *Panorama,* 40.

Figure 34. Louisville—1855

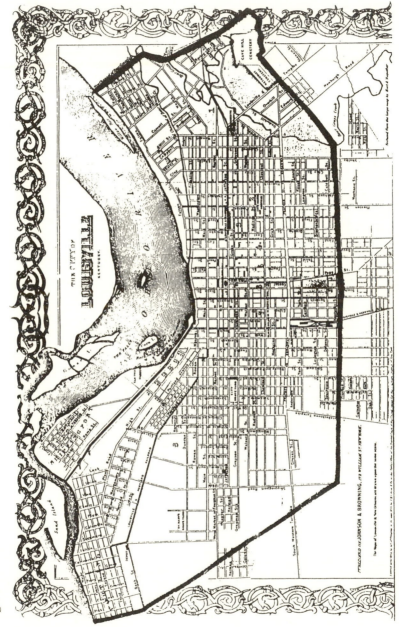

Source: GMLC.

Figure 35. New Orleans—1720

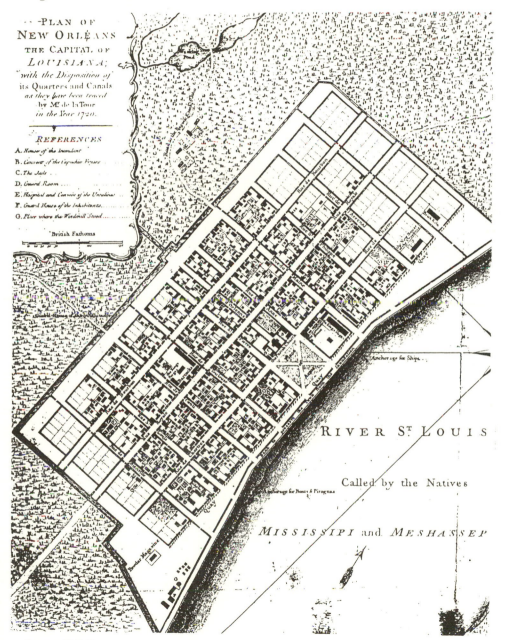

PLAN OF
NEW ORLÉANS
THE CAPITAL OF
LOUISIANA;
with the Disposition of
its Quarters and Canals
as they have been traced
by Mr de la Tour
in the Year 1720.

REFERENCES

A. *House of the Intendant*
B. *Convent of the Capuchin Friars*
C. *The Jail*
D. *Guard Room*
E. *Hospital and Convent of the Ursulines*
F. *Guard House of the Inhabitants*
G. *Place where the Windmill Stood*

British Fathoms

RIVER St LOUIS

Called by the Natives

MISSISSIPI and *MESHASSEP*

Source: GMLC.

Figure 36. New Orleans—1770

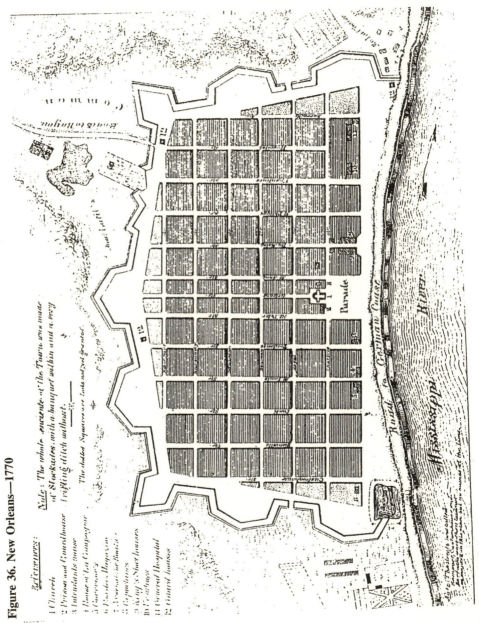

References:

Note: The whole enceinte of the Town was made of Stockades, with a banquet within and a very trifling ditch without.

The dotted Squares are Lots not yet granted.

1 Church
2 Prison and Guardhouse
3 Intendants house
4 House of La Compagnie
5 Governors
6 Parcke Magazin
7 Arsenal or Banks
8 Capuchins
9 King's Storehouses
10 Forstage
11 General Hospital
12 Private houses

Source: GMLC.

Figure 37. New Orleans—1833

Source: H. S. Tanner, *New Universal Atlas* (Philadelphia: By the Author, 1836), 20.

Figure 38. New Orleans—1849

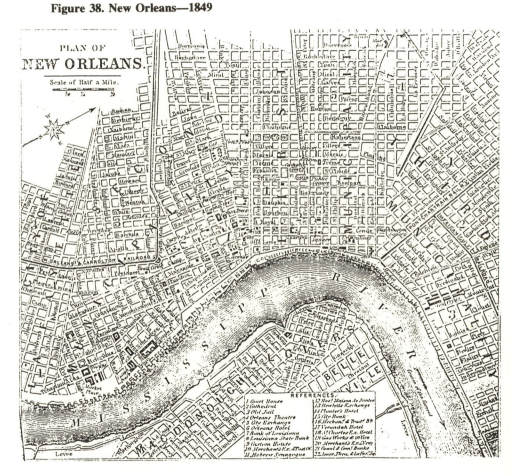

Source: Williams, *Southern and Western Guide* (1853), opp. 132.

Figure 39. New York—1664

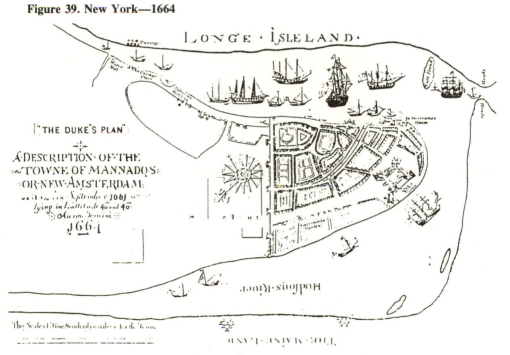

Source: Martha J. Lamb, *History of the City of New York* (New York: A. S. Barnes and
Company, 1877–1880), 1:197.

Figure 40. New York—1695

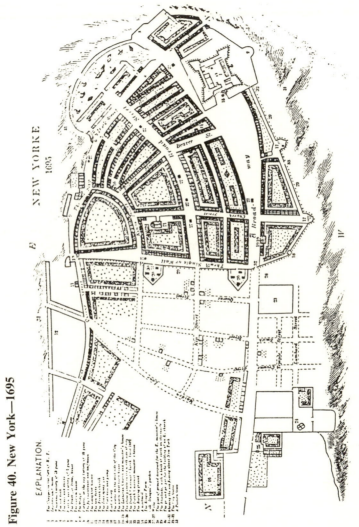

Source: Lamb, *New York,* 1:opp. 420.

Figure 41. New York—1729

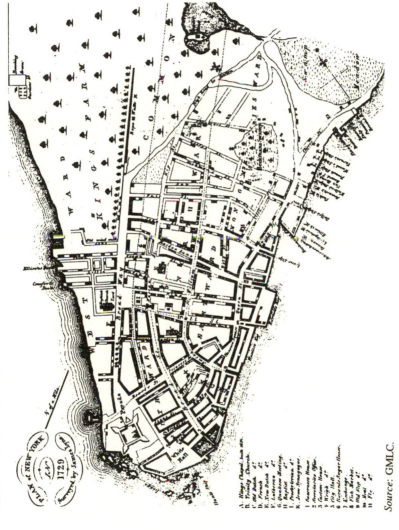

Source: GMLC.

Figure 42. New York—1767

Source: GMLC.

Figure 43. New York—1789

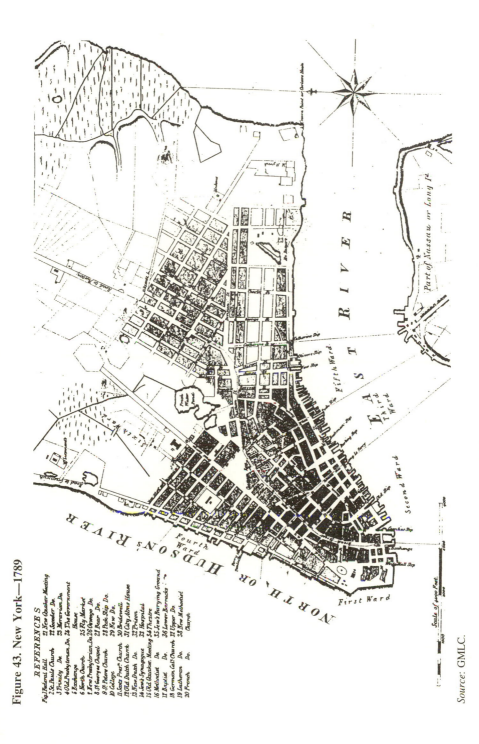

Source: GMLC.

Figure 44. New York—1808

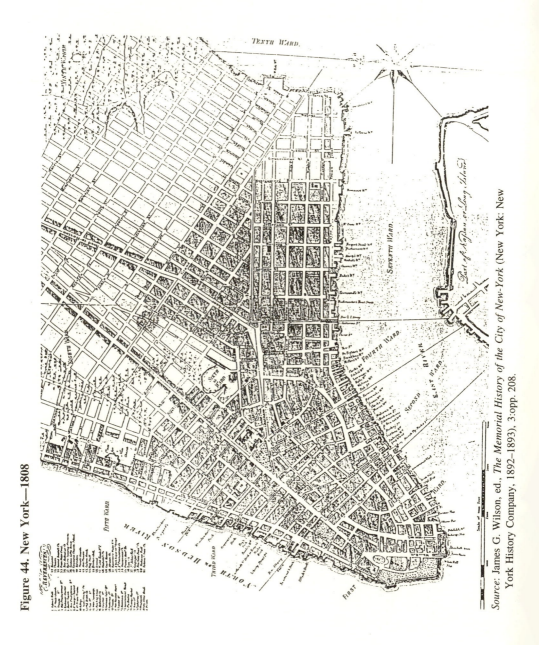

Source: James G. Wilson, ed., *The Memorial History of the City of New-York* (New York: New York History Company, 1892–1893), 3:opp. 208.

Figure 45. New York—1833

Source: Edwin Williams, *New-York As It Is, in 1839* (New York: J. Disturnell, 1833), opp. 192.

Figure 46. New York—1844

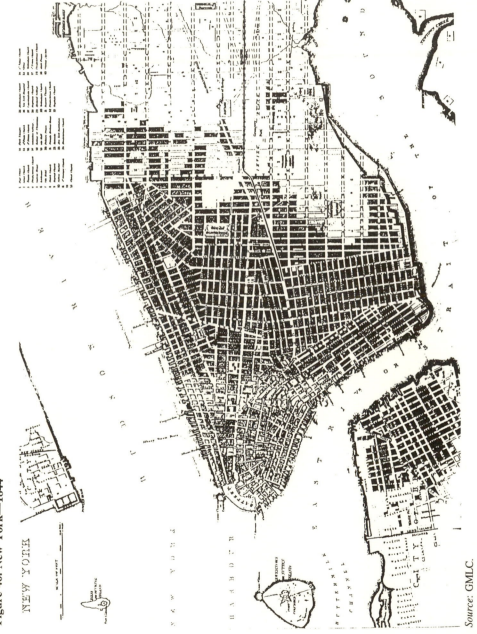

Source: GMLC.

Figure 47. New York—1849

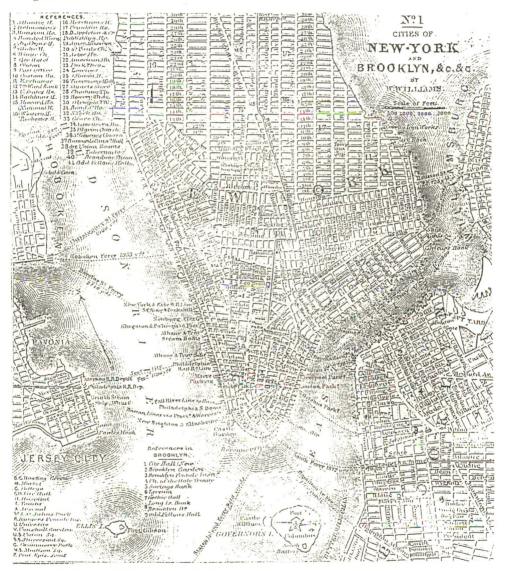

Source: Wellington Williams, *Appleton's Northern and Eastern Travellers' Guide* (New York: Appleton and Company, 1850), frontispiece.

Figure 48. Philadelphia—1682

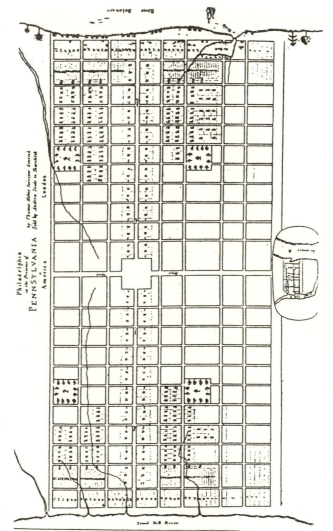

Source: John R. Young, ed., *Memorial History of the City of Philadelphia* (New York: New-York History Company, 1895–1898), 1:32.

Figure 49. Philadelphia—1762

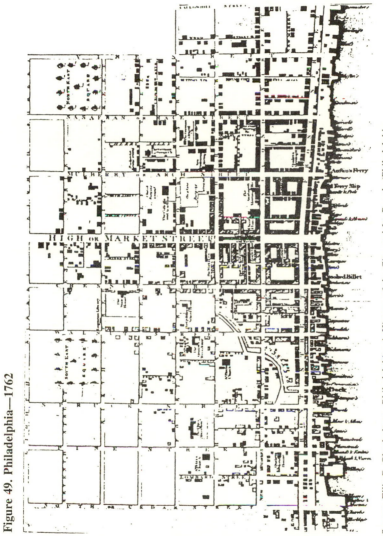

Source: Ellis P. Oberholtzer, *Philadelphia: A History of the City and Its People* (Philadelphia: A. S. J. Clarke Publishing Company, [1912]), 1:217.

Figure 50. Philadelphia—1775

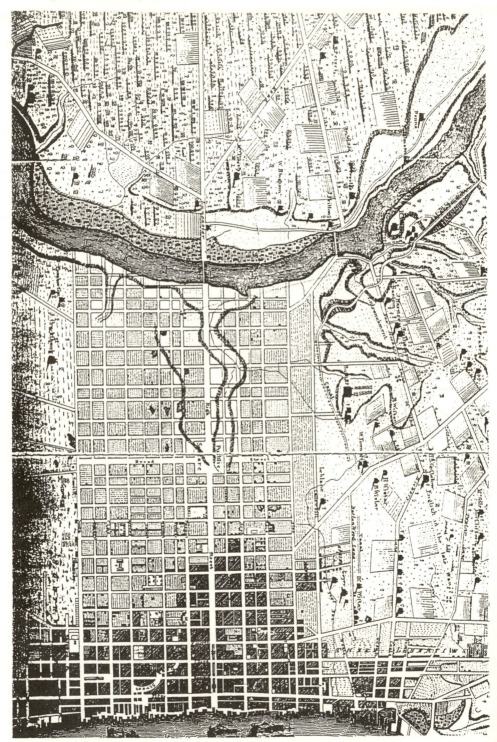

Source: GMLC.

Figure 51. Philadelphia—1836

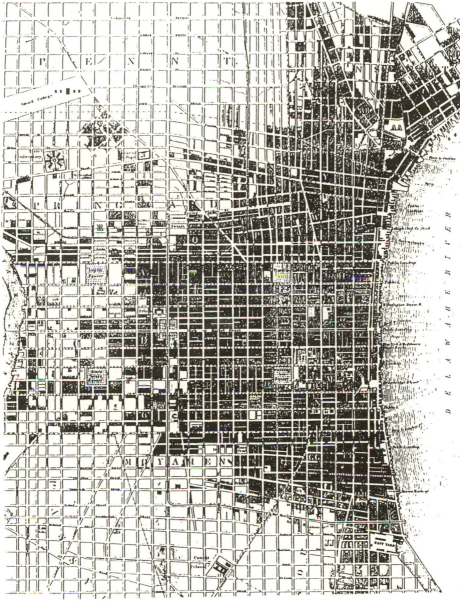

Figure 52. Philadelphia—1851

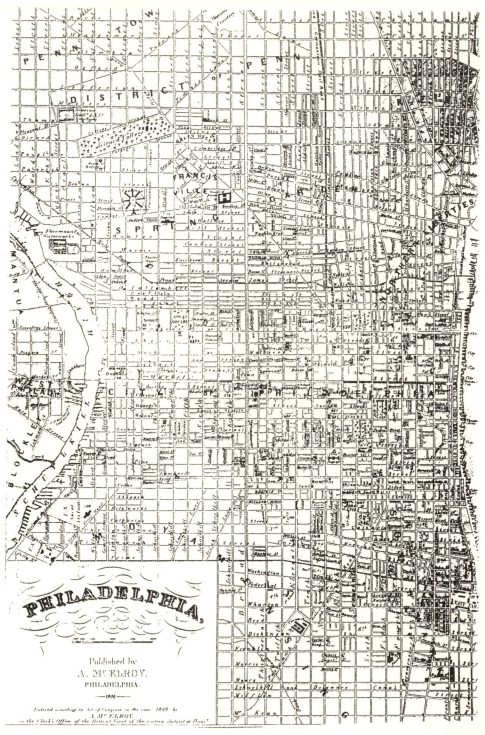

Source: GMLC.

Figure 53. Pittsburgh—1795

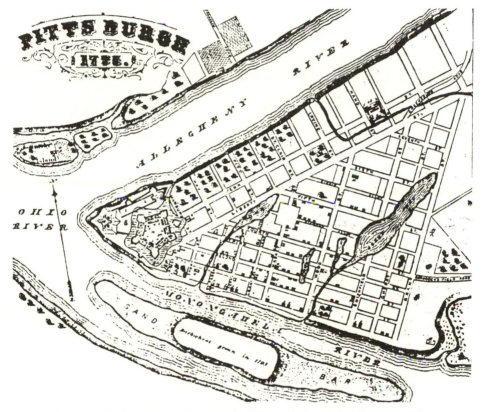

Source: *History of Allegheny County, Pennsylvania* (Chicago: A. Warner and Company, 1889), 484.

Figure 54. Pittsburgh—1800

[PI]TTSBURGH about 1800
showing also
[FO]RTS DUQUESNE and PITT

SCALE IN FEET
500   1000   1500   2000

Source: Leland D. Baldwin, *Pittsburgh: The Story of a City* (Pittsburgh: University of Pittsburgh Press, 1937), map section following index.

Figure 55. Pittsburgh—1826

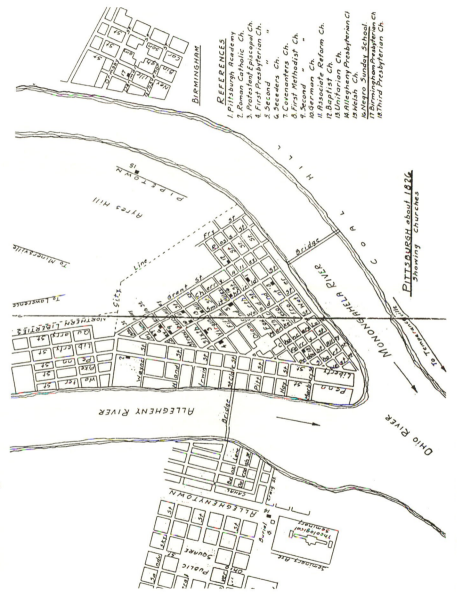

REFERENCES

1. Pittsburgh Academy
2. Roman Catholic Ch.
3. Protestant Episcopal Ch.
4. First Presbyterian Ch.
5. Second   "   "
6. Seceders Ch.
7. Covenanters Ch.
8. First Methodist Ch.
9. Second   "
10. German Ch.
11. Associate Reform Ch.
12. Baptist Ch.
13. Unitarian Ch.
14. Allegheny Presbyterian Ch
15. Welsh Ch.
16. Negro Sunday School
17. Birmingham Presbyterian ch
18. Third Presbyterian Ch.

PITTSBURGH about 1826
Showing Churches

Source: William W. McKinney, Early Pittsburgh Presbyterianism (Pittsburgh: Gibson Press, 1938), 4–5.

Figure 56. Pittsburgh—1845

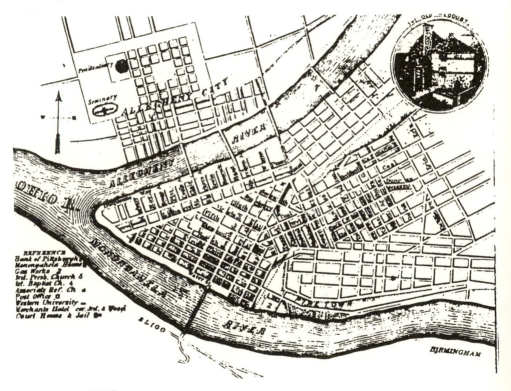

Source: GMLC.

Figure 57. Pittsburgh—1851

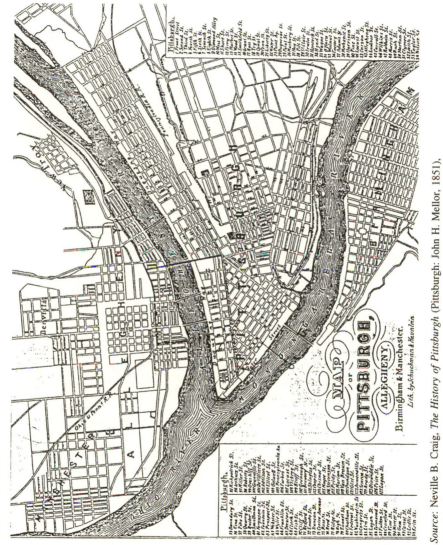

Source: Neville B. Craig, *The History of Pittsburgh* (Pittsburgh: John H. Mellor, 1851), frontispiece.

Figure 58. Providence—1750

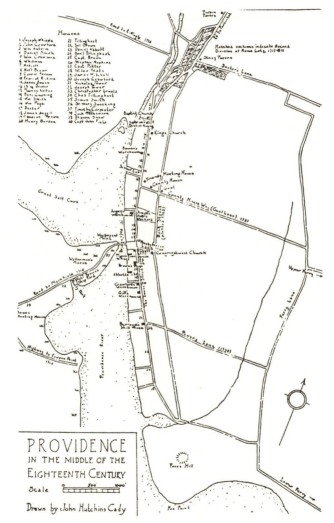

Source: John H. Cady, *The Civil and Architectural Development of Providence, 1636–1950* (Providence: The Book Shop, 1957), 56.

Figure 39. Providence—1803

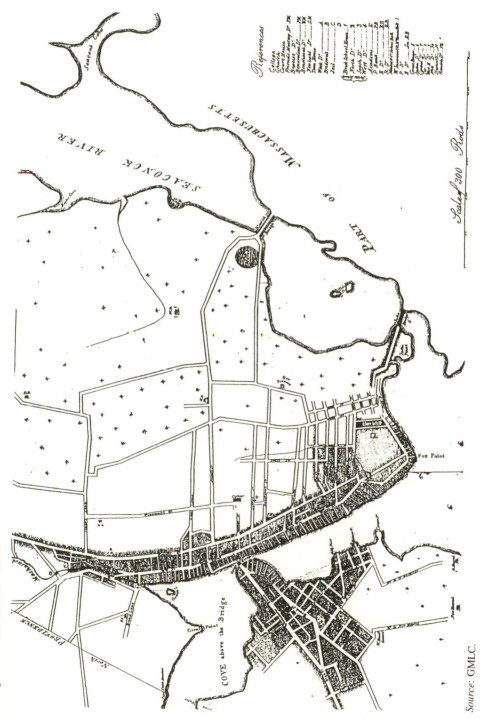

Source: GMLC.

Figure 60. Providence—1832

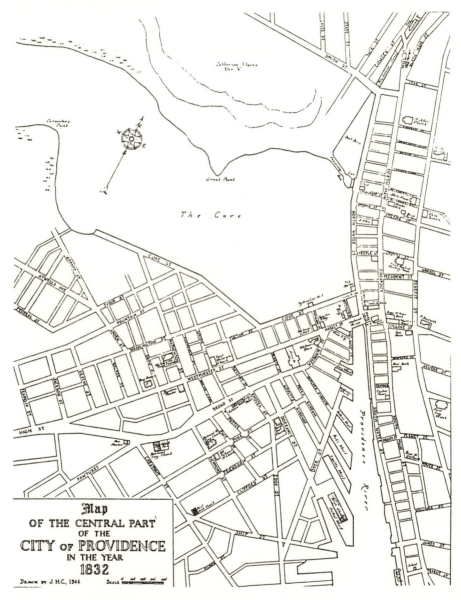

Source: Cady, *Civil and Architectural History*, 93.

Figure 61. Providence—1848

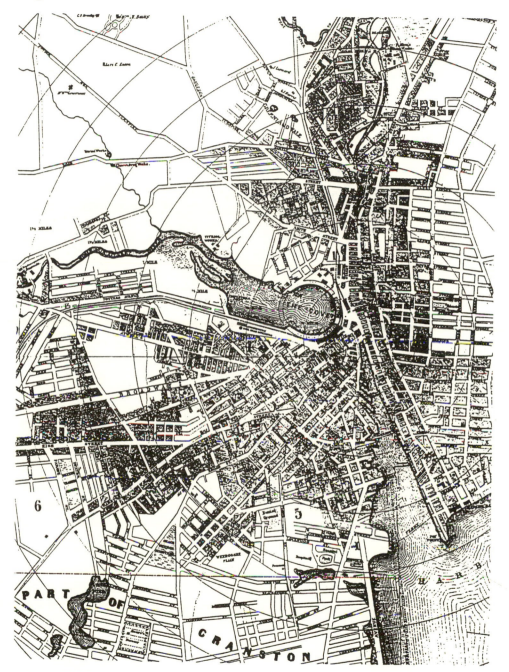

Source: GMLC.

Figure 62. St. Louis—1780

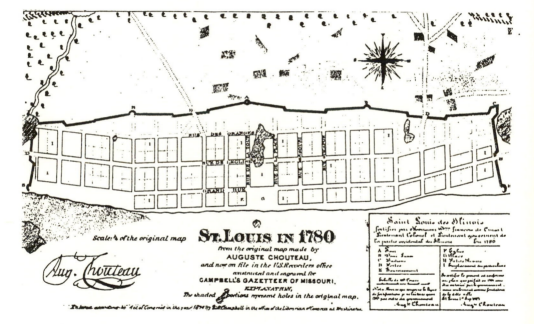

Source: John F. McDermott, *The Early History of St. Louis* (St. Louis: St. Louis Historical Documents Foundation, 1952), unpaged center section.

Figure 63. St. Louis—1804

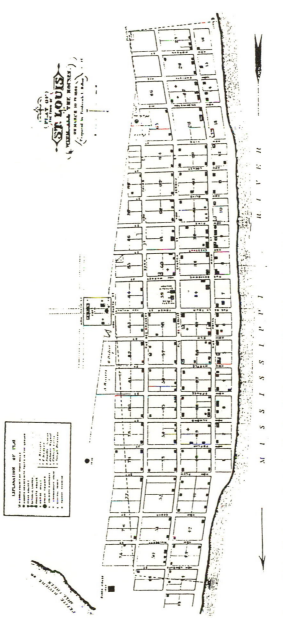

Source: Walter B. Stevens, *St. Louis: The Fourth City, 1763–1909* (Chicago: S. J. Clarke Publishing Company, 1909–1911), 1:opp. 88.

Figure 64. St. Louis—1853

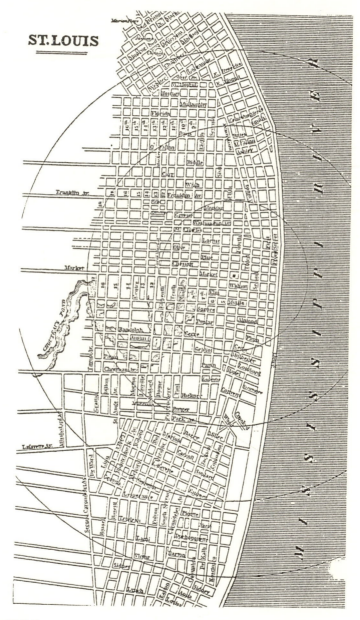

Source: GMLC.

Figure 65. Washington—1790

Source: GMLC.

Figure 66. Washington—1836

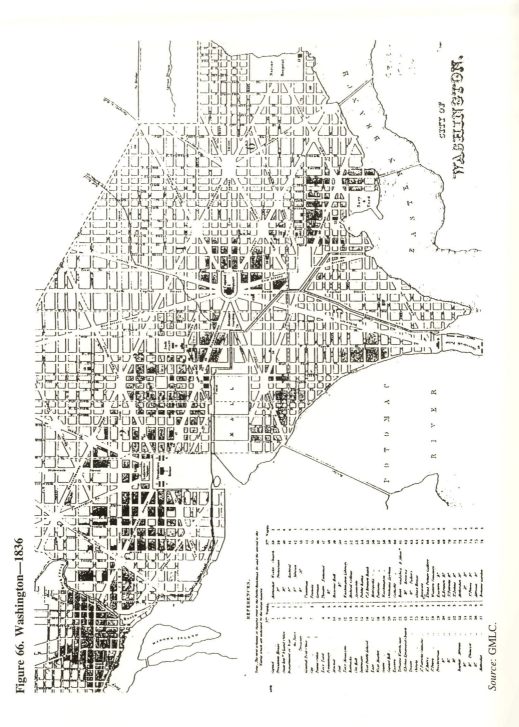

Source: GMLC.

Figure 67. Washington—1845

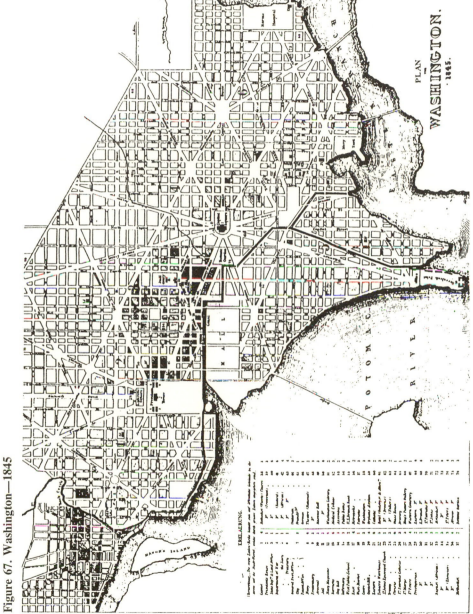

Intergovernmental
Relations

This entire volume has as its purpose the examination of the city as a governmental and political entity. In the United States, with its plethora of governments—parallel, overlapping, and hierarchical—it is inevitable that relationships should exist between these corporate entities. One set of relationships is almost entirely parallel and overlapping—those between the cities and the counties— and these will be briefly explored later in this chapter. Relationships between the cities and the federal government were few (except in the case of Washington) and usually (again, with the exception of Washington) nonhierarchical. But between cities and states there existed both an initial (with a few exceptions) and a continuing relationship of a hierarchical nature. That is, there was a flow of power from the state to the city and restraints were exercised by the former on the latter.

The point of initial contact, of course, was the issuance of a charter that created the city corporation. This type of activity has been fully explored in the first chapter of this volume, as has the subsequent modification of those charters by the states (or, earlier, colonies) and, from time to time, their complete replacement by new charters. To this point in this study, however, the examination of the activities of the states in city affairs has been largely confined to three areas—governmental structure (chapter 1), city finance (chapter 2), and suffrage and elections (chapter 3). There were, however, many other areas in which there were relationships betwen these two governmental entities, usually in the form of grants of power to the cities or the entities in the cities, sometimes in the charters themselves and in other cases in separate legislation.

As has been noted in the previous chapter, city boundaries tended to change over time. But these changes did not result simply from an accretion of population and settled area; boundary changes had to be validated and made legal by state action. In New York and the New England states, where contiguous towns filled the entire occupied areas from an early date, such enlargement could come only at the expense of another political entity. Consequently, expansion would normally be preceded by negotiations to obtain support, or at least acceptance, of the change by the affected adjoining town. But even when such acquiescence was obtained, state action was necessary to legalize the transfer and to avoid interminable litigation about subsequent actions taken by the annexing town. Of this nature were such actions as Dorchester's surrender to Boston of Dorchester Neck (South Boston) in 1804 and of Thompson's Island, farther to the south, in 1834, and the adjustment of the Boston-Brookline boundary in 1825. In Rhode Island the redrawing of the boundary line between the city of Providence and the town of North Providence in 1848 was of the same nature. Similar, too, was the absorption of a portion of the town of Colonie into Albany in 1815.[1]

In other sections of the country the chances of strong opposition to boundary changes were reduced by the limited likelihood that there would be other organized political entities with boundaries in common with those of a city. All of the land was, of course, organized into counties, but (with rare exceptions) the authority of the county included the city so that an extension of the city's boundaries did not diminish the area under the county's jurisdiction or subject to county taxation. The possibility of resistance by residents, of course, remained; the states sometimes specifically considered this possibility and in other cases there is no evidence of such concern. It is certain, for instance, that there was objection to the 1816 expansion of Baltimore's boundaries to include the "precincts," for the city council thought it wise to pass a resolution arguing the wisdom and justice of the legislative action. Hezekiah Niles probably exaggerated the opposition, however, when he asserted that the annexation was "against the consent of nine-tenths, perhaps, of the people of both" the city and the precincts.[2]

In an era of rapidly growing cities, boundary enlargements were numerous and almost routine. No purpose would be served in enumerating them all; a few examples will suffice. The addition to New Orleans of Marigny in 1810 and a new eighth ward upstream in 1818 were only two of many boundary shifts for the Crescent City. Charleston, on the other hand, was a slow-growing city and saw no enlargements (except for filling) until Charleston Neck was annexed in 1849. In 1837 the Pennsylvania legislature extended Pittsburgh's boundaries to encompass a substantial unincorporated territory east of the city, including an area known as the Northern Liberties. The Kentucky General Assembly took a similar action in relation to Louisville in 1827 by extending its boundaries eastward to take in Preston's Enlargement. A few major landholders would appear to have had some concerns about the financial impact of annexation on them, and their acquiescence was apparently secured by a final section in the act, which prohibited the city from collecting any taxes on any land owned by one estate and five individuals. Finally, it was not uncommon for the initial city charter to enlarge considerably the area of governmental jurisdiction beyond that of the previously created town. The city charter of Brooklyn, in 1834, is a good example of this practice: of the nine city wards only five (the smallest) were within the bounds of the village of Brooklyn.[3]

It was possible, of course, that an enlargement of boundaries might be sufficiently extensive to include the whole of a noncontiguous town. Not only did the bounds of Louisville as originally incorporated in 1828 include the town of Shippingport on its northwest corner but the extension of 1837 stretched the city boundaries around the larger town of Portland. Such an action would not be taken casually, of course, as the provisions of the act made clear. The statute recited that the proposed extension of the Lexington and Ohio Railroad to Portland had caused the citizens of that town to petition for annexation to Louisville and required the Louisville authorities to consent "on their record" to such extension. In like fashion, the act transferring a portion of Colonie to Albany in 1815 noted a prior petition by residents of the annexed area, and (even though no other chartered entity was involved) the Kentucky legislature, when providing for the attachment of certain additional lands to Louisville, prefaced the act by reciting that "it is represented to this General Assembly, that sundry property-holders within Preston's enlargement to the town of Louisville . . . are desirous to be added thereto and incorporated therein." Similarly, petitions preceded the annexation of unincorporated territories into Baltimore in 1799 and Cincinnati in 1838.[4]

In a few instances the state (Pennsylvania in these examples) delegated the power of annexation to corporate bodies or to individuals. As might be expected, the approval of both parties was required in these cases. In the spring of 1836 the Pennsylvania legislature authorized the councils of Philadelphia to annex Moyamensing and Passyunk "as soon as" the commissioners of Moyamensing and the supervisors of Passyunk "shall agree thereto." The decision in this case, thus, would be made by elected officials. As it happened, no such annexation took place, though both of these suburbs were among the governmental units making up the consolidated city of Philadelphia in 1854. In June of the latter year the legislature empowered the Pittsburgh councils to annex parcels "within the limits of any section of the said city districts" east of the city along the Monongahela River, upon petition of at least 30 freeholders. Nine years later the act was modified to specify petition of at least 100 qualified electors and to require a favorable vote of the electors in the area to be annexed (containing not fewer than 300 inhabitants).[5]

There were, as might be expected, other circumstances in which state legislators indicated an unwillingness to take action in the absence of requests from the city authorities or to make actions final without the support of urban voters. A major area of operations in which these petitions and ratifications were required was, as has been noted in chapter 1, that related to the city charter and governmental structure; such specifications, it will be recalled, became more prevalent after 1820 and can be seen as associated with the Jacksonian democratic movement. For example, the 1824 state act reshaping the New York city council into boards of aldermen and assistant aldermen, all with two-year terms, was the result of a petition of the city corporation and would be effective only when approved by the city's voters. On more than one occasion the Rhode Island legislature demonstrated its concern for the Providence citizenry by referring a petition for a charter change or the granting of additional power to the city government to the next session of the legislature (Rhode Island had four a year) and requiring the city, in the meantime, to publish the proposed acts, giving notice of "the pendency thereof." Moreover, in 1831 this body had chartered the city of Providence subject to ratification by three-fifths of the town's voters, and more than seven years later had answered a petition for the repeal of the charter by providing for another referendum, with a three-fifths majority being required for a repeal.[6]

More commonly, however, even changes in governmental structure and electoral process were enacted unprovisionally by state legislative bodies, though it is likely that in many cases the initiative came from the city governments affected. From the Maryland legislature came such diverse actions as the 1808 changes in the methods of choosing the mayor and members of the Second Branch of the city council of Baltimore, the changing of the beginning date for the annual meeting of the city council in 1841, and the authorization in 1843 for Baltimore's mayor and councils to hold and administer bequests to the city. The Louisiana legislature changed the qualifications for New Orleans aldermen in 1818 and two years later required (among other provisions) that the mayor visit each section of the "city and faubourgs" at least twice monthly in company with the alderman "and see that the police is well administered." In 1814 the legislature mandated the trustees of the town of St. Louis to publish financial statements every six months, and in 1841 the Providence city tax collectors were required to post performance bonds. The Pennsylvania legislature passed acts specifying the process for filling certain vacancies among Philadelphia officers in 1792, authorizing officials other than the governor to swear in the mayor of that city in 1805, providing for the Philadelphia recorder to be paid, in part, from state funds in 1830, and abolishing the requirement that the mayor of the Quaker City be chosen from the city's aldermen in 1826. The Ohio legislature provided for the direct election of minor officials—e.g., collectors, watchmen, collector of the water works—in Cincinnati in 1840 and regulated the granting of contracts by the city in 1845. The city of Buffalo was authorized by the New York legislature to engage in limited short-term borrowing to bridge the gap between expenditures and tax collections in 1839. These examples of state legislative control over city governmental operations could easily be multiplied a hundredfold.[7]

Integrally connected with city charters and governance structures was the electoral process, and in this area of activity as well the action of the state was frequently necessary to insure legitimacy. This was especially true as the powers vested in city officials and the methods by which they were selected changed significantly over time. Some of these actions have been touched on earlier and only a handful of examples will be given here. For instance, the appropriate state assemblies required voting to be by paper ballot in Albany in 1809, St. Louis in 1842, and Providence in 1840, but exempted Boston from a similar requirement for the whole of the state of Massacuhusetts in 1811. Another state concern was the division of the cities into electoral districts. There were two basic reasons for the creation of such districts: to insure more equitable representation in the city councils and to balance the number of electors using the different polling places. The latter was clearly the dominant concern in Kentucky, where election precincts were required to be established for state and federal elections, and in 1831 each Louisville ward was made a precinct. Since the wards were far too small to be units of state or federal representation, the primary purpose was clearly to facilitate the electoral process. A similar situation existed in the state of New York, where generally applicable legislation was passed in 1841 requiring the common councils in all cities except New York to divide the city into electoral districts, with each ward to be an electoral district unless the number of voters exceeded 500. The purpose of the Louisiana Act of 1825, on the other hand, was obviously to guarantee equitable representation. The mayor of New Orleans was required to take a census of qualified voters in each ward. The council, however, was required not to redraw the ward boundaries but rather to reapportion the aldermanic seats among the existing wards. Electoral pressure, thus, continued to build in New Orleans for the next ten years until the legislature divided the city into three precincts, each with its own polling place, in 1835. And in Philadelphia, despite legislation dividing increasing numbers of wards into two election precincts, voters in all of the electoral subdivisions were still required to cast their ballots at the State House, where separate windows were provided for the voters in each precinct.[8]

Members of state legislative bodies—mostly representing rural and small-town constituencies—tended to have strong doubts about the honesty of urban elections, especially after the rapid increase in the foreign-born residents of the cities in the 1830s. While irregularities in charter elections might cause the legislators little anxiety, the possibility of corrupt voting in state and federal contests was much more threatening. To counteract this possibility assemblies frequently imposed requirements on cities in the conducting of elections that were not mandated elsewhere in the state. One of the most common of these was the creation of some sort of list of qualified voters. As early as 1817 the South Carolina legislature directed Charleston authorities to produce before each election a list of nontaxpayers qualified to vote, with the intention of using this document and the list of taxpayers to establish the right of franchise in a given election. It is true that such lists might facilitate voting in any venue where there were large numbers of electors, but the major concern was clearly the possibility of fraudulent voting. The New York Act of 1840, which required commissioners in each ward to produce an alphabetical list of qualified electors in each precinct, was entitled "An Act to prevent illegal voting in the city of New York. . . ."

Similar provisions existed in Baltimore between 1837 and 1840 and were established in Washington in 1820, in New Orleans in 1835, and in Louisville in 1828.[9]

Closely related to the electoral process was the creation of wards and the drawing of ward boundaries. Wards were both electoral districts for charter (and occasionally other) elections and units through which some types of urban services were administered. The power to create and modify wards must, in order to insure the legitimacy of the city council, flow from the state as the sovereign political entity in the local area. In some instances the state legislature vested the control over ward creation with the cities; in some cases the states retained and exercised that authority; and occasionally the two processes were intermixed. The initial Baltimore charter of 1796, for instance, set the number of wards at eight and specified that they should each "contain, as nearly as may be, an equal number of inhabitants" and directed that the initial division should be accomplished by a body of seven commissioners appointed by the governor and council with subsequent changes to be the responsibility of the corporation. The legislature specified that the number of wards should be fifteen when the population reached 40,000 and that one ward should be added thereafter for every additional 20,000 residents. By 1817 the rapid growth of the Maryland metropolis moved the Assembly to modify these specifications, setting the current number of wards at twelve and projecting fourteen when the population reached 90,000, sixteen at 120,000, eighteen at 160,000, and twenty at 200,000, but leaving the mechanics in the hands of the corporation. Boston's charter of 1822 set the number of wards at twelve and assigned initial responsibility for the division to the selectmen of the town (doubtless because this action was seen as a prerequisite to the elections that would create the city government). Thereafter, the city council was responsible for maintaining equality of population among the twelve wards "as nearly as conveniently may be" by altering the ward boundaries "not oftener that once in ten years." By an act of 1850 the legislature changed the controlling principle from equality of population to equality of legal voters. Louisville's initial charter (1828) specified that the newly elected mayor and council should divide the city into five wards and subsequently alter the ward boundaries "so as to equalize the number of inhabitants in each as nigh as may be," but only after a general census. An 1833 amendment specified that the general census must be of qualified voters. Five years later the number of wards was increased to eight (effective in 1840) with boundary changes every five years, with the council to require a census "of the population and voters" prior to any change. The new charter of 1851 authorized up to twelve wards and enumerations of qualified voters each eight years.[10]

In the case of Providence there were few state restraints. The city was to be divided into six wards. From time to time (but not more frequently than once in five years) the council was to modify the boundaries to insure an equal number of freemen in each ward. Generally speaking, the Washington corporation was also left rather free of restraints. The 1802 charter continued the three divisions of the city previously established by the levy court of the county and gave the council the power to increase the number of wards as "shall seem most conducive to the general interest and convenience." In 1812 the target of an equal number of voters in each ward was added. In 1820 Congress substituted inhabitants for voters and directed that if the council should not act to meet these requirements before the last Monday in May the city should be divided into six wards whose boundaries were specified in the act. In another broadly empowering action the South Carolina legislature, by an act of 1805, authorized the Charleston intendant and wardens to define ward boundaries. But some difficulties apparently arose, for ten years later the legislature, noting that "the constitutional court" had held certain ordinances to be "nugatory" because of the alteration of ward boundaries, declared the Charleston divisions, boundaries, and apportionment to be valid.[11]

In the cases of Cincinnati and St. Louis the role of the state shifted somewhat. The initial city charter of Cincinnati (1819) was actually an amendment to a town charter and made no mention of wards. An act of 1827 divided the city into four wards whose boundaries were specified but gave the council the power to increase the number of wards and amend their boundaries. A proviso was added, however, that prohibited any change in a ward unless approved by a ward meeting held for that purpose. In a new charter in 1834 full and unrestrained power to increase wards and change boundaries was vested in the council. At no time was the aim of achieving equality of population or qualified voters among the wards raised by the Ohio legislature. In the act of 1822 incorporating the city of St. Louis, the Missouri legislature made no mention of wards, and the amendatory act of 1831 merely stated that it was "the duty of the corporate authorities of the city to arrange and reform the wards of the city in such manner as to make them, as nearly as may be, equal in qualified voters." Two years later the legislature required that the city be divided into four wards but made no other specification. The new charter of 1839 repeated the 1833 requirement and confirmed the power of the mayor and aldermen to fix boundaries and establish new wards. The 1839 charter added nothing new on this matter except to acknowledge the existence of the four wards. But the next major act two years later took a different approach, dividing the city into five wards with boundaries specified. The change was designed primarily to accommodate the ward structure to the increased area in the city. The final shift came with the charter of 1843, which directed the city council to divide the city into six wards and subsequently to adjust the boundaries as necessary to provide for an equality of "free white male inhabitants."[12]

In the other seven cases—the four New York cities, the two Pennsylvania towns, and New Orleans—ward changes were accomplished primarily by direct state action. A few examples will suffice to make the point here. In 1812 the Louisiana legislature divided the city of New Orleans into eight wards whose boundaries were specified in the act. The 1730 New York colonial charter divided the city into seven wards whose extent was therein described, and at later dates state legislative acts provided for the creation of new wards and boundaries in 1790, 1803, 1808, 1817, and 1827. New ward lines were drawn in Philadelphia by state legislative acts in 1799, 1825, and 1846. The New York legislature established the boundaries for five wards in Albany in 1826 and ten wards in 1841, and for the four new Brooklyn wards that were created by the first city charter in 1834. The same body divided the newly incorporated city of Buffalo into five wards in 1832 and specified their boundaries in detail. The practices were slightly more mixed in Pittsburgh. There the legislature divided the city into four wards in 1829 but in 1833 directed the city councils to modify the boundaries to secure equality among the wards.[13]

Thus, the state legislatures took an active role in dividing the city into political units and drawing ward lines. Even when the legislators delegated to the city councils the authority for these actions they frequently specified the number of wards to be created or laid down guidelines regarding the principles which were to govern their relative, and sometimes their actual, size.

Perhaps of even more direct concern to state legislators, and particularly to representatives from the nonurban areas, was the question of the representation of the urban residents in the state assemblies. As has already been noted, the fear of the dominance of political power in the state by the relatively large urban population—populations that were frequently perceived as different from and threatening to the rest of the state's people—not infrequently sparked opposition to such institutional changes as the direct election of governors. If a city's growth was relatively slow throughout a substantial portion of the first half of the nineteenth century, the question of representation was likely to be less, or only intermittently, acute. In other instances the urban-rural division might be at least partially submerged in other (e.g., partisan) conflicts. Representation by Charleston in the South Carolina legislature was, for example, never a major issue because it was of far less concern than the determination to preserve the power of the low country in relation to the more rapidly growing western section of the state. Further considerations were that Charleston's growth rate was moderate and that the low country planter elements exercised great influence in the city. Thus Charleston began the century with the relatively large representation of fifteen members in the state House of Representatives, saw an increase to sixteen by the second decade of the century, and to seventeen by the 1840s. Throughout these years the census showed Charleston with roughly 5% to 6% of the state's population, except after the annexation of 1848, when the figure rose to a little under 6.5%.[14]

Though the representation of Charleston in the state legislature was more than adequate (less than 6% of the population and more than 12% of the representatives in 1800) for its size, the situation was far different for residents of Baltimore and Providence. In each state the populations outside the metropolis were extremely wary of conceding to the major cities an equitable influence in the governance of the state. As the century opened, the city of Baltimore had only two representatives in the House of Delegates, about 3% of its membership, although Baltimore's proportion of the state's population was much greater. When, in 1805, an effort was made to increase the city's representation, it was defeated in the lower house by a vote of sixty-four–to–two, with only the Baltimore members supporting the proposition. Similar proposals were beaten back in 1819, 1822, and 1823, never attracting the support of more than a third of the members. In the meantime the city's population increased rapidly, partially by annexation, accounting for almost a fifth of the state's total. It was not until 1836, as a part of a modest reform movement (that also provided for the direct election of the governor) that the city's representation was increased to four, about 5% of the body's membership. Two years later the number was increased to five. By that date about one-fifth of all the state's residents lived in Baltimore; at the end of the half century the figure was 29%.[15]

The situation in Providence was similar to that in Baltimore until 1842. The 1662 charter, which served as the constitution of the state until 1842, specified that Providence and two other towns should elect four representatives, Newport, six, and all other towns, two each. Thus, though the relative populations of the towns changed, and new towns were created, over the next century and a half no change in Providence's level of representation took place. By 1840 the city contained more than a fifth of the state's population and elected one-eighteenth of the representatives. The Dorr Rebellion of 1841 led to the establishment of a new constitution that provided for an apportionment of legislative seats among the towns in accordance with population, but with two restraints—each town was to have at least one representative and no town should elect more than one-sixth of all the members, which were limited to seventy-two. Consequently, in 1842 Providence sent twelve representatives to the seventy-two-member house. Since the census of 1850 showed Providence to contain 28% of the state's population, this still left the city much underrepresented, but to a far lesser degree than previously.[16]

Between these extremes, Boston was an example of a city that was relatively equitably represented in the state legislature. In the 1820s the newly chartered city's representation constituted rather more than a tenth of the assembly members and Boston's proportion of the state's population was somewhat less. In 1830 the city had a tenth of the state's residents and elected almost an eighth of the representatives. Ten years later the city's population share was 12.66% and its proportion of the representation, 10.7%. By the end of the half century the city's representation was probably as equitable as it was possible to achieve—Boston's 11.50% of the state's population elected 11.60% of the members of the General Court. It might be noted that the Massachusetts house membership was quite large and extremely variable, ranging during this period from well over 200 to slightly over 600 members. Since all representatives had to be elected by majorities, and multiple-member constituencies were the rule, there were occasions on which Boston (and doubtless other constituencies) failed to send full delegations to the General Court. In 1826, for example, only fifteen of the twenty-four authorized representatives were chosen in the three elections held during the period authorized by the constitution.[17]

On the whole the New York cities were not dramatically underrepresented in the state legislature, though this was increasingly less true in the largest cities late in the half century. The apportionment of 1826 gave New York City eleven members, about 8.5% of the whole membership; the city's population at this time constituted about a tenth of the state total. The 1836 apportionment gave the city rather more than a tenth of the representation (thirteen) when it contained between an eighth and a ninth of the state's residents. Ten years later the legislature assigned sixteen seats to New York City, about one-eighth of the total, but by this time the city's proportion of the state's population had risen to almost a sixth. Representative seats in the Empire State were assigned by county, and only in New York City were the city and county boundaries coterminous. Among the other major urban centers, only in Kings County (Brooklyn) was the representation assigned by the 1846 apportionment rather less than the population would have justified—2.3% of the representation and about 4% of the population. Albany and Erie (Buffalo) counties, on the other hand, each elected 3.1% of the representation, and that was probably a little above the proportion of the state's residents to be found in these counties at that date. Thus, only in the two largest cities in the state was there observable underrepresentation in the fifth decade of the century, and even there the inequity was not as pronounced as elsewhere.[18]

In Pennsylvania, too, the cities had generally equitable representation in the lower house of the legislature. The constitutions of both 1790 and 1838 provided for an assembly with from 60 to 100 members with the seats to be apportioned among the counties and the city of Philadelphia on the basis of the number of taxable inhabitants. As it happened, Philadelphia was the only one of these cities that consistently contained a smaller and smaller percentage of the state's population (up to 1854). The number of representatives from this city varied from five to seven. Most of the time the city was probably slightly overrepresented, but in 1845 the representation stood at 5% of the legislature and its population constituted a slightly larger proportion of the state's residents than that figure. Allegheny County (Pittsburgh) fared about the same. In both 1832 and 1845 the county had about 4% of the legislative seats; it had a little smaller proportion of the state's population in 1832 and a little larger proportion in 1845.[19]

The situation in the other cities (except for Washington, where there was no question of representation), though different in details, was not unlike the circumstances in one or another of the cities already examined. It is hardly necessary to explore the experiences of all of the cities. The question of representation was one that, in every case, was under the control of the state government. The decision about the level of representation for the urban populations lay always in the hands of representatives who were frequently convinced that there were great differences between them and the urbanites and who often viewed the cities and their people with suspicion, distrust, and, not

uncommonly, hostility. Other factors, of course, also influenced the state legislative decisions about urban representation—power distribution factors in the
state, economic and social interconnections, and notions of the right of equitable
representation in the governments under which people lived come to mind in
individual cases. In any event, underrepresentation was far more common than
overrepresentation, and equity was more likely to be an announced goal than a
reality. Here, as elsewhere, the cities could not avoid intergovernmenal relationships, for they were integral and essential to the political life of the city and
its residents.

It was doubtless inevitable that the political aspects of the city's life should
bring the corporation into more or less continuous interaction with the state that
was its creator, but such continuing interaction took place in other areas of
activity as well. For instance, state action was necessary to enable cities to
engage in a relatively large number of actions that contributed directly to the
building, maintenance, and improvement of the city's infrastructure—streets,
bridges, ferries, wharves, water supply, sewers, and lighting. In some cases the
charters conferred powers in these areas, but even then more ambitious projects
frequently required state authorization, either for the project itself or for its
funding.

For example, the charters of Albany (1801) and Louisville (1828) each gave
the mayor and council broad (but not, in every case, detailed) powers to lay out
and modify streets, but the Kentucky and New York legislatures nevertheless
enacted additional legislation. A rather extensive general grant of power was
added to the Louisville charter as an amendment in 1831, and some years later
the legislature passed another act providing that "the Police Court of Louisville
shall have all the power and authority to open and extend streets and alleys in
the city of Louisville that is vested in the Jefferson Circuit Court." In 1826 the
New York legislature thought it necessary to authorize the city of Albany "to
discontinue and abolish that part of Centre-street situated between Lawrence and
North Ferry-street," and, indeed, the charter had mentioned widening, straightening, and laying out streets, but not closing them.[20]

The situation in Baltimore was quite different. Having been granted very little
power to open, close, or modify streets, especially after the creation of the
Poppleton Plot, the city necessarily invoked the power of the state legislature
for actions affecting individual streets. In the five sessions of the state legislature
between 1832 and 1837, for example, more than sixty pieces of legislation were
passed dealing with individual Baltimore streets—more than two-thirds of all
acts dealing specifically with Baltimore. In 1839 all this changed when the
legislature granted the city authorities extensive powers to deal with street openings, closings, and modifications. Between 1840 and 1850 the Maryland legislature passed only thirteen Baltimore street acts, never more than four in any
year and sometimes none at all.[21]

In no other city was the interrelationship between the state and city governments so continuous as in Baltimore before 1839, but in all of them there were

circumstances that required state action. For one thing, most of the city charters were like that of Albany in not authorizing the city officials to close streets. Only the 1832 charter of Buffalo specifically empowered the corporation to "discontinue" streets, though the 1848 Washington charter did authorize the mayor and councils to close alleys that had previously been opened. None of these alleys, of course, could be found on the L'Enfant/Ellicott plan. The absence of street-closing authorization in almost all of the charters is hardly surprising since most of the cities, as previously noted (see chapter 5), had a recognized plan and the elimination of streets platted on those plans could involve considerable potential financial loss; in the case of the closing of a street already opened, the consequences could be more serious still. Boston, of course, had no preexisting plan, so it is less surprising that the town was empowered by the Massachusetts legislature in 1816 to close, as well as alter, any existing street, lane, or alley.[22] It is only to be expected, therefore, that a number of state acts dealing with city streets involved closing off existing public ways.[23] But a number of state laws also dealt with what appear to have been rather routine street openings, not only in cities whose authority was vague or at least nonspecific, such as Providence, Charleston, and New Orleans, but also in others whose empowerment seemed clear.[24]

Probably the main reason that requests were made for state action in this area—and state actions were often sparked by requests from the city authorities—was that the corporation needed to be certain that its title to land taken to make streets was unquestionable, and that the monetary awards made to prior property owners constituted legal expenditures. This was particularly true when major new streets were constructed through areas already heavily built up, as in the Broad Street and South Street developments in Boston and the construction of East Bay Street in Charleston, when special state legislation seemed absolutely imperative.[25]

Finally, there were those pieces of legislation that were designed to protect, or extricate, or estop the city. In 1847 the Missouri legislature declared that St. Louis had no power to open any streets "through the grounds now enclosed and occupied by the Sisters of the Sacred Heart, and upon which their convent is located; this act being designed to protect them in the enjoyment of the garden and pleasure grounds attached to said convent." But such prohibitions were balanced by protections. Both the Rhode Island (in 1822) and the Ohio (in 1850) legislatures declared that the opening to the public of privately constructed streets did not make them public ways legally, and thus maintainable by charges upon the corporations. Earlier still (in 1795) the Rhode Island Assembly untangled a potentially troublesome problem for Providence when it authorized the town to open a street through the North Burying Ground, replacing the property taken with other land to be used for interments. And at the beginning of the century the Charleston authorities found themselves in an entanglement and had to call upon the state to resolve the problem. The legislature had previously authorized the reconstruction and widening of East Bay Street, but in 1801 the city's actions leading to that end struck an impasse. All of the property owners on East Bay Street had agreed to terms for the cession of the land for the widening with the exception of the heirs of Robert Rapier. One of these heirs was not mentally competent to enter into a contract. The South Carolina legislature, appealed to by the Charleston city council, appointed three commissioners to establish a fair remuneration to be paid to the Rapier heirs and thus validated the tranfer of the property and allowed the project to proceed.[26]

The crucial element was, of course, that the state governments were sovereign governments (as Americans understood that term in the first half of the nineteenth century) and their enactments could legitimatize actions to a far greater degree than city ordinances could. Cities were, after all, subordinate entities— repositories of the powers granted to them by their creators, the states. The state governments' sovereign powers, on the other hand, were subject only to the limitations imposed by the federal constitution and laws in certain areas, their own self-established constitutions, and court interpretations of those (and, perhaps, other common law) restraints.

These comments on the intergovernmental relationships involved in the building of the cities' street systems will serve as an example of those relationships in all areas of infrastructure development. This area was chosen for purposes of illustration because of its universality among all cities and its diversity of details. Street paving and drainage were as universal but lacked some measure of diversity. The intergovernmental relationships there and elsewhere were essentially the same as in the area of street layout. That is, general authorization to pave and drain were common but some specific authorization was also frequent. The major specific aspects dealt with were the procedures for establishing and collecting the assessments which funded most of these activities and, less frequently, the apportionment of costs between the corporation and the landholder. Bridges and ferries were usually mentioned in the charters of, or legislation addressing, those cities whose geography and topography made such transportation facilities important. Generally speaking, the city authorities were given the power to build bridges, regulate and maintain harbors and docks, locate ferries, regulate rates, and, in the case of ferries, regulate frequency of service. Street lighting and water supply were universally authorized by state action, though the former commonly preceded the latter in the time of its introduction. Bridge building and operation, water delivery, and street lighting frequently involved private corporations, and these entities, of course, could be created only by state, not city, action. The actual development and introduction of these elements of the cities' infrastructures will be dealt with in a subsequent volume of this work. The financial support of these facilities obviously involved the cities in the raising of money by assessment, taxation, and loans; these matters have already been addressed in chapter 2 of this volume.

Another area of governmental operations important to urban dwellers involved the inspection and regulation of private activities for the benefit of the whole population—for example, the operation of a market, or the inspection of salt pork, or the prohibition of economic activities deemed harmful to individuals and society—which might generically be denominated as protective. In these instances, as was the case in the building and maintenance of the urban infrastructure, the sovereign power of the state was necessarily involved, either to act itself or to empower the city corporation to act.[27]

One of the commonest of these activities was the establishment and operation of markets, an activity designed to facilitate the feeding of the urban population. All of these cities not only had markets—with rare exceptions multiple markets—but also exerted control over them and established regulations for them. Although markets were set up in a few towns very early and on local initiative, in almost every case the cities were empowered by state or colonial authorities to operate the markets or had their established practices confirmed by such action. In the cases of Albany and New York the authorization came with the colonial charters of 1686 and 1730. The Albany charter provided for the setting of market days and made the mayor clerk of the market, and the New York charter specifically spoke to the establishment of a market and designated the mayor as clerk. In 1701 the proprietary charter granted to Philadelphia had provided for a market to be held on Wednesdays and Saturdays and directed the mayor to appoint a clerk, who, in this case, was to exercise a wide range of related powers. These provisions were also embodied in the first post-Revolutionary city charter for the Quaker City in 1789. The Maryland legislature, in 1783, before Baltimore was chartered, acted to regulate the market established in that town. This was not an uncommon practice in relation to settlements that had not been granted city charters; the Kentucky legislature also passed market legislation for Louisville at about the turn of the century. In the latter case, however, the Assembly decided to vest some of the responsibility and authority in the town trustees. That body was given the power to locate the market in 1802 when the legislature rescinded its earlier act requiring placement on the Public Square. In the same year as the Maryland legislation the South Carolina Assembly, in the charter that first created Charleston as a political entity, conferred upon that city the power to regulate markets within its boundaries.[28]

Market activities in the New England towns would seem to have developed in the early days with considerably less oversight by the colonial government than was the case in New York (doubtless a direct reflection of the differences between proprietary or royal and corporate or charter colonial governments). Bostonians, for example, initially opposed markets as monopolistic in nature and tending to raise the prices of provisions. That town had mixed, but intermittent, experiences with markets in the mid-1700s, but the selectmen were routinely enacting market regulations by the end of the century. Providence grew much more slowly, having a population only a quarter to a third that of Boston in the early nineteenth century, and doubtless had less need than the larger town for market facilities. In 1813 the Rhode Island legislature empowered the town meeting of Providence to establish and regulate a market. The first charter of the city in 1831, while granting considerably expanded authority, also, like many such documents, transferred to the city authorities all powers previously exercised by the town government. Brooklyn's experience was in some respects similar. It, too, was an early foundation which grew slowly; markets had existed intermittently in the early years of the nineteenth century. A market ordinance was passed by the trustees in 1828 and the first city charter authorized the city council to select a "Clerk for each market."[29]

In some other cases state action preceded the chartering of the cities. In 1804 the town council of Pittsburgh was authorized to regulate the market and to appoint a clerk; eleven years later the Ohio Assembly empowered the Cincinnati town council to appoint clerks of the market. It was also common, however, for the legislatures to addresss this matter in the initial city charters. Buffalo's charter of 1832, for instance, authorized the council to name a clerk of the market; that of Washington in 1802 gave the city government the power to establish and regulate markets; and in 1822 the St. Louis charter conferred on that city the authority to regulate markets. In the case of New Orleans, the authorization to establish and inspect a market came by a separate act in 1816, rather more than a decade after the city was first chartered.[30]

The granting of power by a state legislature did not necessarily end the relationship between these two governments in the matter of markets. For one thing, the degree of empowerment differed greatly from city to city. Additionally, other circumstances might arise which would move state legislators to intervene or city authorities to request additional state legislation. It was no accident that continuing state involvement was more marked in those cities whose grants of authority were less comprehensive. Several acts of the Maryland legislature, for example, dealt with the creation of new markets—for the sale of livestock in 1793, in the Eastern Precincts in 1808, in the Western Precincts in 1811, and Richmond Market in 1834. All of these dealt with the powers of commissioners named to acquire land, and some included specific market regulations. In 1790 the state authorized the commissioners named to erect a market at the west end of the "Bason," and to sell off some adjoining land to reimburse themselves for the considerable personal debt they had contracted when the cost exceeded the funding provided. And in the 1840s the city petitioned the legislature for, and obtained, a grant of power of condemnation to extend the Bel-Air Market.

There was also a considerable amount of state legislation respecting Philadelphia markets, especially in the late eighteenth and early nineteenth centuries. An act of 1786 authorized the city wardens to extend the High Street Market to Fourth Street, and beyond if needed later. This act was supplemented by additional legislation in 1795 which required the exclusion of butchers from the western half of the market and the free vending by country people in one-half of the new buildings. An act of 1804, which authorized the Philadelphia corporation to establish markets anyplace in the city and make regulations therefor, retained the requirement that half of any buildings erected "remain free for the use of the country people attending said market''; six years later the state consented to an annual stall rental, not to exceed twenty dollars, for the ''country people.'' Even with the large amount of freedom granted to the city in the 1804 act (confirmed by further legislation in 1810) it was still thought necessary for the legislature specifically to authorize the establishment of a fish market in 1812. In cities with broad and specific grants of authority regulating markets, state action was less common. Even so, the New York legislature authorized the Albany mayor to appoint superintendents of markets in 1802, and in 1816 the corporation of New York, believing its powers to be inadequate to the task, sought and obtained legislation empowering the city to acquire property to establish a market in the second ward.[31]

There were dozens of areas in which the city governments undertook protective activities. They are worthy of the more extensive treatment which they will receive in a subsequent volume of this study, but at this juncture it is sufficient to note that these powers (though simply assumed by some of the earliest established towns) were normally derived from the state and conferred upon the cities by legislative act. The number of specific authorizations for protective action grew as the nature of urban life became increasingly complex. The earliest charters conveyed relatively slight, but not insignificant, powers in this area. The 1701 charter of Philadelphia, though conferring broad and nonspecific ordinance powers, made only one reference to protective activity. The mayor, as heretofore noted, was to name a clerk of the market, ''who shall have assize of bread, wine, beer, wood and other things.'' That is to say, he would have the responsibility and the power to insure, personally or through his deputies, the quality and quantity of the materials listed when offered for sale in the city. The latter portion of the statement would appear to grant almost unlimited power in this area, but it did not differ significantly from other early grants. The 1686 Albany charter gave the mayor, as clerk of the market, ''assize . . . of bread, wine, beer and wood, and other things to the office of Clerk of the Market belonging or concerning.'' In the case of Albany the mayor was also empowered to license sellers of alcoholic beverages, and the corporation was authorized to build a public weigh-house. The New York charter of the same year conferred the most extensive powers to take protective action of any of these early eighteenth-century charters. Here the mayor was also to license liquor sales and the corporation was given the ''assizes . . . of bread, wine, beer, ale, and all other victuals and things whatsoever.'' But in addition, the corporation was to name gaugers of liquor, measurers of salt, grain, and ''other merchandise measurable,'' surveyors and packers of ''bread, flour, beef, pork, and other provisions,'' public carriers, and ''garblers''—that is, those who inspect materials and remove foreign objects.[32]

As the years passed more and more authority in this area was granted to the urban governments. An examination of the relevant provisions in two late charters—those of Louisville and St. Louis in 1851—will illustrate the range of authority granted by that date.

There were basically three ways in which the cities exercised their protective functions—through inspection by city officers, licensing by the corporation, and prohibition by city ordinances. Licensing was often nothing more than a means of raising revenue; in this context only the licensing processes that were normally associated with regulation or prohibition will be noted. The 1851 charters of both cities provided for the gauging of liquors, oils, and other liquids; the inspection of barreled and packaged foodstuffs such as beef, pork, flour, meat, lard, tallow, and butter; and weighing and measuring of hay (in St. Louis), coal, wood, and lime. The St. Louis charter specified the establishment of weights and measures, and as a practical matter this was necessary to carry out most inspections. Both charters authorized inspection of lumber, stone, and other building material, and that of St. Louis retained a section common to earlier documents authorizing the regulation of brick size. Both legislatures empowered the cities to license liquor retailers, theatrical performances and other public exhibitions, public transportation vehicles (carts, drays, carriages, wagons), games (bowling alleys and shooting galleries in Louisville, billiard houses in St. Louis), auctions, and auctioneers. The St. Louis document specified the power of the corporation to set rates for transportion services (and added porters to the list), but that was usual in any event, and Louisville's charter conferred the power to fix ferry rates and measure and mark the capacity of vehicles carrying wood, coal, and lime. St. Louis could also license and regulate pawnbrokers, money-changing brokers, hawkers, and peddlers (an interesting combination of employments to be grouped in one section), and Louisville authorities could name members of a Board or Institute of Pharmacy which, in turn, must certify the competence of apothecaries before they could be licensed by the city, which would also regulate their trade.

The Louisville city council might prohibit the market practices of forestalling, regrating, and engrossing; while that of St. Louis, more modestly, was only authorized to prohibit forestalling of poultry, butter, eggs, and fruit, but was specifically empowered to regulate the vending of meat, poultry, and vegetables, which other cities did routinely with market ordinances. The St. Louis corporation could regulate the weight, quality, and price of bread and the rates and practices of chimney sweepers. Both councils might prohibit the erection of wooden buildings in any part of the city (the concern here was the spread of fire), and St. Louis', in addition, could specify the "manner and order of the building of partition and parapet walls and of partition fences," a practice fairly common in the cities. Louisville's authorization "to prohibit the erection of manufacturing establishments deemed likely to create the danger of fire or producing unpleasant effluvia" was somewhat more inclusive than usual charter empowerments. Finally, the Louisville charter provided for the appointment of a number of officers to examine the work done by the building trades—inspectors of brick and stone work, of carpenter's work, of painter's work, and of plasterer's work.[33]

But, of course, the states' authorization of regulatory control did not occur only with the enactment of a new charter; individual pieces of legislation expanded the cities' regulatory powers (or, sometimes, restricted them) as the legislators perceived changes in the needs of society. These circumstances can be illustrated by seizing almost randomly upon acts affecting each of these cities. Albany was empowered to license butchers and liquor retailers in 1802 and livery stables and hackney carriages in 1814. In 1837 the Maryland legislature authorized the mayor of Baltimore to name three commissioners to fix carriage rates in the city and in 1841 restricted wood sales in Baltimore to sellers licensed by the corporation, but five weeks later the legislature exempted wood wharves in the city from these restrictions and permitted the corporation to except others. In 1850 the Philadelphia councils obtained the power to regulate omnibusses, and sixty years earlier the corporation had been give the authority (in an act primarily concerned with streets) to set rates charged by draymen, carters, wagoners, porters, wood sawyers, and chimney sweeps. The New York City authorities were given the power to regulate boardinghouses in 1803 and to license pawnbrokers in 1812. The Ohio legislature, in 1845, empowered the Cincinnati city council to appoint gaugers of spirits, molasses, and linseed oil; and in 1832 a Rhode Island act specified in considerable detail how the surveyor general appointed by the Providence authorities should measure and evaluate lumber. The interests of the states extended beyond initial authorizing legislation to include revision and extension. In 1840 the Rhode Island legislature empowered the city of Providence to name two additonal measurers of grain, salt, and sea coal; Massachusetts' act of 1830 authorized the Boston corporation to adopt ordinances and regulations governing the inspection and measurement of lumber, replacing an earlier measure of 1784; and the Kentucky Assembly, in 1849, repealed a prior prohibition on Louisville's licensing ninepin and tenpin alleys.[34]

In some cases the states regulated or prohibited activity in the cities directly rather than authorizing action by the city authorities. The New York legislature, for instance, in 1818 provided for the governor and council to name the gaugers of fish oil for New York and Brooklyn and in 1822 made the same provision for the inspectors of flaxseed in New York. Similarly, by an act of 1827 the governor and Senate were to appoint the weighers of cotton and hay in New Orleans. But it was the Maryland legislature that was most active in this kind of activity. That body provided for the governor and council to appoint two inspectors of salt provisions in Baltimore in 1827, two inspectors of sole leather in 1832, an inspector of lime in 1836, two inspectors of hay and straw in 1837, and a "practical chemist" to be an inspector of guano in 1847.[35]

And, finally, there were, of course, circumstances in which the state intervened to restrict the exercise of powers already possessed, or that could be inferred to be possessed, by city governments. Such actions would normally occur when the advantages of nonurban interests appeared to be threatened. The determination of the Pennsylvania legislators to insure free access to the Philadelphia market for the "country people" has already been noted. Two other examples will suffice to illustrate this predilection. In 1808 the Maryland Assembly passed an act supplementary to an earlier law which gave the Baltimore government the power to preserve the paving on the streets of that city by regulating such matters as weight and wheel width of carriages, carts, wagons, drays, and the like. The 1808 act declared that these powers could not be exercised in relation to vehicles employed in the city less than two months per year—that is, used to transport goods into the city rather than to move goods about the city. In somewhat similar circumstances the Louisiana legislature declared in 1843 that both the city corporation and governments of the municipalities were "incompetent" to pass or enforce any ordinance or regulation that would result in the imposition of a "charge of any nature whatsoever" on any "good, produce, wares, and merchandise, of whatsoever kind or nature, landed in, or shipped from, the corporate limits of said city." In all of these cases it would seem clear that the state intended to limit city authority for the benefit of nonurban residents.[36]

There were various other areas in which the states gave the cities the power to act to provide services to their residents or to preserve order; these grants of power (as in other cases previously noted) were sometimes accompanied by limitations or requirements. Some of these were so obviously necessary—for example, to maintain a police function, to assist in providing fire protection, to suppress riots, to operate a city court to enforce ordinances—that they will not be here considered as an aspect of intergovernmental relations, though each will be explored in some detail in subsequent volumes. Others would appear to have been integral to the establishment of the city as a corporate entity—for example, the right to hold property—and will not be discussed here, even though supplementary legislation was considered necesary in some specific cases. One or two examples of these additional areas of city-state interaction will suffice at this juncture.

One circumstance that many urban residents found distasteful, annoying, and dangerous was the presence in the city streets of various animals, especially hogs. In only a few instances—Buffalo in 1832, Brooklyn in 1834, and Albany in 1842, for instance—did the city charters include specific grants of authority to "restrain and regulate the running at large" of these normally rural denizens. It is quite likely, of course, that such empowerment might well have been considered to be subsumed in the general ordinance powers to preserve order and provide for the health of inhabitants which was routinely granted to city corporations, but the state legislature, in a number of cases, passed statutes specifically addressing this problem. New York was authorized in 1821 to prohibit by ordinance swine running at large and to declare such swine forfeit. Hogs were already, by that date, an ancient nuisance; Governor Stuyvesant in 1648 had banned hogs between the fort and the Freshwater Pond, except in enclosures. Early action was also taken in Philadelphia, where the colonial legislature prohibited swine running at large in 1705. In 1822 the state Assembly gave the "exclusive right and privilege of taking up any swine, hogs, shoats, or pigs" to the overseers of the poor, who were to dispose of the animals for the benefit of the poor. Four years later the "privilege" was transferred to the councils. When Providence, in 1845, was given "full power to enact ordinances and regulations prohibiting horses, cattle, sheep, hogs, goats and geese from going at large," it is likely that some challenge had been raised to the city's earlier actions. The Maryland legislature early took steps (largely ineffective) to protect Baltimore's residents from this annoyance by prohibiting swine from running at large within five miles of the city.[37]

Two other areas of concern by urban government that frequently sparked state legislative action were public health and support for the poor. Some public health function authorizations were built into the governing documents of more than half of these cities. The initial charters of Baltimore (1796), Washington (1802), St. Louis (1822), Boston (1822), Louisville (1828), Buffalo (1832), and Brooklyn (1834) all contained some form of provision enabling the corporation to address public health concerns, as did Cincinnati's 1834 charter and the Philadelphia consolidation charter of 1854 (which established a health department in the urban government), though health matters had doubtless been dealt with by predecessor governments in most of these cases. The clause in the Washington charter was very limited, simply authorizing the city government to take action to prevent the introduction of contagious diseases into the city, while that in Baltimore's was general and nonspecific. The St. Louis charter statements were generally empowering, with specific responsibilities noted. Charter provisions directed the appointment of health officers or members of boards of health (or assigned such functions to elected officials) in Boston, Buffalo, Cincinnati (1834), and Louisville, and specific responsibilities were assigned to a board of health in Brooklyn.[38]

Two other considerations must be kept in mind here: 1) the state governments acted through regular (noncharter) legislation to authorize individual city governments (or, sometimes, *all* town or city governments in the state) to play an active role in public health matters, and 2) cities doubtless engaged in similar activities under the authority conferred by the general ordinance powers they possessed—that is, to pass ordinances for the safety and convenience of their residents. By 1818, for example, Philadelphia's participation in health matters was well established and extensive (under one or both of these empowerments), and a broad state statute of January 29 of that year was clearly aimed at consolidating and extending that activity. A board of health existed, but it was metropolitan in nature, with the city authorities naming only about half of the members. (Incidentally, this means that Pittsburgh also had extensive power in this area, for its initial [1816] city charter conferred upon that corporation all of the powers of the Philadelphia government.) A similar act of the Massachusetts legislature in 1816 shows Boston to have been engaged in extensive health-related activities before its initial city charter casually disposed of the matter by assigning to the city corporation all the powers of the predecessor town and making councilmen members of the board of health. Indeed, as early as 1797 Boston's voters were authorized to elect members of this board. In 1816 the

Rhode Island Assembly made all town councils boards of health, and in 1823 the New York legislature passed a lengthy and detailed act dealing with public health matters in the city of New York, including the selection of members of the board of health. A year later the Assembly designated the trustees of Brooklyn village members of the board of health.[39]

There were even a few times when state legislatures were willing to go beyond authorizing corporation action, appropriating state funds to assist cities whose treasuries had been depleted by epidemics or whose needs for medical facilities seemed to justify assistance. There were several instances of state aid to city hospitals but a single example will serve. In 1792 the New York legislature pledged £2,000 annually to the "Society of the Hospital of the City of New York" for five years; in 1795 the contribution was increased to £4,000 and the time extended to 1800. Less common was reimbursement by the state of city expenditures for public health purposes. But in the years about the turn of the century, when epidemics seemed to follow close on the heels of each other, several such transactions took place. In 1796 the New York legislature appropriated more than £255 for Albany and almost £3,312 for New York to offset the expenses of combating "infectious diseases" in the summer and fall of 1795. Three years later the Pennsylvania Assembly directed that state funds be used to reimburse the sheriff of Philadelphia city and county for the expenses incurred during the "prevalence of the late contagious fever," and in 1801 the state agreed to service and retire a $45,000 loan contracted in 1799 to relieve the distress caused by a recent epidemic. More unusual was the South Carolina legislature's decision in 1837 to appropriate $12,000 to indemnify Charleston for damages recovered and recoverable because of the burning, by order of city authorities, of the brig *Amelia* and its cargo, while in quarantine, in order to prevent the introduction of cholera into the city.[40]

As was the case with health affairs, the city charters frequently said little or nothing about care of the poor. To a considerable degree this was probably because the local responsibility for the care of indigents was long established and the mechanisms were already in place. Additionally, the counties sometimes retained these responsibilities even after the creation of urban corporations within their boundaries. The initial charters of Boston (1822) and Brooklyn (1834) contained provisions for the election of overseers of the poor, but each also provided for the transfer of the powers of the town in this area to the new corporations. The first charters of Charleston (1783) and Washington (1802) did not address processes but did authorize the councils to provide for the support of the poor, and Philadelphia's consolidation charter of 1854 also directed the election of guardians of the poor while requiring certain of the existing arrangements to be continued until changed by the councils. Albany's 1801 charter acknowledged the matter only by limiting the power of the overseers to extend support to the poor, and in New York (1730) and Louisville (1828) the only sections dealing with the poor were those authorizing the corporation to build or acquire buildings to be used as almshouses.[41]

The state legislatures, of course, enacted a variety of measures affecting the support of the poor in the cities. A few examples will serve to illustrate their concerns. The Maryland Assembly took a somewhat unusual course in using nongovernmental entities to address this problem. In 1831 it chartered a corporation of private subscribers to build and operate a House of Reform and three years later directed that two-fifths of the money derived from fees on immigrants (which went to support the poor) should be given to the German and Hibernian Societies. South Carolina, in 1820, took a rather more conventional approach by appropriating several thousand dollars to the Charleston authorities to assist them in supporting the transient poor. A quarter of a century later the Ohio legislature authorized the Cincinnati council (which had the power in this area routinely held by the township trustees) to provide medical and pharmaceutical assistance to the city's poor even if they were not in the public hospital. Of course, authorizing action did not necessarily cause that action to occur. In 1841 the Louisiana Assembly authorized each of the New Orleans municipalities to establish a House of Refuge for Juveniles (such institutions normally admitted many poor children), but six years later the legislature found it necessary to repass the measure. The New York Assembly, in 1812, gave the city officers of New York another instrumentality for dealing with the poor (and enabled them to cut costs) when it authorized the commissioners of the almshouse to bind out poor children to persons residing outside the city boundaries but within the state. The Pennsylvania legislature moved relatively quickly to deal with the problems related to the care of the poor posed by the early development of contiguous suburbs. The 1803 act "for the consolidation and amendment of the laws, as far as they respect the Poor" provided for a single body of guardians for Philadelphia, Southwark, and Northern Liberties. And in 1794 and 1795 the Rhode Island Assembly made three special grants, totaling almost £58, to the town trustees of Providence "for the Support of divers French Exiles from St. Domingo."[42]

State legislatures, obviously, were continuously involved with many other aspects of the life of the urban corporations and their citizens than those dealt with here. State actions (sometimes requirements) were necessary, for example, to enable the cities to provide fire and police protection, supply their residents with water, educate their children, and borrow money. All of these activities are dealt with in a later volume of this study and the role of the states is considered there.

One other point might be noted specifically, however. By the exercise of its incorporating power a state legislature created not only the urban governmental entities but also a wide variety of other corporations that played influential roles in city life. In this way legal existence was given to churches, fraternal orders, beneficial societies, insurance companies, banks, moral uplift bodies, charitable organizations, bridge companies, private cemeteries, libraries, gas companies, water works, and manufacturing concerns. Of particular interest were special-purpose societies empowered to establish and manage almshouses, houses of correction, orphanages, houses for widows, asylums for unmarried pregnant women, reform schools for juveniles, various kinds of schools, and many other institutions, not a few of which were quasi-governmental in nature. These city-state interactions, too, will be discussed in other contexts.

There was much less interaction between city and county governments, and the relationship here was clearly not one of power hierarchy. In a few cases there was no real difference between the county and the city. New York City and County had identical boundaries, and although there were some county institutions—for example, courts—they were essentially just additional city functions staffed by additional city officials. It was highly indicative that "the mayor, recorder, and aldermen of the city of New-York" were also the county supervisors. The situation in Boston was not very different. By a series of acts—most notably in 1822, 1823, 1831, and 1833—the corporation of Boston was given all the power of the Suffolk County government, and Chelsea, the only other town in the county, was relieved from all county taxation; the Boston mayor and council even had the power to license innkeepers in Chelsea. The city of Philadelphia, of course, similarily became (in 1854) coterminous with Philadelphia County, but Baltimore took a different course, being separated entirely from Baltimore County in 1851. In the meantime, however, Baltimore City had gradually expanded its area of independence from, and its share of the power in, Baltimore County government. As early as 1818 the corporation was given the appointment of constables for "that part of Baltimore County within the limits of the city," and five years later received the appointment of a majority of the trustees for the poor. Perhaps the most significant step was the 1827 Maryland statute providing for the election of commissioners for Baltimore County. In these commissioners, when elected, would be vested "all the power, rights and privileges, lawfully exercised by, and all property, estate and effects, vested in the justices of the levy court of Baltimore county, so far as regards the said county *without the limits of the city of Baltimore* [emphasis mine]." Those powers and effects, *within* Baltimore city were vested in the mayor and city council.[43]

In both Albany and Brooklyn the supervisors of the county continued to exercise certain authority over the cities, the most notable of which was the annual approval of the cities' budgets. In addition, the overseers of the poor were county officers. In the first of these instances the potential for difficulties was considerably minimized as the cities gained larger representation on the boards of supervisors. Until 1833, for example, Brooklyn had only one member on the six-man board, but with the issuance of the city charter in 1834 its representation rose to half of the membership. While the care of the poor remained the responsibility of these counties (Albany and Kings), the cities had representatives on the appropriate bodies, and the two governments, in each case, appear to have cooperated amicably to meet a growing obligation, abolishing distinctions between city and county poor and cooperatively erecting poor-houses.[44]

This was the general pattern in all these cities—accommodation and cooperation with occasional irritation. The Jefferson County Court was, for instance, prohibited from authorizing ferries within the boundaries of Louisville but permitted to appoint inspectors of barreled provisions landed in the city. An 1833 Kentucky act provided for the equal sharing of the expenses of county offices, but apparent disagreement led to another, more specific, statute seven years later. Both governments agreed, however, jointly to construct, occupy, and maintain a courthouse. In Pittsburgh, Allegheny County retained the power to regulate the opening of streets contrary to the existing street plan and in 1820 was required to provide accommodations for the Pittsburgh public schools and to appoint the initial city school committee. The relationship of the city of Washington and Washington County was largely nonexistent, except for taxation. In 1804, following the incorporation of the city, the levy court of the county was prohibited from taxing persons and property within the city. The members of the court, however, complained about the loss of revenue, and in 1812 Congress required the city to pay one-half of all county expenses, excluding those for roads and bridges, despite the fact that the seven-man levy court consisted entirely of persons residing outside the limits of Washington. It was not until 1848 that four residents of the city were added to the court, raising the total membership to eleven, at a time when the city residents made up more than three-quarters of the entire District population. In St. Louis (in addition to the usual access to the courts) city assessors were, in 1845, appointed by the county court and city school taxes were, in 1849, paid to the county collector. In this same period the question was raised of separating the city from the county, and the Missouri legislature authorized a referendum on the matter, but prohibited city residents from voting on the issue. The proposal was defeated by a more than two-to-one majority of the county voters.[45]

Although there were some areas of friction, cooperation between county and city governments would appear to have been more nearly the norm than the exception. Perhaps this was because (and perhaps despite the fact that) there were in each case two governments, both subordinate to the state, existing in close proximity—indeed, usually with overlapping boundaries—with some shared responsibilities but with administrative functions that were, for the most part, separate from each other. The case of the Louisville/Jefferson County courthouse, which has been noted, was by no means unusual. In 1849 Buffalo and Erie County launched a similar project, and in 1835 the city of Baltimore and Baltimore County jointly financed repairs of the courthouse. In like manner the city and county of Albany, after contributing jointly for years to the operation and upkeep of the jail, undertook the construction of a new one together in 1809.[46] To these examples might be added many cases of cooperative funding and operation of various functions, especially corrections and poor relief, several of which have been previously noted.

Finally, there were, as might be expected, contacts among the various cities. These were inevitably more intermittent than the intergovernmental relationships heretofore examined in this chapter because there were no governmental connections among the cities comparable to the ties that bound the cities to their state and county governments. Intercity contacts, thus, were devoid of any trace of legal requirement and were often informal in nature. It did not follow that such relationships were less important than those involving counties and states; indeed, being voluntary, they flowed from a recognition that there were many and important commonalities in all contemporary (and some historical) urban experiences. In some measure, these contacts were generic, sharing undifferentiated bodies of urban information. There was, for example, a widespread exchange of charters, ordinances, and regulations among cities. This was done more formally among a number of northeastern towns—Boston, New York, Philadelphia, Baltimore, and Washington—and requests and acknowledgements passed back and forth among city councils. At least one mayor, in his annual message, commented, "I should be happy if the members of the Council would avail themselves of the opportunity thereby presented, of examining the various regulations contained in them, and which would doubtless lead to many enactments which the experiences of the other cities has induced them to adopt and enforce." In other cases the exchange was less formal but no less influential; one of the most striking examples of the importance of intercity contacts was the direct quotation in the New Orleans charter of 1852 of whole sections from the 1849 New York charter.[47]

The cities also sought, in the experience of the other towns, assistance in dealing with specific issues; poor relief and education, in particular, moved city officials to look for procedures that other urban centers had found workable. There was sometimes an element of circularity in these inquires. When the New York Association for Improving the Condition of the Poor was proposing to begin operations in the mid-1840s, the AICP agent was dispatched to Boston, Philadelphia, and Baltimore to examine the circumstances in each of these cities. In 1849, when the Boston Society for the Prevention of Pauperism was preparing to initiate its program, it sent two representatives to New York on a fact-finding mission; these strongly recommended the program they observed to the members of the Boston society. The previous year the mayor of Baltimore, at a mass meeting of persons concerned with the issue of poor relief, appointed a committee to make recommendations about organizing poor relief in that city. The committee, like its counterpart in Boston, was favorably impressed by New York practices and shortly thereafter a Baltimore chapter of the AICP was founded. The development of public educational systems and practices was, in like manner, informed by the experiences of other cities. In the summer of 1829 the Louisville city council appropriated money to pay the expenses of a trip by Louisville educational leader Mann Butler to New York to examine the schools of that city. And before establishing Central High School in Philadelphia, the school controllers sent a four-man committee to New York and Boston to observe similar schools in operation. In 1839 the Baltimore commissioners of public schools recommended that the city obtain the plans of schoolhouses recently constructed in Boston and Philadelphia, and in the previous year the Providence committee on schoolhouses (with the permission of the city council) had dispatched a subcommittee to Boston and three other Massachusetts towns before reporting on proposed construction in their city.[48]

In a wide variety of other governmental undertakings reference or inquiry was made regarding the experience of other cities. The earliest (1791) building regulations in Washington contained material from several sections of a Philadelphia ordinance of 1782, transmitted in a letter from Thomas Jefferson to George Washington. Both Cincinnati in 1845 and Washington in 1831, when planning the establishment of a house of refuge for juvenile offenders, had recourse to experiences elsewhere. Washington's board of inspectors for the penitentiary noted in its report that "similar institutions at Philadelphia, New York, and Boston, have been the means of reclaiming numerous idle and dissolute boys and girls," and in Cincinnati the impetus came from "a few philanthropic persons . . . who had seen the happy results of similar institutions" in those same cities. Before action was taken in the latter city "a person was delegated to visit the Houses of Refuge and Corrections then in operation." Public health concerns also stimulated contact among the cities. For example, in 1827 the Baltimore board of health received two requests from the Charleston health department for "vaccine matter," which were "carefully attended to"; in 1848 the Philadelphia board of health sent a committee to visit the New York quarantine station on Staten Island to obtain clearer intelligence regarding an outbreak of cholera; and the next year a committee of that same body asked the boards of "Baltimore, New Orleans, Charleston, New York, Boston &c" to join in urging upon Congress the desirability of levying a tax on immigrants to be used for public health purposes. The supplying of water to city residents—a project not unrelated to public health—was also the subject of intercity inquiry. The proposal in New York just before the turn of the century was supposed to have been sparked by Albany's plans of 1796; an 1824 report on proposals to "introduce pure water" into Boston examined the systems of Philadelphia, Richmond, and Cincinnati (as well as a number of foreign cities, ancient and modern); and Robert Mills' article published in the *National Intelligencer* in 1849 urging an end to Washington's reliance on springs and the construction of a citywide water delivery system, examined (in variable detail) the facilities of Philadelphia, New York, Cincinnati, Baltimore, Boston, Albany, Providence, Richmond, and Troy.[49]

The list might be extended greatly. New York, in 1838, sought information on street operations from Baltimore, Philadelphia, and Boston, and in 1846 Baltimore sent a committee to obtain similar information from Philadelphia. In 1851 the Baltimore corporation decided that the contract with the Gas Light Company to light the streets of the city should specify "similar sized burners as are now used in the public lamps of Phiadelphia." Although not directly related to the subject of this chapter, it might be noted that nongovernmental bodies and individual urbanites also possessed intercity awareness. The impetus for the establishment of the New York Historical Society in 1808 came in part from the connection of one of its founders, John Pintard, with the creation of a similar body in Boston in 1791. The convening of an 1806 Baltimore meeting of merchants to complain to the federal government about the violations of neutral rights on the high seas was sparked by earlier gatherings in New York and Philadelphia. The creation of an apprentices' library in Philadelphia was inspired by earlier action of the same sort in Boston, and the directors of the St. Louis Mercantile Library were quick to compare its growth with those of Boston, New York, Philadelphia, and Cincinnati. And a New York committee investigating the feasibility of establishing a savings bank in 1819 wrote for information to existing banks in Boston, Baltimore, Philadelphia, and Salem.[50]

It would appear that there was, in the perceptions of many city leaders, the concept of an urban community transcending individual cities, of which they were a part. This sense of belonging transcended the recognition of certain commonalities of experience and can be seen at work as both city leaders and other citizens came to the aid of residents of other towns who had suffered from disasters.

Fire was a calamity that every urbanite had reason to fear. In 1820 the mayor of Washington named three persons in each ward to collect contributions to aid the Savannah residents suffering from a recent fire. Nine years later Boston churches, with the aid of a council appropriation, raised almost $2,250 for fire victims in Augusta, Georgia. In 1838 and in 1845 Washington's mayor was involved in raising funds to aid sufferers from the ravages of fire in Charleston and Pittsburgh. But help was not confined to dollars; when New York was in the grips of the holocaust of 1835—the most extensive New York conflagration of the century—assistance came from not only Brooklyn and Newark but also from Philadelphia, which sent the Franklin Fire Company and 400 additional firemen.[51]

Cooperation, mutual advancement, and compassionate assistance do not, of course, constitute the whole of intercity relationships. Rivalry—especially commercial rivalry—constituted a major element in the perceived commonality of urban life. This aspect will be touched on in the next chapter and, consequently, will not be examined here. But one more affirmative manifestation of rivalry should be mentioned. In a number of instances the ingrained interurban rivalry formed a base to permit advocates of change or improvement to garner support by presenting the proposal in the form of a challenge—an appeal to local residents to insure that their city would "measure up" to the level of achievement of a perceived rival. An 1812 plea for support for the Baltimore General Dispensary included an observation that "in Philadelphia very liberal legacies have been left to the Dispensary of that city; and it is not believed that there is any less disposition in Baltimoreans, than in their brethren of Philadelphia, . . . to offer all 'those sacrifices, with which God is well pleased.' " A similar argument was employed at the middle of the century in New York by persons calling for an increase in public hospitals. Enumerating the hospital capacities in that city and in New Orleans, the advocates concluded that, excluding the Marine Hospital, with its restricted and transient clientele, the two cities had about the same number of hospital beds despite the fact that the population of New Orleans was only a third of that of New York. And somewhat later, in 1859, a New York State Senate committee set up to examine the operations of the New York City health department observed caustically that in Providence, Philadelphia, and Boston "the best medical talent is employed to protect the public health," but in New York "this idea is practically discarded."[52]

There were, thus, many manifestations of intercity relations in the first half of the nineteenth century. The rapid growth of urban population in this era was coupled with expansion of the cities' services and responsibilities and technological changes of considerable magnitude. Given these circumstances, it was hardly surprising that the urban areas, which appeared to experience the greatest impact of both the growth and the change, should feel a certain kinship, which would, in turn, foster both cooperation and competition—a sort of sibling rivalry.

These various intergovernmental relations which have been briefly examined here might be seen as a natural concomitant of the corporate nature of all these governmental entities. They existed as legal, but fictitious, persons, having the power not only to perform certain acts that are essential to the operation of whole bodies of individuals (e.g., raise taxes, maintain the public peace, supply services to large number of individuals), but also to act in ways that only persons otherwise could (e.g., to sue and be sued, to own property, to make contracts). It was, then, only natural (indeed, inevitable) that the same sorts of relationships should emerge among city corporations as among real (as distinct from legal) persons. These included hierarchical relationships (e.g., worker-employer, parent-child, elder-younger—state-city, nation-city), longitudinal relationships (e.g., coworkers in the same location—city-county), and, finally, occupational relationships (e.g., people following the same employment in different geographic areas—city-city). Thus, these relationships may be seen as inevitable, given the nature of cities and the American governmental structures.

Chapter 7

Urban Mercantilism

The existence of urban mercantilism has been vaguely perceived by various authors on a number of occasions. Arthur M. Schlesinger, Sr., used the term *urban imperialism* casually in 1933 and 1940 and noted that the expression had been employed by a contemporary observer in the late nineteenth century.[1] In 1961 Julius Rubin commented on the utility of the phrase *municipal mercantilism* suggested by Julius P. Cairns in an M.A. thesis submitted to the Graduate School of Columbia University in 1950.[2] Moreover, there are numerous studies that narrate the effects of this concept (generally without identifying or analyzing it) in the histories of individual cities.[3] But none of these scholars have thought it necessary to examine the elements that comprise urban mercantilism, or to relate this concept specifically to typical events in antebellum American cities.

Both *mercantilism* and *imperialism* are words that have generally been used with reference to national states. But the terms have much relevance to certain aspects of the history of many antebellum (and later) American cities. Mercantilism, Gustav Schmoller said, is nothing more than economic state making.[4] Urban mercantilism doubtless seemed to its practitioners to be nothing more than economic city making.

The most obvious aspect of mercantilism is that it rests primarily on commercial activity. Some scholars, such as Henri Pirenne, argue that the city is first and foremost a market—indeed, if there is no market, there is no true city. Erwin A. Gutkind adds that it is not possible to assess accurately the development of any city apart from its hinterland.[5] While there are considerable doubts about the absolute accuracy of these assertions when applied to twentieth-century metropolises, they have a much higher degree of validity in structuring the study of antebellum American cities.

The apparently irresistible tendency to speak of the rise of urban-industrial

America tends partially to obscure the fact that throughout more than half of the nineteenth century urban America and industrial America were by no means coterminous. Not only had commercial considerations been determinative in the initial location and early growth of all of the major nineteenth-century cities (except Washington), but, further, most of these cities remained firmly tied to their original mercantile bases until well into the second half of the century. Industry—in the sense of production for a more than local market—was throughout much of this period far more frequently a large town/small city, than a metropolitan, activity. There was no compelling reason for a shift of the urban economic base to occur until railroad development radically changed the distribution economics of both raw materials and manufactured goods, the widespread introduction of cheap steam power cut factories loose from water power sites, and access to urban labor pools became a significant consideration for plant location. Hence, the major American cities continued to rest firmly on commercial foundations for a substantial part of the century.[6]

But this is not to say that the mercantilists were unaware of the economic advantages that accrue to manufacturers. Both theorists and practitioners of mercantilism in the seventeenth and eighteenth centuries stressed the desirability of importing raw materials and exporting manufactured goods. Their primary concern, however, was the production of cheaper merchandise for export, with the additional expectation of recapturing industrial wages and the value added by manufacture for the domestic economy. The nineteenth-century urban mercantilists were equally perceptive. They were not unwilling to engage in manufacturing activities themselves and they expended considerable effort in promoting industrial development (though they were by no means insistent upon locating those establishments within their cities) and in attracting raw materials to their local markets. But in almost every case, they viewed these activities as adjuncts to the basic economic livelihood of the city—commerce.

Earlier mercantilists strongly urged the necessity of keeping shipping facilities under the control of the commercial entity with which they were identified. The urban mercantilists of the antebellum United States were even more impressed by the need to develop and dominate transportation routes. For them the matter of the carrying profit was of much less importance than the fact that throughout the era (and beyond) such facilities increasingly became major weapons in the fight for markets. At best, the control of these transportation routes made it possible to exclude rivals from the market area, and at the very least it still conferred a significant competitive advantage upon the mercantile interests exercising control.

For the urban mercantilist—like his seventeenth-and eighteenth-century counterparts—was desirous of establishing a favorable balance of trade. Indeed, it can be argued that, personally, he was much more vitally concerned with market development than his European predecessors, for, unlike them, the nineteenth-century American urban mercantilist was normally only an "exporter," and not both an "exporter" and an "importer." This is merely to say that he was a more specialized mercantile operator. Consequently, urban merchants frequently took little or no toll from the raw materials "imported" from their hinterlands. This marketing of agricultural commodities was, in many cities, increasingly in the hands of agents representing nonlocal economic interests. Hence, those activities of the urban mercantilists that related to the movement of raw materials were designed primarily to assist in financing their sales within the market area, with a secondary interest in some instances in reducing the cost of (i.e., increasing the profit on the sale of) manufactured goods produced locally and marketed regionally.

Like earlier mercantilists, the urban mercantilist of the antebellum era considered trade at any given time to have certain finite limits. He was, consequently, excessively jealous of any sales made by merchants of other cities, even when individual competition was not directly involved—it was, in any event, "lost" trade. Undoubtedly this view of commerce encouraged the development of the concept of a "natural" or "legitimate" market area. All trade within the shifting and not too clearly defined bounds of this mercantile province was considered "tributary" to the dominant commercial city and any intrusion was to be strongly resisted.

And, finally, mercantilism—at least effective mercantilism—assumed the existence of a political entity closely identified with the well-being of and attentive to the demands of the commercial elements. In the case of national mercantilism, this entity could (indeed, should) extend its area of political control and exclude commercial competition from these imperial possessions while, at the same time, using its financial resources to assist the mercantile activity of its citizens. The American city clearly had no power to engage in such political expansion or commercial exclusion. But the city government was, nevertheless, an important instrumentality for forging and employing other weapons in the competition for markets. The urban merchants were thoroughly aware of the utility of this governmental instrumentality and quickly established (and usually maintained) a congruity of sentiment between commercial interest and political leadership. Charles N. Glaab states the situation bluntly when, in reference to Kansas City (at a somewhat later date), he says,

The members of the City Council were selected almost by consensus of the business leadership and were chosen from its ranks. Government functioned informally: policy was made in the Chamber of Commerce, through the columns of [Robert T.] Van Horn's newspaper [the *Western Journal of Commerce*], or at meetings of the business leaders.[7]

In practice, circumstances varied rather widely, but somewhat similar conditions prevailed in almost every major city during a substantial part of the first century after American independence. Richard C. Wade, citing numerous examples, correctly asserts that "urban affairs [in the western cities in the early nineteenth century] were managed not merely by merchants, but usually by the most successful ones."[8]

Mercantilism, therefore, can clearly be said to have had an urban dimension. Certainly attempts to create mercantile spheres of influence have long been quite common in America. When the Plymouth settlers dispatched Myles Standish to seize Thomas Morton and his companions at Merry Mount in 1628, they were doubtless at least as disturbed by the threat that the newer colony posed to Plymouth's exploitation of the Indian trade as they were by the inhabitants' revels and their "ungodlyness." Later, communities engaging in commercial competition found the development of transportation routes essential to their purpose (see below). So obvious to contemporary observers was the role of governmental and mercantile institutions in the developing of such facilities that railroad critic and historian Charles Francis Adams, Jr., in an 1868 article on Boston's relative commercial decline, could observe (citing Henry T. Buckle), "Yet it is unquestionably true . . . that it is only in Asia and semi-barbarous countries that the course and extent of trade are regulated by the original [i.e., topographical] features of the country, but in Europe and among advanced nations its determining cause is the skill and energy of man."[9]

As Adams noted, the instrumentalities involved were human institutions and their activities were directed by individuals. Hence, the key to the development of aggressive urban mercantilism, obviously, was conscious individual identification on the part of mercantile operators with their cities of residence. That is, a hardware merchant of Baltimore must think of himself primarily as a member of the Baltimore mercantile community, and secondarily as a wholesaler of hardware. This identification of individual merchants with their urban centers (which was essential to the employment of urban governments as instruments of market development) was obvious to many contemporary observers and can easily be documented by reference to newspaper files, diaries, letters, and (above all) the types of activities urged upon the inhabitants and governments of almost every American city of this era.[10] Some commentators have seen this element of individual identification as a pecularily American phenomenon. George M. Young argues that in England this sense of "civic self-consciousness . . . had to be built up by slow degrees. In America it was there from the first. The best society of Philadelphia was trying to improve and glorify Philadelphia. The best society of Manchester was trying to get out of it."[11]

Clearly, for many antebellum American urbanites, the city evoked a type of identification that bore many resemblances to nationalism. State and regional loyalties tend to be exclusive as well as expansive—that is, commonly manifested in attempts to prevent intrusions, to exclude "foreigners" from the profits to be made within the unit, and to defend internal institutions from attack from without. By the nature of the case, these urban loyalties could not generally inspire or support this type of commercial imperialism. Residents of urban communities, however, frequently exhibited a number of traits that would justify the use of the term *urban mercantilism* when discussing their activities. Among these traits and conditions were (1) the existence of a self-conscious commercial community identifying itself with a political entity; (2) the existence of a fairly

well-defined (though shifting) view of the legitimate market area of this mercantile community (lying, of necessity, outside the bounds of the political entity); (3) a willingness to use the municipality as an instrumentality to underwrite
capital investment for long-range group benefit and for political action to defend
the preferential position of the commercial community; and (4) a willingness to
act cooperatively in other enterprises and activities.[12] This sense of community
did not, of course, prevent merchants from competing actively among themselves within the bounds of the city's market area, but when nonlocal forces
threatened the integrity of that sphere of influence, their urban loyalties came
to the fore. Such loyalties they saw as mere extensions of self-interest and they
would have endorsed without qualification (though they doubtless would have
reversed the word order) the remarks of a later urban leader—Thomas L. Johnson—about the necessity of "making men's ambitions and pecuniary interests
identical with the welfare of the city."[13] Indeed, the identification with the city
could be almost mystical. William Carr Lane, eight times mayor of St. Louis in
the 1820s and 1830s, declared that

the fortunes of inhabitants may fluctuate; you and I may sink into oblivion, and even
our families may become extinct, but the progressive rise of our city is morally certain;
the causes of its prosperity are inscribed upon the very face of the earth, and are as
permanent as the foundations of the soil and sources of the Mississippi.[14]

But, as has been noted, urban mercantilism rested not just on an identification
of urbanites with their city as an entity, but also with dominance of commerce
in the cities' economies. The observation of Scotch traveler Robert Baird in
1849 that "New Orleans is pre-eminently a city of trade" could have been
echoed for almost all major American cities of this era. More important in the
flourishing of urban mercantilism was the open recognition of this fact by the
local population and, especially, the urban leadership. "The prosperity of New-
York has always depended chiefly upon its commerce," wrote "A New
Yorker" (Daniel Curry) in 1853. "It has indeed other sources of prosperity, . . .
but these are only incidental, while commerce is the source of life and activity
to the whole." Great metropolises and small cities alike embraced this economic
truth without regret or sense of loss. Writing about "ante-bellum days" from a
perspective of half a century, Louisville manufacturing booster Charles F. Hub-
lein exaggerated only slightly, if at all, when he observed that

Louisville people, while including . . . some of the most daring and sagacious manufacturers and financiers, were, on the whole, indifferent to manufactures; looking upon
banking and merchandising as the exclusive, or at least the preferred mercantile operations, and rather desired the factories, if established hereabouts at all, to locate a good
distance.

Even those who opposed this preoccupation acknowledged its prevalence. The editor of the *Pittsburgh Gazette* in 1818 bemoaned what he characterized as "merchantilmania" and pleaded for a shift of the city's capital into industrial activity.[15]

Cities thus relying upon commerce for their prosperity inevitably find themselves in competiton for markets—at least in this era. Diane Lindstrom observed in her study *Economic Development in the Philadelphia Region, 1780–1850* that historians' assertions that the period 1810–1850 was characterized by the "rise of a national market" were not supported by the evidence in the case of Philadelphia. Nor are they reflected in contemporary observations. Even those who might claim mercantile dominance in the nation for their own city saw that status as singular. John A. Dix, who in 1827 characterized New York as "THE GREAT COMMERCIAL EMPORIUM OF THE CONFEDERACY," alone possessing "the character of a general mart, where the domestic productions of all sections of the country have been collected for exportation, and where the importations from foreign countries have concentrated for general distribution," insisted that "every city, excepting New York, has been a particular emporium." "Boston," he specified,

has been the market for New-England, Philadelphia for Pennsylvania and portions of the contiguous states, Baltimore for Maryland, Charleston for South Carolina, and New-Orleans for the country upon the Gulf of Mexico and the Mississippi; and to those limits their respective commercial operations have been restricted.[16]

Contemporary residents of the smaller cities took the same view. Cincinnatians Benjamin Drake and E. D. Mansfield, in 1826, designated their city as the distribution center for that portion of Ohio west of the Muskingum, most of Indiana, and "large portions of Kentucky and Missouri." A decade later Gabriel Collins, somewhat grandiloquently, said of Louisville, "As a grocery market, she is not inferior, at least as it regards the country dealer, to New Orleans or New York," and added that "in the dry goods business her success is but little less signal." Collins was wholly vague about the extent of Louisville's market area, mentioning "country dealers" and "the other large cities of the Ohio river."[17]

Although some mention was made (particularly in the case of the seaboard cities, e.g., New York, New Orleans, and Charleston) of collecting the produce of the countryside, it is notable that the tributary hinterlands of most of these commercial cities were normally defined by the area in which the cities' wholesalers supplied the local retailers, using specifically such statements as "mostly the country dealers within her sphere of influence, have found it to their advantage to purchase of her merchants." Dix stated the matter even more bluntly (though with something less than crystal clarity). "It may be laid down as a principle," he wrote, "that the dimensions of a city, which is purely commercial in its character, will be in a compound proportion to the wealth and resources of the country, which it supplies, and to the degree, in which it is tributary to the supply of that country.'' Drake and Mansfield, too, spoke of the role of Cincinnati as that of a distribution center. And writing a century later Harry A. Mitchell described the commercial importance of antebellum St. Louis in terms of the number of wholesale grocery and dry goods houses and their sales.[18]

Quite naturally, urban political and mercantile leaders were jealous of their commercial hinterlands and were quick to resist the ''rival projects of other cities'' which might result in their being ''deprived'' of their trade dominance in these areas. At the same time they vigorously pursued proposals that seemed to promise successful intrusion into the trade areas of their competitors.[19]

The major instruments that urban mercantile leaders saw as available to them in the struggle to control and expand their cities' hinterlands were those related to the improvement of transportation facilities. There were, in essence, three alternatives that presented themselves to those who would use these instruments to outflank or defeat the competition and enhance their own trade position— secure private investment capital from the city's economic leadership, provide public capitalization by the city itself, or persuade some other persons or governments to finance the appropriate transportation works. The anxiety, the determination, and the imagination of the urban mercantilists were reflected in a Philadelphia council resolution in 1846. It declared that

a large portion of our western trade, once enjoyed almost exclusively by Philadelphia, has already been diverted from her, and the remainder is seriously endangered by the rival projects of other cities and states. And . . . a continuous railway, connecting this city with the Ohio river at Pittsburg [*sic*], and with the lakes, by means of the railroad from Pittsburg to Cleveland, and other roads extending westward now in progress or contemplated, will not only restore to Philadelphia that portion of the trade of which she has been deprived, but add immensely to the amount of her internal and foreign commerce, enhance the value of real estate, augment the corporate income, lessen the burden of taxation on the citizen, and greatly increase the general prosperity,

and then authorized the borrowing of $2,500,000 to purchase 50,000 shares of Pennsylvania Railroad stock, provided an equal amount should be taken by other subscribers.[20] Nor was this position extreme among antebellum American cities. Writing more than a century later, an economic historian would say, ''Indeed, Providence entrepreneurs so clearly recognized the significance of transportation as an instrument for extending, consolidating, and protecting their economic influence that Rhode Island's transportation history is almost exclusively the story of the efforts to expand the Providence hinterland.''[21]

Perhaps no city was a better example of urban mercantilism than Baltimore. The merchants of this burgeoning port—between 1790 and 1820 Baltimore had grown three times a fast as Charleston, twice as rapidly as Boston, one and three-quarters as swiftly as Philadelphia, and even one and one-quarter as fast as New York—were deeply perturbed by the potential expansion of the market of its more northerly competitors as the Erie Canal neared completion and the vision of the Pennsylvania canal/rail scheme began to emerge. Consequently, in the 1820s Baltimoreans, and their city, began a search for instrumentalities to defend and extend their market area. There were three established avenues of the city's trade: oceangoing commerce moving through the port of Baltimore, the Potomac River, and the Susquehanna Valley. Baltimore merchants (and, because of their dominance, the city corporation) were prepared to exploit every trade route and to employ all available technologies. As early as 1818 Baltimore merchants were urged to support turnpike and canal projects to gain market access to the Ohio Valley region through Wheeling, and in 1824 the Maryland legislature authorized the city itself to construct a canal to the head of tidewater on the Susquehanna and from there to Conewaga Falls, subject to the approval of the Pennsylvania Assembly. As it turned out, this somewhat unfocused project came to naught, but the Baltimore corporation did (with state approval) spend $50,000 over a ten-year period to remove obstructions in the Susquehanna, and was empowered in 1827 to raise money by borrowing or taxation to purchase an unspecified amount of stock in the Pennsylvania and Maryland Canal Company. Nor were the needs of the city's bay and ocean commerce neglected. The corporation was authorized by the state (1839) to subscribe $25,000 in the stock of the Baltimore and Chesapeake Steam Towing Company, and Baltimore interests secured the incorporation in 1850 of the Baltimore and Susquehanna Steam Company, whose purpose was declared to be "the navigation of the Chesapeake Bay, and its tributary streams." Moreover, the city spent hundreds of thousands of dollars over these years on dredges and icebreakers to keep the harbor open to commerce.[22]

But Baltimore was particularly notable in employing cutting-edge transportation technology in its mercantilistic activities. Alarmed by the completion of the Erie Canal and the projection of the "Pennsylvania State System," Baltimoreans, in 1826 and 1827, cast about for some method of securing access to the trans-Appalachian market for their mercantile community. Not blessed with the unique topographical circumstances that made possible the Erie Canal and justifiably dubious about the ability of the Pennsylvania project to afford competitive market access (though the Susquehanna improvements were designed to tap that system), they embarked, under the leadership of Philip E. Thomas and George Brown, both important city bankers, on the Baltimore and Ohio railroad project, despite the fact that existing railway technology was almost certainly inadequate to meet the terrain challenges involved. In 1826 the state legislature chartered the Baltimore and Ohio Railroad Company, and authorized that corporation to issue stock in the amount of $3,000,000 (with liberty to increase the amount) of which one-third was to be reserved for state subscriptions and one-sixth for Baltimore purchase. The city was to name two members of the board of directors. Ten years later the legislature authorized additional subscriptions by Baltimore of up to $3,000,000, with the city to name one additional director for each 5,000 shares of stock held. At the same time the Assembly authorized the city to levy a special tax to fund such stock purchases.

In addition, by the late 1830s Baltimore was providing funding on a somewhat more modest scale for the completion of the Baltimore and Susquehanna Railroad, and the city's internal improvement debt mounted dramatically. The burden of funding this debt fell entirely upon the taxpayers within the direct taxation limits, but the state legislature granted a measure of relief by authorizing the city to collect the internal improvement tax throughout the whole urban area, ignoring (for this tax only) the limits of direct taxation.[23]

Thus, the city of Baltimore, in its corporate capacity, played an extraordinarily active role in developing the transporation instruments to exploit and extend the city's market area. Baltimore's activity in this arena was made possible by legislative grants of significant additional taxing authority (the implementation of which was approved by the local government and the electorate). By 1850 the city held company securities representing a total investment in transportation works in excess of $5,000,000—$3,929,877 in the Baltimore and Ohio Railroad, $450,000 (plus an $850,000 loan) in the Baltimore and Susquehanna, $380,000 in the Susquehanna Canal, and $29,500 in five turnpike companies.[24]

Although Baltimore was unusual in the scope of its urban mercantilistic activities, there was nothing unique about any one of these undertakings. Other cities invested in these same sorts of enterprise during this era. The city of Albany, for example, purchased stock in three turnpike companies—the Great Western, the Bethlehem, and the Farmers'—and Louisville invested in the Louisville and Portland Turnpike, all before 1836. The latter city also held $50,000 worth of stock in the Ohio Bridge Company in the same period. The Philadelphia corporation was also convinced that bridges could contribute to the commercial advancement of the city, making a modest investment in the Schuylkill Permanent Bridge Company and obtaining legislative authorization in 1839 to borrow up to $80,000 to purchase the bridge. In 1850 the legislature approved the city's borrowing another $100,000 to modify the bridge to carry railway cars.[25]

City expenditures on harbor improvements and maintenance were even more common. After the bitter winter of 1835–1836 had closed the Delaware River to navigation for fifty-two days, the mercantile community of Philadelphia clamored for relief. In March 1837 the city, inspired by Baltimore's success, authorized a $70,000 loan to build an iceboat and promised an annual appropriation of $12,000 to defray operating expenses and to retire the loan. The vessel was put into use in December of that year. But other barriers, of course, were less transient than ice. In 1819, in a rare example of individual commitment, the residents of Pittsburgh personally removed the three major obstructions to navigation between that city and Wheeling, Virginia, on the "ripples" near Montour Island. Closer to home, almost two decades later (1836) the corporation borrowed $30,000 for "improvements along the Monongahela River front." Because of the heavy burden of silt borne by the Mississippi, maintaining full access for steamboats to the St. Louis waterfront was a continuing problem for the city authorities. In a fourteen-year period (1837–1851) St.

Louis borrowed almost a third of a million dollars for harbor improvements, leaving aside any expenditures from its regular revenue. The Hudson was a very different river and, consequently, Albany's dredging expenditures ranged from a few hundred to a few thousand dollars. For the merchants, the city's harbor facilities constituted the portal through which they gained access to the nation's and the world's waterborne commerce—the nearest link in a commercial chain essential to their success, indeed, their survival. For the merchants and the mercantile urban corporations, there was a feeling of close connection with their ports. After having secured the location of the Cunard Line terminus in Boston harbor in 1840 by an offer of free wharf facilities, the city caused a channel to be cut through the ice four years later to enable the *Britannia* "to go to sea, that it might not be said that she was detained in the harbor because Boston was frozen up."[26]

Of course, it was possible to rely too heavily on port facilities and the related waterborne commerce. In 1847 B. H. Payne, in two separate articles in *DeBow's Review*, warned New Orleans mercantile interests that western commerce would be diverted from the Crescent City by the railways and urged that some action be taken to counteract this development. But it was a sad commentary on New Orleans' fixation on the Mississippi that Payne could think of nothing more innovative to recommend than the improvement of wharf facilities in the Third Municipality to provide greater security and faster movement of river-borne commodities.[27]

Most cities' authorities, however, were not as complacent as those of New Orleans, who ignored even Payne's modest program.[28] Instead they, like their compatriots (and competitors) in Baltimore, saw their interests and aspirations overleap the city boundaries to encompass their hinterlands and the avenues of trade that tied them to the metropolises. The earliest transporation works that demanded heavy capitalization (that is to say, excluding turnpikes) to attract extensive urban funding were canals. While American cities and their merchants might invest a few tens of thousands of dollars in turnpike stocks, the canal investments might run to hundreds of thousands. Moreover, the canals usually lay well out in the hinterland and frequently made no direct connection with the city itself.

For some urban centers canal connections—even highly important canal connections—made no financial demands upon the city government or, in some cases, even the mercantile establishment. The tremendously successful Erie Canal (which project originated at a meeting in New York City convened by its then mayor DeWitt Clinton in 1815) and the largely unsuccessful Pennsylvania canal/rail scheme (strongly agitated for by both Philadelphia and Pittsburgh and their commercial communities) were state ventures, and New York, Albany, Buffalo, Philadelphia, and Pittsburgh had, largely, a free ride. There were also some cities—for example, St. Louis, New Orleans, and Charleston—that were not well placed topographically to profit from canal development. But other urban centers saw canals as instruments of mercantilistic hinterland exploitation or, in a few instances, as threats to their mercantile position. Even these towns sometimes proceeded very cautiously. Cincinnatians, for example, doubted the advantages to them of the Little Miami and Great Miami canals, which reached the Ohio east and west of the city (and were able to generate adequate financial support elsewhere), but invested $200,000 in the Louisville and Portland Canal Company, which constructed a canal around the Falls of the Ohio at Louisville. Pittsburgh residents had subscribed for stock in an earlier company with the same aim, but Louisvillians themselves were ambivalent about such an improvement, fearing its disadvantages to that city would be greater than its benefits, and the town invested its public improvement money elsewhere.[29]

Only Washington, of these cities, came close to matching Baltimore's $380,000 commitment of public money to a canal project. And the nation's capital, like its municipal neighbor, found such investments financially unrewarding. Some decades later Baltimore still held Baltimore and Susquehanna Tidewater Canal stock, listing it as an unproductive asset. Washington was more fortunate; of the $1,250,000 debt it created to purchase Chesapeake and Ohio Canal stock, the federal government agreed to assume $1,000,000 in 1837, but ten years later the city was still channeling lesser amounts of funds into the company for continuing construction. Personal subscriptions by Washingtonians amounted to another $233,600. The Washington City Canal, which ran from Rock Creek to the Eastern Branch (Anacostia), was at length completed. But from its opening in 1815 it was plagued by silting and inadequate water levels. The city bought out the company in 1831 for $50,000 and invested another $60,000 in improving and widening the canal. This proved an utter failure, but fortunately the federal government appropriated $150,000 to aid the city in the undertaking.[30]

Even those cities which had less to gain from canal development or whose most obvious desires for canal access to their hinterlands were fulfilled by works undertaken by other instrumentalities occasionally assumed a more active role. In the late eighteenth and early nineteenth centuries, for example, long before the construction of the Erie Canal, let alone Pennsylvania's competitive canal/rail system, was even contemplated, Philadelphia interests, seeking connections with the Chesapeake, promoted the Chesapeake and Delaware Canal. When the company was incorporated by Maryland (1799) and Delaware (1801) it was with the clear understanding that Pennsylvania and its metropolis would provide more than one *quid pro quo*: the removal of obstructions in the Susquehanna River, the transfer of Delaware land records to that state, and a modification of the Philadelphia quarantine law. When the company was organized in 1803 more than half the directors were residents of the Quaker City. Philadelphian Matthew Carey was largely responsible for the renewal of interest in the company in the 1820s, and investors (even purchasers of one or two shares) and banks in that city furnished most of the capital which secured the canal's completion in 1829.

Some years earlier a Philadelphia management had been installed and the head-quarters moved to that city.[31]

In the 1820s and 1830s New York bankers made heavy investments in Ohio canal companies to extend the city's commercial influence in the area opened by the completion of the Erie Canal, and somewhat earlier Providence merchants pushed the building of the Blackstone Canal, which gave that city a useful connection with Worcester, Massachusetts.[32]

But it was railway corporations that, more than any other transportation enterprises, attracted the interest of the mercantile cities and stimulated the visions of commercial aggrandizement of their residents. It quickly became apparent to ambitious urban mercantile communities that the railroad freed them from the limitations imposed by geography as did no other then available form of "artificial" tranportation work, and it was also gradually borne upon them that railways tended to concentrate commercial activity in nodal cities serving multiple rail lines, expanding their hinterlands and subordinating the smaller cities and relegating them to more limited mercantile roles. It was also true, of course, that railways, requiring expensive preparation and construction throughout their entire length (as canals, for example, frequently did not), made heavy demands for capital, which, in many sections of the country, necessarily implied public investment in the corporations.

As has been noted, Baltimore was perhaps the preeminent example of municipal activity in this arena. Deeply wedded to the success of the Baltimore and Ohio, in particular, the city's commitment went beyond stock purchases; in the panic year of 1837 the "railroad notes" issued by that cash-starved corporation were accepted in payment of city dues by Baltimore officials. Ultimately the steady determination of the Maryland metropolis paid off. Rather more than a quarter of a century after the first subscriptions the city saw the completion of the Baltimore and Ohio to Wheeling (1853) and the Baltimore and Susquehanna to Sunbury (1855).[33]

But Baltimore had many active, if not always successful, imitators in its efforts to use rail lines to enlarge its commercial hinterland. Charleston, indeed, was, like Baltimore, early in the race. In 1828 the city council appropriated a modest $20,000 for the purchase of 200 shares of stock in the South Carolina Railway and Canal Company, which, in the next five years, built the Charleston and Hamburg Railroad, connecting the city with the Savannah River. Then the longest railroad in the world (136 miles), it enabled Charleston merchants to tap into the Georgia and western South Carolina cotton trade, intercepting the downriver traffic to Savannah—a substantial gain at very small cost. The city's other major urban mercantilistic effort involving railroads was not an unqualified success. In the mid-1830s a grandiose scheme was concocted to connect Charleston with the Ohio Valley by rail (the Charleston, Louisville, and Cincinnati Railway), and the South Carolina metropolis responded in 1837 with, first, a $100,000 loan to assist the C, L, and C in the acquisition of the Charleston and Hamburg and, second, a purchase of $50,000 worth of C, L, and C stock. Caught in the 1837 panic, the larger enterprise collapsed, leaving only a remnant—the South Carolina Railroad, from Charleston to Columbia. It was, on the whole, not an insubstantial return for such limited investments; by 1858 the receipts of cotton in Charleston were more than double what they had been thirty years earlier.[34]

In the 1830s other major cities followed the same courses. In 1837 the New York legislature authorized the city of Albany to issue $250,000 in bonds to purchase stock in the Albany and Stockbridge Railroad, and by 1844 the city's support for the construction of this line—the New York section of Boston's Western Railroad—had reached $1,000,000. Somewhat later the city issued $125,000 in bonds as a loan to an earlier Albany road—the Mohawk and Hudson, completed in 1833—and also guaranteed other loans to this company.[35]

In the trans-Appalachian region other cities also entered the railroad competition in the 1830s. New Orleans purchased $500,000 of stock in the New Orleans and Nashville Railroad, which, unfortunately, went bankrupt in 1842. After an interlude of quiet the Crescent City reentered the lists in the 1850s with investments in railway stocks in excess of $4,000,000, including $2,000,000 in the New Orleans, Jackson, and Great Northern, and $1,500,000 in the New Orleans, Opelousas, and Great Western. Louisville was somewhat more fortunate with its initial railway venture. Authorized by a legislative act of February 28, 1835, the city invested $140,000 in the Lexington and Ohio Railroad the following year. The line at least survived, though for years only the Louisville-Portland segment was open for use. Like New Orleans, the Falls City took a much more active role in the 1850s. After the Kentucky legislature incorporated the Louisville and Nashville Railroad in 1850, and refused to provide state funding for railways, the city became the primary financier of the L & N; the first city subscription of $200,000 came in April 1852 and was followed by $500,000 a year later. By 1857 Louisville's investment in this line amounted to $1,925,000. Cincinnati, too, began its subscription to railways in 1836 and continued its activity until such actions were prohibited by the Ohio constitution of 1851. During that time the city provided various railroads (e.g., the Little Miami, the Ohio and Mississippi) with some $600,000 in subscriptions and loans. Twice that much had been conditionally subscribed to the Charleston, Louisville, and Cincinnati ($200,000), which collapsed in the 1837 panic, and the Ohio and Mississippi ($1,000,000), which was not chartered by the Illinois legislature before the Ohio constitution prohibition became effective.[36]

The citizens of St. Louis, too, evinced their interest in railroad development in the 1830s, though their financial involvement in such activity was somewhat delayed, doubtless at least in part by the relative smallness of both the population and the available public and private capital. A convention was held in that city in April 1835, consisting of delegates from eleven Missouri counties, which addressed the need for rail transportation in the city's hinterland. The body recommended the construction of two rail lines terminating in St. Louis—one to Fayette and the other to the iron and lead mines in southern Missouri. The

St. Louis County Court responded by appropriating $2,000 for surveys. Three years later the Board of Aldermen voted to subscribe for $500,000 worth of stock in the St. Louis and Belleview Mineral Railroad, but Mayor William Carr Lane vetoed the ordinance.[37]

In the meantime, in 1836 and 1839, two conventions were held in St. Louis to offer support for the development of the city's eastern connections—specifically for a connection with Boston currently being promoted by Bay State capitalists. The economic distress after 1837, and especially following 1839, doubtless contributed to both the suspension of activity in this area and the fact that neither of the two railways chartered by the Missouri legislature in January 1837 were ever built.[38]

It would be well into the next decade before the residents of St. Louis resumed their fight for rail connections, both east and west. In late December 1846 a mass meeting in the city appointed a committee to petition the state legislature to authorize the city residents, by vote, to subscribe $500,000 to the Ohio and Mississippi Railroad. This line originated in Cincinnati and at this juncture had not been chartered in either Indiana, Ohio, or Illinois. These states acted favorably, however, in 1848, 1849, and 1851, respectively. St. Louis residents were well represented among the incorporators or on the boards of directors of at least the Indiana and Illinois corporations. In the meantime, the Missouri legislature had, in February 1849, authorized the city, subject to a referendum, to subscribe $500,000 to the company, and the voters had approved the proposal (including a special tax to fund the debt) by a "heavy majority." The city's subscription followed later in the same year. A construction contract was let in November 1851 and the work was completed in August 1857.[39]

While all this activity was taking place to the east, St. Louis also turned her eyes westward. On February 20, 1849, a mass meeting was held in the city to support a proposal to charter the Pacific Railroad Company of Missouri, to run from St. Louis to the western boundary of Van Buren County. Less than a month later the state legislature chartered the corporation, with a list of incorporators packed with the names of St. Louis mayors, aldermen, councilmen, and mercantile leaders. Early the following year the corporation was organized and the subscription books opened. Over 2,000 shares were taken in a little over a week and ward committees were formed to canvass the population. In addition to the hundreds of thousands of dollars subscribed by the city's residents, they also voted their approval for a city subscription of $500,000 later in the same year (1850). The 1851 St. Louis city charter prohibited such subscriptions, but this section was amended in 1853 to permit support for in-state railway corporations. The city continued its activities in this area and by the end of the 1850s held $1,500,000 in railway stock.[40]

Farther to the east, the two Pennsylvania cities both had vital mercantile interests in the completion of a rail line linking the Atlantic and the Ohio Valley and terminating in, respectively, Philadelphia and Pittsburgh. There was, nevertheless, an area of considerable difference between the two. For Philadelphia mercantile interests, the connection with Pittsburgh was well-nigh essential, but for the Pittsburgh commercial community the connection with Philadelphia was only one option, to be measured against others in terms of cost, benefit, and, indeed, the likelihood of completion.

In 1828, doubtless stimulated by the success of the Erie Canal, the Pennsylvania legislature chartered the Pennsylvania Railroad Company, with a heavy Philadelphia interest—five of the nine incorporators were from that city. Work progressed slowly and it was not until early in the next decade that the question of a connection with the Delaware River at Philadelphia arose. At that point the state legislature provided that no part of the line (which was to enter the city along Callowhill Road) east of the Schuylkill should be built until the city should engage to construct the line from Vine and Broad, down Broad to South (Cedar) Street. This the city council agreed to do and in January 1833 appropriated $25,000 for that purpose. This still left the road well back from the river, and three eastern connections—through Southwark, through Northern Liberties, and along Market Street—were subsequently constructed. This construction was strongly supported by the Board of Trade, to reduce the ruinously high drayage costs. These small contributions were apparently the whole of the corporation's financial involvement in this work. This was certainly a minimal public contribution to a railway of great economic importance to the city's commercial interests. The line ran through Lancaster to Columbia, on the Susquehanna (for which reason it was called the Columbia Railroad), giving Philadelphia access to the state canal-railroad line which was completed to Pittsburgh in 1834.[41]

In the meantime, Pittsburgh's mercantile and political leaders began to agitate for a connection with the Baltimore and Ohio Railroad almost as soon as that company was chartered in 1826, and, indeed, the B & O obtained a Pennsylvania charter to build such a branch. But when it became apparent that years would elapse before the Baltimore road reached the Appalachians, Pittsburgh leaders, despite long-standing distrust, turned their attention to Philadelphia. It took the western Pennsylvanians only a short time to realize that the "State System" would probably never be adequate for their needs. By 1836 (two years after the completion of the "system") they were agitating for a direct rail link to the Quaker City. Not unaware of the potential advantages associated with stimulating a little competition, a Pittsburgh convention two years later urged the city council to subscribe $1,000,000 to the B & O if it should be extended to that city.[42]

By the mid-1840s increasing numbers of Pennsylvanians had come to a conclusion that some Pittsburghers had reached a decade earlier—the "State System" was inadequate to its purpose. In 1843 the B & O's Pennsylvania charter had expired, with no work done in that state, and the company immediately sought a renewal. But despite growing support among western Pennsylvania legislators, little was accomplished. This was largely because of increased activity on the part of Philadelphia and its mercantile leadership. Having come to realize that the interests of the Quaker City themselves were ill served by a policy that concentrated on combating in the state legislature potential Baltimore competition, the city's legislators and merchants backed the chartering of the Pennsylvania Railroad in 1846, with a capitalization of $7,500,000 and permission to increase that to $10,000,000. The corporation was authorized to build a line to Pittsburgh, and the act further provided that if, by July 30, 1847, the company had $3,000,000 subscribed and $1,000,000 paid in, and fifteen miles of track under contract, the law granting the B & O right-of-way to Pittsburgh would be null and void. The project was actively promoted among Philadelphia residents—the first annual report showed 2,600 subscribers, about 1,800 of whom held five shares or fewer—and the city subscribed $2,500,000 in 1847. The conditions were met and the B & O's entry into western Pennsylvania was greatly inhibited. Six years after the charter was granted cars ran from Philadelphia to Pittsburgh, and two years later the last reliance on inclined planes in the mountains was abandoned.

Nevertheless, in 1853 the Pittsburgh and Connelsville Railroad scheme (the B & O connection) was revived and the line received a Maryland charter as well. The city of Baltimore pledged to guarantee $1,000,000 of the P & C bonds if an additional $2,000,000 could be raised; the city of Pittsburgh committed $500,000; and Allegheny County added another $750,000.[43]

Thus, Pittsburgh continued to foment and foster the competition between these two Atlantic ports as each fought to attach the Ohio Valley to its hinterland. By the mid-1850s the corporation of Pittsburgh had contracted a public debt in aid of railway companies in the amount of $1,800,000. The involvement of Philadelphia was much greater. At the time of the consolidation of the city and its suburbs (1854) Philadelphia's subscriptions to railway corporations amounted to $6,100,000, and an additional $2,500,000 had been subscribed by Northern Liberties, Spring Garden, and Richmond.[44]

For a few cities, of course, the resort to public funding for railroads was unnecessary. Either their location or their political or economic dominance substantially guaranteed that they would be termini of major rail lines, or they were so situated as to profit only minimally from such connections, or the supply of private capital was adequate to the needs. Boston, for example, became the hub of seven rail lines in New England doubtless in large part because of its earlier developed mercantile dominance combined with the large supply of capital in the hands of its residents. The $2,000,000 in private subscriptions to the Western Railroad was obtained, in part, by a house-to-house canvass of that city. It was ironic that this, Boston's most ambitious undertaking, was the only line that failed fully to accomplish its purpose. Designed to siphon off the flood of commerce, originating as far away as the Great Lakes, that rushed down the Hudson Valley by river and rail, it could not give Boston a victory over the nation's preeminent magnet of trade, New York.[45]

A similar effort by Providence was, predictably, even less likely to prevail. Though normally content to extract commercial benefit from the railways capitalized by Boston and New York interests, the city of Providence, in 1851, embarked on an ambitious effort to challenge New York mercantile dominance in both the Connecticut and Hudson river valleys, investing $500,000 in the Hartford, Providence, and Fishkill Railroad. The road opened to Hartford in 1854 but went into bankruptcy before the end of the decade.[46]

Cities were not, of course, the only political entities that could be used by mercantile interests to finance transportation works to facilitate hinterland development. States were frequent sources of public capital for turnpikes, canals, and railroads. But cities had attributes that made them more viable instrumentalites of mercantilism. For all the economic diversity that was a hallmark of urbanism, the mercantile community (merchants and their employees, associates, and beneficiaries) was overwhelmingly dominant; only the established landed elite (often the descendants of the founders), fearing increases in property taxes, mounted an organized opposition to city subscription proposals. States, faced with the conflicting demands of rival economic groups—especially agriculturists—often followed divergent paths simultaneously and funded, frequently inadequately, various nonrelated and sometimes competing projects. Even the mercantile interests in different parts of the states had different and conflicting aspirations. But the cities were sufficiently small in area to render such sectional divisions highly unlikely, and, if such differences did emerge, relatively insignificant. Both Pennsylvania and Maryland, for example, developed programs for state funding of transportation works which were multitargeted, diffuse, and occasionally conflicting—a logical response to the political pressures exerted by differing constitutencies.[47] But during the same period Baltimore, Philadelphia, and Pittsburgh were pursuing much more focused activity, strongly supported by a more unified mercantile community.

The concentration of liquid capital in the cities was, of course, what made possible the financing of programs designed to benefit the relatively homogeneous mercantile interests. The holders of these funds—acquired by successful commercial activity—were easily convinced of the value to their own enterprises of the construction of turnpikes, canals, and railroads, or the development of port facilities, or the dredging of harbors, or the employment of icebreakers. They not only purchased corporation stocks but also carried out extensive campaigns to convince other residents of their cities that their interests, too, could best be served by their purchase of such securities, either on their own behalf or, on a grander scale, through the instrumentality of the governmental entity that was their city. Outside of the urban environment such unity of economic interest (real or apparent) was much less frequently coupled with capital availability.

Finally, the dominance of urban governmental leadership by members, allies, or representatives of the mercantile elite meant that the city as a political entity became an instrument of support for the commercial community. Thus, public as well as private capital could be tapped for the development of instruments for mercantile growth and the extension of the hinterland areas of commercial dominance. In many instances, public capital was essential to the construction of expensive transportation works. The substantial identity between the commercial and the political leadership was crucial in securing the authorization by the state legislature of the cities' purchase of transportation company stocks or the guaranteeing of private corporation loans; the urban governmental decisions to provide the public funding authorized; and, as was frequently necessary, the approval by the electorate of special taxes to fund such stock purchases.

These, then, were the circumstances that fostered the emergence and growth of urban mercantilism in the United States in the nineteenth century. It was, moreover, urban mercantilism that made possible the rapid development of transportation works in the country during that same period. And a further consequence of the prevalence of urban mercantilism was the increasing influence of the cities in American life as the United States moved gingerly toward its destiny as an urban nation.

Conclusion

This volume may be seen as examining the corporate environment in which American urbanism took root. This milieu can, of course, only be perceived as a dynamic, living organism—never static and, therefore, impossible to depict accurately as a structure or a diagram. Rather, it must be seen as an interaction of multiple forces with constantly shifting valences and relationships within equally constantly changing parameters.

Just as a human organism cannot be accurately observed—and certainly not understood—from a solely physical point of view, so, too, must we include shifting concepts, ambitions, fears, aspirations, and levels of knowledge in any viable depiction of the corporate entity that is one formulation of the city. The task of this volume is made more difficult by the intention to generalize about the nature and role of urban political entities in the United States in the antebellum era—to explore the legal/political milieu in which the strong roots of American urbanism developed.

It should come as no surprise that both diversity and commonality strongly mark this experience. Like all same-species organisms there are many simularities imposed by inheritance (shared history) and common generic experience, yet each complex organism is different in many particulars. But what is lost in neatness is made up in vitality, and the honest observer neither tries to force all units to fit a mold of commonality nor, in despair, embraces utter randomness.

In the fluid and transmuting urban environment occurs that economic, social, and, in the broadest sense, cultural development—involving many more elements than elsewhere and shifting even more rapidly, acting in and reacting with, changing and changed by the environment—that produces the kaleidoscopic cultural mosaic that is urbanism. It can no more be described with precision than can the human psyche, because it defies encapsulation. But it can be perceived, as a performance is perceived, and experienced retrospectively. And it is to this end that this work has been undertaken—first to describe organically the legal/political urban environment, and then to depict other major elements of the American urban exerience. This latter task will be addressed in subsequent volumes.

Notes

CHAPTER 1

1. Henry R. Stiles, *A History of the City of Brooklyn* (Brooklyn: by subscription, 1867–1870), 1:378; H. Perry Smith, *History of the City of Buffalo and Erie County* (Syracuse: D. Mason & Co., 1884), 2:38; Frederick L. Billon, *Annals of St. Louis in Its Territorial Days from 1804 to 1821* (St. Louis: Nixon-Jones, 1888), 1; Daniel Drake, *Natural and Statistical View, or Picture of Cincinnati and the Miami Country* (Cincinnati: Looker & Wallace, 1815), 173–74; Wilhelmus B. Bryan, *A History of the National Capital* (New York: Macmillan Company, 1914–1916), 1:169–71, 285–87, 445–46; Samuel Burch, *A Digest of the Laws of the Corporation of the City of Washington, to the First of June, 1823* (Washington: James Wilson, 1823), 4–7.

2. William W. Howe, *Municipal History of New Orleans*, Series 7, No. 4 of *Johns Hopkins Studies in Historical and Political Science* (Baltimore: Johns Hopkins University, 1889), 8–14; John S. Kendall, *History of New Orleans* (Chicago: Lewis Publishing Co., 1922), 1:48–72.

3. Louisville, City Council, *Charter of the City of Louisville of 1851, and Ordinances of the City . . . , also a Collection of Acts of the General Assembly of Kentucky, from the Establishment of the Town of Louisville in May, 1780 to March 15, 1869* (Louisville: Bradley & Gilbert, 1869), 9–10, 18–20; Erasmus Wilson, *Standard History of Pittsburg [sic], Pennsylvania* (Chicago: Goodspeed Publishing Company, 1898), 679.

4. Albany, Common Council, *Laws and Ordinances of the Mayor, Aldermen and Commonality of the City of Albany, Passed on the 6th Day of June, 1808* (Albany: Webster & Skinner, 1808), 91–111; John Hardy, *Manual of the Corporation of the City of New York [1870]* (New York: n.p., 1871), 4–8; Wilbur F. Coyle, *Records of the City of Baltimore (City Commissioners), 1797–1813* (Baltimore: City Library, 1906), i–x; Charleston, City Council, *A Digest of the Ordinances of the City Council of Charleston, from the Year 1783 to Oct. 1844, to Which Are Annexed the Acts of the Legislature Which Relate Exclusively to the City of Charleston* (Charleston: Walker & Burke, 1844),

339–41; Philadelphia, City Council, *Ordinances of the Corporation of the City of Philadelphia* (Philadelphia: Moses Thomas, 1812), 63–78; Ellis P. Oberholtzer, *Philadelphia:
A History of the City and Its People* (Philadelphia: S. J. Clarke Publishing Co., [1912]),
1:343; Carl Bridenbaugh, *Cities in Revolt: Urban Life in America, 1743–1776* (New
York: Alfred A. Knopf, 1959), 218.

5. George G. Wilson, *Town and City Government in Providence* (Providence: Tib-
bitts & Preston, 1889), 53–58; Howard K. Stokes, *The Finances and Administration of
Providence*, Extra volume 25 of *Johns Hopkins University Studies in Historical and
Political Science* (Baltimore: The Johns Hopkins Press, 1903), 134–35; Charles Shaw,
A Topographical and Historical Description of Boston (Boston: Oliver Spear, 1817),
153; Caleb H. Snow, *A History of Boston* (Boston: Abel Bowen, 1828), 364–65; John
Koren, *Boston, 1822–1922: The Story of Its Government and Principal Activities during
One Hundred Years* (Boston: Boston Printing Department, 1923), 6–10; Boston Registry
Department, *A Volume of Records Relating to the Early History of Boston Containing
Boston Town Records, 1814 to 1822* (Boston: Municipal Printing Office, 1906), 37:44,
48, 255, 263, 265.

6. Albany, Common Council, *Ordinances, 1808*, 91–111; Samuel L. Mitchell, *The
Picture of New York; or the Travellers' Guide* (New York: I. Riley and Company, 1807),
29–32; New York, Common Council, *The Charter of the City of New-York* (New York:
Childs and Devoe, 1836), 35–95.

7. The previous paragraphs are based on the following: Baltimore, City Council,
Ordinances of the Corporation of the City of Baltimore [1797–1802] (Baltimore: John
Cox, 1875), 19–21; Coyle, *Records of the Baltimore City Commissioners, 1797–1813*,
i–x; Charleston, *Year-Book—1881* (Charleston: News and Courier Book Presses, 1881),
342–43; Charleston, City Council, *Ordinances, 1783–1844*, 339–41; Philadelphia, City
Council, *A Digest of the Acts of the Assembly Relating to the City of Philadelphia*
(Philadelphia: J. H. Jones, 1856), 9–26; George C. Rogers, Jr., *Charleston in the Age of
the Pinckneys* (Norman: University of Oklahoma Press, 1969), 50–51; Edward P. Allinson and Boies Penrose, *Philadelphia, 1681–1887: A History of Municipal Development*
(Philadelphia: Allen, Lane and Scott, 1887), 67. The 1789 Philadelphia charter, before
its amendment in 1796, provided for the election of the aldermen, who elected the mayor
from their number and, with the council, mayor, and recorder, constituted the city council.
In Baltimore the two councils met separately, although the charter is not entirely clear
as to the intent of the framers.

8. Walter F. Dodd, *The Government of the District of Columbia* (Washington: John
Byrne and Company, 1909), 36–37; Kendall, *History of New Orleans*, 1:70–73; New
Orleans, City Council, *A Digest of the Ordinances, Resolutions, By-Laws, and Regula-
tions of the Corporation of New-Orleans, and a Collection of the Laws of the Legislature
Relative to the Said City* (New Orleans: Gaston Brusle, 1836), 283–95; Washington, City
Council, *A Digest of the General Acts of the Corporation of the City of Washington*
(Washington: J. Gideon, Jr., 1818), 5–8.

9. Boston, City Council, *The Charter of the City of Boston, and Ordinances Made
and Established by the Mayor, Aldermen, and Common Council, with Such Acts of the
Legislature of Massachusetts, As Relate to the Government of the Said City* (Boston:
True and Green, 1827), 3–20; Leonard P. Curry, *The Free Black in Urban America,
1800–1850: The Shadow of the Dream* (Chicago: University of Chicago Press, 1981),
217–20; Koren, *Boston, 1822–1922*, 9–11; Louisville, City Council, *Charter and*

Ordinances (1869), 33–53; Pittsburgh, City Council, *A Digest of the Acts of the Assembly Relating to, and the General Ordinances of the City of Pittsburgh from 1804 to Sept. 1, 1886* (Harrisburg: Edwin K. Meyers, 1887), 1–15; St. Louis, City Council, *The Revised Ordinances of the City of St. Louis, Revised and Digested by the City Council, in the Year 1850* (St. Louis: Chambers and Knapp, 1850), 49–55; Philadelphia, City Council, *Digest of Acts* (1856), 9–22; Ohio, Legislature, *Acts Passed at the First Session of the Seventeenth General Assembly of the State of Ohio, Begun and Held in the Town of Columbus, December 7, 1818* (Chillicothe, Ohio: George Naskee, 1819), 170–80.

10. Boston, Registry Department, *Boston Town Records, 1814–1822*, 37:254–65; Elihu H. Shepard, *The Autobiography of Elihu H. Shepard* (St. Louis: George Knapp and Company, 1869), 103; Marshall S. Snow, ed., *History of the Development of Missouri and Particularly of Saint Louis* (St. Louis: National Press Bureau, 1908), 92.

11. Stokes, *Finances and Administration of Providence*, 162–63; William R. Staples, *Annals of the Town of Providence from Its First Settlement, to the Organization of the City Government, in June, 1832* (Providence: Knowles and Vose, 1843), 396–400. For the riot of 1831, see Curry, *Free Black in Urban America*, 102–3. See also Howard P. Chudacoff and Theodore C. Hirt, "Social Turmoil and Government Reform in Providence, 1820–1832," *Rhode Island History* 31 (Winter 1972): 21–33.

12. Providence, City Council, *The Charter and Ordinances of the City of Providence; With the Acts of the General Assembly Relating to the City* (Providence: Weeden and Cory, 1835), 3–12; Stokes, *Finances and Administration of Providence*, 168–69; Wilson, *Government in Providence*, 66–68.

13. Stiles, *History of Brooklyn*, 2:238–43.

14. Brooklyn, Common Council, *Acts Relating to the City of Brooklyn, and the Ordinances Thereof* (Brooklyn: J. Douglas, 1836), 3–35; J. N. Larned, *A History of Buffalo, Delineating the Evolution of the City* (New York: Progress of the Empire State Company, 1911), 1:188; New York, Legislature, *An Act to Incorporate the City of Buffalo, Passed April 20, 1832* (Buffalo: David M. Day, 1832), 3–26.

15. Baltimore, City Council, *The Ordinances of the Mayor and City Council of Baltimore . . . , 1833* (Baltimore: Sands and Neilson, 1833), 103–4; Charleston, *Year-Book—1881*, 347.

16. New Orleans, City Council, *Digest of Ordinances* (1836), 301; Washington, City Council, *Digest of Acts* (1818), 9; John A. Dix, *Sketch of the Resources of the City of New-York* (New York: G. & C. Carrill, 1827), 22; Albany, Common Council, *Laws and Ordinances of the Common Council of the City of Albany, Revised and Revived, December 1837* (Albany: Alfred Southwick, 1838), 37; Allinson and Penrose, *Philadelphia*, 65; Wilson, *History of Pittsburg*, 702.

17. Wilson, *History of Pittsburg*, 702; Washington, City Council, *Charter of Washington, Being the Acts of Incorporation [1820–1848]* (Washington: Robert A. Waters, 1859), 4; David T. Valentine, *Manual of the Corporation of the City of New-York, for the Year 1850* (New York: McSpedon and Baker, 1850), 239; David T. Valentine, *Manual of the Corporation of the City of New-York, for 1854* (New York: McSpedon and Baker, 1854), 486; Albany, Common Council, *Laws and Ordinances of the Common Council of the City of Albany, Revised and Revived, April 14, 1845* (Albany: Weed & Parsons, 1845), 104–5; Allinson and Penrose, *Philadelphia*, 65.

18. See p. 6, above; *The Cincinnati Almanac for 1839* (Cincinnati: Glezen and Shepard, 1839), 34; Louisville, City Council, *Charter and Ordinances* (1869), 68, 75;

Albany, Common Council, *Ordinances, 1845*, 104–5 (New York legislative act of February 13, 1840).

19. This table is slightly misleading in one respect—because of the dates of the changes in the method of mayoral election in a number of cities it understates the extent of unrestricted council elections. Actually, the councils were authorized to select the mayors in three-fifths of these cities at one time or another during the period 1812–1840: Albany (1836–1840), Brooklyn (1834–1840), Buffalo (1832–1840), Cincinnati (1819–1827), Louisville (1836–1838), New York (1821–1834), Philadelphia (1826–1839), Pittsburgh (1833), and Washington (1812–1820).

20. David T. Valentine, *Manual of the Corporation of the City of New-York for 1856* (New York: McSpedon & Baker, 1856), 26; New Orleans, City Council, *Digest of Ordinances* (1836), 517–18. See also sources listed in notes 16, 17, and 18, above. In 1843 the vote required to override the veto of the mayor of St. Louis was changed from a majority of the elected members to three-fifths of those voting. See St. Louis, City Council, *The Revised Ordinances of the City of St. Louis, Revised and Digested by the City Council, in the Year 1850* (St. Louis: Chambers & Knapp, 1850), 105. It is interesting to note, however, the early appearance of both popularly elected mayors and mayoral veto powers in southern cities. In 1820 all three of the cities with directly elected mayors (Charleston, New Orleans, and Washington) and all three in which the mayors had veto powers (Baltimore, New Orleans, and Washington) were southern.

21. Boston, City Council, *The Charter and Ordinances of the City of Boston, Together with the Acts of the Legislature Relating to the City* (Boston: Moore & Crosby, 1856), 22; Brooklyn, Common Council, *The Charter of the City of Brooklyn, and the Special Laws Relating Thereto; Together with the Ordinances for the Government of the City* (Brooklyn: George C. Bennett, 1857), 22; Buffalo, Common Council, *Revised Charter of the City of Buffalo* (Buffalo: Brunck, Held & Co., 1856), 14; Louisville, City Council, *Revised Ordinances of the City of Louisville, Including the Charter of 1851* (Louisville: Louisville Courier Steam Printing House, 1854), 12–14; Alexander Walker, *City Digest: Including a Sketch of the Political History of New Orleans* (New Orleans: Daily Delta Office, 1852), 7; Valentine, *Manual of New-York, 1856*, 39; Philadelphia, City Council, *Digest of Acts* (1856), 33–34; Providence, City Council, *The Charter and Ordinances of the City of Providence together with the Acts of the General Assembly Relating to the City* (Providence: Knowles, Anthony and Co., 1854), 22.

22. New Orleans, City Council, *Digest of Ordinances* (1836), 301; Washington, City Council, *Digest of Acts* (1818), 9; Louisville, City Council, *Charter and Ordinances* (1869), 75; Valentine, *Manual of New-York, 1856*, 29; Brooklyn, Common Council, *Charter and Ordinances* (1857), 39; Buffalo, Common Council, *Revised Charter* (1856), 6; Philadelphia, City Council, *Digest of Acts* (1856), 33; Cincinnati, City Council, *An Act Incorporating the City of Cincinnati, and the Ordinances of Said City, Now in Force* (Cincinnati: Morgan, Fisher and L'Hommedieu, 1828), 5.

23. Louisville, City Council, *Charter and Ordinances* (1869), 69; Louisville, City Council, *Revised Ordinances* (1854), 12–14; Valentine, *Manual of New York, 1856*, 31, 40; Walker, *City Digest of New Orleans*, 6; Philadelphia, City Council, *Digest of Acts* (1856), 33; Buffalo, Common Council, *Revised Charter* (1856), 44–45.

24. Valentine, *Manual of New York, 1856*, 26; St. Louis, City Council, *Revised Ordinances, 1850*, 58; Louisville, City Council, *Revised Ordinances* (1854), 8; Walker, *City Digest of New Orleans*, 2. The Ohio legislature in 1834 authorized the city of Cincinnati to establish a bicameral council by ordinance, if approved by the electorate, but the city

did not elect to make the change. See Cincinnati, City Council, *An Act Incorporating the City of Cincinnati, and a Digest of the Ordinances of Said City, of a General Nature, Now in Force* (Cincinnati: Lodge, L'Hommedieu & Company, 1835), 22–23.

25. Edward Waite, *The Washington Directory, and Congressional and Executive Register, for 1850* (Washington: Columbus Alexander, 1850), 180; Oliver Farnsworth, *The Cincinnati Directory* (Cincinnati: Morgan, Lodge and Company, 1819), 80; Charles Cist, *Sketches and Statistics of Cincinnati in 1851* (Cincinnati: William H. Moore & Company, 1851), 87–88; New Orleans, City Council, *Digest of Ordinances* (1836), 517; Walker, *City Digest of New Orleans*, 2; Boston, City Council, *A Catalogue of the City Councils of Boston, 1822–1908* (Boston: City of Boston Printing Department, 1909), 240; *The Providence Directory* (Providence: H. H. Brown, 1850), 252; Smith, *History of the City of Buffalo*, 2:138; *Philadelphia As It Is* (Philadelphia: P. J. Gray, 1833), 24; *McElroy's Philadelphia Directory for 1850* (Philadelphia: Edward C. and John Biddle, 1850), 28, 246–47; J. Stoddard Johnston, ed., *Memorial History of Louisville from Its First Settlement to the Year 1896* (Chicago: American Biographical Printing Company, [1896]), 1: 646–47; Charles Keemle, *The St. Louis Directory for the Years 1836–37* (St. Louis: C. Keemle, 1836), 34–35; *Greene's St. Louis Directory, for 1851* (St. Louis: Charles & Hammond, 1850), xx–xxi. Obviously, two-chamber councils are likely to have more members than single-house councils. Consequently, all comparisons of council size are made between the larger of the two councils or between a single-body council and the larger chamber in a two-house council.

26. Joel Munsell, *The Annals of Albany* (Albany: Joel Munsell/Munsell and Nowland, 1850–1859), 6:125, 10:303–4, 312–14; J. Fry, *The Albany Register, and Albany Directory for the Year 1815* (Albany: H. C. Southwick, Packard, and Van Benthuysen, and Churchill and Abbey, 1815), 9–10; U.S., Census Office, *Return of the Whole Number of Persons within the Several Districts of the United States* (Washington: William Duane and Son, 1802), 44; U.S., Census Office, *Census for 1820* (Washington: Gales and Seaton, 1821), 9* [Page numbers with asterisks are numbered as they appear in the original source.]; U.S., Census Office, *Fifth Census; or Enumeration of the Inhabitants of the United States, 1830* (Washington: Duff Green, 1832), 36–37 (third pagination); U.S., Census Office, *Sixth Census or Enumeration of the Inhabitants of the United States, As Corrected at the Department of State, in 1840* (Washington: Blair and Rives, 1841), 82–83; U.S., Census Office, *The Seventh Census of the United States: 1850* (Washington: Robert Armstrong, 1853), 92.

27. J. Thomas Scharf, *History of Baltimore City and County* (Philadelphia: Louis H. Everts, 1881), 188–89; U.S., Census Office, *Census, 1800*, 68; U.S., Census Office, *Aggregate Amount of Each Description of Persons Within the United States of America, and the Territories Thereof, Agreeable to Actual Enumeration Made According to Law, in the Year 1810* (Washington: n.p., 1811), 53; U.S., Census Office, *Census, 1820*, 20*; U.S., Census Office, *Census, 1830*, 80–81 (third pagination); U.S., Census Office, *Census, 1840*, 194–95; U.S., Census Office, *Census, 1850*, 221.

28. Isaac Harris, *Harris' Pittsburgh & Allegheny Directory*, (Pittsburgh: A. A. Anderson, 1839), 194; U.S., Census Office, *Census, 1810*, 44; U.S., Census Office, *Census, 1820*, 15*; U.S., Census Office, *Census, 1840*, 160–61; George T. Fleming, *History of Pittsburgh and Its Environs* (New York: American Historical Society, Inc., 1822), 2:85; Wilson, *History of Pittsburg*, 717–18.

29. Henry McCloskey, *Manual of the Common Council of the City of Brooklyn, for 1865* (n.p., n.d.), xxii; U.S., Census Office, *Census, 1830*, 50–51 (third pagination); U.S.,

Census Office, *Census, 1840*, 118–19; U.S., Census Office, *Census, 1850,* 99; New York, Secretary of State, *Census of the State of New-York, for 1855* (Albany: Charles Van Benthuysen, 1857), xxii. The population of Ward Eleven in 1855 exceeded 22,000.

30. Sources for Table 1.3: see sources listed in notes 25–29; U.S., Census Office, *Census, 1830,* 22–23, 24–25, 36–37, 38–39, 50–51, 64–65, 68–69, 80–81, 94–95, 105– 6, 114–15, 126–27, 160–61 (third pagination); U.S., Census Office, *Census, 1840,* 52– 53, 88–89, 118–19; U.S., Census Office, *Census, 1850,* 52, 67, 92, 96, 99, 102, 158, 179, 221, 234, 339, 474, 612, 662, 830; *Cohen's New Orleans and Lafayette Directory* (New Orleans: The Daily Delta, 1852), 260; Scharf, *History of Baltimore,* 188; Charleston, *Year-Book—1881,* 371; Charles T. Greve, *Centennial History of Cincinnati and Representative Citizens* (Chicago: Biographical Publishing Company, 1904), 1:508; Johnston, *History of Louisville,* 1:646; Valentine, *Manual of New-York, 1850,* 237–38; Andrew Rothwell, *Laws of the Corporation of the City of Washington, to the End of the Thirtieth Council—June, 1833* (Washington: F. W. deKrafft, 1833), 323; "An Abstract of the Census of the Several Counties of the State of Missouri, for the Year 1828," *Journal of the Senate of the State of Missouri, at the First Session of the Fifth General Assembly, Begun and Held at the City of Jefferson, on Monday the Seventeenth Day of November, in the Year of Our Lord, One Thousand Eight Hundred and Twenty-eight* (Jefferson City: Calvin Gunn, 1828), unpaged. The populations of Providence (1831), Buffalo (1832), and Brooklyn (1824) are interpolated from the 1830 and 1840 U.S. censuses by assigning an equal amount of the population increase during the decade to each of the intercensal years. Since the growth of urban populations depends heavily on in-migration, which varies, sometimes widely, from year to year, it is believed that this simpler method of calculating population for intercensal years will create no more distortion than more complex approaches. The 1830 U.S. census reported the Missouri data by counties only. Consequently, an 1828 figure from a local enumeration has been substituted for St. Louis.

31. Walker, *City Digest of New Orleans,* 2; "Report of the Committee Appointed to Apportion the Representation of the State," 5, in Louisiana, Legislature, Senate, *Official Reports of the Senate of the State of Louisiana* (New Orleans: Emile LeSere, 1854). See also sources relevant to these cities cited in note 30.

32. Greve, *History of Cincinnati,* 1:656; Valentine, *Manual of New-York, 1856,* 38– 39; U.S., Census Office, *Census, 1850,* 102, 830; U.S., Census Office, *Preliminary Report of the Eighth Census. 1860* (Washington: Government Printing Office, 1862), 337, 381.

33. Philadelphia, City Council, *Digest of Acts* (1856), 28–30; U.S., Census Office, *Census, 1850,* 179; U.S., Census Office, *Preliminary Census, 1860,* 431–32; J. D. B. DeBow, *Statistical View of the United States* (Washington: A. O. P. Nicholson, 1854), 375.

34. The reference here is to offices, not officers. In a number of cases several individuals held a given office. In 1831, for instance, only the ward offices of warden and clerk (aside from the mayoral and council offices) were elective in Providence, but a warden and a clerk were elected in each ward. It should also be noted that the number of elective offices indicated should be understood as a minimum number. By virtue of general state legislation city residents voted for a number of other offices—national, state, county, township, special district, and, in some instances, doubtless, municipal.

35. Albany, Common Council, *Ordinances, 1808,* 64, 67; Coyle, *Records of the Baltimore City Commissioners, 1797–1813,* i–x; Boston, City Council, *Charter and Ordinances* (1827), 4, 14–15; Brooklyn, Common Council, *Acts and Ordinances* (1836), 6– 7, 20, 31; New York, Legislature, *An Act to Incorporate the City of Buffalo, 1832,* 4;

Charleston, *Year-Book—1881*, 342–43; Ohio, Legislature, *Acts, 1818–1819*, 175–180; Louisville, City Council, *Charter and Ordinances* (1869), 47; New Orleans, City Council, *Digest of Ordinances* (1836), 283–95; New York, Common Council, *Charter* (1836), 46; Philadelphia, City Council, *Digest of Acts* (1856), 9–26; Pittsburgh, City Council, *Digest of Acts* (1887), 6–15; Providence, City Council, *Charter and Ordinances* (1835), 4; St. Louis, City Council, *Revised Ordinances, 1850*, 49–55; Washington, City Council, *Digest of Acts* (1818), 5–7.

36. In all of these discussions of elective offices public school officials—for example, members of school committees, inspectors, directors, trustees—have been excluded from consideration. Such officers were directly elected, usually on a ward basis, in all cities except Baltimore, Charleston, New Orleans, and Washington. Also excluded, obviously, are mayors and council members.

37. Albany, Common Council, *Laws and Ordinances of the Common Council of the City of Albany, Revised and Revived May 5, 1856* (Albany: W. C. Little and Company, 1856), 324–37; *Hearnes' Brooklyn Directory, 1851–1853* (Brooklyn: n.p., 1851), 20–21; Buffalo, Common Council, *Revised Charter* (1856), 4–5; Cincinnati, City Council, *Laws and General Ordinances of the City of Cincinnati* (Cincinnati: By order of the City Council, 1853), 42–45; Louisville, City Council, *Revised Ordinances* (1854), 15–21; Johnston, *History of Louisville*, 1:94; Valentine, *Manual of New-York, 1856*, 31–40; Philadelphia, City Council, *Digest of Acts* (1856), 34–55; Wilson, *Government in Providence*, 67; St. Louis, City Council, *Revised Ordinances, 1850*, 90–91, 107; Thomas S. Barclay, *The Movement for Municipal Home Rule in St. Louis* (Columbia: University of Missouri Press, 1943), 16; Washington, City Council, *Charter of Washington* (1859), 22–23. The terminal years for which the count of elective offices was taken are as follows: Albany, 1851; Baltimore, 1850; Boston, 1854; Brooklyn, 1851; Buffalo, 1853; Charleston, 1850; Cincinnati, 1852; Louisville, 1851; New Orleans, 1852; New York, 1853; Philadelphia, 1854; Pittsburgh, 1850; Providence, 1850; St. Louis, 1853; Washington, 1848.

38. Sidney I. Pomerantz, *New York: An American City, 1783–1803* (Port Washington, N.Y.: Ira J. Friedman, 1965; originally published in 1938), 139–44; Edmund P. Willis, "Social Origins of Political Leadership in New York City from the Revolution to 1815" (Ph.D. dissertation, University of California, Berkeley, 1967), 49–53. Freemen of the city (who could acquire that status by purchase) created after 1777 could also vote in city elections. Free black males could vote if, in addition to satisfying the other requirements, they presented their certificates of freedom.

39. Edward Pessen, "Political Democracy and the Distribution of Power in Antebellum New York City," in Irwin Yellowitz, ed., *Essays in the History of New York City: A Memorial to Sidney Pomerantz* (Port Washington, N.Y.: Kennikat Press, 1978), 71; James G. Wilson, ed., *The Memorial History of the City of New-York* (New York: New-York History Company, 1892–1893), 3:381–82; Valentine, *Manual of New-York, 1856*, 29.

40. Brooklyn, Common Council, *Acts and Ordinances* (1836), 8; New York, Legislature, *An Act to Incorporate the City of Buffalo, 1832*, 5; Cincinnati, City Council, *An Act Incorporating the City of Cincinnati* (1835), 21; Louisville, City Council, *Charter and Ordinances* (1869), 34, 53, 55, 77; Louisville, City Council, *Revised Ordinances* (1854), 58; Coyle, *Records of the Baltimore City Commissioners, 1797–1813*, ii; Philadelphia, City Council, *Digest of Acts* (1856), 25; Charleston, *Year-Book—1881*, 348.

41. Albany, Common Council, *Ordinances, 1808*, 67; Albany, Common Council, *Or-*

dinances, 1837, 35–36, 77; St. Louis, City Council, *Revised Ordinances, 1850*, 54, 66, 80, 91.

42. Kendall, *History of New Orleans*, 1:72; New Orleans, City Council, *Digest of Ordinances* (1836), 305, 315, 507; James K. Greer, "Politics in Louisiana, 1845–1861," *Louisiana Historical Quarterly* 12 (July 1929): 415.

43. Boston, City Council, *Charter and Ordinances* (1827), 8; Boston, City Council, *Charter and Ordinances* (1856), 26; George Adams, *The Boston Directory, for the Year 1851* (Boston: George Adams, 1851), Appendix, 10.

44. Washington, City Council, *Digest of Acts* (1818), 5; Washington, City Council, *Charter of Washington (1859)*, 21, 25.

45. Pittsburgh, City Council, *Digest of Acts* (1887), 121–22; Providence, City Council, *Charter and Ordinances* (1835), 10; Stokes, *Finances and Administration of Providence*, 168–69. There were, of course, other suffrage requirements (e.g., residence, citizenship, age, sex) and, additionally, some persons (e.g., paupers, persons under guardianship, felons, persons *non compos mentis*) otherwise qualified to vote were specifically excluded. While municipal law on these matters differed in some small particulars among these cities, the basic limitations and restrictions were common to all and are not discussed here. On the matter of black suffrage, see Curry, *Free Black in Urban America*, 216–24.

46. J. L. Dawson and H. W. DeSaussure, *Census of the City of Charleston, South Carolina, for the Year 1848* (Charleston: J. B. Nixon, 1849), 36; Pomerantz, *New York*, 143–44; St. Louis, City Council, *Revised Ordinances, 1850*, 54, 66, 80, 91.

47. Albany, Common Council, *Ordinances, 1808*, 91–111; Albany, Common Council, *Laws and Ordinances, Revised 1856*, 282–83; New York, Common Council, *Charter* (1836), 48; Valentine, *Manual of New-York, 1856*, 24–36; Boston, City Council, *Charter and Ordinances* (1827), 5–7; Boston, City Council, *Charter and Ordinances* (1856), 4–10; Providence, City Council, *Charter and Ordinances* (1835), 3; Pittsburgh, City Council, *Digest of Acts* (1887), 7; Philadelphia, City Council, *Digest of Acts* (1856), 25, 30; Charleston, *Year-Book—1881*, 343. Unless otherwise stated, these discussions address only the qualifications specified for mayors and members of the city councils.

48. Coyle, *Records of the Baltimore City Commissioners, 1797–1813*, ii; Baltimore, City Council, *The Ordinances of the Mayor and City Council of Baltimore* (Baltimore: John D. Toy, 1826), 28–30, 39–40; Charleston, City Council, *Ordinances, 1783–1844*, 343; Washington, City Council, *Digest of Acts* (1818), 5, 6, 9, 10; Washington, City Council, *Charter of Washington* (1859), 5, 6, 19–30.

49. Brooklyn, Common Council, *Acts and Ordinances* (1836), 6; Brooklyn, Common Council, *Charter and Ordinances* (1857), 20, 34–35; New York, Legislature, *An Act to Incorporate the City of Buffalo, 1832*, 4; Buffalo, Common Council, *Revised Charter* (1856), 5; Cincinnati, City Council, *An Act Incorporating the City of Cincinnati* (1828), 5, 7; Cincinnati, City Council, *An Act Incorporating the City of Cincinnati* (1835), 6, 9, 21; Cincinnati, City Council, *Ordinances* (1853), 34; St. Louis, City Council, *Revised Ordinances, 1850*, 50, 51, 60–61, 72, 77, 84, 89.

50. Howe, *Municipal History of New Orleans*, 14; New Orleans, City Council, *Digest of Ordinances* (1836), 305, 315, 507; Walker, *City Digest of New Orleans*, 2.

51. Louisville, City Council, *Charter and Ordinances* (1869), 34, 53, 70, 75; Louisville, City Council, *Revised Ordinances* (1854), 9, 13.

52. Albany, Common Council, *Ordinances, 1808*, 66; Philadelphia, City Council, *Ordinances of the Corporation of, and Acts of the Assembly Relating to the City of Phil-*

adelphia (Philadelphia: Crissy and Markley, 1851), 62; Pittsburgh, City Council, *Digest of Acts* (1887), 1; Baltimore, City Council, *Ordinances* (1826), 38; New York, Common Council, *Charter* (1836), 127–28.

53. Baltimore, City Council, *Ordinances* (1826), 38–40; Whitman H. Ridgeway, *Community Leadership in Maryland, 1790–1840: A Comparative Analysis of Power in Society* (Chapel Hill: University of North Carolina Press, 1979), 84. The convention unanimously ratified the charter changes in February 1808, some three months after the legislature had acted.

54. Boston, Registry Department, *Boston Town Records, 1814–1822*, 37:254–65; Snow, *History of Boston*, 365–68; Boston, City Council, *Charter and Ordinances* (1827), 3–20.

55. Staples, *Annals of Providence*, 396–99.

56. Wilson, *History of New-York*, 3:384–85; Valentine, *Manual of New-York, 1856*, 36; John Hardy, *Manual of the Corporation of the City of New York [1870]* (New York: n.p., 1871), 8; New York, Common Council, *Charter* (1836), 223–55; Allen C. Clark, "Colonel William Winston Seaton and His Mayoralty," *Records of the Columbia Historical Society* 29–30 (1928):69; Washington, City Council, *Laws of the Corporation of the City of Washington [1848]* (Washington: John T. Towers, 1848), 37–44, 121; Washington, City Council, *Charter of Washington (1859)*, 19–30; Jacob Judd, "The History of Brooklyn, 1834–1855: Political and Administrative Aspects" (Ph.D. dissertation, New York University, 1959), 51–57; Attia M. Bowmer, "The History of the Government of the City of Louisville, 1780–1870" (M. A. thesis, University of Louisville, 1948), 62–63; Greve, *History of Cincinnati*, 1:508; St. Louis, City Council, *Revised Ordinances, 1850*, 55.

57. Louisville, City Council, *Revised Ordinances* (1854), 64; Bowmer, "Government of Louisville, 1780–1870," 67, 79.

58. J. H. Hollander, *The Financial History of Baltimore*, Extra Volume 20 of *Johns Hopkins University Studies in Historical and Political Science* (Baltimore: The Johns Hopkins Press, 1899), 126–27; Greve, *History of Cincinnati*, 1:508–9; Judd, "History of Brooklyn, 1834–1855," 51–57.

59. New Orleans, City Council, *Digest of Ordinances* (1836), 497–521 (quotations from pp. 501, 503–5); Kendall, *History of New Orleans*, 1:124–26; Henry C. Castellanos, *New Orleans As It Was* (New Orleans: L. Graham and Son, 1895), 147, 155.

60. Baltimore, City Council, *Ordinances* (1826), 55; Brooklyn, Common Council, *Acts and Ordinances* (1836), 17, 19, 21–22; St. Louis, City Council, *Revised Ordinances, 1850*, 95, 116, 118; Walker, *City Digest of New Orleans*, 41.

61. Washington, City Council, *Digest of Acts* (1818), 11–12; Washington, City Council, *Charter of Washington (1859)*, 7, 15, 20–22.

62. Greve, *History of Cincinnati*, 1:508.

63. Valentine, *Manual of New-York, 1856*, 27, 31–34; Valentine, *Manual of New-York, 1854*, 499–502; Ira M. Leonard, "New York City Politics, 1841–1844: Nativism and Reform" (Ph.D. dissertation, New York University, 1965), 234–35.

64. Philadelphia, City Council, *A Digest of the Ordinances of the Corporation of the City of Philadelphia, and of the Acts of the Assembly, Relating Thereto* (Philadelphia: S. C. Atkinson, 1834), 57; Philadelphia, City Council, *A Digest of the Ordinances of the Corporation of the City of Philadelphia, and Acts of Assembly Relating Thereto* (Philadelphia: J. Crissy, 1841), 235–36; Philadelphia, City Council, *Digest of Acts* (1856), 3; Philadelphia, Common Council, *Journal of the Common Council, of the City of Phila-*

delphia for 1838–9 (Philadelphia: J. Van Court, 1839), 113, 121; Philadelphia, Common Council, *Journal of the Common Council of the City of Philadelphia, for 1840–41* (Philadelphia: J. Van Court, 1841), 79.

65. Brooklyn, Common Council, *Acts and Ordinances* (1836), 8–10; Boston, City Council, *Charter and Ordinances* (1856), 15–16, 18; Louisville, City Council, *Revised Ordinances* (1854), 17, 19; Providence, City Council, *Charter and Ordinances* (1835), 65–66; Philadelphia, City Council, *Digest of Acts* (1856), 49–50; Valentine, *Manual of New-York, 1856,* 31, 41; Buffalo, Common Council, *Revised Charter* (1856), 5, 22–23, 26–27; Brooklyn, *A Law to Revise and Amend the Several Acts Relating to the City of Brooklyn, Adopted in Convention* (Brooklyn: Lees and Foulkes, 1818), 62–63. Most of the officers appointed by the Brooklyn council in 1834 were later made elective.

66. Boston, City Council, *Charter and Ordinances* (1827), 10; Josiah Quincy, *A Municipal History of the Town and City of Boston, during Two Centuries. From September 17, 1630, to September 17, 1830* (Boston: Charles C. Little and James Brown, 1852), 60–61; Boston, City Council, *Charter and Ordinances* (1856), 18, 23, 24; Koren, *Boston, 1822–1922,* 11.

67. Koren, *Boston, 1822–1922,* 10–11; Justin Winsor (ed.), *The Memorial History of Boston, Including Suffolk County, Massachusetts, 1630–1880* (Boston: James R. Osgood and Company, 1880–1881), 3:221; the quotation is from Koren.

68. James Cheetham, *Annals of the Corporation, Relative to the Late Contested Elections* (New York: Dennison and Cheetham, 1802), 9–10; Mitchell, *Picture of New York,* 31.

69. Providence, City Council, *Charter and Ordinances* (1835), 4–5.

70. Philadelphia, City Council, *Digest of Acts* (1856), 53; Valentine, *Manual of New-York, 1856,* 40.

71. James Bryce, *The American Commonwealth,* 2nd ed. (London: Macmillan and Company, 1891), 1:609; Mitchell, *Picture of New York,* 31.

CHAPTER 2

1. J. H. Hollander, *The Financial History of Baltimore,* Extra Volume 20 of *Johns Hopkins University Studies in Historical and Political Science,* edited by Herbert Baxter Adams (Baltimore: The Johns Hopkins Press, 1899), 381.

2. Sources for Table 2.1: Joel Munsell, *The Annals of Albany* (Albany: J. Munsell, 1854), 5:30–31; Hollander, *Financial History of Baltimore,* 379; Charles P. Huse, *The Financial History of Boston from May 1, 1822, to January 31, 1909,* Vol. 15 of *Harvard Economic Studies* (Cambridge: Harvard University Press, 1916), 368–69; Boston, Committee of Finance, *Seventh Annual Report of the Committee of Finance of the Town of Boston* ([Boston]: n.p., 1819), 1–3; Minutes of the Trustees of the Town of Louisville, February 26, 1819, Louisville City Records, University of Louisville Archives, University of Louisville, Louisville, Kentucky, Project 10A, Series I, Reel 1, p. 232; *Niles' Weekly Register* (October 21, 1820), 128; New York City, Comptroller, *Annual Report of the Comptroller, with the Accounts of the Corporation, for the Year Ending May 11, 1818* (New York: Thomas P. Low, 1818), 5; Erasmus Wilson, ed., *Standard History of Pittsburg [sic], Pennsylvania* (Chicago: Goodspeed Publishing Company, 1898), 691; Howard K. Stokes, *The Finances and Administration of Providence,* Extra Volume 25 of *Johns Hopkins University Studies in Historical and Political Science* (Baltimore: The Johns

Hopkins Press, 1903), 404; L. U. Reavis, *Saint Louis: Future Great City of the World* (St. Louis: Gray, Baker, and Company, 1875), Appendix, 202. The Louisville data are drawn from a tax levy ordinance rather than from a statement of revenue collected.

3. In computing the per capita revenue, the gross revenue was divided by the interpolated population for that year (not by the 1820 population). In computing the population of a city for a given year one-tenth of the population growth for the decade was assigned to each of the intercensal years. Since urban populations were heavily impacted by in-migration, which could vary widely from year to year (and concerning which there are no reliable data), it is believed that this method of calculating urban populations between censuses will create no more distortion than the employment of more complex methods.

4. Expenditures are discussed on pp. 64–84, below, but it might be noted at this point that Baltimore made no expenditures on schools in 1817 and spent practically nothing on public charities, while Boston spent more than a quarter of its revenues on these items. See Hollander, *Financial History of Baltimore*, 380; Huse, *Financial History of Boston*, 348–49.

5. See sources listed in note 2 (except that for Pittsburgh).

6. Sources for Table 2.3: Hollander, *Financial History of Baltimore*, 382; James H. Thompson, "The Financial History of Pittsburgh: The Early Period, 1816–1865," *Western Pennsylvania Historical Magazine* 33 (March–June 1950): 55; Washington, City Council, *Laws of the Corporation of the City of Washington* (Washington: Way and Gideon, 1819), 9–13; Lemuel Shattuck, *Report to the Committee of the City Council Appointed to Obtain the Census of Boston for the Year 1845* (Boston: John H. Eastburn, 1846), Appendix, 59; Henry A. Ford and Kate B. Ford, *History of Cincinnati, Ohio* (Cleveland: L. A. Williams and Company, 1881), 61; *DeBow's Review* 6 (September 1848): 231; Edwin Williams, *The New-York Annual Register for the Year of Our Lord 1837* (New York: G. and C. Carrill and Company, 1837), 343; Providence, Board of Assessors, *A List of Persons Assessed in the City Tax of . . . 1848* (Providence: H. H. Brown, 1848), 90; Donatien Augustin, *A General Digest of the Ordinances and Resolutions Passed by the City Council of New Orleans* (New Orleans: Jerome Bayon, 1831), 393–95. See also sources cited in note 2 for Baltimore, Boston, St. Louis, New York, Providence, and Louisville. See also note 3.

7. Sources for Table 2.4: Providence, Board of Assessors, *List of Persons Assessed, 1848*, 91–92; David T. Valentine, *Manual of the Corporation of the City of New-York for 1854* (New York: McSpedon and Baker, 1854), 205–6; Peter Force, *A National Calendar for 1820* (Washington: Davis and Force, 1820), 119; Shattuck, *Census of Boston for 1845*, Appendix, 59; William G. Bishop, *Manual of the Common Council of the City of Brooklyn for 1861–1862* (Brooklyn: George C. Bennett, 1861), 456; *Philadelphia in 1824* (Philadelphia: H. C. Carey and I. Lee, 1824), 45; Reavis, *St. Louis*, Appendix, 212; Ben Casseday, *The History of Louisville, from Its Earliest Settlements to the Year 1852* (Louisville: Hull and Brother, 1852), 160; Scharf, *History of Baltimore*, 186.

8. J. Thomas Scharf, *History of Baltimore City and County* (Philadelphia: Louis H. Everts, 1881), 186; *Niles' Weekly Register* (January 4, 1817), 305; Shattuck, *Census of Boston for 1845*, Appendix, 59. See also sources listed in note 7. For some discussion of tax delinquency, see pp. 54–55, below.

9. Sources for Table 2.5: Albany, City Chamberlain, *Report of the Chamberlain to the Hon. the Common Council, of the Receipts and Expenditures of the City of Albany, for the Year Ending on the 8th October, 1833: With a Review Statement of the Receipts*

and Expenditures from Oct. 1826 to Oct. 1833 (Albany: Hoffman and White, 1833), 12–24; Baltimore, City Council, The Ordinances of the Mayor and City Council of Baltimore ... 1836 (Baltimore: Lucas and Deaver, 1836), Appendix, 57–60; Boston, Auditor, Twenty-fourth Annual Report of the Receipts and Expenditures of the City of Boston and County of Suffolk (Boston: John H. Eastburn, 1836), 16–26; Charleston, City Council, A Report Containing a Review of the Proceedings of the City Authorities from First September, 1838, to First August, 1839 (Charleston: W. Riley, 1839), 7; The Cincinnati Almanac for 1839 (Cincinnati: Gleason and Shepard, 1839), 52–53; Louisville, Common Council, Minutes of the Common Council, February 28, 1833, Louisville City Records, University of Louisville Archives, University of Louisville, Project 10A, Series II, Reel 4, 142–43; Edwin Williams, The New-York Annual Register for the Year of Our Lord 1835 (New York: Edwin Williams, 1835), 307; Philadelphia, Common Council, Minutes of the Common Council of the City of Philadelphia, for 1835–6 (Philadelphia: J. Van Court, 1836), 111–12; Stokes, Finances and Administration of Providence, 404–12; Reavis, St. Louis, Appendix, 212; Andrew Rothwell, Laws of the Corporation of the City of Washington, to the End of the Thirtieth Council—June 1833 (Washington: F. W. DeKrafft, 1833), 419. Where it is possible to determine the balances on hand at the beginning of the fiscal year, these have been excluded from the receipts.

10. Because of nonavailability of data, all of the cities listed in Table 2.1 are not included in Table 2.5. The seven cities mentioned in this paragraph appear in both lists. Investigators should be aware of the very considerable difficulty encountered in using in comparative analysis the Boston data supplied by Huse (Financial History of Boston, 348–49, 368–69). He does not, at any time, include loans in his list of receipts (though some limited borrowing might be included in the "miscellaneous" category). The total receipts recorded by Huse in 1835, for example, are less than 45 percent of the total reported by the auditor. Neither the auditor nor Huse reported assessments for street improvements, since the city of Boston was not authorized to levy such assessments. See John Koren, Boston, 1822 to 1922: the Story of Its Government and Principal Activities during One Hundred Years (Boston: Boston Printing Department, 1923), 152–53.

11. See note 3 for the interpolation of urban populations for intercensal years.

12. See sources in note 10. The Charleston City Council report of 1835 lists a single entry of $116,281 under the head of "Taxes." This figure has been disaggregated on the basis of the percentage distribution between property and other taxes in the following year. The estimated property tax figure ($81,676) includes taxes collected on slaves, carriages, horses, and so forth. See Theodore D. Jervey, Robert Y. Hayne and His Times (New York: Macmillan, 1909), 500–501.

13. Washington, City Council, A Digest of the General Acts of the Corporation of the City of Washington (Washington: J. Gideon, Jr., 1818), 11–12; Rothwell, Laws of Washington, 1833, 491.

14. Reavis, St. Louis, Appendix, 212.

15. Niles' Weekly Register (December 6, 1823), 210; The Picture of New-York and Stranger's Guide to the Commercial Metropolis of the United States (New York: A. T. Goodrich, 1828), 189–90; Edwin Williams, The New-York Annual Register for the Year of Our Lord 1830 (New York: J. Leavitt, 1830), 212–13; Edwin Williams, The New-York Annual Register for the Year of Our Lord 1831 (New York: Jonathan Leavitt and Collins and Hannay, 1831), 350; Edwin Williams, The New-York Annual Register for the Year of Our Lord 1832 (New York: J. Seymour, 1832), 213; Edwin Williams, The

New-York Annual Register for the Year of Our Lord 1833 (New York: Peter Hill, 1833), 249; Edwin Williams, *The New-York Annual Register for the Year of Our Lord 1834* (New York: Edwin Williams, 1834), 263–64; Hollander, *Financial History of Baltimore*, 380.

16. See sources listed in note 10.

17. In some cases, however, these vehicles were taxed as personal property and the income so reported by the appropriate city officers.

18. See sources listed in note 10 relating to Baltimore, Charleston, Cincinnati, Louisville, New York, Providence, St. Louis, and Washington; Jervey, *Robert Y. Hayne*, 500–501.

19. Sources for Table 2.8: See sources in note 10 for Baltimore, Boston, Charleston, Cincinnati, Louisville, New York, Philadelphia, Providence, St. Louis, and Washington; Albany, City Chamberlain, *Report of the Chamberlain to the Common Council, Showing the Receipts and Expenditures of the City of Albany, from May 1, 1850, to April 30, 1851* (Albany: Weed, Parsons, and Company, 1851), 60; Hollander, *Financial History of Baltimore*, 384; Shattuck, *Census of Boston for 1845*, Appendix, 59; William G. Bishop, *Manual of the Common Council of the City of Brooklyn for 1860–1861* (Brooklyn: George C. Bennett, 1860), 459; Cincinnati, City Auditor, *Seventh Annual Report of the City Auditor* (Cincinnati: Gazette Steam Printing House, 1860), 63; *The Louisville Directory for the Year 1832* (Louisville: Richard W. Otis, 1832), 114; David T. Valentine, *Manual of the Corporation of the City of New-York for 1859* (New York: Charles W. Barker, 1859), 520; Philadelphia, Common Council, *Journal of the Common Council of the City of Philadelphia, for 1836–7* (Philadelphia: J. Van Court, 1837), Appendix, 6; Wilson, *History of Pittsburg*, 707; Providence, Board of Assessors, *List of Persons Assessed, 1848*, 91; *DeBow's Review* 6 (September 1848), 231.

20. Sources for Table 2.9: Albany, City Chamberlain, *Report, 1850–1851*, 60; Hollander, *Financial History of Baltimore*, 384; Shattuck, *Census of Boston for 1845*, Appendix, 59; Bishop, *Manual of Brooklyn, 1861–1862*, 459; Jervey, *Robert Y. Hayne*, 500–501; Cincinnati, City Auditor, *Report* (1860), 63; *Louisville Directory for 1832*, 115; Albert E. Fossier, *New Orleans: The Glamour Period, 1800–1840* (New Orleans: Pelican Publishing Company, 1857), 54–55; David T. Valentine, *Manual of the Corporation of the City of New-York for 1855* (New York: McSpedon and Baker, 1855), 206; *Hazard's Register* (May 27, 1840), 350; Wilson, *History of Pittsburg*, 707; Providence, Board of Assessors, *List of Persons Assessed, 1848*, 91; *DeBow's Review* 6 (September 1848):231; [John Sessford], "The Sessford Annals," *Columbia Historical Society Records* 11 (1908), 297, 299. See also note 3.

21. Computed from data in Tables 2.3 and 2.8. See also note 3.

22. *Hazard's Register* (May 27, 1840), 350; Hollander, *Financial History of Baltimore*, 384.

23. Sources for Table 2.10: Albany, City Chamberlain, *Report, 1850–1851*, 13–19; Baltimore, City Council, *The Ordinances of the Mayor and City Council of Baltimore . . . , 1851* (Baltimore: James Lucas, 1851), Appendix, 29–39; Boston, Auditor, *Auditor's Thirty-Ninth Report of the Receipts and Expenditures of the City of Boston, and the County of Suffolk, for the Financial Year 1850–51* (Boston: J. H. Eastburn, 1851), 189–91; Thomas P. Teale, *Municipal Register of the City of Brooklyn, and Manual of King's County, from the Earliest Period Up to the Present Time* (Brooklyn: E. B. Spooner, 1848), 117–20; Cincinnati, Auditor, *Report* (1860), 64–65; Louisville, Common Council, Minutes, March 31, 1851; *DeBow's Review* 3 (April 1847):346; David T. Valentine,

Manual of the Corporation of the City of New-York, for the Year 1850 (New York: McSpedon and Baker, 1850), 195–208; Philadelphia, Common Council, *Journal of the Common Council of the City of Philadelphia, for 1849–50* (Philadelphia: King and Baird, 1850), Appendix, 228–29; Reavis, *St. Louis*, Appendix, 212; Washington, City Council, *Laws of the Corporation of the City of Washington . . . [1851]* (Washington: John T. Towers, 1851), 279–87.

24. Boston, New York, Albany, New Orleans, Charleston, Providence, and Philadelphia ranked fourth, first, tenth, sixth, fifth, eighth, and second in size in 1810; Baltimore ranked third. See U.S., Bureau of the Census, *Twelfth Census of the United States, Taken in the Year 1900: Population* (Washington: Government Printing Office, 1901), 1:430–33; J. D. B. DeBow, *Statistical View of the United States* (Washington: A. O. P. Nicholson, 1854), 192.

25. The New Orleans figures are for total receipts only and those for Cincinnati are separated only into tax and other receipts. Satisfactory analysis of the St. Louis figures is inhibited by the fact that only four revenue sources are specifically designated (taxes, licenses, water works, and wharfage) and all other receipts are lumped under a "miscellaneous" category. Receipts in this latter category leaped from less than $20,000 in 1847 to more than $120,000 (almost a quarter of the whole) in 1850, and may include some loan receipts.

26. See sources for Albany, Boston, Philadelphia, Pittsburgh, New York, and St. Louis in note 23. Providence was the only other city (New Orleans being excluded because of the nonavailability of disaggregated data) with per capita receipts above five dollars.

27. See sources in note 23.

28. In rank order (1830s): Washington, Providence, Louisville, New York, Baltimore, Philadelphia, Cincinnati, Boston, St. Louis, Albany.

29. An analysis of the eleven cities common to both Table 2.6 and Table 2.11 essentially duplicates the findings for the tables as a whole. The range and standard deviation dropped by 6.2 and 4.3 percentage points, respectively, while the mean and median rose by 8.35 and 10.9 percentage points.

30. Sources for Table 2.12: See sources listed in note 23 for these cities; Albany, City Chamberlain, *Report, 1850–51*, 60; Hollander, *Financial History of Baltimore*, 384; Huse, *Financial History of Boston*, Appendix, 376; Bishop, *Manual of Brooklyn, 1860–1861*, 465; Cincinnati, City Auditor, *Report* (1860), 63; Legislative Records of the City of Louisville, University of Louisville Archives, Louisville, Kentucky, Record Group 100, Box 3; Edward D. Durant, *The Finances of New York City* (New York: The Macmillan Company, 1898), 372; Philadelphia, Common Council, *Journal, 1849–1850*, Appendix, 250; *The Providence Directory* (Providence: H. H. Brown, 1855), xvii; Washington, City Council, *Laws of the Corporation of the City of Washington* (Washington: John T. Towers, 1850), 424.

31. Sources for Table 2.13: See sources for Albany, Baltimore, Boston, Brooklyn, Cincinnati, Louisville, Providence, and St. Louis in note 30; Charleston, City Council, Committee on Ways and Means, *The Disabilities of Charleston for Complete and Equal Taxation, and the Influence of State Taxation on Her Prospects* (Charleston: Walker, Evans, and Company, 1857), 46; New Orleans, Comptroller, *Comptroller's Report, Embracing a Detailed Statement of the Receipts and Expenditures of the City of New Orleans, from April 12th, 1852, to January 1st, 1853* (New Orleans: Cook, Young, and Company, 1853), 144; David T. Valentine, *Manual of the Corporation of the City of New-York, for the Year 1851* (New York: McSpedon and Baker, 1851), 209; Philadelphia,

Common Council, *Journal, 1849–50*, Appendix, 229; Washington, City Council, *Laws of the Corporation of the City of Washington* (Washington: John T. Towers, 1846), 335.

32. The situation in Brooklyn in the 1830s was the reverse of that in Baltimore. It had the lowest property tax rate ($0.233 per $100 assessed value) and the highest per capita assessment ($1,085.12). See Tables 2.8 and 2.9.

33. See sources in note 23. These data excluded a wide variety of miscellaneous items (e.g., sale of paving stones, receipts from almshouses, use of city seal, fines and forfeitures, sale of manure) which are almost always individually small amounts and in the aggregate exceed 5% of the revenue in only three cities. The St. Louis data are very slightly disaggregated, leaving a miscellaneous block amounting to 23.22% of the total receipts. Miscellaneous receipts for Louisville amount to 6.7% of the total, largely because of an unspecified "bills receivable" entry that comprises almost three-quarters of the miscellaneous block. A similar situation exists in Charleston, where miscellaneous expenditures comprised 19.8% of the total, with "notes payable" amounting to almost the whole (97%) of that component.

34. Albany, Baltimore, Boston, Charleston, Louisville, New York, Philadelphia, Providence, St. Louis, and Washington.

35. Baltimore, City Council, *The Ordinances of the Mayor and City Council of Baltimore* (Baltimore: James Lucas, 1849), Appendix, 47.

36. The cities are Albany, Boston, Charleston, New York, Philadelphia, and Providence.

37. For example, Huse, *Financial History of Boston*, 41; Charles Cist, *The Cincinnati Miscellany, or Antiquities of the West* (Cincinnati: n.p., 1845–1846), 2:158; John C. Schwab, "History of the New York Property Tax," American Economics Association *Publications* 5 (September 1890):85.

38. Albany, City Chamberlain, *The Chamberlain's Report to the Common Council, Showing the Receipts and Expenditures of the City of Albany, from May 1, 1840, to May 1, 1841* (Albany: Hoffman, White, and Visscher, 1841), 7–13. See also Hollander, *Financial History of Baltimore*, 382; New York, City Comptroller, *Annual Statement of the Funds of the Corporation of the City of New York Ending December 31, 1848* (New York: McSpedon and Baker, 1849), 89.

39. New York, City Comptroller, *Annual Statement of the Funds of the Corporation of the City of New York, for the Year Ending December 31, 1849* (New York: McSpedon and Baker, 1850), 113. See also Hollander, *Financial History of Baltimore*, 99, 382.

40. Samuel Osgood, *New York in the Nineteenth Century* (New York: New York Historical Society, 1867), 66–67; New York City, City Comptroller, *Annual Report of the Comptroller, with the Accounts of the Corporation of the City of New-York for the Year Ending the 31st Day of December, 1830* (New York: Peter Van Pelt, 1831), 11–16; Williams, *New-York Annual Register for 1832*, 231; Williams, *New-York Annual Register for 1837*, 340; Edwin Williams, *The New-York Annual Register for the Year of Our Lord 1840* (New York: David Felt and Company, 1840), 375; New York City, City Comptroller, *Annual Statement of the Funds of the Corporation, for the Year Ending December 31, A. D. 1840* (New York: Jared W. Bell, 1841), 23; Valentine, *Manual of New-York, 1851*, 208; Hollander, *Financial History of Baltimore*, 384; Baltimore, City Council, *The Ordinances of the Mayor and City Council of Baltimore* (Baltimore: Lucas and Deaver, 1831), Appendix, 93–97; Baltimore, City Council, *The Ordinances of the Mayor and City Council of Baltimore* (Baltimore: Joseph Robinson, 1832), Appendix, 119–24; Baltimore, City Council, *The Ordinances of the Mayor and City Council of*

Baltimore (Baltimore: Sands and Neilson, 1833), Appendix, 89–95; Baltimore, City Council, *The Ordinances of the Mayor and City Council of Baltimore* (Baltimore: Lucas and Deaver, 1837), 497–98; Baltimore, City Council, *The Ordinances of the Mayor and City Council of Baltimore* (Baltimore: Lucas and Deaver, 1842), Appendix, 91–92; Baltimore, City Council, *The Ordinances of the Mayor and City Council of Baltimore* (Baltimore: Lucas and Deaver, 1843), Appendix, 45–47; Shattuck, *Census of Boston for 1845*, Appendix, 59; Elias H. Derby, *Boston: A Commercial Metropolis in 1850* (Boston: Redding and Company, 1850), 14; Boston, Auditor, *Report, 1850–51*, 19–21; Teale, *Municipal Register of Brooklyn (1848)*, 117; Charleston, City Treasurer, "City Accounts" statement for 1848–1849, Charleston City Treasury Records, City of Charleston Archives and Records, Charleston, South Carolina, Records Group 6, Box 1; Cincinnati, City Auditor, *Report, 1860*, 62; Cist, *Cincinnati Miscellany*, 2:158; Louisville, Common Council, Minutes, March 2, 1832, February 18, 1833, February 27, 1834, March 23, 1835, March 21, 1836, March 27, 1837, March 26, 1838, March 29, 1841, April 4, 1842, April 14, 1845, March 30, 1846, March 29, 1847, March 31, 1851; Philadelphia, Common Council, *Journal of the Common Council of the City of Philadelphia, for 1841–42* (Philadelphia: J. Van Court, 1842), Appendix, 113, 118; Philadelphia, Common Council, *Journal of the Common Council of the City of Philadelphia, for 1842–43* (Philadelphia: J. Van Court, 1843), Appendix, 132; Philadelphia, Common Council, *Journal of the Common Council of the City of Philadelphia, for 1845–46* (Philadelphia: R. Beresford, 1846), Appendix, 119; Philadelphia, Common Council, *Journal of the Common Council of the City of Philadelphia, for 1846–1847* (Philadelphia: R. Beresford, 1847), Appendix, 176; Philadelphia, Common Council, *Journal of the Common Council of the City of Philadelphia, for 1847–8* (Philadelphia: King and Baird, 1848), Appendix, 190; Philadelphia, Common Council, *Journal of the Common Council of the City of Philadelphia, for 1848–49* (Philadelphia: King and Baird, 1849), Appendix, 24; Philadelphia, Common Council, *Journal, 1849–50*, Appendix, 229, 240; Philadelphia, Common Council, *Journal of the Common Council of the City of Philadelphia, for 1850–51* (Philadelphia: King and Baird, 1851), Appendix, 262; *Providence Directory* (1855), xvii; Richard Edwards and M. Hopewell, *Edwards' Great West and Her Commercial Metropolis, Embracing a General View of the West, and a Complete History of St. Louis* (St. Louis: Edwards' Monthly, 1860), Appendix, 610; Washington, City Register, *Annual Report of the Register of the City of Washington* (Washington: Way and Gideon, 1830), 1; Washington, City Register, *Annual Report of the Register of the City of Washington* (Washington: Way and Gideon, 1831), 3; Washington, City Register, *Annual Report of the Register of the City of Washington* (Washington: Way and Gideon, 1832), 9; Washington, City Register, *Annual Report of the Register of the City of Washington* (Washington: Jacob Gideon, Jr., 1834), 11.

41. Sources for Table 2.17: Albany, City Chamberlain, *Report, 1833*, 12; Baltimore, City Council, *The Ordinances of the Mayor and City Council of Baltimore . . . 1850* (Baltimore: James Lucas, 1850), Appendix, foldout chart following 234; Boston, [Auditing Department], *Third Annual Report of the Commitee of Finance* (n.p., 1815), 12; *Picture of New-York* (1828), 97; James Mease, *The Picture of Philadelphia* (Philadelphia: B. and T. Kite, 1811), 195–96; Wilson, *History of Pittsburg*, 692; Stokes, *Finances and Administration of Providence*, 384; Wilhelmus B. Bryan, *A History of the National Capital* (New York: Macmillan, 1914–1916), 2:98.

42. Albany's indebtedness is obviously a pronounced anomaly during this period. If that city is excluded, the mean per capita debt for the remaining seven cities drops by

more than a third, from $6.00 to $3.98; the range falls by almost two-thirds, from $22.03 to $7.79; and the standard deviation declines from 6.57 to 2.84. The median per capita debt is, of course, affected only slightly, dropping from $2.54 to $2.05.

43. Albany, City Chamberlain, *Report, 1833*, viii; Cuyler Reynolds, *Albany Chronicles* (Albany: J. B. Lyon, 1906), 395; Durant, *Finances of New York*, 33; Mease, *Picture of Philadelphia* (1811), 695–96.

44. Munsell, *Annals of Albany*, 8:135; Albany, City Chamberlain, *Report, 1833*, 12–14; Baltimore, City Council, *Ordinances, 1850*, Appendix, foldout chart following 234; Hollander, *Financial History of Baltimore*, 178; Baltimore, City Register, Annual Summaries of City Revenues and Expenditures (ms.), Baltimore City Archives, Baltimore, Maryland, Record Group 32, Ser. 8, Vol. 1 (1797–1828), Summary of 1818; Huse, *Financial History of Boston*, 378; Daniel Curry, *New York: Historical Sketch of the Rise and Progress of the Metropolitan City of America* (New York: Carlton and Phillips, 1853), 518; *Picture of New-York* (1828), 172, 188; Williams, *New-York Annual Register for 1830*, 212; Durant, *Finances of New York*, 374; *Philadelphia in 1824*, 170; *Philadelphia 1830–1*. (Philadelphia: E. L. Cary and A. Hart, 1830), 187; Daniel Bowen, *A History of Philadelphia* (Philadelphia: D. Bowen, 1839), 97–99; Philadelphia, City Council, Watering Committee, *Annual Report of the Watering Committee for the Year 1850* (Philadelphia: Crissy and Markley, 1851), 35; Thompson, "Financial History of Pittsburgh, 1816–1865," 60; George T. Fleming, *History of Pittsburgh and Its Environs* (New York: The American Historical Society, 1922), 2:66–67; Stokes, *Finances and Administration of Providence*, 284; *The Rhode-Island Register, and United States Calendar, for the Year of Our Lord Christ, 1826* (Providence: Carlile and Brown, [1825]), 59; *The Rhode-Island Register, and United States Calendar, for the Year of Our Lord Christ, 1827* (Providence: Carlile and Brown, [1826]), 59; *The Rhode-Island Register, and United States Calendar, for the Year of Our Lord Christ, 1829* (Providence: H. H. Brown, [1828]), 35; Bryan, *National Capital*, 2:98; Washington, City Council, *Laws of the Corporation of the City of Washington, [1818–1827]* ([Washington: Way and Gideon, [1818–1827]), Appendix, 3–7; Washington, City Council, *Laws of the Corporation of the City of Washington, [1828]* (Washington: Way and Gideon, 1827 [sic; 1828]), ii–iii; Jonathan Elliot, *Historical Sketches of the Ten Miles Square Forming the District of Columbia* (Washington: J. Elliot, 1830), 187–89.

45. Sources for Table 2.18: In constructing this table I have attempted to obtain figures for the year 1835. When such data have not been located, figures for the closest earlier year available (as indicated) have been substituted. See Albany, City Chamberlain, *Report of the Chamberlain to the Common Council, Showing the Receipts and Expenditure of the City of Albany, from May 1, 1848, to May 1, 1849* (Albany: Weed, Parsons and Company, 1850), 231; Baltimore, City Council, *Ordinances, 1836*, Appendix, 11; Huse, *Financial History of Boston*, 378; Cincinnati, City Auditor, *Report*, (1860), 65; Louisville, Common Council, Minutes, March 23, 1835; Durant, *Finances of New York*, 374; Philadelphia, Common Council, *Journal of the Common Council, of the City of Philadelphia, for 1837–8* (Philadelphia: J. Van Court, 1838), 11; Wilson, *History of Pittsburg*, 701; Stokes, *Finances and Administration of Providence*, 384; Washington, City Register, *Annual Report of the Register of the City of Washington* (Washington: Jacob Gideon, Jr., 1835), 9–10.

46. Washington, City Register, *Report* (1835), Appendix, 1–2; Bryan, *National Capital*, 2:124–27.

47. Baltimore, City Council, *The Ordinances of the Mayor and City Council of Bal-*

timore (Baltimore: Bailey and Francis, 1830), Appendix, 73, 77; Baltimore, City Council, *Ordinances* (1831), Appendix, 80–81; Baltimore, City Council, *Ordinances* (1832), Appendix, 113, 115; Baltimore, City Council, *Ordinances* (1833), Appendix, 87–88, Baltimore, City Council, *The Ordinances of the Mayor and City Council of Baltimore* (Baltimore: James Lucas and E. K. Deaver, 1834), Appendix, 91, 95; Baltimore, City Council, *The Ordinances of the Mayor and City Council of Baltimore* (Baltimore: Lucas and Deaver, 1835), Appendix, 75, 79; Josiah Quincy, *A Municipal History of the Town and City of Boston, during two Centuries, from September 17, 1630, to September 17, 1830* (Boston: Charles C. Little and James Brown, 1852), 274; Louisville, Common Council, Minutes, February 27, 1834; Williams, *New-York Annual Register for 1837*, 338; Philadelphia, Common Council, *Journal of the Common Council of the City of Philadelphia, for 1838–9* (Philadelphia: J. Van Court, 1839), Appendix, 112; Thompson, "Financial History of Pittsburgh, 1816–1865," 61; Stokes, *Finances and Administration of Providence*, 149; *Rhode-Island Register, 1826*, 59; *Rhode-Island Register, 1827*, 56; *The Rhode-Island Register, and United States Calendar, for the Year of Our Lord Christ, 1830* (Providence: H. H. Brown, [1829]), 36; Washington, City Register, *Report* (1835), 9–10.

48. Sources for Table 2.19: Albany, City Chamberlain, *Report, 1850–1851*, 56–57; Baltimore, City Council, *The Ordinances of the Mayor and City Council of Baltimore* (Baltimore: Joseph Robinson, 1840), Appendix, 6; Huse, *Financial History of Boston*, 378; Charleston, City Council, *Report Containing a Review of the Proceedings of the City Authorities from the 4th September, 1837, to the 1st August, 1838* (Charleston: Thomas C. Eccles, 1838), 9; Cincinnati, City Auditor, *Report*, (1860), 65; Louisville, Common Council, Minutes, March 26, 1838; Durant, *Finances of New York*, 374; Philadelphia, Common Council, *Journal for 1837–8*, 701; Stokes, *Finances and Administration of Providence*, 384; James N. Primm, *The Lion of the Valley: St. Louis, Missouri* (Boulder, Colo.: Pruett Publishing Company, 1981), 159; Washington, City Council, *Laws of the Corporation of the City of Washington* (Washington: Jacob Gideon, Jr., 1839), 457. The Philadelphia figure is for November 1837.

49. See sources listed in notes 45 and 48. Note: the figures at the bottom of the last two columns are the changes in the means, not the mean of the changes in the individual cities.

50. Stokes, *Finances and Administration of Providence*, 165, 384; Charleston, City Council, *Review of Proceedings, 1837–38*, 8–9; Primm, *Lion of the Valley*, 258–59.

51. See the data in Tables 2.18 and 2.19. These calculations have employed the adjusted figure for Washington in 1835.

52. Durant, *Finances of New York*, 374; Williams, *New-York Annual Register for 1840*, 376–77; Baltimore, City Council, *Ordinances, 1836*, Appendix, 479; Baltimore, City Council, *Ordinances of the Mayor and City Council of Baltimore* (Baltimore: John D. Toy, 1839), Appendix, 71; Baltimore, City Council, *Ordinances of the Mayor and City Council of Baltimore* (Baltimore: Joseph Robinson, 1841), Appendix, 4–5; Carter Goodrich and Harry A. Segal, "Baltimore's Aid to Railroads: A Study in the Municipal Planning of Internal Improvements," *Journal of Economic History* 13 (Winter 1953): 6; Philadelphia, Common Council, *Journal for 1837–8*, 11; Huse, *Financial History of Boston*, 349, 369; Louisville, Common Council, Minutes, March 27, 1838.

53. Sources for Table 2.21: Albany, City Chamberlain, *Report, 1850–1851*, 33; Hollander, *Financial History of Baltimore*, 188; Huse, *Financial History of Boston*, 378; Teale, *Municipal Register of Brooklyn* (1848), 118–20; J. L. Dawson and H. W. De-

Saussure, *Census of the City of Charleston, South Carolina, for the Year 1848* (Charleston: J. B. Nixon, 1848), 175; Cincinnati, City Auditor, *Report, 1860,* 65; Louisville, Common Council, Minutes, March 31, 1851; *DeBow's Review* 3 (April 1847): 346; Durant, *Finances of New York,* 274; Philadelphia, Common Council, *Journal, 1849–1850,* 237–39; *Bywater's Philadelphia Business Directory and City Guide, for the Year 1851* (Philadelphia: Maurice Bywater, n.d.), 174; Wilson, *History of Pittsburg,* 723; Stokes, *Finances and Administration of Providence,* 384; William Hyde and Howard L. Conrad, eds., *Encyclopedia of the History of St. Louis* (St. Louis: The Southern History Company, 1899), 2:381; Washington, City Council, *Laws* (1850), 423.

54. There is, consequently, a rather high rank order correlation (Spearman: .815) between population and total debt among the cities listed in Table 2.21. The correlation (Pearson) between the actual (rather than rank order) figures is higher still—r: .925. Similarly, the correlation between the *numerical* growth in the populations (1830–1850) and the *gross* indebtedness is both substantial and positive (r: .853). The rank order (Spearman) correlation is considerably lower (.645), but still positive. This contrasts strongly with the negative correlations between *percentage* population growth and *per capita* indebtedness (see above).

55. Albany, City Chamberlain, *Report, 1850–1851,* 36; Munsell, *Annals of Albany,* 2: 286; Baltimore, City Council, *Ordinances, 1836,* Appendix, 479; Baltimore, City Council, *Ordinances* (1839), Appendix, 71; Goodrich and Segal, "Baltimore's Aid to Railroads," 6–7; Huse, *Financial History of Boston,* 378–80; *Hunt's Merchants' Magazine* 25 (August 1851): 228; Cincinnati, Water Department, *Forty-fifth Annual Report of the Water Department of the City of Cincinnati for the Year Ending December 31, 1880* (Cincinnati: Robert Clarke, [1881]), Appendix, 12; Valentine, *Manual of New-York, 1851,* 192; Philadelphia, Common Council, *Journal, 1849–1850,* 237–39; *Bywater's Philadelphia Business Directory, 1851,* 174.

56. Albany, City Chamberlain, *Report, 1833,* 13; Hollander, *Financial History of Baltimore,* 188–89; Gabriel Collins, *The Louisville Directory, for the Years 1843–'44* ([Louisville]: A. S. Tilden, 1843), 177–80; J. Stoddard Johnston, ed., *Memorial History of Louisville from Its First Settlement to the Year 1896* (Chicago and New York: American Biographical Publishing Company, [1896]), 1:68; "Balance Sheet," July 1, 1851, in Legislative Records of the City of Louisville, Box 3; Louisville, Common Council, Minutes, March 30, 1840, March 29, 1841, April 4, 1842, April 14, 1845; John S. Kendall, *History of New Orleans* (Chicago and New York: Lewis Publishing Company, 1822), 1:143; John Calhoun, *Digest of the Ordinances and Resolutions of the Second Municipality of New-Orleans, in Force May 1, 1840* (New Orleans: F. Cook and A. Levy, 1840), 163; Isaac Harris, *Harris' Business Directory of the Cities of Pittsburgh and Allegheny* (Pittsburgh: A. A. Anderson, 1844), 103; Thompson, "Financial History of Pittsburgh, 1816–1865," 60; Wilson, *History of Pittsburg,* 341–42, 361, 432, 691–92, 712, 720; Washington, City Council, *Laws, [1818–1827],* Appendix, 2; Washington, City Register, *Report, 1835,* 10; Elliot, *Ten Miles Square,* 187–89; Richard T. Farrell, "Cincinnati in the Early Jackson Era, 1816–1834: An Economic and Political Study" (Ph.D. dissertation, Indiana University, 1967), 153–54; *Picture of New-York* (1828), 104–5; Martha J. Lamb, *History of the City of New York* (New York: A. S. Barnes and Company, 1877–1880), 2:648; Hyde and Conrad, *Encyclopedia of the History of St. Louis,* 1:379–80; Philadelphia, Common Council, *Journal, 1838–9,* Appendix, 115; Philadelphia, Common Council, *Journal of the Common Council of the City of Philadelphia, for 1840–41* (Philadelphia: J. Van Court, 1841), Appendix, 79; Philadelphia, Common

Council, *Journal, 1842–43*, Appendix, 131; Philadelphia, Common Council, *Journal of the Common Council of the City of Philadelphia, for 1844–45* (Philadelphia: For the Common Council, 1845), Appendix, 23; Philadelphia, Common Council, *Journal, 1846–1847*, Appendix, 175; Philadelphia, Common Council, *Journal, 1847–8*, Appendix, 189; Philadelphia, Common Council, *Journal, 1850–51*, Appendix, 261.

57. Sources for Table 2.23: Munsell, *Annals of Albany*, 5:30–31; Hollander, *Financial History of Baltimore*, 379; Boston, Committee of Finance, *Report* (1819), 2–7; Charleston, City Treasurer, "City Accounts" for 1821; *Niles' Weekly Register* (October 21, 1820), 128; New York, City Comptroller, *Report, 1818*, 5; Mease, *Picture of Philadelphia* (1811), 194; Stokes, *Finances and Administration of Providence*, 414–30; J. Thomas Scharf, *History of Saint Louis City and County* (Philadelphia: Louis H. Everts, 1883), 1: 653; Rothwell, *Laws of Washington, 1833*, 291.

58. See sources listed in note 57, except *Niles' Weekly Register* and Scharf.

59. The percentage reduction in per capita expenditures produced by the exclusion of debt service charges for the other six cities common to the listings in Table 2.23 and Table 2.24 were as follows: Charleston, 18%; Albany, 15%; Boston, 21%; Providence, 13%; Baltimore, 4%; Philadelphia, 6%.

60. See sources listed in note 58.

61. Sources for Table 2.26: Albany, City Chamberlain, *The Chamberlain's Report to the Common Council, Showing the Receipts and Expenditures of the City of Albany, from May 1, 1844, to May 1, 1845* (Albany: Weed and Parsons, 1845), 21–28; Baltimore, City Council, *Ordinances, 1836*, Appendix, 60–65; Boston, Auditor, *Report* (1836), 27–48; Ralph F. Weld, *Brooklyn Village, 1816–1834* (New York: Columbia University Press, 1938), 46; Charleston, City Council, *Review of Proceedings, 1837–38*, 7–9; Cincinnati, City Auditor, *Report* (1860), 64–65; Louisville, Common Council, Minutes, March 21, 1836; Fossier, *New Orleans*, 86–87; Williams, *New-York Annual Register for 1835*, 306–08; Philadelphia, Common Council, *Minutes for 1835–6*, 112–13; Stokes, *Finances and Administration of Providence*, 414–30; Washington, City Council, *Laws of the Corporation of the City of Washington, [1836–1837]* (Washington: Jacob Gideon, Jr., 1836 [*sic*; 1837?]), 237–38.

62. Physical facilities includes streets, walkways, gutters, sewers, docks, wharves, harbor improvements, markets, and water delivery facilities. Human services includes education, poor relief, and public health (including street cleaning). Public safety includes police, watch, corrections, fire protection, and street lighting.

63. See sources listed in note 62.

64. See sources in note 62 and explanation in note 60.

65. See sources in note 62.

66. Sources for Table 2.30: Albany, City Chamberlain, *Report, 1850–1851*, 14–29; Baltimore, City Council, *Ordinances, 1851*, Appendix, 28–38; Boston, Auditor, *Report, 1850–51*, 186–90; Teale, *Municipal Register of Brooklyn* (1848), 118–20; Charleston, Treasurer, "City Accounts" for 1848–1849; Cincinnati, City Auditor, *Report* (1860), 64–65; Louisville, City Council, Minutes, March 31, 1851; New Orleans, Comptroller, *Report, 1852–53*, 142–44; Valentine, *Manual of New-York, 1851*, 195–205; Philadelphia, Common Council, *Journal, 1849–1850*, Appendix, 241–42; Philadelphia, Common Council, *Journal, 1848–49*, Appendix, 32–37; Wilson, *History of Pittsburg*, 721–22; Stokes, *Finances and Administration of Providence*, 414–30; Washington, City Council, *Laws [1851]*, 209–11, 279–87.

67. A single city—Providence—had shown a decline in per capita expenditures between the 1810s and the 1830s.

68. U.S., Bureau of the Census, *Historical Statistics of the United States, Colonial Times to 1857* (Washington: Government Printing Office, 1960), 115.

69. See sources listed in note 66.

70. For a fuller discussion of city debts, see pages 55–64, above.

71. See sources listed in note 66 and explanation in note 60.

72. The Brooklyn data are excluded from both calculations.

73. See sources listed in note 66.

74. The actual (as opposed to percentage) gap was almost unchanged, declining from forty-eight cents to forty-seven cents per capita.

75. Tables 2.23, 2.24, and 2.25 (1809–1821) are partial exceptions because of the unusually large number of years involved and the volatility of the price index during those years. Even there, the ranking of cities by per capita gross expenditures is only slightly affected, with only New York (1816; wholesale price index = 151) moving by as many as two rank positions (from first to third) and with one-half of the rank positions being unchanged. See U.S., Bureau of the Census, *Historical Statistics*, 115–16.

76. See sources listed in notes 57, 62, and 66; U.S., Bureau of the Census, *Historical Statistics*, 115–16. In compiling the figures for Tables 2.36 and 2.37 the data for each city have been converted to constant (1835) dollars and all per capita and percentage figures have been recalculated for each city and each array of cities.

CHAPTER 3

1. U.S. Congress, Joint Committee on Printing, *Biographical Directory of the American Congress, 1774–1961* (Washington: Government Printing Office, 1961), 1622–23; hereafter cited as *BDAC*.

2. Richard G. Miller, *Philadelphia—The Federalist City: A Study in Urban Politics, 1789–1801* (Port Washington, N.Y.: Kennikut Press, 1976), 65, 83–85, 96, 100, 121.

3. Howard B. Rock, *Artisans of the New Republic: The Tradesmen of New York in the Age of Jefferson* (New York: New York University Press, 1979), 36; Sidney I. Pomerantz, *New York: An American City, 1783–1803*, 2nd ed. (Port Washington, N.Y.: Ira F. Friedman, 1965), 69.

4. Pomerantz, *New York, 1783–1803*, 93, 128–29; Joel Munsell, *The Annals of Albany* (Albany: Joel Munsell, 1850–1859), 4:307; *BDAC*, 1226; David T. Valentine, *Manual of the Corporation of the City of New-York for 1854* (New York: McSpedon and Baker, 1854), 447.

5. Munsell, *Annals of Albany*, 3:170–71; Albert P. Langtry, ed., *Metropolitan Boston: A Modern History* (New York: Lewis Historical Publishing Company, 1929), 1:77; George C. Rogers, Jr., *Charleston in the Age of the Pinckneys* (Norman: University of Oklahoma Press, 1969), 117–18; Clarkson A. Collins III, "Pictures of Providence in the Past, 1790–1820: The Reminiscences of Walter P. Danforth," *Rhode Island History* 10 (April 1851): 58; Erasmus Wilson, ed., *Standard History of Pittsburg [sic], Pennsylvania* (Chicago: Goodspeed Publishing Company 1898), 743–53.

6. Valentine, *Manual of New-York, 1854*, 447–50; Rock, *Artisans of New Republic*, 33; John Cheetham, *Annals of the Corporation, Relative to the Late Contested Election* (New York: Denniston and Cheetham, 1802), 9–10. The New York charter electorate

consisted of two elements–£20 ($50) freeholders and "freemen." The latter were indi-
viduals who were given their status by governmental action and often (probably usually)
did not meet the freeholder criteria. Legally no one but freemen could act as cartmen or
as innkeepers, and since there was a continually increasing demand for cartmen, in particular, the usual practice had been to make applicants freemen and then grant them
licenses. Betwen 1783 and 1792 some 688 persons had been made freemen, almost 400
of them cartmen. But during the next eleven years only 56 freemen had been named and
none of these were cartmen. Varick's opponents charged that he had licensed many
cartmen and innkeepers but refused to make them freemen, thus restricting the growth
of the charter electorate.

7. Valentine, *Manual of New-York, 1854*, 451–55; Rock, *Artisans of New Republic*,
33; Pomerantz, *New York, 1783–1803*, 72.

8. Mary L. Booth, *History of the City of New York* (New York: W. R. C. Clark,
1867), 2:688–89; Martha J. Lamb, *History of the City of New York* (New York: A. S.
Barnes and Company, 1877–1880), 2:490; Valentine, *Manual of New-York, 1854*, 451–
66; Rock, *Artisans of New Republic*, 33. Because of the number of uncontested seats it
is difficult to calculate the party percentages of the total vote with acceptable accuracy
for the city council elections.

9. Miller, *Philadelphia—The Federalist City*, 100, 136, 142–43; Eliza Cope Harrison, ed., *Philadelphia Merchant: the Diary of Thomas Cope* (South Bend, Ind.: Gate-
way Editions, 1978), 29–30, hereafter cited as Cope, *Diary*; J. Thomas Scharf and
Thompson Wescott, *A History of Philadelphia* (Philadelphia: L. G. Everts and Company,
1884), 1:513; Herman L. Collins and Wilford Jordan, *Philadelphia: A Story of Progress*
(Philadelphia: Lewis Historical Publishing Company, 1941), 1:169.

10. Miller, *Philadelphia—The Federalist City*, 142–43.

11. John R. Young, *Memorial History of the City of Philadelphia* (New York: New-
York History Company, 1895–1898), 2:199–202; Scharf and Wescott, *History of Philadelphia*, 1:557; Philadelphia *United States Gazette* (October 13, 1808, October 11, 1809,
October 10, 1810, October 9, 1811, October 11, 1815); Washington *Daily National Intelligencer* (October 16, 1813); *The Charleston Courier* (October 20, 1814).

12. Munsell, *Annals of Albany*, 4:315, 5:25; Dixon R. Fox, *The Decline of Aristoc-
racy in the Politics of New York*, Vol. 84, No. 128 of *[Columbia University] Studies in
History, Economics, and Public Law* (New York: Columbia University Press, 1919), 118;
Lemuel Shattuck, *Report to the Committee of the City Council Appointed to Obtain the
Census of Boston for the Year 1845* (Boston: John H. Eastburn, 1846), 34.

13. Wilson, *History of Pittsburg*, 747–49, 753; *The Pittsburgh Gazette* (October 9,
1810; September 13, 17, October 18, 1811; September 25, October 1, 16, 1812; March
26, May 21, 1813).

14. John H. Wolfe, *Jeffersonian Democracy in South Carolina* (Chapel Hill: University of North Carolina Press, 1940), 182, 274, 279; *The Charleston Courier* (February
9, 1803, October 10, 1804, October 11, 15, 17, 1806, October 11, 1808, October 11,
1810, October 15, 18, 1812, October 13, 1814); Charleston, *Year Book—1881* (Charleston: News and Courier, [1882]), 367.

15. Pomerantz, *New York, 1783–1803*, 114; Scharf and Wescott, *History of Phila-
delphia*, 2081–82; Edmund P. Willis, "Social Origins of Political Leadership in New
York City from the Revolution to 1815" (Ph.D. dissertation, University of California,
Berkeley, 1967), 237–39; Fox, *Decline of Aristocracy*, 89–93; David H. Fischer, *The

Revolution of American Conservatism: The Federalist Party in the Era of Jeffersonian Democracy (New York: Harper and Row, 1965), 117–19.

16. *Niles' Weekly Register* (May 18, 1816); *Providence Daily Journal* (April 22, May 7, 1830, April 21, 28, 1831, April 19, 26, November 22, 1832, April 18, 1833, April 17, 1834, April 16, 1835); *Albany Evening Journal* (April 19, 1834).

17. Shattuck, *Census of Boston for 1845*, 34–37; John B. Blake, *Public Health in the Town of Boston, 1630–1822* (Cambridge: Harvard University Press, 1959), 230–31, 236n; Boston, City Council, *A Catalogue of the City Councils of Boston, 1822–1908 . . . and of the Selectmen of Boston, 1634–1822, also of Various Other Town and Municipal Officers* (Boston: City of Boston Printing Department, 1909), 369; *Niles' Weekly Register* (April 20, June 8, 1822, 128, 240, May 7, 1825, 178, May 19, 1827, 198–99); Justin Winsor, ed., *The Memorial History of Boston, Including Suffolk County, Massachusetts, 1630–1880* (Boston: James R. Osgood and Company, 1880–1881), 3:224; *Bowen's Boston News-Letter and City Record* (May 27, 1826, 274–75); Caleb H. Snow, *A History of Boston* (Boston: Abel Bowen, 1828), 410–11.

18. Shattuck, *Census of Boston for 1845*, 37; *Niles' Weekly Register* (December 27, 1828), 283; Josiah Quincy, *A Municipal History of the Town and City of Boston, during Two Centuries, from September 17, 1630, to September 17, 1830* (Boston: Charles C. Little and James Brown, 1852), 257–58.

19. Edward Pessen, "Did Labor Support Jackson?: The Boston Story," *Political Science Quarterly* 59 (June 1949):271–72; Shattuck, *Census of Boston for 1845*, 35–37; *Niles' Weekly Register* (April 6, May 11, June 22, 1833, 83, 161, 268, December 13, 1834, 237); Richard Hildreth, *My Connection with the Atlas Newspaper* (Boston: Whipple and Damrell, 1839; a pamphlet).

20. *Pittsburgh Gazette* (October 11, 1819, October 2, 1820, October 11, 1822); Carnegie Library of Pittsburgh, *Pittsburgh in 1816* (Pittsburgh: Carnegie Library, 1916), 9; Wilson, *History of Pittsburg*, 756; James A. Kehl, *Ill Feeling in the Era of Good Feeling: Western Pennsylvania's Political Battles, 1815–1825* (Pittsburgh: University of Pittsburgh Press, 1956), 208.

21. Wilson, *History of Pittsburg*, 693, 759, 765–66, 769–70; *Pittsburgh Gazette* (November 19, 1827); Melvin G. Holli and Peter d'A. Jones, eds., *Biographical Dictionary of American Mayors, 1820–1980: Big City Mayors* (Westport, Conn.: Greenwood Press, 1981), 336–37; hereafter cited as *BDAM*.

22. Wilson, *History of Pittsburg*, 773–74, 779, 781–82; *BDAM*, 222; William A. Sullivan, "The Pittsburgh Workingmen's Party," *Western Pennsylvania Historical Magazine* 34 (September 1951), 152–61.

23. Munsell, *Annals of Albany*, 6:125–26, 7:140, 152, 159, 164, 8:95, 108–9, 127–28, 158–59; Fox, *Decline of Aristocracy*, 299; *Albany Argus* (September 26, 1827).

24. Munsell, *Annals of Albany*, 9:174, 192, 217–18; Edwin Williams, *The New-York Annual Register for the Year of Our Lord 1831* (New York: Jonathan Leavitt and Collins and Hannay, 1831), 40; *Niles' Weekly Register* (October 9, 1830), 105.

25. Munsell, *Annals of Albany*, 9:232–33, 256–59,273–74, 282, 10:242, 248; Edwin Williams, *The New-York Annual Register for the Year of Our Lord 1835* (New York: Edwin Williams, 1835), 47.

26. Valentine, *Manual of New-York, 1854*, 466–75; Booth, *History of New York*, 2: 706; John Hardy, *Manual of the Corporation of the City of New York [1870]* (New York: n.p., 1871), 739–40.

27. Hardy, *Manual of New York [1870]*, 740; Valentine, *Manual of New-York, 1854*, 476–82, quotations from 476, 479, and 480.

28. Ira Cohen, "The Auction System in the Port of New York, 1817–1837" (Ph.D. dissertation, New York University, 1969), 122–23; Hardy, *Manual of New York [1870]*, 740; *Niles' Weekly Register* (November 15, 1828), 178.

29. *Niles' Weekly Register* (November 14, 1829), 177; Hardy, *Manual of New York [1870]*, 740.

30. Hardy, *Manual of New York [1870]*, 741–42; Valentine, *Manual of New-York, 1854*, 480–89; Edwin Williams, *The New-York Annual Register for the Year of Our Lord 1834* (New York: Edwin Williams, 1834), 39–43; *BDAC*, 86–119, *passim*. The remarkable consistency of Republican victories in congressional races is, at least in part, the result of a broader suffrage in the early years of this period for Assembly contests, the provisions of which governed congressional races, than for gubernatorial, state Senate, and charter elections.

31. Members of the Philadelphia Select and Common Councils were elected at large and, consequently, only in the case of very narrowly balanced elections would there ever be any party divisions in these bodies.

32. Scharf and Wescott, *History of Philadelphia*, 1:584, 588; Young, *History of Philadelphia*, 2:207–8; *Niles' Weekly Register* (October 15, 1825), 97; Philadelphia *United States Gazette* (November 16, 1818, October 11, 1821, October 10, 1822, October 16, 1823, October 13, 1824); *BDAC*, 1581; Philip S. Klein, *Pennsylvania Politics, 1817–1832* (Philadelphia: Historical Society of Pennsylvania, 1840), 407–8; Glover Moore, *The Missouri Controversy, 1819–1821* (Lexington: University of Kentucky Press, 1953), 340.

33. After the 1825 division Philadelphia consisted of a range of eight wards in the eastern section of the city, along the Delaware River, and a range of seven wards in the western section, along the Schuylkill River. The dividing line between the ranges was Seventh Street. See Ellis P. Oberholtzer, *Philadelphia: A History of the City and Its People* (Philadelphia: S. J. Clarke Publishing Company, [1912]), 2:opp. 112.

34. Philadelphia *United States Gazette* (October 11, 1826, October 11, 1827); *Niles' Weekly Register* (October 14, 1826), 102, (October 13, 1827), 98; *Hazard's Register of Pennsylvania* 2 (October 11, 1828):224, (November 22, 1828):305; Louis H. Arky, "The Mechanics' Union of Trade Associations and the Foundation of the Philadelphia Workingmen's Movement," *Pennsylvania Magazine of History and Biography* 86 (April 1952):170.

35. *Hazard's Register of Pennsylvania* 4 (October 17, 1829):256; William A. Sullivan, "Did Labor Support Andrew Jackson?" *Political Science Quarterly* 62 (December 1947):572–73.

36. *Hazard's Register of Pennsylvania* 6 (October 23, 1830):268–69, 8 (October 8, 1831):256; Sullivan, "Did Labor Support Jackson?" 573.

37. *Hazard's Register of Pennsylvania* 10 (October 13, 1832):237–38, (October 27, 1832):268–69, (November 10, 1832):301, 12 (October 12, 1833):239, (October 26, 1833):260–61, 14 (October 25, 1834):268–69, 16 (October 17, 1835):251, (October 24, 1835):270–71. It might be noted that the Anti-Masons never showed much strength in Philadelphia. See Young, *History of Philadelphia*, 2:178.

38. *Charleston Courier* (October 17, 1816, October 8, 13, 15, 17, 1818, October 12, 1820, January 13, 1821, October 14, 17, 19, 1822).

39. Ibid. (February 13, 1823, September 3, 1824, October 6, 7, 10, 14, 1824).

40. Ibid. (October 7, 10, 11, 1828, September 3, 7, 8, October 17, 1829).

41. Ibid. (August 31, September 4, 6, 7, October 14, 15, 1830).

42. Ibid. (September 7, October 13, 1831, September 5, October 13, 1832, September 4, 1833, September 3, October 16, 1834, September 9, 1835).

43. Thomas P. Teale, *Municipal Register of the City of Brooklyn, and Manual of Kings County, from the Earliest Period Up to the Present Time* (Brooklyn: E. B. Spencer, 1848), 43; Williams, *New-York Annual Register for 1831*, 45; Williams, *New-York Annual Register for 1835*, 50–51; William G. Bishop, *Manual of the Common Council of the City of Brooklyn for 1861–1862* (Brooklyn: George C. Bennett, 1861), 308; Henry R. Stiles, *A History of the City of Brooklyn* (Brooklyn: n.p., 1867–1870), 2:251; Jacob Judd, "The History of Brooklyn, 1834–1855: Political and Administrative Aspects" (Ph.D. dissertation, New York University, 1959), 198–212.

44. William Ketchum, *An Authentic and Comprehensive History of Buffalo, with Some Account of Its Early Inhabitants, Both Savage and Civilized* (Buffalo: Rockwell, Barber, and Hill, 1865),1:169; Henry W. Hill, ed., *Municipality of Buffalo, New York: A History, 1774–1923* (New York and Chicago: Lewis Historical Publishing Company, 1923), 1:95–96, 165; Elijah D. Efner, "The Adventures and Enterprises of Elijah D. Efner," *Publications of the Buffalo Historical Society* 4 (1896):42; Williams, *New-York Annual Register for 1831*, 43; Williams, *New-York Annual Register for 1834*, 45.

45. Allen C. Clark, "Col. Benjamin G. Orr, Mayor," *Records of the Columbia Historical Society* 28 (1926):6; Allen C. Clark, "Samuel Nichols Smallwood, Merchant and Mayor," *Records of the Columbia Historical Society* 28 (1926):30; Allen C. Clark, "Mayors of the Corporation of Washington: Thomas Carberry," *Records of the Columbia Historical Society* 19 (1916):66–67; Allen C. Clark, "General Roger Chew Weightman, a Mayor of the City of Washington," *Records of the Columbia Historical Society* 22 (1919):66; Wilhelmus B. Bryan, *A History of the National Capital* (New York: The Macmillan Company, 1914–1916), 2:161–63; Washington *Daily National Intelligencer* (June 5, 1822).

46. Washington *Daily National Intelligencer* (June 6, 1826, June 8, 1830, June 6, 1832, June 4, 1834); Allen C. Clark, "Joseph Gales, Junior, Editor and Mayor," *Records of the Columbia Historical Society* 23 (1920):101; Allen C. Clark, "General John Peter Van Ness, a Mayor of Washington, His Wife Marcia, and Her Father, David Burnes," *Records of the Columbia Historical Society* 25 (1923):109.

47. BDAM, 183–84, 258–59, 331–32, 345–46; *Niles' Weekly Register* (October 10, 1818), 112, (October 12, 1822), 96, (November 13, 1824), 162, (October 7, 1826), 82–84; Henry E. Shepherd, ed., *History of Baltimore, Maryland* (n.p.: S. B. Nelson, 1898), 79–80; Archibald Hawkins, *The Life and Times of Hon. Elijah Stansbury* (Baltimore: John Murphy and Company, 1874), 58.

48. BDAM, 331–32; *Niles' Weekly Register* (November 15, 1828), 177, (October 17, 1829), 122, (October 9, 1830), 107, (October 20, 1832), 5, (October 12, 1833), 104, (October 25, 1834), 117, (September 12, 1835), 23; *The Maryland Pocket Almanac, for the Year of Our Lord 1833* (Annapolis: J. Hughes, [1833]), 25; *The Maryland Pocket Almanac, for the Year of Our Lord, 1835* (Annapolis: J. Hughes, [1835]), 84.

49. *Cincinnati Advertiser* (October 15, 1822, October 16, November 3, 1824, October 28, 1829, October 20, November 7, 1832); Charles T. Greve, *Centennial History of Cincinnati: and Representative Citizens* (Chicago: Biographical Publishing Company, 1904), 1:584; Richard T. Farrell, "Cincinnati in the Early Jackson Era, 1816–1834: An Economic and Political Study" (Ph.D. dissertation, Indiana University, 1967), 180–81.

The *Cincinnati Advertiser* was published under various titles and is here, as elsewhere, cited only as *Cincinnati Advertiser*.

50. *Cincinnati Advertiser* (October 20, 1832, October 12, 1833, October 15, 1834, April 11, October 17, 1835).

51. See Arndt M. Stickles, *The Critical Court Struggle in Kentucky* ([Bloomington, Indiana]: Graduate Council, Indiana University, 1929); Richard P. McCormick, *The Second American Party System* (Chapel Hill: University of North Carolina Press, 1966), 212–15.

52. *Louisville Public Advertiser* (August 12, 1820, August 11, 1821, August 7, 1824, November 13, 1824).

53. Ibid. (July 23, August 3, 1825, August 5, 9, 12, 1826, August 9, November 11, 1828).

54. Ibid. (August 4, 1829, February 26, August 5, 1831, August 7, 1834, March 3, August 6, 1835).

55. Ernest Kirschten, *Catfish and Crystal* (Garden City, N.Y.: Doubleday and Company, 1960), 136–42; Kenneth W. Keller, "Alexander McNair and John B. C. Lucas: The Background of Early Missouri Politics," *Bulletin of the Missouri Historical Society* 33 (July 1977):242–43; St. Louis *Missouri Gazette* (August 17, 1816, September 13, 1817, August 7, 1818); *St. Louis Enquirer* (December 8, 1819, May 6, 1820); J. Thomas Scharf, *History of Saint Louis City and County* (Philadelphia: Louis H. Everts, 1883), 1: 652.

56. St. Louis *Missouri Republican* (July 31, August 7, 1822, April 9, 1823, July 26, August 9, November 8, 1824); *BDAM*, 207–8.

57. St. Louis *Missouri Republican* (August 5, 10, 1826); Scharf, *History of St. Louis*, 1:163–64; *BDAM*, 184; Elihu H. Shepard, *The Early History of St. Louis and Missouri: From Its First Explorations by the White Man in 1673 to 1843* (St. Louis: Southwestern Book and Publishing Company, 1870), 118.

58. William H. Pease and Jane H. Pease, *The Web of Progress: Private Values and Public Styles in Boston and Charleston, 1828–1843* (New York: Oxford University Press, 1985), 80; *Charleston Courier* (September 2, 1835, September 5, 7, October 5, 13, 1836, September 6, 1837, September 3, 5, 1838, September 7, 1840, September 6, 1841, September 5, October 10, 1842, September 4, 1843, September 1, 1845, September 7, 1846, September 4, 1848, September 2, October 15, 1850).

59. *Charleston Courier* (October 13, 1842, October 12, 17, 1844, October 10, 16, 1846).

60. *The Maryland Pocket Annual, for the Year of Our Lord 1839* (Annapolis: Jeremiah Hughes, [1839]), 195–96, 209–10; *Niles' National Register* (October 7, 1843), 87; (October 21, 1843), 116.

61. *The Tribune Almanac for the Years 1838 to 1868, Inclusive* (New York: The New York Tribune, 1868), 1:(1850) 43, (1851) 47, hereafter cited as *Trib. Almac.*, with appropriate year; *Niles' National Register*, October 22, 1842, 128. Election data for this period were collected from various issues of *Niles' Weekly Register* (before September 2, 1837) and *Niles' National Register* (after September 2, 1837); *The Maryland Pocket Annual, for the Year of Our Lord, 1838* (Annapolis: Jeremiah Hughes, [1838]), 125, 131; *Maryland Pocket Annual, 1839*, 195–96, 209–10; *The Maryland Pocket Annual, for the Year of Our Lord 1841* (Annapolis: Jeremiah L. Hughes, [1841]), 116–17; *The Maryland Pocket Annual, for the Year of Our Lord 1842* (Annapolis: Jeremiah L. Hughes, [1842]), 92, 146; *The Maryland Pocket Annual, for 1846* (n.p.: 1846), 3–4; Daniel H. Craig,

Craig's Business Directory and Baltimore Almanac; for 1842 (Washington: R. Farnham, 1842), 72; Hawkins, *Elijah Stansbury*, 124–25.

62. See sources listed in note 61. The long, narrow wards, which were common in Baltimore until the late 1840s, make it difficult to analyze the voting pattern satisfactorily.

63. Valentine, *Manual of New-York, 1854*, 492–95; Hardy, *Manual of New York [1870]*, 743; *Trib. Almac., 1838*, 4; *Trib. Almac., 1839*, 10; Leon Hershkowitz, "The Native American Democratic Association in New York City, 1835–1836," *New York Historical Society Quarterly* 46 (January 1962):57–58.

64. Valentine, *Manual of New-York, 1854*, 495–96; Hardy, *Manual of New York [1870]*, 743; Leo Hershkowitz, "New York City, 1834–1840: A Study in Local Politics" (Ph.D. dissertation, New York University, 1960), 257.

65. *Trib. Almac., 1844*, 44; Valentine, *Manual of New-York, 1854*, 496–504; Hardy, *Manual of New York [1870]*, 744–45.

66. Hardy, *Manual of New-York [1870]*, 745.

67. Valentine, *Manual of New-York, 1854*, 502–18.

68. Ibid., 506–9.

69. Hardy, *Manual of New York [1870]*, 745–46; *Trib. Almac., 1845*, 43.

70. Hardy, *Manual of New York [1870]*, 746–48; Valentine, *Manual of New-York, 1854*, 512–19; *Trib. Almac., 1849*, 59; *Trib. Almac., 1851*, 42.

71. See sources listed in notes 63–70.

72. Asa Greene, *A Glance at New York* (New York: A. Greene, 1837), 166–68; Hardy, *Manual of New York [1870]*, 742; *Trib. Almac., 1839*, 11; U.S. Census Office, *Sixth Census or Enumeration of the Inhabitants of the United States, As Corrected at the Department of State, in 1840* (Washington: Blair and Rives, 1841), 115.

73. Louis D. Scisco, *Political Nativism in New York State* (New York: Columbia University Press, 1901), 31–32; *Hazard's Register of Pennsylvania* 2 (April 4, 1840): 243, 3 (October 21, 1840):271; New York City, Common Council, *Proceedings of the Boards of Aldermen and Assistant Aldermen, Approved by the Mayor, from May 31, 1842, to May 3, 1843, Inclusive* (New York: Thomas Snowden, 1843), 50–58; George Combe, *Notes on the United States of North America during a Phrenological Visit in 1838–9–40* (Philadelphia: Carey and Hart, 1841), 2:182; Bayard Tuckerman, ed., *The Diary of Philip Hone, 1828–1851* (New York: Dodd, Mead and Company, 1889), 2:49–50.

74. *Cincinnati Advertiser* (October 12, November 9, 1836); *Niles' Weekly Register* (November 23, 1836), 131; *Trib. Almac., 1838*, 33. The three Whig townships were Storrs, Fulton, and Miami.

75. *Cincinnati Advertiser* (April 4, October 10, 1839); *BDAM*, 170.

76. *Cincinnati Advertiser* (April 10, October 17, 31, 1840).

77. *Daily Cincinnati Commercial* (April 4, 1844, April 9, 1845); *BDAM*, 340.

78. *Daily Cincinnati Commercial* (October 21, 1845).

79. Ibid., (October 5, 1846, April 7, October 14, 1847, April 5, November 8, 1848, April 5, 6, 1849, October 14, 1850).

80. See sources in notes 77, 78, and 79.

81. *Louisiana Courier* (November 10, 1836, July 6, 1838); John S. Kendall, *History of New Orleans* (Chicago: Lewis Publishing Company, 1922), 1:145, In 1836 the First and Second Municipalities almost exactly evenly divided 84.5% of the vote cast.

82. *Louisiana Courier* (April 7, July 10, November 5, 1840, July 5, 1842); Earl F. Niehaus, *The Irish in New Orleans, 1800–1860* (Baton Rouge: Louisiana State University

Press, 1965), 78; *Niles' National Register* (August 1, 1840), 346; Kendall, *History of New Orleans*, 1:156.

83. *Louisiana Courier* (July 5, 1843, April 2, November 7, 1844); Kendall, *History of New Orleans*, 1:158; *Trib. Almac., 1845*, 48.

84. *Niles' National Register* (July 13, 1844), 320; Zenon Caveliler et al., *An Address to the Citizens of Louisiana on the Subject of the Recent Election in New Orleans* (New Orleans: The Bee Office, 1844), 14–15, and *passim*; *Louisiana Courier* (April 12, July 2, 1844).

85. *Louisiana Courier* (November 4, 1845); James K. Greer, "Politics in Louisiana, 1845–1861," *Louisiana Historical Quarterly* 12 (July 1929):415–16; Kendall, *History of New Orleans*, 1:162–63; [New Orleans] *Daily Picayune* (January 22, April 7, 1846, April 16, November 3, 1847).

86. *Daily Picayune* (April 4, November 8, 1848, April 13, November 7, 1849); *Trib. Almac., 1850*, 51; *Trib. Almac., 1852*, 45; Kendall, *History of New Orleans*, 1:165.

87. See sources listed in notes 81–86; Leon Cyprian Soule, "The Know-Nothing Party in New Orleans: A Reappraisal" (Ph.D. dissertation, Tulane University, 1960), 3; Greer, "Politics in Louisiana, 1845–1861," 392–93.

88. Teale, *Municipal Register of Brooklyn*, 71; *New York Commercial Advertiser*, April 12, 1837; Judd, "History of Brooklyn," 25–26.

89. *New York Commercial Advertiser* (April 14, 1838, November 8, 1839); Edwin Williams, *The New-York Annual Register for the Year of Our Lord 1840* (New York: David Felt and Company, 1840), 222; *Providence Daily Journal* (April 17, 1840); Stiles, *History of Brooklyn*, 2:262; O. L. Holley, *The New York State Register for 1843* (Albany: J. Disturnell, 1843), 82.

90. *Brooklyn Eagle* (November 8, 1841, April 15, 1842, April 2, 15, November 11, 1843, April 12, 1844, April 12, November 14, 1845); Holley, *New York State Register, 1843*, 82.

91. Teale, *Municipal Register of Brooklyn*, 83; *Brooklyn Eagle* (April 10, 1844); O. L. Holley, *The New York State Register, for 1845* (Albany: J. Disturnell, 1845), 81.

92. *Brooklyn Eagle* (April 4, 1846, April 13, 1849, April 10, November 8, 1850); Teale, *Municipal Register of Brooklyn*, 149.

93. *Brooklyn Eagle* (April 15, 1846, April 10, November 7, 1850); Teale, *Municipal Register of Brooklyn*, 150; Judd, "History of Brooklyn," 199–211.

94. *Brooklyn Eagle* (November 5, 1846, April 16, 1847, November 9, 1848, November 17, 1849, November 8, 1850); Judd, "History of Brooklyn," 78–79.

95. *BDAM*, 16–17, 292–93, 367–68, 378–79, 392–93; Williams, *New-York Annual Register for 1840*, 218; Holley, *New York State Register, 1843*, 77; H. Perry Smith, *History of the City of Buffalo and Erie County*, Vol. 2 (Syracuse: D. Mason and Company, 1884), 2: 101–2.

96. *BDAM*, 149, 195, 248; Holley, *New York State Register, 1843*, 77; Holley, *New York State Register, 1845*, 76.

97. *BDAM*, 7, 20, 155, 333, 338; *Cincinnati Daily Commercial* November 8, 1848; *Trib. Almac., 1851*, 41–42.

98. *BDAM*, 91, 94, 207–8; *Niles' Weekly Register* (August 26, 1837, 405); *Niles' National Register* (August 29, 1840, 406, November 7, 1840, 151); *Trib. Almac., 1841*, 30; Shepard, *Early History of St. Louis*, 153.

99. *BDAM*, 240–41, 293, 397; Shepard, *Early History of St. Louis*, 163, 167–68; *Niles' National Register* (April 13, 1844), 101; Walter B. Stevens, *St. Louis: The Fourth*

City, 1764–1909 (St. Louis: S. J. Clarke Publishing Company, 1909–1911), 1:130–31; Halvor G. Melom, "The Economic Development of St. Louis, 1803–1846" (Ph.D. dissertation, University of Missouri, 1947), 329–36; Russell M. Nolen, "The Labor Movement in St. Louis Prior to the Civil War," *The Missouri Historical Review* 34 (October 1939):25–27.

100. *BDAM*, 293; Richard Edwards and M. Hopewell, *Edwards' Great West and Her Commercial Metropolis, Embracing a General View of the West, and a Complete History of St. Louis, from the Landing of Lingueste, in 1764, to the Present Time* (St. Louis: Edwards' Monthly, 1860), 388; *St. Louis Daily Union* (November 12, 1846, April 6, 1847).

101. *BDAM*, 193–94; *St. Louis Daily Union* (August 4, 1847, April 5, August 9, November 8, 1848, April 4, 1849).

102. Eugene T. Wells, "St. Louis and Cities West, 1820–1880: A Study in History and Geography" (Ph.D. dissertation, University of Kansas, 1951), 76; St. Louis *Missouri Republican* (April 7, 1841, April 3, 1850); *St. Louis Daily Union* (April 17, 1847, April 15, November 8, 1848, April 4, 1849).

103. *Louisville Daily Journal* (May 14, 1840); *Louisville Morning Courier* (August 9, 1849, May 8, 1850); *Niles' National Register* (December 28, 1844), 272. The 142 elections examined obviously do not constitute all of the contests taking place in these five cities over the fifteen-year period, and there are doubtless some Whig defeats to be found in the excluded elections (Thomas A. Davis, for example, actually did eventually obtain a small majority in the Boston mayoral race, on the eighth trial). But the original universe (for all fifteen cities) of elections was formed on the basis of availablity of data, coverage of all of the years of the period, and inclusion of races for different offices (except in the case of Washington, where only the mayoral races are used or usable).

104. See, among other sources, *BDAM, passim;* Shattuck, *Census of Boston for 1845,* 133–38; *Providence Daily Journal, passim; Louisiana Morning Courier, passim; Louisville Daily Journal, passim; Trib. Almac., passim; Niles' National Register, passim;* Young, *History of Philadelphia,* 2:222–25; M. Theopane Geary, *A History of Third Parties in Pennsylvania, 1840–1860* (Washington: Catholic University of America, 1938), *passim;* Washington *Daily National Intelligencer, passim;* Bryan, *History of the National Capital,* 2:*passim.*

105. See sources listed in note 104.

106. Munsell, *Annals of Albany,* 10:327–28, 361–62; Holley, *New York State Register, 1845,* 488; L. G. Hoffman, *Hoffman's Albany Directory, and City Register, for the Years 1837–8* (Albany: L. G. Hoffman, 1837), 5. See also Munsell, *Annals of Albany,,* 1: *passim,* 10: *passim;* O. L. Holley, *The New York State Register, for 1844* (Albany: J. Disturnell, 1844), Appendix, 20; Holley, *New York State Register, 1845,* 488; O. L. Holley, *The New York State Register, for 1846* (Albany: J. Disturnell, 1846), 93; Cuyler Reynolds, *Albany Chronicles: A History of the City Arranged Chronologically* (Albany: J. B. Lyon, 1906), 559; Williams, *New-York Annual Register for 1840,* 212.

107. See sources cited in note 106.

108. Wilson, *Standard History of Pittsburg,* 779–86; John M. Boucher, *A Century and a Half of Pittsburg [sic] and Her People* ([New York]: The Lewis Publishing Company, 1908), 1:424; *BDAM,* 231–32.

109. Wilson, *Standard History of Pittsburg,* 787–93; *BDAM,* 155, 362–63.

110. *BDAM,* 173, 194; Geary, *Third Parties in Pennsylvania,* 122.

111. *BDAM*, 3, 159–60; Wilson, *Standard History of Pittsburg*, 799; *Niles' National Register* (January 23, 1847), 334.

112. *BDAM*, 15–16; Wilson, *Standard History of Pittsburg*, 799–800; *Pittsburgh Gazette*, January 9, 1850.

113. Pittsburgh *Daily Commercial Journal* (November 12, 1848, November 11, 1849); *Pittsburgh Gazette* (October 12, 1850); Wilson, *Standard History of Pittsburg*, 779.

CHAPTER 4

1. The word *tenancy* is here used to denote a period of continuous service. The word *term* is not so employed in this analysis because mayoral terms differed in length from city to city and from time to time in the same city. Additionally, a number of mayors served parts of terms. Data for these and following observations are drawn from Melvin G. Holli and Peter d'A. Jones, eds., *Biographical Dictionary of American Mayors, 1820–1980: Big City Mayors* (Westport, Conn.: Greenwood Press, 1981), hereafter cited as *BDAM*; Cuyler Reynolds, *Albany Chronicle: A History of the City Arranged Chronologically* (Albany: J. B. Lyon, 1906), 389, 423, 431, 447, 459, 473, 495, 507, 521, 533, 545, 551, 565, 571, 591, 601; George R. Howell and Jonathan Tenney, eds., *History of the County of Albany, N.Y., from 1609 to 1886* (New York: W. W. Munsell and Company, 1886), 662–65; J. Thomas Scharf, *History of Baltimore City and County* (Philadelphia: Louis H. Everts, 1881), 187; William G. Bishop, *Manual of the Common Council of the City of Brooklyn for 1860–1861* (Brooklyn: George C. Bennett, 1860), 308; Jacob Judd, "The History of Brooklyn, 1834–1855: Political and Administrative Aspects" (Ph.D. dissertation, New York University, 1959), 198–243; H. Perry Smith, ed., *History of the City of Buffalo and Erie County* (Syracuse: D. Mason and Company, 1884), 2:135–38; Charleston, *Year Book—1881* (Charleston: News and Courier, [1882]), 368–74; Charleston, City Council, *A Digest of the Ordinances of the City Council of Charleston, from the Year 1783 to Oct. 1844* (Charleston: Walker and Burke, 1844), 436; Robert L. Black, *The Cincinnati Orphan Asylum* (Cincinnati: Robert L. Black, 1952), 14; J. Stoddard Johnston, ed., *Memorial History of Louisville from Its First Settlement to the Year 1896* (Chicago and New York: American Biographical Publishing Company, [1896]), 645–46; David T. Valentine, *Manual of the Corporation of the City of New York for 1853* (New York: McSpedon and Baker, 1853), 414–26; John R. Young, ed., *Memorial History of the City of Philadelphia* (New York: New York History Company, 1895–98), 1:408, 443, 498–500; Providence, City Council, *Providence City Manual; or Organization of the Municipal Government, June 1, 1863* (Providence: Knowles, Anthony and Company, 1863), 117; Walter B. Stevens, *St. Louis: The Fourth City, 1764–1909* (St. Louis and Chicago: S. J. Clarke Publishing Company, 1909–1911), 1:121–37; James D. Morgan, "Robert Brent, First Mayor of Washington City," *Records of the Columbia Historical Society* [hereafter *RCHS*] 2 (1899):236–51; Maud Burr Morris, "William A. Bradley, Eleventh Mayor of the Corporation of Washington," *RCHS* 25 (1923):105–39; Ainsworth R. Spofford, "The Life and Labors of Peter Force, Mayor of Washington," *RCHS* 2 (1899):219–35; Allen C. Clark, "Col. Benjamin G. Orr, Mayor," *RCHS* 28 (1926):1–22; *idem*, "Daniel Rapine, Second Mayor," *RCHS* 25 (1923):194–215; *idem*, "General John Peter Van Ness, a Mayor of the City of Washington, His Wife Marcie, and Her Father, David Burnes," *RCHS* 22 (1919):125–204; *idem*, "General Roger Chew Weightman, a Mayor of the City of Washington," *RCHS* 22 (1919):62–

104; *idem* "James Heighe Blake, the Third Mayor of the Corporation of Washington," *RCHS* 24 (1927):136–63; *idem*, "Joseph Gales, Junior, Editor and Mayor," *RCHS* 23 (1920):86–144; *idem*, "Mayors of the Corporation of Washington: Thomas Carberry," *RCHS* 19 (1916):61–98; *idem*, "Walter Lenox, the Thirteenth Mayor of the City of Washington," *RCHS* 20 (1917):167–93; and a large number of city directories for all fifteen of the cities.

2. Because the issue here is one of the influence of shifting party victories on average length of tenancy, these comments are based entirely on mayoral party affiliation. As indicated in the previous chapter (on the basis of a much more comprehensive analysis), Baltimore and Charleston (in its own way) were solidly Democratic and New York tended toward that party. Cincinnati and New Orleans were closely contested by the major parties; Brooklyn, Buffalo, and St. Louis leaned heavily toward the Whigs; and the other cities were solidly or nearly solidly Whig.

3. Nativity data have been located for 148 of the 202 mayors who served during the first half of the nineteenth century.

4. Grocers are separately listed because it is often not possible to determine whether the individual was a wholesale or a retail dealer in groceries. Grocers *known* to be wholesalers are included in the merchant category.

5. Moses Y. Beach, *The Wealth and Biography of the Wealthy Citizens of the City of New York* (New York: The Sun Office, 1846); Edward Pessen, "The Wealthiest New Yorkers of the Jackson Era: A New List," *The New-York Historical Society Quarterly* 54 (April 1970):145–72.

6. Abner Forbes, *The Rich Men of Massachusetts* (Boston: Redding and Company, Hotchkiss and Company, Fetridge and Company, M. V. Spencer, 1852).

7. Boston, Assessing Department, *List of Persons, Copartnerships, and Corporations, Who Were Taxed on Six Thousand Dollars and Upward, in the City of Boston in the Year 1850* (Boston: J. H. Eastburn, 1851).

8. John Lomis and Alfred S. Peace, *The Wealthy Men and Women of Brooklyn and Williamsburg* (Brooklyn: A. S. Peace, 1847).

9. See note 5, above.

10. Five of the mayors were certainly, and two others probably, deceased.

11. A Merchant of Philadelphia, *Memoirs and Autobiography of Some of the Wealthy Citizens of Philadelphia, with a Fair Estimate of Their Estates* (Philadelphia: The Bookseller, 1846).

12. Providence, Board of Assessors, *A List of Persons Assessed in the City Tax of $169,381.16 . . . Ordered by the City Council, June 1850* (Providence: H. H. Brown, 1850); "The Wealthy Population of St. Louis," *Hunt's Merchants' Magazine* 25 (October 1851):476.

13. See Albany city directories for 1813, 1821, 1829, 1832, 1838, 1843, 1850.

14. See Providence directories for 1828, 1832, 1841, and 1850.

15. See Brooklyn directories for 1828, 1829, 1834, 1838, 1839, 1843, 1845, 1851; New York directories for 1805, 1816, 1835, 1840, 1850; Boston directories for 1818, 1825, 1835, 1846, 1851; *New York As It Is* (New York: T. R. Tanner, 1840), 123–51.

16. See Buffalo directories for 1828, 1832, 1835, 1838, 1844; Philadelphia directories for 1807, 1817, 1820, 1830, 1840, 1851; Washington directories for 1822, 1834, 1841, 1853; Cincinnati directories for 1819, 1829, 1837, 1844, 1851; Baltimore directories for 1810, 1814, 1824, 1835, 1842, 1851.

17. See New Orleans directories for 1823, 1824, 1834, 1849, 1851; St. Louis direc-

tories for 1821, 1836, 1845. It might be noted, however, that there was only a single bank in St. Louis.

18. See Pittsburgh directories for 1815, 1839, 1841, 1844; Charleston directories for 1806, 1819, 1829, 1831, 1835, 1837, 1840, 1849; Louisville directories for 1832, 1836, 1844, 1848.

19. The figures given, as indicated, are, in every case, the proportion of those mayors serving in these corporate offices who were connected with two or more institutions.

20. It might be suggested that this conclusion is, perhaps, suspect in the case of Charleston, where the twenty-six mayors included eight planters, who might be presumed to have been less likely to hold bank and insurance company directorships than would merchants and lawyers. Actually, planters constituted a slightly larger percentage (37.5%) of the mayors who held offices or directorates in these financial institutions than planters formed of the whole body of mayors during the first half of the nineteenth century (30.77%).

21. Listings of councilmen, aldermen, trustees, and selectmen were developed from the following sources: Joel Munsell, *The Annals of Albany* (Albany: J. Munsell, 1850–1857; Munsell and Rowland, 1858–1859), 1:39, 5:47, 6:125–26, 8:108–9, 127–28, 158–59, 9:174, 192, 217–18, 232–33, 273–74,286–87, 10:242, 269, 279–80, 292, 302–4, 313–14, 327–28, 340, 349–50, 361–62, 370, 378; Albany city directories for 1814, 1816, 1820, 1834–1835, 1837–1838, 1849–1850; *Albany Evening Journal*, April 10, 13, 1848, April 9, 10, 1850; *Albany Argus*, September 20, 1820, September 26, 1827; Scharf, *History of Baltimore*, 187–90; Boston, City Council, *A Catalogue of the City Councils of Boston, 1822–1908 . . . and of the Selectmen of Boston, 1634–1822* (Boston: City of Boston Printing Department, 1903); William G. Bishop, *Manual of the Common Council of the City of Brooklyn for 1861–1862* (Brooklyn: George C. Bennett, 1861), 306–12; Henry McCloskey, *Manual of the Common Council of the City of Brooklyn, for 1865* (n.p., n.d.), 305–25; Smith, *History of Buffalo*, 2:133–38; Charleston, *Year Book—1881*, 368–74; Henry A. Ford and Kate B. Ford, *History of Cincinnati, Ohio* (Cleveland: L. A. Williams, 1881), 67; Charles T. Greve, *Centennial History of Cincinnati and Representative Citizens* (Chicago: Biographical Publishing Company, 1904), 1:447, 508, 539; Cincinnati city directories for 1819, 1834, 1836–1837, 1844, 1846; *Cincinnati Advertiser* [some variations in title] (April 8, 1829, April 7, 1830, April 9, 1831, April 6, 1833, April 11, 1835, April 10, 1840); *Daily Cincinnati Commercial* [some variations in title] (April 10, 1845, April 8, 1846, April 7, 1847, April 5, 1848, April 5, 1849, April 4, 1850); Johnston, *History of Louisville*, 1:645–47; David T. Valentine, *Manual of the Corporation of the City of New-York, for the Year 1850* (New York: McSpedon and Baker, 1850), 228–49; Philadelphia city directories for 1801, 1802, 1804, 1806, 1807, 1813, 1818, 1825, 1839, 1840, 1841, 1845, 1850, 1851; Philadelphia *United States Gazette* (October 14, 1802, October 14, 1807, October 13, 1808, October 9, 1809, October 10, 1810, October 15, 1811, October 14, 1813, October 11, 1815, October 9, 1816, October 16, 1818, October 11, 1821, October 10, 1822, October 16, 1823, October 13, 1824, October 11, 1826, October 11, 1827, October 12, 1836); Philadelphia *Public Ledger* (October 11, 1837, October 14, 1841, October 13, 1842, October 12, 1843, October 16, 1845, October 15, 1846, October 14, 1847, October 12, 1848); *Hazard's Register of Pennsylvania* 2 (October 11, 1828):224, 4 (October 17, 1829):256, 6 (October 23, 1830):268–69, 8 (October 15, 1831):256, 10 (October 13, 1832): 237–38, 12 (October 12, 1833):239, 14 (October 25, 1834):268–69, 16 (October 17, 1835):251; William R. Staples, *Annals of the Town of Providence from Its First Settlement, to the Organization*

of the City Government, in June, 1832, Vol. 5 of *Collections of the Rhode Island Historical Society* (Providence: Knowles and Vose, 1843), 653–59; Richard M. Bayles, *History of Providence County, Rhode Island* (New York: W. W. Preston and Company, 1891), 1:317–24; J. Thomas Scharf, *History of Saint Louis City and County* (Philadelphia: Louis H. Everts, 1883), 2:720–21; Andrew Rothwell, *Laws of the Corporation of the City of Washington, to the End of the Thirteenth Council—June 1833* (Washington: F. W. DeKrafft, 1833), 317–25; Washington, City Council, *Laws of the Corporation of the City of Washington [1834–35]* (Washington: Jacob Gideon, Jr., 1835), 323; Washington, City Council, *Laws of the Corporation of the City of Washington [1835–36]* (Washington: Jacob Gideon, Jr., 1836), 209; Washington, City Council, *Laws of the Corporation of the City of Washington [1836–37]* (Washington: Jacob Gideon, Jr., 1836 [*sic*; 1837?]), 209; Washington, City Council, *Laws of the Corporation of the City of Washington [1837–38]* (Washington: Jacob Gideon, Jr., 1838), 321; Washington, City Council, *Laws of the Corporation of the City of Washington [1838–39]* (Washington: Jacob Gideon, Jr., 1839), 323; Washington, City Council, *Laws of the Corporation of the City of Washington [1839–40]* (Washington: Jacob Gideon, Jr., 1840), 55; Washington, City Council, *Laws of the Corporation of the City of Washington [1840–41]* (Washington: Jacob Gideon, Jr., 1841), 201; Washington *Daily National Intelligencer* (June 9, 1841, June 8, 1842, June 6, 1843, June 4, 1844, June 3, 1846, June 8, 1847, June 7, 1848, June 5, 1849, June 4, 1850); Washington city directory for 1846. Occupations have been located in the city directories of these thirteen cities and in Judd, ''The History of Brooklyn, 1834–1855.'' Analysis and comments on the following pages rest on these sources.

22. The term *councilman* is here used generally to encompass aldermen, trustees, and members of all other council bodies.

23. See note 4, above.

24. The government officials and employees component may be somewhat inflated. In a number of directories the only designation for some residents who served as councilmen was ''inspector,'' ''magistrate,'' ''notary,'' ''commissioner,'' ''collector,'' or similar titles indicating minor (and doubtless part-time) government employment. In the absence of indications of other occupations, these councilmen are tabulated in the government official or employee category. It is possible that the artisan and shopkeeper segment may also be slightly skewed upward because I have placed all ''traders,'' ''dealers,'' and ''vendors'' (e.g., dry goods, liquor, or lumber) in this category unless the directory entry clearly indicates that the individual was engaged in wholesale or mercantile (as opposed to retail and shopkeeping) operations. All figures given here are percentages of the 3,995 councilmen for whom occupational activities have been determined.

25. The actual numbers of merchants involved were twelve, six, and nine, respectively.

26. The actual numbers were three, three, and two, respectively.

27. There are so many gaps in the Cincinnati data that the number of apparent single-year councilmen may be significantly greater than the reality. It is likely that this circumstance contributes to the unusually high (but *not* the highest) percentage of such councilmen (54.43%). All further comment on council members' time in office will be based on a universe of twelve cities, excluding Cincinnati.

28. A city/occupational cell consists of the councilmen following employments in a given occupational grouping in a single city. Since there are eleven occupational groupings (including both those of unknown occupation and ''other'') and twelve cities in this analytical universe, there are 132 city/occupation cells. Of these, 49 were excluded from

this particular discussion because they contained fewer than ten councilmen. These excluded cells included all of those with 0.00% and 100.00% single-year council members (7 and 4, respectively,) and 10 vacant cells (8 of them in the planter/farmer category).

29. Forbes, *Rich Men of Massachusetts*; Beach, *Wealthy Citizens of New York* (1846); Merchant of Philadelphia, *Wealthy Citizens of Philadelphia*.

30. See the sources listed in notes 12–18.

CHAPTER 5

1. George R. Howell and Jonathan Tenney, eds., *History of the County of Albany, N.Y., from 1609 to 1886* (New York: S. S. Munsell, 1886), 504–5; Albany Map (1698), Albany Map (1794), Geography and Maps Division, Library of Congress, Washington, D.C., hereafter cited as GMLC.

2. Albany Map (1756–1757), Albany Map (1794), GMLC.

3. Daniel Van Pelt, *Leslie's History of Greater New York* (New York: Arkell Publishing Company, 1898), 1:between 26 and 27; I. N. Phelps Stokes, *The Iconography of Manhattan Island* (New York: Robert H. Dodd, 1915–1928), 1:plate 51, 2: frontispiece, plate 82; New York Map (1729), New York Map (1730), New York Map (1755), GMLC.

4. Stokes, *Iconography*, 2:frontispiece; New York Map (1755), GMLC.

5. New York Map (1755), GMLC.

6. New York Map (1789), New York Map (1799), GMLC.

7. Boston Map (1728), Boston Map (1739), GMLC; James H. Stark, *Stark's Antique Views of the Town of Boston* (Boston: Photo-Electrotype Engraving Company, 1901), opposite 44.

8. Boston Map (1800), GMLC.

9. Robert M. Bayles, ed., *A History of Providence County, Rhode Island* (New York: W. W. Preston, 1891), 1:140–41; John H. Cady, *The Civic and Architectural Development of Providence, 1663–1950* (Providence: The Book Shop, 1957), 56.

10. Providence Map (1803), GMLC.

11. Henry R. Stiles, *A History of the City of Brooklyn* (Brooklyn: By subscription, 1867–1870), 1:23–24, 45–47, opposite 62; J. T. Bailey, *An Historical Sketch of the City of Brooklyn and the Surrounding Neighborhood* (Brooklyn: By the author, 1840), 12; Martha J. Lamb, *History of the City of New York* (New York: A. S. Barnes and Company, 1877–1880), 1:124; Brooklyn Map (1816), Brooklyn Map (1835), Brooklyn Map (1845), Brooklyn Map (1854), GMLC.

12. Brooklyn Map (1816), GMLC; New York, Legislature, *Laws of the State of New-York, Passed at the Thirty-Ninth Session of the Legislature* (Albany: J. Buel, 1816), 95, hereafter cited as New York, *Session Laws*, with appropriate date.

13. Daniel Bowen, *A History of Philadelphia* (Philadelphia: D. Bowen, 1839), 5. Another scholar makes no mention of Babylon but does note that the original plan was intended to include 10,000 acres, but that only 1,280 acres were surveyed and platted. See Ellis P. Oberholtzer, *Philadelphia: A History of the City and Its People* (Philadelphia: S. J. Clarke Publishing Company, [1912]), 1:29–30. This, too, seems highly unlikely. The nature of Penn's drawing clearly indicates that the general river lines were known by observation. A plan to cover 10,000 acres, with the same east-west dimensions restricted by the Delaware and Schuylkill Rivers, measured along the High Street line, would have required such a city to extend more than nine and a quarter miles from north to south—more than ten times the width of the established city.

14. Philadelphia Map (1683), GMLC; John R. Young, ed., *Memorial History of the City of Philadelphia* (New York: New York History Company, 1895–1898), 1:32; John F. Watson and Willis P. Hazard, eds., *Annals of Philadelphia and Pennsylvania, in the Olden Time* (Philadelphia: Edwin S. Stuart, 1884), 1:166–67.

15. Philadelphia Map (1775), GMLC; Bowen, *History of Philadelphia*, 8.

16. William A. Courtenay, comp., *The Centennial of Incorporation* (Charleston: News and Courier Book Press, 1884), 144; Mrs. St. Julian Ravenel, *Charleston: The Place and the People* (New York: The Macmillan Company, 1906), 13–16; Robert G. Rhett, *Charleston: An Epic of Carolina* (Richmond, Va.: Garrett and Massie, 1940), 11; Charleston Map (1704), GMLC. The observations on the nature of the "Grand Model" are based on the assumption that it was accurately reflected in the actual form of early Charleston as shown in the map of 1704.

17. Charleston Map (1739), Charleston Map (1790), GMLC.

18. Charleston Map (1790), GMLC.

19. Clayton C. Hall, ed., *Baltimore: Its History and Its People* (New York: Lewis Publishing Company, 1912), 1:12–13, opposite 14; J. Thomas Scharf, *History of Baltimore City and County* (Philadelphia: Louis H. Everts, 1881), 1:52; Baltimore Map (1799), GMLC.

20. Scharf, *History of Baltimore*, 1:52, Hall, *Baltimore*, 1:14–15.

21. Baltimore Map (1799), Baltimore Map (1836), GMLC.

22. Hall, *Baltimore*, 1:15, 18; Scharf, *History of Baltimore*, 1:52, Baltimore Map (1799), GMLC.

23. John S. Kendall, *History of New Orleans* (Chicago and New Orleans: Lewis Publishing Company, 1922), 1:2–6, 23; New Orleans Map (1720), New Orleans Map (1798), GMLC.

24. Sarah H. Killikelly, *The History of Pittsburgh: Its Rise and Progress* (Pittsburgh: B. C. and Gordon Montgomery Company, 1906), 74, 78, 81.

25. Ibid., 80–84; Pittsburgh Map (1787), GMLC.

26. *History of Allegheny County, Pennsylvania* (Chicago: A. Warner and Company, 1889), 484; Pittsburgh Map (1795), GMLC.

27. Elihu H. Shepard, *The Early History of St. Louis and Missouri, from Its First Exploration by White Men in 1673 to 1848* (St. Louis: Southwestern Book and Publishing Company, 1870), 11, 73; St. Louis Map (1764), GMLC; Frederic L. Billon, *Annals of St. Louis in Its Territorial Days from 1804 to 1821* (St. Louis: Nixon-Jones Printing Company, 1888), 23.

28. Shepard, *Early History of St. Louis*, 63; St. Louis Map (1804), GMLC. Main Street (east-west) had originally been laid out with a width of thirty-six feet, but some property holders overbuilt the street lines and the actual width was about thirty feet. See Billon, *Annals of St. Louis, 1804–1821*, 23.

29. J. Stoddard Johnston, ed., *Memorial History of Louisville from Its First Settlements to the Year 1896* (Chicago and New York: American Biographical Publishing Company, [1896]), 1:39–42.

30. There is a reference to a narrow street (thirty feet wide) called Water, which is not located on any map. This may have been the street in question. Henry McMurtrie, *Sketches of Louisville and Its Environs* (Louisville: S. Penn, 1819), 111–12.

31. Johnston, *Memorial History of Louisville*, 1:42–43.

32. Ibid.; Raymond C. Riebel, *Louisville Panorama* (Louisville: Liberty National Bank and Trust Company, 1954), 10; McMurtrie, *Sketches of Louisville*, 111–13.

33. Daniel Drake, *Natural and Statistical View, or Picture of Cincinnati and the Miami Country* (Cincinnati: Looker and Wallace, 1815), frontispiece, 129–30; Charles T. Greve, *Centennial History of Cincinnati and Representative Citizens* (Chicago: Biographical Publishing Company, 1904), 1:86; Lewis A. Leonard, *Greater Cincinnati and Its People* (Cincinnati: Lewis Historical Publishing Company, 1927), 1:76–77; Cincinnati Map (1792), GMLC.

34. Drake, *Picture of Cincinnati*, 130–31; Leonard, *Greater Cincinnati*, 1:99; Cincinnati Map (1792), GMLC.

35. Washington Map (1790), Washington Map (1800), GMLC.

36. Washington Map (1800), GMLC; William Tindell, *Origin and Government of the District of Columbia* (Washington: Government Printing Office, 1912), 24–25.

37. Washington Historical Map (1801–1802; published 1931), GMLC.

38. Henry W. Hill, ed., *Municipality of Buffalo, New York: A History, 1720–1923* (New York and Chicago: Lewis Historical Publishing Company, 1923), 2:61–101.

39. Ibid., 2: opposite 144; H. Perry Smith, ed., *History of the City of Buffalo and Erie County* (Syracuse: D. Mason and Company, 1884), 2:28, 28n; Samuel M. Welch, *Home History. Recollections of Buffalo during the Decade from 1830 to 1840, or Fifty Years Since* (Buffalo: Peter Paul and Brother, 1891), 6; Buffalo Map 1804), GMLC. These terms, *east-west* and *north-south*, are only approximate; the village streets were not laid out precisely along these lines.

40. Buffalo Map (1804), GMLC. The words *extended* and *extension* are used in this paragraph to indicate the projection of the streets on the survey, not their construction.

41. Ibid.

42. Washington Map (1800), Washington Map (1851), GMLC; Wilhelmus Bryant, *A History of the National Capital* (New York: The Macmillan Company, 1914–1916), 1: 507, 507n.

43. Buffalo Map (1804), Buffalo Map (1836), Buffalo Map (1847), GMLC; Hill, *Municipality of Buffalo*, 1:opposite 88. See note 39, above.

44. Philadelphia Map (1802), Philadelphia Map (1836), Philadelphia Map (1849), GMLC. For a contemporary complaint about some of these practices, see *Niles' National Register* 56 (August 10, 1839):272.

45. Oberholtzer, *Philadelphia*, 2:85–87; Watson and Hazard, *Annals of Philadelphia*, 3:397–98.

46. Baltimore Map (1799), GMLC; Maryland, *Laws Made and Passed by the General Assembly of the State of Maryland, at a Session Begun . . . on Monday the Second Day of December, Eighteen Hundred and Sixteen* (Annapolis: Jonas Green, 1817), 160–63, hereafter cited as Maryland, *Session Laws*, with appropriate date; *Niles' Weekly Register* 12 (March 1, 1817):16; Thomas W. Griffith, *Annals of Baltimore* (Baltimore: William Wooddy, 1833), 217–18, 235–37; Maryland, *Session Laws* (1817–1818), 157–63; Baltimore, City Council, *The Ordinances of the Mayor and City Council of Baltimore, 1839* (Baltimore: John D. Toy, 1839), 90–96.

47. Baltimore Map (1799), Baltimore Map (1836), GMLC.

48. Baltimore Map (1799), Baltimore Map (1801), Baltimore Map (1836), GMLC; Baltimore, City Council, *The Ordinances of the Mayor and City Council of Baltimore . . . , 1850* (Baltimore: James Lucas, 1850), Appendix 11.

49. Kendall, *History of New Orleans*, 1:61, 70; New Orleans Map (1803), New Orleans Map (1839), GMLC; New Orleans Sanitary Commission, *Report . . . on the Epidemic Yellow Fever, of 1853* (New Orleans: Picayune Office, 1854), opposite 213;

B. M. Norman, *Norman's New Orleans and Environs* (New Orleans: B. M. Norman, 1845), 181–82; Alexander Walker, *City Digest: Including a Sketch of the Political History of New Orleans* (New Orleans: Daily Delta Office, 1852), 12–14.

50. Pittsburgh Map (1815), GMLC; Erasmus Wilson, ed., *Standard History of Pittsburg, [sic], Pennsylvania* (Chicago: The Goodspeed Publishing Company, 1898), 709, 899; Neville B. Craig, *The History of Pittsburgh* (Pittsburgh: John H. Mellor, 1851), frontispiece; George T. Fleming, *Fleming's Views of Old Pittsburgh[:] A Portfolio of the Past* (Pittsburgh: The Crescent Press, 1832), 3:639.

51. Kentucky, General Assembly, *Acts Passed at the First Session of the Twenty-sixth General Assembly for the Commonwealth of Kentucky* (Frankfort: Kendall and Russells, 1818), 473–75, hereafter cited as Kentucky, *Session Laws*, with appropriate dates; Riebel, *Louisville Panorama*, 40; Louisville, City Council, *A Collection of the Acts of Virginia and Kentucky, Relative to Louisville and Portland: With the Charter of Louisville and the Amendments Thereto* (Louisville: Prentice and Weissinger, 1839), 44–45, 100–101, hereafter cited as Louisville, *Collected Ordinances* (1839); Louisville, City Council, *Charter of the City of Louisville of 1851, and Ordinances of the City . . . , also a Collection of Acts of the General Assembly of Kentucky* (Louisville: Bradley and Gilbert, 1869), 33, 54, 60, 73–74, hereafter cited as Louisville, *Charter and Ordinances* (1869); *Coulton's Atlas of the World* (New York: J. H. Coulton and Company, 1856), 1:34; McMurtrie, *Sketches of Louisville*, 114–15.

52. Cincinnati Map (1792), Cincinnati Map (1839), Cincinnati Map (ca. 1850 [sic]; after 1853), GMLC; Leonard, *Greater Cincinnati*, 1:6–7; Wellington Williams, *Appleton's Southern and Western Travellers' Guide* (New York: D. Appleton and Company, 1853), opposite 19; Cincinnati, City Council, *Charter, Amendments, and General Ordinances, of the City of Cincinnati* (Cincinnati: Day and Company, 1850), 334–35; Greve, *History of Cincinnati*, 1:981.

53. Charleston Map (1790), GMLC; Williams, *Appleton's Southern and Western Travellers' Guide* (1853), opposite 115; South Carolina, General Assembly, *Acts and Resolutions of the General Assembly of the State of South Carolina, Passed in December, 1822* (Columbia: Daniel Faust, 1823), 57, hereafter cited as South Carolina, *Session Laws*, with appropriate date; South Carolina, *Session Laws* (1849), 579–80; James Silk Buckingham, *The Slave States of America* (London: Fisher, Son, and Company, [1842]), 1:559.

54. Walter B. Stevens, *St. Louis: The Fourth City, 1764–1909* (St. Louis: S. J. Clarke Publishing Company, 1909–1911), 1:opposite 88; St. Louis Map (1835), St. Louis Map (1842), St. Louis Map (1851), GMLC; William Hyde and Howard L. Conard, eds., *Encyclopedia of the History of St. Louis* (St. Louis: The Southern History Company, 1899), 4:1951; Missouri, General Assembly, *Laws of the State of Missouri, Passed by the First Session of the Tenth General Assembly* (City of Jefferson: Calvin Gunn, 1838[sic]), 156, hereafter cited as Missouri, *Session Laws*, with appropirate date; Missouri, *Session Laws* (1841), 129; Billon, *Annals of St. Louis, 1804–1821*, 22–23; J. Thomas Scharf, *History of Saint Louis City and County* (Philadelphia: Louis H. Everts, 1883), 1:757–58; St. Louis, City Council, *The Revised Ordinances of the City of St. Louis* (St. Louis: Chambers and Knapp, 1850), 67–70.

55. Brooklyn Map (1816), Brooklyn Map (1835), GMLC; William G. Bishop, *Manual of the Common Council of the City of Brooklyn for 1861–1862* (Brooklyn: George C. Bennett, 1861), opposite 302.

56. Donald E. Simon, "The Public Park Movement in Brooklyn, 1824–1873" (Ph.D.

dissertation, New York University, 1972), 39–94; Stiles, *History of Brooklyn*, 3:616–17; Brooklyn, Common Council, *Acts Relating to the City of Brooklyn, and the Ordinances Thereof* (Brooklyn: J. Douglas, 1836), 3–5; New York, *Session Laws* (1845), 76–77.

57. Albany Map (1794), Albany Map (1841), GMLC; *Hoffman and Munsell's Albany Directory and City Register, for 1851–52* (Albany: Joel Munsell, 1851), opposite 161.

58. James G. Wilson, ed., *The Memorial History of the City of New York* (New York: New-York History Company, 1892–1893), 3:opposite 208; Stokes, *Iconography*, 1:Plates 70, 79, 5:1531–32; New York Map (1807), GMLC; New York, *Session Laws* (1807), 125–30; James Ford, *Slums and Housing, with Special Reference to New York City* (Cambridge, Mass.: Harvard University Press, 1963), 1:84.

59. *Picture of New-York and Stranger's Guide to the Commercial Metropolis of the United States* (New York: A. T. Goodrich, 1828), 140–41; Stokes, *Iconography*, 1:472, 5:1531; New York, *Session Laws* (1814), 206–8; New York, *Session Laws* (1824), 7–9; New York, *Session Laws* (1829), 400.

60. New York Map (1803), New York Map (1834), New York Map (1845), GMLC; Stokes, *Iconography*, 1:Plate 79; James Hardie, *The Description of the City of New-York* (New York: Samuel Marks, 1827), 146–47; New York, *Session Laws* (1793), 434–36; New York, *Session Laws* (1795), 622–24.

61. Quoted in Stokes, *Iconography*, 1:472.

62. Providence Map (1803), Providence Map (1849), GMLC; Cady, *Civic and Architectural Development of Providence*, 90–93; Asa Greene, *A Glance at New York* (New York: A. Greene, 1837), 2–3.

63. Providence Map (1849), GMLC; Bayles, *History of Providence*, 1:286–88; Providence, City Council, *The Charter and Ordinances of the City of Providence Together with the Acts of the General Assembly Relating to the City* (Providence: Knowles, Anthony, and Company, 1854), 194–95.

64. Carl David Arfwedson, *The United States and Canada in 1832, 1833, and 1834* (London: Richard Bentley, 1834), 1:131; Timothy Dwight, *Boston at the Beginning of the 19th Century*, Vol. 5, No. 136 of *Old South Leaflets* (Boston: Directors of the Old South Walk, 1903), 1–3; Josiah Quincy, *A Municipal History of the Town and City of Boston, during Two Centuries* (Boston: Charles C. Little and James Brown, 1852), 194–96, quotation from 195; John Koren, *Boston, 1822–1922* (Boston: City of Boston Printing Department, 1933), 153; Boston Map (1800), Boston Map (1850), GMLC.

65. Walter M. Whitehill, *Boston: A Topographical History* (Cambridge: Harvard University Press, 1955), 85–88.

66. Arfwedson, *U.S. and Canada*, 1:131; Boston Map (1800), Boston Map (1833), Boston Map (1846), GMLC; Whitehill, *Boston: A Topographical History*, 74–78; Thomas C. Simonds, *History of South Boston* (Boston: David Clapp, 1857), 72–77; Caleb H. Snow, *A History of Boston* (Boston: Abel Bowen, 1828), 318–19; Massachusetts, General Court, *Acts and Laws, Passed by the General Court of Massachusetts, at the Session Begun and Held, . . . on Thursday, the twelfth Day of January, Anno Domini, 1804* (Boston: Young and Minns, [1804]), 412–21, hereafter cited as Massachusetts, *Session Laws*, with appropriate date. Some thirty years later, when the East Boston Company had acquired title to all of the land on Noddle's Island and the city extended its authority over the area, it was the gridiron concept that shaped the survey there, though there were several diagonal streets. Justin Winsor, ed., *The Memorial History of Boston, Including Suffolk County, Massachusetts, 1630–1881* (Boston: James R. Osgood and Company, 1880–1881), 4:38–39.

67. Massachusetts, *Session Laws* (January 1804), 462–64; Whitehill, *Boston: A Topographical History*, 79–84; Boston Map (1800), Boston Map (1833), GMLC.

68. Whitehill, *Boston: A Topographical History*, 88–95, 128–29; Snow, *History of Boston*, 3; Boston Map (1833), GMLC.

69. Whitehill, *Boston: A Topographical History*, 107–10; Winsor, *Memorial History of Boston*, 4:39–40.

70. Whitehill, *Boston: A Topographical History*, 96–98; Boston Map (1800), Boston Map (1833), GMLC; Dwight, *Boston at the Beginning of the 19th Century*, 1.

71. Dwight, *Boston at the Beginning of the 19th Century*, 1; Boston Map (1800), Boston Map (1833), GMLC; Nathaniel B. Shurtleff, *A Topographical and Historical Description of Boston* (Boston: Alfred Mudge and Son, 1871), 320–27, 378–79, 382–87; Winsor, *Memorial History of Boston*, 4:60–61; I. Smith Homans, *Sketches of Boston, Past and Present* (Boston: Phillips, Sampson, and Company, 1851), 196–98; Quincy, *Municipal History of Boston*, 113–16; Christopher R. Eliot, "The Boston Public Garden: Horace Gray, Sr., Charles Francis Barnard," *Proceedings of the Bostonian Society* 58 (1939):39.

CHAPTER 6

1. Massachusetts, *Session Laws* (January 1804), 412–14; Massachusetts, *Session Laws* (January 1825), 593–94; Rhode Island, *Session Laws* (January 1848), 9; New York, *Session Laws* (1814–1815), 45–48. In this chapter considerable use will be made of state laws published at the end of each legislative session. These are generically known as "Session Laws," though they never, in my experience, bear such a designation on the title page. As might be expected, they are published by a number of different publishers, even over short periods of time. These laws, whatever their published title, are easily located in law libraries under the designation "Session Laws." Consequently, the citation format shown above will be used throughout this chapter.

2. Thomas W. Griffith, *Annals of Baltimore* (Baltimore: William Wooddy, 1833), 217; Baltimore, City Council, *Ordinances of the Corporation of the City of Baltimore, from 1815 to 1822, Inclusive* (Baltimore: John Cox, 1876), 201–202; *Niles' Weekly Register* (March 1, 1817), 16.

3. Louisiana, *Session Laws* (1810), 12; Louisiana, *Session Laws* (1818), 44; Charleston, City Council, *Ordinances of the City of Charleston, from the 19th of August 1849, to the 14th of September 1854 and the Acts of the General Assembly Relating to the City of Charleston . . . during the Same Interval* (Charleston: A. E. Miller, 1854), 178–79; Pennsylvania, *Session Laws* (1836–1837), 29–30; Kentucky, *Session Laws* (1826–1827), 175–76; New York, *Session Laws* (1834), 90–92.

4. Kentucky, *Session Laws* (1826–1827), 175; Kentucky, *Session Laws* (1836–1837), 276–78; New York, *Session Laws* (1814–1815), 45–48; Baltimore, City Council, *Ordinances of the Corporation of the City of Baltimore, [1797–1802]* (Baltimore: John Cox, 1875), 192–93; Charles T. Greve, *Centennial History of Cincinnati and Representative Citizens* (Chicago: Biographical Publishing Company, 1904), 1:511.

5. Pennsylvania, *Session Laws* (1835–1836), 245–46, 749–54; Pennsylvania, *Session Laws* (1845), 88–89.

6. New York, *Session Laws* (1823), 162–66; Rhode Island, *Session Laws* (October 1831), 31–33; Rhode Island, *Session Laws* (June 1834), 15; Rhode Island, *Session Laws* (January 1839), 69–72; Rhode Island, *Session Laws* (October 1841), 14.

7. Maryland, *Session Laws* (1807–1808), Chapter 152; Baltimore, City Council, *The Ordinances of the Mayor and City Council of Baltimore . . . , 1841* (Baltimore: Joseph Robinson, 1841), 69; Baltimore, City Council, *The Ordinances of the Mayor and City Council of Baltimore . . . , 1843* (Baltimore: Lucas and Deaver, 1843), 69; Louisiana, *Session Laws* (1818), 38–40; Louisiana, *Session Laws* (1820), 66–70; Missouri (Territory), *Session Laws* (1813–1814), 63–65; Rhode Island, *Session Laws* (June 1841), 9; Pennsylvania, *Session Laws* (December 1791), 182–83; Pennsylvania, *Session Laws* (1804–1805), 36–37; Pennsylvania, *Session Laws* (1819–20), 133; Pennsylvania, *Session Laws* (1825–1826), 356–57; Ohio, *Session Laws* (1839–1840), 157–59; Ohio, *Session Laws* (1844–1845), 355–56; New York, *Session Laws* (1819), 18–22.

8. Missouri, *Session Laws* (1843), 106; New York, *Session Laws* (1808–1809), 137–44; New York, *Session Laws* (1841), 289–91; Rhode Island, *Session Laws* (January 1840), 40; Massachusetts, *Session Laws* (May 1811), 392–93; Kentucky, *Session Laws* (1831–1832), 28–29; Louisiana, *Session Laws* (1824–1825), 178–82; Louisiana, *Session Laws* (1835), 179–82; Pennsylvania, *Session Laws* (1841), 44–46; Pennsylvania, *Session Laws* (1847), 226–28. New York City was excluded from the effect of the 1841 statute because similar provisions had been made for it a year earlier. See New York, *Session Laws* (1840), 52–58.

9. South Carolina, *Session Laws* (December 1817), 41–43; New York, *Session Laws* (1840), 52–58; Baltimore, City Council, *The Ordinances of the Mayor and City Council of Baltimore . . . , 1840* (Baltimore: Joseph Robinson, 1840), 73; Louisiana, *Session Laws* (1835), 179–82; Louisville, City Council, *Charter of the City of Louisville of 1851, and Ordinances of the City . . . , also a Collection of Acts of the General Assembly of Kentucky, from the Establishment of the Town of Louisville in May, 1780, to March 15, 1869* (Louisville: Bradley and Gilbert, 1869), 35; Washington, City Council, *Charter of the City of Washington, Being the Acts of Incorporation [1820–1848]* (Washington: Robert A. Waters, 1859), 6.

10. Wilbur F. Coyle, *Records of the City of Baltimore (City Commissioners), 1797–1813* (Baltimore: City Library, 1906), i–ii; Baltimore, City Council, *The Charter of the Province of Maryland; The Declaration of Rights of 1776, and Acts of the General Assembly of Maryland, Relating to Baltimore-Town and City, from 1729 to 1830* (Baltimore: John Cox, 1879), 314; Boston, City Council, *The Charter of the City of Boston, and Ordinances Made and Established by the Mayor, Aldermen, and Common Council, with Such Acts of the Legislature of Massachusetts, as Relate to the Government of Said City* ((Boston: True and Greene, 1827), 3–4; Boston, City Council, *The Charter and Ordinances of the City of Boston, Together with the Acts of the Legislature Relating to the City* (Boston: John H. Eastburn, 1850), 482–83; Louisville, City Council, *Charter of Louisville* (1869), 34, 57, 77; Louisville, City Council, *Revised Ordinances of the City of Louisville, Including the Charter of 1851* (Louisville: Louisville Courier Steam Printing House, 1854), 9–10.

11. Providence, City Council, *The Charter and Ordinances of the City of Providence, with the Acts of the General Assembly Relating to the City* (Providence: Weeden and Cary, 1835), 8–9; Washington, City Council, *A Digest of the General Acts of the Corporation of the City of Washington* (Washington: J. Gideon, Jr., 1818), 5, 14; Washington, *Charter [1820–1848]*, 14–15; South Carolina, *Session Laws* (1805), 64–65; South Carolina, *Session Laws* (1815), 58–59.

12. Ohio, *Session Laws* (1818–1819), 175–80; Ohio, *Session Laws* (1826–1827), 41–42; Ohio, *Session Laws* (1833–1834), 245; St. Louis, City Council, *The Revised Ordi-*

nances of the City of St. Louis, Revised and Digested by the City Council, in the Year 1850 (St. Louis: Chambers and Knapp, 1850), 49–55, 57, 58; Missouri, *Session Laws* (1835–1836), 30; Missouri, *Session Laws* (1838–1839), 156; Missouri, *Session Laws* (1840–1841), 130; Missouri, *Session Laws* (1842–1843), 114.

13. New Orleans, City Council, *A Digest of the Ordinances, Resolutions, By-Laws, and Regulations of the Corporation of New-Orleans, and a Collection of the Laws of the Legislature Relative to Said City* (New Orleans: Gaston Brusle, 1836), 299–303; New York, Common Council, *The Charter of the City of New-York* (New York: Childs and Devoe, 1836), 38–42; New York, *Session Laws* (1789–1791), 217–18; New York, *Session Laws* (1803), 59–62; New York, *Session Laws* (1808), 58–60; New York, *Session Laws* (1817), 341–43; New York, *Session Laws* (1826), 184–86; New York, *Session Laws* (1827), 57–58; New York, *Session Laws* (1832), 297–98; New York, *Session Laws* (1834), 90–92; New York, *Session Laws* (1841), 48–51; Pennsylvania, *Session Laws* (December 1799), 556–58; Pennsylvania, *Session Laws* (1824–1825), 130–37; Pennsylvania, *Session Laws* (1829–1830), 13–14; Pennsylvania, *Session Laws* (1833–1834), 4–5; Pennsylvania, *Session Laws* (1841), 48–56.

14. *Charleston Courier* (October 17, 1806, October 15, 1812, October 13, 1842); J. D. B. DeBow, *Statistical View of the United States* (Washington: A. O. P. Nicholson, 1854), 40, 192. All subsequent statements about population are drawn from the latter source.

15. Griffith, *Annals of Baltimore*, 182; J. Thomas Scharf, *History of Baltimore City and County* (Philadelphia: Louis H. Everts, 1881), 121; Baltimore, City Council, *The Ordinances of the Mayor and City Council of Baltimore . . . , 1836* (Baltimore: Lucas and Deaver, 1836), 135; *The Maryland Pocket Annual, for the Year of Our Lord 1838* (Annapolis: Jeremiah Hughes, [1838]), 196; *Niles' National Register* (November 13, 1849), 166.

16. Francis N. Thorpe, *The Federal and State Constitutions, Colonial Charters, and Other Organic Laws of the States, Territories and Colonies* (Washington: Government Printing Office, 1909), 6:3214, 3228, 3258; Peter J. Coleman, *The Transformation of Rhode Island, 1790–1860* (Providence: Brown University Press, 1963), 256.

17. Justin Winsor, ed., *The Memorial History of Boston, Including Suffolk County, Massachusetts, 1630–1880* (Boston: James R. Osgood and Company, 1880–1881), 3: 297–98; *Bowen's Boston News-Letter and City Record* (May 27, 1826), 274–75.

18. New York, *Session Laws* (1826), 335–37; New York, *Session Laws* (1836), 653–55; New York, *Session Laws* (1846), 48–50; U.S., Census Office, *The Seventh Census of the United States: 1850* (Washington: Robert Armstrong, 1853), 92, 97, 100.

19. Thorpe, *Charters*, 5:3098, 3104; Washington *National Intelligencer* (October 16, 1813); *Hazard's Register of Pennsylvania* (October 27, 1832), 268; *Niles' National Register* (November 1, 1845), 135; U.S., Census Office, *Sixth Census or Enumeration of the Inhabitants of the United States, As Corrected at the Department of State, in 1840* (Washington: Blair and Rives, 1841), 26; U.S., Census Office, *Census, 1850*, 159. It should be noted that cities tended to have smaller percentages of taxable inhabitants in their populations than did the more rural counties.

20. Albany, Common Council, *Laws and Ordinances of the Mayor, Aldermen, and Commonality of the City of Albany, . . . 1808* (Albany: Websters and Skinner, 1808), 70–71; Louisville, City Council, *Charter of Louisville* (1869), 38–40; Kentucky, *Session Laws* (1837–1838), 87–88; New York, *Session Laws* (1826), 93.

21. Maryland, *Session Laws* (1832–1837, 1840–1850), *passim*; Baltimore, City Coun-

cil, *The Ordinances of the Mayor and City Council of Baltimore . . . , 1839* (Baltimore: John D. Toy, 1839), 96–97.

22. New York, Legislature, *An Act to Incorporate the City of Buffalo, Passed April 20, 1832* (Buffalo: David M. Day, 1832), 14–20; Washington, *Charter [1820–1848]*, 21; Boston, City Council, *The Charter and Ordinances of the City of Boston, Together with the Acts of the Legislature Relating to the City* (Boston: J. H. Eastburn, 1834), 256–57.

23. E.g., New York, *Session Laws* (1818), 701–6; South Carolina, *Session Laws* (1835), 24–25; South Carolina, *Session Laws* (1836), 49–50; South Carolina, *Session Laws* (1838), 39.

24. E.g., Rhode Island, *Session Laws* (January 1848), 3; Alexander Walker, *City Digest: Including a Sketch of the Political History of New Orleans* (New Orleans: Daily Delta Office, 1852), 30–36; South Carolina, *Session Laws* (1794), 51–52; South Carolina, *Session Laws* (1816), 49–50; New York, *Session Laws* (1828), 335–36.

25. Massachusetts, *Session Laws* (1831–1832), 774–75; Massachusetts, *Session Laws* (1834), 84; South Carolina, *Session Laws* (November 1795), 26–27 [first pagination]; South Carolina, *Session Laws* (December 1797), 122–23 [second pagination].

26. Missouri, *Session Laws* (1846–1847), 226; Rhode Island, *Session Laws* (October 1795), 5–7; Rhode Island, *Session Laws* (January 1822), 9–10; Ohio, *Session Laws* (1849–1850), 696–700; South Carolina, *Session Laws* (1801), 109–11.

27. The reader is again reminded that we are here concerned only with the interaction between the states and the cities, and that the activities of city governments in these areas will be dealt with in a subsequent volume.

28. Albany, Common Council, *Ordinances* (1808), 102, 109; New York, Common Council, *Charter* (1836), 59, 65; Philadelphia, City Council, *A Digest of the Acts of Assembly Relating to the City of Philadelphia* (Philadelphia: J. H. Jones, 1856), 4, 6, 21; Scharf, *History of Baltimore*, 201; Louisville, City Council, *A Collection of the Acts of Virginia and Kentucky, Relative to Louisville and Portland: With the Charter of Louisville and the Amendments Thereto* (Louisville: Prentice and Weissinger, 1839), 20; Charleston, City Council, *A Digest of the Ordinances of the City Council of Charleston, from the Year 1783 to Oct. 1844, to Which Are Annexed the Acts of the Legislature Which Relate Exclusively to the City of Charleston* (Charleston: Walker and Burke, 1844), 339.

29. Josiah Quincy, *A Memorial History of the Town and City of Boston during Two Centuries* (Boston: Charles C. Little and James Brown, 1852), 1013; Boston, Registry Department, *A Volume of Records Relating to the Early History of Boston Containing Minutes of the Selectmen's Meetings, 1799 to, and Including, 1810* (Boston: Municipal Printing Office, 1904), 33:80; Providence, City Council, *Charters and Ordinances* (1835), 13; Brooklyn, Common Council, *Acts Relating to the City of Brooklyn, and the Ordinances Thereof* (Brooklyn: J. Douglas, 1836), 80; Brooklyn, City Council, *Ordinances of the Village of Brooklyn* (Brooklyn: G. L. Black, 1828), 28–30.

30. Pittsburgh, City Council, *A Digest of the Acts of Assembly Relating to, and the General Ordinances of the City of Pittsburgh from 1804 to Sept. 1, 1886* (Harrisburg: Edwin K. Meyers, 1887), 3; Lewis A. Leonard, *Greater Cincinnati and Its People* (Chicago and Cincinnati: Lewis Publishing Company, 1927), 1:10; New York, Legislature, *An Act to Incorporate the City of Buffalo, 1832*, 7; Washington, City Council, *Digest of Acts* (1818), 6–7; St. Louis, City Council, *Revised Ordinances, 1850*, 52; Louisiana, *Session Laws* (1816), 92.

31. Maryland, *Session Laws* (1790), Chapter 17; Maryland, *Session Laws* (1793),

Chapter 59; Maryland, *Session Laws* (1807–1808), Chapter 160; Maryland, *Session Laws* (1811–1812), 14–16; Baltimore, City Council, *The Ordinances of the Mayor and City Council of Baltimore . . . , 1834* (Baltimore: James Lucas and E. K. Deaver, 1834), 75; Baltimore, City Council, *Ordinances, 1840*, 43; Baltimore, City Council, *The Ordinances of the Mayor and City Council of Baltimore . . . , 1844* (Baltimore: Lucas and Deaver, 1844), 51, 99–100; John F. Watson and Willis P. Hazard, *Annals of Philadelphia and Pennsylvania, in the Olden Times* (Philadelphia: Edwin S. Stuart, 1884), 3:187; Pennsylvania, *Session Laws* (December 1794), 654–55; Pennsylvania, *Session Laws* (1809–1810), 119–20; Pennsylvania, *Session Laws* (1812–1813), 4; Philadelphia, City Council, *Ordinances of the Corporation of the City of Philadelphia* (Philadelphia: Moses Thomas, 1812), 107, 118; Albany, Common Council, *Ordinances, 1808*, 77; New York, *Session Laws* (1816), 50–56.

32. Albany, Common Council, *Ordinances, 1808*, 1–2, 103, 109; New York, Common Council, *Charter* (1836), 59–60, 63, 66–67; Philadelphia, City Council, *Digest of Acts* (1856), 4–6.

33. Louisville, City Council, *Revised Ordinances* (1854), 17–18, 29–32, 39, 45–46, 60–61; St. Louis, Common Council, *Digest of the Charter and Revised Ordinances of the City of St. Louis* (St. Louis: McKee, Fishback, and Company, 1866), 94–95.

34. New York, *Session Laws* (1802), 219–22; New York, *Session Laws* (1803), 189–201; New York, *Session Laws* (1812), 390–92; New York, *Session Laws* (1814), 254; Baltimore, City Council, *The Ordinances of the Mayor and City Council of Baltimore . . . , 1837* (Baltimore: Lucas and Deaver, 1837), 91–93; Baltimore, City Council, *Ordinances, 1841*, 70–71, 97; Pennsylvania, *Session Laws* (December 1790), 280–82; Pennsylvania, *Session Laws* (1850), 469; Rhode Island, *Session Laws* (June 1832), 7–13; Rhode Island, *Session Laws* (June 1840), 3; Boston, City Council, *Charter and Ordinances* (1834), 216–17; Kentucky, *Session Laws* (1848–1849), 386.

35. New York, *Session Laws* (1818), 54–56; New York, *Session Laws* (1822), 148–49; Louisiana, *Session Laws* (1827), 172–76; Maryland, *Session Laws* (1826–1827), Chapter 137; Baltimore, City Council, *The Ordinances of the Mayor and City Council of Baltimore . . . , 1832* (Baltimore: Joseph Robinson, 1832), 107–11; Baltimore, City Council, *Ordinances, 1836*, 131; Baltimore, City Council, *Ordinances, 1837*, 86–87; Baltimore, City Council, *The Ordinances of the Mayor and City Council of Baltimore . . . , 1847* (Baltimore: James Lucas, 1847), 129–30.

36. Maryland, *Session Laws* (1808), Chapter 116; Louisiana, *Session Laws* (1843), 55.

37. New York, Legislature, *An Act to Incorporate the City of Buffalo, 1832*, 11; Brooklyn, Common Council, *Acts and Ordinances* (1836), 13; Albany, Common Council, *Laws and Ordinances of the Common Council of the City of Albany, Revised and Revived May 5, 1856* (Albany: W. C. Little and Company, 1856), 296; New York, *Session Laws* (1819–1820), 63–64; Martha J. Lamb, *History of the City of New York* (New York: A. S. Barnes and Company, 1877–1880), 1:139; Pennsylvania, *Session Laws* (1821–1822), 108; Pennsylvania, *Session Laws* (1825–1826), 277; Rhode Island, *Session Laws* (January 1845), 55; Maryland, *Session Laws* (1797–1798), Chapter 11.

38. Coyle, *Records of Baltimore Commissioners, 1797–1813*, vi; Boston, City Council, *Charter and Ordinances* (1827), 14; Brooklyn, Common Council, *Acts and Ordinances* (1836), 13, 15, 30; New York, Legislature, *An Act to Incorporate the City of Buffalo, 1832*, 23–25; Cincinnati, City Council, *An Act Incorporating the City of Cincinnati, and a Digest of the Ordinances of Said City, of a General Nature, Now in Force*

(Cincinnati: Lodge, L'Hommedieu and Company, 1835), 9, 11; Louisville, City Council, *Charter of Louisville* (1869), 41; Philadelphia, City Council, *Digest of Acts* (1856), 53; St. Louis, City Council, *Revised Ordinances, 1850*, 52; Washington, City Council, *Digest of Acts* (1818), 6.

39. *Digest of the Acts of Assembly Relative to the Board of Health: With the Rules of the Board* (Philadelphia: Thomas B. Town, 1846), 16–37; Pittsburgh, City Council, *Digest of Acts* (1887), 9; Boston, City Council, *Charter and Ordinances* (1827), 158–68; Massachusetts, *Session Laws* (January 1799), 251–54; Rhode Island, *Session Laws* (February 1816), 44–46; New York, *Session Laws* (1823), 64–82; New York, *Session Laws* (1824), 241–44.

40. New York, *Session Laws* (1792), 375; New York, *Session Laws* (1795), 581; New York, *Session Laws* (1789–1796), 710–16; New York, *Session Laws* (1801), 4; Pennsylvania, *Session Laws* (December 1798), 371–72; South Carolina, *Session Laws* (1837), 21.

41. Boston, City Council, *Charter and Ordinances* (1827), 15; Brooklyn, Common Council, *Acts and Ordinances* (1836), 31; Charleston, City Council, *Digest of Ordinances, 1783–1844*, 339; Washington, City Council, *Digest of Acts* (1818), 7; Philadelphia, City Council, *Digest of Acts* (1856), 42; Albany, Common Council, *Ordinances*, (1808), 76; New York, Common Council, *Charter* (1836), 64; Louisville, City Council, *Charter of Louisville* (1869), 41–42.

42. Baltimore, City Council, *The Ordinances of the Mayor and City Council of Baltimore . . . , 1821* (Baltimore: Lucas and Deaver, 1831), 89–90; South Carolina, *Session Laws* (1820), 90; Ohio, *Session Laws* (1844–1845), 166; Louisiana, *Session Laws* (1841), 46–48; Louisiana, *Session Laws* (1847), 203; New York, *Session Laws* (1812), 392; Pennsylvania, *Session Laws* (1802–1803), Chapter 154; Rhode Island, *Session Laws* (June 1794), 15; Rhode Island, *Session Laws* (October 1794), 3; Rhode Island, *Session Laws* (May 1795), 20.

43. New York, *Session Laws* (1811), 152; Boston, City Council, *Charter and Ordinances* (1834), 210; Boston, City Council, *Charter and Ordinances* (1850), 76–78, 470; Abel Bowen, *Bowen's Picture of Boston, or the Citizen's and Stranger's Guide to the Metropolis of Massachusetts, and Its Environs* (Boston: Lilly Wait and Company, 1833), 18; Philadelphia, City Council, *Digest of Acts* (1856), 28–30; Scharf, *History of Baltimore*, 62–63; Maryland, *Session Laws* (1817–1818), 197, Maryland, *Session Laws* (1822–1823), 102–5; Maryland, *Session Laws* (1826–1827), Chapter 217.

44. George R. Howell and Jonathan Tenney, *History of the County of Albany, N.Y., from 1609 to 1886* (New York: W. W. Munsell and Company, 1886), 80–82, 87–91; William G. Bishop, *Manual of the Common Council of the City of Brooklyn for 1861–1862* (Brooklyn: George C. Bennett, 1861), 82–83, 326–51; Henry R. Stiles, *The Civil, Political, Professional and Ecclesiastical History and Commercial and Institutional Record of the County of Kings and the City of Brooklyn, N.Y., from 1683 to 1884* (New York: W. W. Munsell and Company, 1884), 396–409, 463–64; New York, *Session Laws* (1832), 77–79.

45. Kentucky, *Session Laws* (1835–1836), 124–25; Kentucky, *Session Laws* (1827–1828), 162; Kentucky, *Session Laws* (1839–1840), 244–45; Kentucky, *Session Laws* (1846–1847), 268–69; Louisville, City Council, *Charter of Louisville* (1869), 61; Pennsylvania, *Session Laws* (1827–1828), 105–7; Pennsylvania, *Session Laws* (1830–1831), 311–14; Pennsylvania, *Session Laws* (1831–1832), 11–12; William Tindall, *Origin and Government of the District of Columbia* (Washington: Government Printing Office,

1912), 28–29; Thomas S. Barclay, *The Movement for Municipal Home Rule in St. Louis* (Columbia: University of Missouri Press, 1943), 18–19; St. Louis, City Council, *Revised Ordinances, 1850*, 118–20; Missouri, *Session Laws* (1842), 402.

46. Baltimore, City Council, *The Ordinances of the Mayor and City Council of Baltimore . . . 1835* (Baltimore: Lucas and Deaver, 1835), 67–69; New York, *Session Laws* (1800), 181–83; New York, *Session Laws* (1808–1809), 168–71; New York, *Session Laws* (1849), 165–67.

47. New York, Common Council, *Proceedings of the Boards of Aldermen and Assistant Aldermen, and Approved by the Mayor, from May 6, 1833, to May 25, 1835* (New York: Common Council, 1835), 114; New York, Common Council, *Proceedings of the Boards of Alderman and Assistant Aldermen, Approved by the Mayor, from May 13, 1845, to May 12, 1846 Inclusive* (New York: J. L. O'Sullivan, 1846), 326; Washington, City Council, *Acts of the Corporation of the City of Washington* (Washington: A. & G. Way, 1808), 19–20; Washington, City Council, *Acts of the Corporation of the City of Washington* (Washington; A. & G. Way, 1811), 56; Washington, City Council, *Laws of the Corporation of the City of Washington* (Washington: Way and Gideon, 1834), 30; Baltimore, City Council, *The Ordinances of the Mayor and City Council of Baltimore . . . , 1845* (Baltimore: James Lucas, 1845), 54; Baltimore, City Council, *The Ordinances of the Mayor and City Council of Baltimore . . . , 1848* (Baltimore: James Lucas, 1848), Appendix 10 (quotation); David T. Valentine, *Manual of the Corporation of the City of New-York for 1856* (New York: McSpeedon and Baker, 1856), 29–31; Walker, *City Digest of New Orleans*, 4–5.

48. New York Association for the Improvement of the Condition of the Poor, *First Annual Report . . . for the Year 1845* (New York: John F. Trow and Company, 1845), 34; *Journal of the [Boston] Society for the Prevention of Pauperism* 1 (April 1849):22–25; Clayton C. Hall, ed., *Baltimore: Its History and Its People* (New York: Lewis Publishing Company, 1912), 1:661–62; Elizabeth W. Chenault, "The Development of Louisville, Town and City, from the Earliest Beginnings to 1830" (M.A. thesis, University of Louisville, 1963), 111–12; Franklin S. Edmonds, *History of the Central High School of Philadelphia* (Philadelphia: J. B. Lippincott Company, 1902), 34; Baltimore, City Council, *Ordinances, 1840*, Appendix 54–55; Providence Committee to Superintend the Erection of School Houses, *Report to the City Council . . . on the Re-Organization of the Public Schools* (Providence: Knowles and Voss, 1846), 4.

49. Appleton C. Clark, Jr., "Origin of the Building Regulations," *Records of the Columbia Historical Society* 4 (1901):168–72; Board of Inspectors for the Penitentiary for the District of Columbia, *Report* (January 24, 1831), *Ho. Exec. Doc.* No. 66, 31 Cong. 2 Sess., 2–3; Cincinnati, House of Refuge, Board of Directors, *First Annual Report* (Cincinnati: Dumas and Lawyer, 1852), 3; Philadelphia, Board of Health, *Statistics of Cholera* (Philadelphia: King and Baird, 1849), 6; Baltimore, City Health Department, *The First Thirty-Five Annual Reports, 1825–1849* (Baltimore: Baltimore Commissioner of Health, 1953), January 1, 1828 (unpaged); Baltimore, City Council, *The Ordinances of the Mayor and City Council of Baltimore . . . , 1850* (Baltimore: James Lucas, 1850), Appendix 83; Sidney I. Pomerantz, *New York: An American City, 1783–1803* (Port Washington, N.Y.: Ira J. Friedman, 1965), 281–82; Robert Mills, *Water-Works for the Metropolitan City of Washington* (Washington: Lemuel Towers, 1853), 25.

50. Baltimore, City Council, *The Ordinances of the Mayor and City Council of Baltimore . . . , 1846* (Baltimore: James Lucas, 1846), 109; New York, Common Council, *Proceedings of the Boards of Aldermen and Assistant Aldermen, and Approved by the*

Mayor, from May 7, 1838, to May 14, 1839 (New York: Common Council, 1839), 23;
Baltimore, City Council, *The Ordinances of the Mayor and City Council of Baltimore
. . . , 1851* (Baltimore, James Lucas, 1851), 101; Lamb, *History of New York*, 2:505;
Griffith, *Annals of Baltimore*, 183; Dorothy C. Barck, ed., *Letters from John Pintard to
His Daughter Eliza Noel Pintard Davidson, 1816–1833* (New York: New-York Historical
Society, 1940–1941), 1:271; Brad Luckingham, "A Note on the Significance of the
Merchant in the Development of St. Louis Society As Expressed in the Philosophy of
the Mercantile Library Association, 1846–1854," *The Missouri Historical Review* 57
(January 1963):186; Society for the Prevention of Pauperism in the City of New York,
Documents Relative to Savings Banks, Intemperance, and Lotteries (New York: E. Con-
rad, 1819), 5–7.

51. Washington, City Council, *Laws of the Corporation of the City of Washington,
[1818–1827]* ([Washington]: Way and Gideon, [1818–1827]), 46; Quincy, *Municipal
History of Boston*, 293–94; Washington, City Council, *Laws of the Corporation of the
City of Washington . . . , [1838]* (Washington: Jacob Gideon, Jr., 1838), 319; Washington, City Council, *Laws of the Corporation of the City of Washington . . . , [1845]* (Washington: John J. Towers, 1845), 53; Lowell M. Limpus, *History of the New York Fire
Department* (New York: E. P. Dutton and Company, 1940), 151–57. Charitable donations
of this sort might, of course, represent public relations efforts by mercantile communities
with extensive commercial connections (or ambitions for such) with the affected city.
Washington has been used as an example in this instance at least in part because it was
not possessed of any significant mercantile establishment.

52. Baltimore General Dispensary, *An Address to the Citizens of Baltimore and Its
Vicinity, Containing a Concise Account of the Baltimore General Dispensary* (Baltimore:
Benjamin Edes, 1812), 6; *A Plea for Hospitals* (New York: Barker, Godwin and Com-
pany, 1851), 1–3; New York, Legislature, Senate, Select Committee to Investigate the
Health Department of the City of New York, Report, Senate Document No. 49 (Albany:
n.p., 1859), 10–11.

CHAPTER 7

1. Arthur M. Schlesinger, *The Rise of the City* (New York: Macmillan, 1933), 86;
Arthur M. Schlesinger, "The City in American History," *Mississippi Valley Historical
Review* 17 (June 1940):50.

2. Julius Rubin, *Canal or Railroad? Imitation and Innovation in the Response to the
Erie Canal in Philadelphia, Baltimore, and Boston*, Vol. 51 (N.S.), Pt. 7 of *Transactions
of the American Philosophical Society* (Philadelphia: American Philosophical Society,
1961), 14.

3. For example, ibid.; Wyatt W. Belcher, *The Economic Rivalry between St. Louis
and Chicago, 1850–1880* (New York: Columbia University Press, 1947); Charles N.
Glaab, *Kansas City and the Railroads: Community Policy in the Growth of a Regional
Metropolis* (Madison: State Historical Society of Wisconsin, 1962); James W. Livingood,
The Philadelphia-Baltimore Trade Rivalry, 1780–1860 (Harrisburg: Pennsylvania
Historical and Museum Commission, 1947).

4. Gustav Schmoller, *The Mercantile System and Its Historical Significance* (New
York: Macmillan, 1897), 50–51.

5. Oscar Handlin and John Burchard, eds., *The Historian and the City* (Cambridge:
The MIT Press and Harvard University Press, 1963), 28, 264.

6. The city as a commercial center will be dealt with in a later volume of this study.

7. Glaab, *Kansas City and the Railroads*, 47.

8. Richard C. Wade, *The Urban Frontier* (Chicago: University of Chicago Press, 1964), 78.

9. Charles F. Adams, Jr., "Boston," *North American Review* 106 (January 1868), 14.

10. For a brief discussion of this point, see Wade, *Urban Frontier*, 79.

11. George M. Young, "Puritans and Victorians," in *Daylight and Champaign* (London: Jonathan Cope, 1937), 229.

12. Later (primarily in the post–Civil War era) a fifth practice might be identified: the use of a rhetoric that appealed to local and regional pride and identified competitors as residents of "foreign" cities.

13. Quoted in Charles N. Glaab and Theodore A. Brown, *A History of Urban America* (New York: Macmillan, 1967), 215.

14. Ernest Kirschten, *Catfish and Crystal* (Garden City, N.Y.: Doubleday and Company, 1960), 43–44.

15. Robert Baird, *Impressions and Experiences of the West Indies and North America in 1849* (Philadelphia: Lea and Blanchard, 1850), 194; Daniel Curry, *New-York: Historical Sketch of the Rise and Progress of the Metropolitan City of America* (New York: Carlton and Phillips, 1853), 330; J. Stoddard Johnston, ed., *Memorial History of Louisville from its First Settlement to the Year 1896* (Chicago and New York: American Biographical Publishing Company, [1896]), 1: 78; F. Frank Crall, "Half Century of Rivalry between Pittsburgh and Wheeling," *Western Pennsylvania Historical Magazine* 13 (October 1930): 242.

16. Diane Lindstrom, *Economic Development in the Philadelphia Region, 1780–1850* (New York: Columbia University Press, 1978), vii; John A. Dix, *Sketch of the Resources of the City of New-York* (New York: G. and C. Carrill, 1827), 81–82.

17. Benjamin Drake and E. D. Mansfield, *Cincinnati in 1826* (Cincinnati: Morgan, Lodge, and Fisher, 1827), 71; Gabriel Collins, *The Louisville Directory, for the Year 1836* (Louisville: Prentice and Weissinger, 1836), vii.

18. Collins, *Louisville Directory* (1836), vii; Drake and Mansfield, *Cincinnati in 1826*, 71; Dix, *Resources of New-York*, 86–87; Harry A. Mitchell, "The Development of New Orleans as a Wholesale Center," *The Louisiana Historical Quarterly* 27 (October 1944): 954. For sources showing an interest in hinterlands as sources of supply, see Sheppard C. Leakin, "Mayor's Communication," in Baltimore, City Council, *The Ordinances of the Mayor and City Council of Baltimore . . . 1840* (Baltimore: Joseph Robinson, 1840), Appendix, 3; *Hazard's Register of Pennsylvania* 3 (November 4, 1840): 293.

19. For example, Leakin, "Mayor's Message," Baltimore, City Council, *Ordinances, 1840*, Appendix, 3; Philadelphia, City Council, *Ordinances of the Corporation of, and Acts of Assembly Relating to the City of Philadelphia* (Philadelphia: Crissy and Markley, 1851), 303–4.

20. Philadelphia, City Council, *Ordinances and Acts* (1851), 303–4.

21. Peter J. Coleman, *The Transformation of Rhode Island, 1790–1860* (Providence: Brown University Press, 1963), 161.

22. William Hollins, *Remarks on the Intercourse of Baltimore with the Western Country* (Baltimore: Joseph Robinson, 1818), *passim*; Maryland, *Session Laws* (1826–1827), Chapter 11; Maryland, *Session Laws* (1849–1850), Chapter 159; Baltimore, City Council, *The Ordinances of the Mayor and City Council of Baltimore, 1839* (Baltimore: John D.

Toy, 1839), 36–37. On dredges and icebreakers, see, for example, Baltimore, City Council, *Ordinances of the Mayor and City Council of Baltimore, 1836* (Baltimore: Lucas and Deaver, 1836), Appendix, 10; Baltimore, City Council, *Ordinances of the Mayor and City Council of Baltimore, 1834* (Baltimore: James Lucas and E. K. Deaver, 1834), 47–48.

23. U.S., Census Office, *Report on the Social Statistics of the Cities* (Washington: Government Printing Office, 1887), 2:12; J. Thomas Scharf, *History of Baltimore City and County* (Philadelphia: Louis H. Everts, 1881), 316; Baltimore, *Ordinances, 1836,* 135–36; Baltimore, City Council, *Ordinances of the Mayor and City Council of Baltimore, 1837* (Baltimore: Lucas and Deaver, 1836), 90.

24. Baltimore, City Register, *Report in Reference to City Property* (Baltimore: J. Lucas, 1851), 16–19.

25. Albany, City Chamberlain, *Report of the Chamberlain to the Honorable the Common Council, of the Receipts and Expenditures of the City of Albany, from May 1835 to May 1836* (Albany: E. W. and C. Skinner, 1836), 5; Collins, *Louisville Directory* (1836), 80; Philadelphia, Common Council, *Journal of the Common Council of the City of Philadelphia, for 1841–42* (Philadelphia: J. Van Court, 1842), 115; Philadelphia, City Council, *A Digest of the Ordinances of the Corporation of the City of Philadelphia and of Acts of the Assembly Related Thereto* (Philadelphia: J. Crissy, 1841), 13–15; Philadelphia, City Council, *Ordinances and Acts (1851)*, 351–52.

26. Charles R. Baker, "Philadelphia, 1836–9: Transportation and Development," *Philadelphia History* 2 (1933):349; Philadephia, City Council, *Digest of Ordinances* (1841), 195–97; Robert C. Albion, *The Rise of New York Port, 1815–1860* (New York: Charles Scribner's Sons, 1934), 33; Catherine E. Reiser, *Pittsburgh's Commercial Development* (Harrisburg: Pennsylvania Historical and Museum Commission, 1951), 143; Erasmus Wilson, ed., *Standard History of Pittsburg, Pennsylvania* (Chicago: Goodspeed Publishing Company, 1898), 708; William Hyde and Howard L. Conrad, eds., *Encyclopedia of the History of St. Louis* (St. Louis: The Southern History Company, 1899), 1: 380–82; Albany, Common Council, *Laws and Ordinances of the Common Council of the City of Albany, Revised and Revived, December, 1837* (Albany: Alfred Southwick, 1838), 77–78; Joel Munsell, *The Annals of Albany* (Albany: Munsell and Newland, 1850–1859), 10:272; Albany, City Chamberlain, *Report of the Finance Committee, to the Common Council, on the Annual Report of the Chamberlain, for the Year Ending May 1, 1847* (Albany: Weed, Parsons, and Company, 1847), 28; Elliot A. Rosen, "The Growth of the American City, 1830 to 1860. Economic Foundations of Urban Growth in the Pre–Civil War Period" (Ph.D. dissertation, New York University, 1954), 49–50; Justin Winsor, ed., *The Memorial History of Boston, Including Suffolk County, Massachusetts, 1630–1880* (Boston: James R. Osgood and Company, 1880–1881), 4:169, 226.

27. B. H. Payne, "New Orleans, Her Commerce and Her Duties," *DeBow's Review* 3 (February 1847):39–48; B. H. Payne, "Contests for the Trade of the Mississippi Valley," *DeBow's Review* 3 (February 1847):98–111.

28. John G. Clark, "New Orleans and the River: A Study in Attitudes and Responses," *Louisiana History* 8 (Spring 1967):117–135.

29. Martha J. Lamb, *History of the City of New York* (New York: A. S. Barnes and Company, 1877–1880), 2:670–72; Richard I. Shelling, "Philadelphia and the Agitation in 1825 for the Pennsylvania Canal," *Pennsylvania Magazine of History and Biography* 62 (April 1938):175–205; John Melish, *Travels through the United States of America,*

in the Years 1806 & 1807, and 1809, 1810, 1811 (London: George Crowe and Company, 1818), 379; Richard T. Farrell, "Cinncinnati in the Early Jackson Era, 1816–1834: An Economic and Political Study" (Ph.D. dissertation, Indiana University, 1967), 92–99; Wilson, *History of Pittsburg*, 87, 117–18; Louisville, Common Council, Minutes of the Common Council, Louisville City Records, Project 10A, Ser. II, University of Louisville Archives, Louisville, Kentucky, Reel 4, 21, 27 March 1836.

30. Scharf, *History of Baltimore*, 183; Wilhelmus B. Bryan, *A History of the National Capital* (New York: Macmillan, 1914–1916), 2:108n, 124–27; Washington, City Council, *Laws of the Corporation of the City of Washington . . . [1847]* (Washington: John T. Tower, 1847), 48–50; Washington, City Council, *Laws of the Corporation of the City of Washington . . . [1834]* (Washington: Way and Gideon, 1833 [sic, 1834]), Appendix, 9; Andrew Rothwell, *Laws of the Corporation of the City of Washington, to the End of the Thirteenth Council—June 1833* (Washington: F. W. DeKrafft, 1833), 463.

31. Ralph D. Gray, "Philadelphia and the Chesapeake and Delaware Canal," *The Pennsylvania Magazine of History and Biography* 84 (October 1960): 401–423.

32. Albion, *Rise of New York Port*, 90; Rosen, "Growth of the American City," 98.

33. Carter Goodrich, *Government Promotion of American Canals and Railroads, 1800–1890* (New York: Columbia University Press, 1960), 80; U. S., Census Office, *Social Statistics of Cities*, 2:13; Clayton C. Hall, ed., *Baltimore: Its History and Its People* (New York and Chicago: Lewis Publishing Company, 1912), 1:484–85.

34. Charleston, City Council, *Report Containing a Review of the Proceedings of the City Authorities from the 4th September, 1836, to the 1st August, 1837* (Charleston: Thomas C. Eccles, 1838), 13–14; Goodrich, *Government Promotion*, 103–5; Rosen, "Growth of the American City," 139–41. The rail connections were not, of course, the only reason for the increase of cotton receipts.

35. Albany, City Chamberlain, *The Chamberlain's Report, to the Common Council, Showing the Receipts and Expenditures of the City of Albany, from May 1, 1843, to May 1, 1844* (Albany: Weed and Parsons, 1844), 6, 15; Albany, Common Council, *Laws and Ordinances, 1837*, 141–43; Rosen, "Growth of the American City," 129; Munsell, *Annals of Albany*, 1:46–47.

36. Merl E. Reed, *New Orleans and the Railroads: The Struggle for Commercial Empire, 1830–1866* (Baton Rouge: Louisiana State University Press 1866), 13, 83–84; Louisville, City Council, *A Collection of the Acts of Virginia and Kentucky, Relative to Louisville and Portland: With the Charter of Louisville and the Amendments Thereto* (Louisville: Prentice and Wissenger, 1839), 75; Louisville, City Council, Minutes, Vol. 4, March 21, 26, 1836; *History of the Ohio Falls Cities and Their Counties* (Cleveland: L. A. Williams and Company, 1882), 1:316–17; Goodrich, *Government Promotion*, 137–38.

37. J. Thomas Scharf, *History of St. Louis City and County* (Philadelphia: Louis H. Everts, 1883), 2:139–40; Eugene T. Wells, "St. Louis and Cities West, 1820–1880: A Study in History and Geography" (Ph.D. dissertation, University of Kansas, 1951), 141.

38. Scharf, *History of St. Louis*, 2:140–41.

39. Richard Edwards and M. Hopewell, *Edwards' Great West and Her Commercial Metropolis, Embracing a General View of the West, and a Complete History of St. Louis, from the Landing of Ligueste, in 1764, to the Present Time* (St. Louis: Edwards' Monthly, 1860), 359; Scharf, *History of St. Louis*, 2:1179–81; Walter B. Stevens, *St. Louis: The Fourth City, 1764–1909* (City of Jefferson: Hampton and Boone, 1849), 159–61.

40. Scharf, *History of St. Louis*, 2:1142–43; Thomas S. Barclay, *The Movement for Municipal Home Rule in St. Louis* (Columbia: University of Missouri Press, 1943), 22n.

41. Ellis P. Oberholtzer, *Philadelphia: A History of the City and Its People* (Philadelphia: S. J. Clarke Publishing Company, [1912]), 2:150–52; Philadelphia, Councils, *A Digest of the Ordinances of the Corporation of the City of Philadelphia, and of the Acts of the Assembly, Relating Thereto* (Philadelphia: A. C. Atkinson, 1834), 205–6; Joseph C. Clark, Jr., "The Railroad Struggle for Pittsburgh: Forty-three Years of Philadelphia-Baltimore Rivalry, 1838–1871," *Pennsylvania Magazine of History and Biography* 48 (January 1924): 2; J. Thomas Scharf and Thompson Wescott, *A History of Philadelphia* (Philadelphia: L. H. Everts and Company, 1884), 3:2174–76.

42. Wilson, *History of Pittsburg*, 131–34.

43. Clark, "The Railroad Struggle for Pittsburgh," 3–5; Scharf and Wescott, *History of Philadelphia*, 3:2190.

44. Clark, "The Railroad Struggle for Pittsburgh," 15–16; George T. Fleming, *History of Pittsburgh and Its Environs* (New York: American Historical Society, 1922), 2: 90; Oberholtzer, *Philadelphia*, 2:316–17.

45. Goodrich, *Government Promotion*, 128; Rosen, "Growth of the American City," 131–32; Josiah Quincy, *A Municipal History of the Town and City of Boston, during Two Centuries. From September 17, 1630, to September 17, 1830* (Boston: Charles C. Little and James Brown, 1852), 295–96; William S. Rossiter, ed., *Days and Ways in Old Boston* (Boston: R. H. Stearns, 1915), 18–24.

46. Goodrich, *Government Promotion*, 130: Howard K. Stokes, *The Finances and Administration of Providence* (Baltimore: The Johns Hopkins Press, 1903), 195; Providence, City Council, *The Charter and Ordinances of the City of Providence Together with the Acts of the General Assembly Relating to the City* (Providence: Knowles, Anthony, and Company, 1854), 130–33; John H. Cady, *The Civil and Architectural Development of Providence, 1636–1950* (Providence: The Book Shop, 1957), 18–19.

47. See pp. 229–32, above; Carter Goodrich and Harry H. Segal, "Baltimore's Aid to Railroads: A Study in the Municipal Planning of Internal Improvements," *Journal of Economic History* 13 (Winter 1953):85.

Index

About the Author

LEONARD P. CURRY is Professor of History at the University of Louisville. His book, *The Free Black in Urban America, 1800–1850: The Shadow of the Dream* (1981), was nominated for the Pulitzer Prize in History at the request of the chair of the history panel.

ISBN 0-313-30277-4

90000>

EAN

9 780313 302770

HARDCOVER BAR CODE